The Economics of Governmental Activity

The Economics
of Governmental Activity

DAVID N. HYMAN

NORTH CAROLINA STATE UNIVERSITY AT RALEIGH

HOLT, RINEHART AND WINSTON, INC.

New York   Chicago   San Francisco
Atlanta   Dallas   Montreal   Toronto   London   Sydney

To Amy, who entered during Chapter 5.

Preface

This book provides a microeconomic analysis of governmental activity. Its purpose is to make the student aware of the economic basis for governmental activity and the consequences of alternative public policies. Recent developments in welfare economics, the theory of the state, the choice of political institutions, and public policy are integrated with more traditional principles of public finance and expenditure theory. The theory is applied to many current social problems in the United States including pollution, tax and expenditure policy, and intergovernmental fiscal relations.

The text differs from most public finance books in that it includes a major section on welfare economics as it relates to the theory of governmental activity. The concept of economic efficiency is defined precisely and implications for resource allocation are derived for the student. Both positive and normative approaches to determining the role of government in achieving economic efficiency are discussed. Recent developments in the theory of externalities are included in this section and then applied to the theories of governmental regulation of private action and public expenditure. The text also includes a chapter on collective choice and political institutions. The theory of taxation is presented in general terms at first and then applied to taxes on income, consumption, and wealth.

An attempt has been made to motivate the student by integrating relevant examples with the theory. In most cases the examples relate to current social problems in the United States. When necessary, political and economic institutions are described for the student's benefit. Recent empirical studies are cited when useful in providing information to students on the likely effects of alternative policies. The text includes a discussion of such current and proposed policies as revenue sharing, negative income taxation, and the Tax Reform Act of 1969.

This text is intended for use in junior-level courses in public finance or public policy. It has been assumed that students have had at least one course in price theory. Students weak in price theory are likely to find the early chapters useful as a review of some basic principles. Theoretical concepts are defined when they are introduced so as to avoid later confusion by the student. Although the book is designed for use primarily by undergraduates, some instructors might find it useful in graduate courses either as a supplement or as a basic text.

There is no discussion of fiscal policy or macroeconomic theory in this book. The stabilization aspects of governmental activity are usually included in courses in money and banking or macroeconomics and the inclusion of this topic in a public finance course often involves needless repetition for the student. Instructors desiring to include stabilization policy in this course might easily supplement this book with a short macroeconomic text.

The author is indebted to many friends and colleagues for criticism and encouragement during the preparation of this book. Professor Edgar K. Browning of the University of Virginia reviewed the entire manuscript in its early version and provided extensive criticism and suggestions for improvement. Helpful criticism was also provided by Professor Wallace Oates of Princeton University and William Beranek of the University of Pittsburgh.

Many of my colleagues at North Carolina State University read portions of the manuscript correcting errors and providing helpful hints for improving the exposition. These include Richard E. Sylla, Bruce Gardner, Thomas J. Grennes, Edward W. Erickson, and Michael B. McElroy. Early versions of parts of this text were used in the author's undergraduate Public Finance course in the Fall of 1970. The students who served as guinea pigs were helpful in providing criticism to the author and answering a detailed questionnaire on the text. The classroom tryout along with the enthusiasm displayed for the text by some students encouraged the author that the text could serve its purpose well.

The author is indebted to Mrs. Dawn Mitchell for her skillful typing of the pages of the final and earlier versions of the manuscript. Additional typing was done by Mrs. Dianne Graham with expertise rivaling that of Mrs. Mitchell.

DAVID N. HYMAN

Raleigh, North Carolina
December 1972

Contents

INTRODUCTION

Industrial Society and Governmental Activity

THE PROBLEMS OF THE 1970s

In the United States, where technology has been developed permitting man to travel to the moon, build complex computers, and transplant human organs as medical therapy, many seemingly more mundane but nagging problems remain to be solved. One does not have to be particularly sophisticated to realize that the substance of many of these problems is not technological but social in nature: poverty in the midst of wealth, racial conflict, growing crime, inadequate educational facilities, pollution, and urban decay.

A recent State of the Union Address by the President of the United States emphasizes the urgent need for solutions. Thus, the President tells us that: "The time has come for a new quest—a quest not for a greater quantity of what we have but for a new quality of life in America." In order to achieve this "new quality" he lists three priorities requiring immediate action. The first deals with a total reform of the welfare system designed to alleviate some of the misery of poverty. Second, the President suggests a fundamental overhaul of our federalist structure designed to channel resources to local governments. This suggestion, in part, reflects a realization of the importance of the problems of the cities and the need to reallocate resources to solve these problems. And third, the President advocates "equal voting rights, equal employment opportunity, and new opportunities for expanded ownership" to help resolve racial conflict. In addition, the President refers to problems involved in winning "the war against criminal elements" and their relationship to municipal expenditure patterns.

1

Considerable stress is put on pollution problems by President Nixon:

> The great question of the seventies is: Shall we surrender to our surroundings
> or shall we make our peace with nature and begin to make reparations for the
> damage we have done to our air, to our land, and to our water? . . .
> We still think of air as free. But clean air is not free. And neither is clean
> water. The price tag on pollution control is high. Through our years of past
> carelessness we incurred a debt to nature and now that debt is being called.[1]

How are the President's priorities established? Are they the "correct"
priorities? How can viable solutions to these social problems be formulated in
the face of the conflicts they represent? To what extent can solutions be
achieved through private initiative? When is governmental action desirable?
Questions such as these must be investigated to understand both the problems
and alternative solutions.

THE ALLOCATION OF RESOURCES, DISTRIBUTION OF WEALTH, AND GOVERNMENTAL ACTIVITY

Social problems share one important quality—they all have a vital economic
aspect. In this sense, they involve questions concerning the allocation of resources among alternative uses and the distribution of income and wealth
among households. Poverty involves, among other things, the distribution of a
nation's income and wealth among the populace. Acceptable solutions to
pollution problems may involve increases in costs of operation for many
business firms and a consequent diversion of resources from current uses to
alternatives. For example, citizens of this nation may have to be content with
fewer automobiles and use of alternative modes of transport such as bicycles
and mass transit to secure the benefits of less pollution. Similarly, a solution
to problems of the cities may entail a reallocation of resources from the
"private sector" of the economy to the "public sector." Thus, households may
have to be content with fewer televisions and other commodities in exchange
for more policemen and public schools.

This text concentrates on the economic aspects of social problems and the
role of government in supplying services to citizens in order to find acceptable
solutions to the problems. Insofar as governmental activity requires real resources to achieve its objectives, the private sector of the economy will have
to surrender command over these resources to free them for use by the public
sector.

For example, to supply national defense services the government has to
acquire steel, labor power, and other inputs necessary to support armed forces

[1] For a transcript of the President's speech, see the *New York Times*, January 23, 1970,
p. 22.

and maintain aircraft, tanks, ships, and other capital equipment. A municipal government must acquire trucks and other equipment to effectively administer the collection and disposal of garbage. To acquire these resources governments usually levy taxes that induce households to surrender their command over resources to the public sector. The dollars that governments collect in taxes merely represent "property rights," or "purchasing power," to acquire scarce resources. In real terms, taxes induce private households to exchange private goods such as clothing and radios for public services such as schools or police protection representing alternative uses of the economy's wealth. Thus, governmental activity designed to satisfy social needs often requires diversion of resources from private uses.

But not all forms of governmental activity require the withdrawal of resources from private use. In some cases, the government merely serves as an agent to redistribute command over private goods and services among households. Such activity does not require real resources beyond that amount of labor and capital necessary to administer the transfer of income among households. Thus, the income maintenance programs designed to alleviate poverty merely redistribute income from upper-income households to those households with incomes below the poverty level. Governmental activities that represent a redistribution of purchasing power among citizens are called "transfer payments," while those activities that actually divert resources away from private uses to supply public services are referred to as "exhaustive expenditures."

A number of questions must be posed to study governmental activity in any society. These include the following:

1. How do citizens of a nation collectively make choices among issues of common interest to all of them?
2. How many and what kinds of activities should government undertake?
3. What effects do alternative governmental policies have on social objectives?
4. What effect does the financing of governmental activity have on social objectives?

In the process of answering such questions one can propose a solution to the problem of determining the optimal dollar value of resources the government should extract from the private sector to accomplish its tasks. Currently, the federal government alone spends over 20 percent of gross national product to provide public services and transfer income among households. Total federal, state, and local expenditure accounts for over 30 percent of gross national product. Is 30 percent too much or too little? Could some of the activities undertaken by government be better accomplished by private enterprise? Could some governmental activities be dispensed with completely? Or, on the other hand, should government undertake more activities?

A government's expenditure plan and the sources of finance for these expenditures in a given year is summarized in a budget. Alternative expenditure and financing plans are represented by different budgets. The "best," or *optimal budget,* can be determined by seeking answers to the four questions previously listed.

PUBLIC FINANCE

The title of this book needs to be explained. The subject matter to be covered is the area of economics usually called "public finance." But this term is misleading for it tends to focus attention on the *financing* of governmental activity. Although obtaining the revenue necessary to conduct governmental activity is an important part of this study, it represents only part of the problem. As the previous paragraph would seem to indicate, many of the vital questions that must be answered concern the amount and kinds of activities that governments undertake. Consequently, rather than determining only the optimal pattern of finance, the objective of this book is the determination of the optimal level and mix of *both* governmental expenditures and sources of financing. Hence, the author has chosen to title this text *The Economics of Governmental Activity.*

Many of the famous nineteenth-century English economists (such as Ricardo, Mill, and Edgeworth) analyzed governmental activity by concentrating on the revenue side of the budget. The kinds of activities that governments undertook were often taken for granted and hence the expenditure side of the budget usually escaped rigorous analysis.[2] This is not to say that the classical economists did not study the expenditure problem at all but rather that their approach was usually somewhat vague. They viewed the problem of taxation to be independent of the problem of determining the level of public expenditure.

Although there was some integration of public expenditure and finance analysis by European economists in the latter part of the nineteenth century, the approach did not enter the mainstream of English and American economic thought until the mid-twentieth century. The Swedish economists Knut Wicksell and Erik Lindahl emphasized the political nature of the problems of

---

[2] Adam Smith, writing in the late eighteenth century, established three major categories of governmental activity: (1) protecting the community from violence and invasion by foreign powers, (2) establishing an exact administration of justice, and (3) providing certain public institutions and public works that would not be profitable for private enterprise to supply. See Adam Smith, *The Wealth of Nations,* The Modern Library, Random House, New York, 1937, Book 5.

These categories are somewhat broad and open to interpretation. For an analysis of Smith's elaboration on the criteria for governmental activity the reader may wish to consult Jacob Viner's provocative analysis, "Adam Smith and Laissez Faire" reprinted in Joseph J. Spengler and William R. Allen (eds.), *Essays in Economic Thought,* Rand McNally, Chicago, 1960, especially pp. 318–328.

determination of an optimal budget. These and other writers analyzed the basis for public expenditure and emphasized the interdependencies between the revenue and expenditure sides of the budget.[3] In the late 1940s and early 1950s the American economists Howard Bowen, Richard Musgrave, and Paul Samuelson did further work on public-expenditure theory and in recent years a number of significant contributions have been made by James Buchanan.[4]

In discussing governmental activity the author of this book specifies conditions under which households will find it mutually advantageous to surrender their command over resources to public authorities and the alternative policies that permit governmental activity to improve economic welfare. In addition, the author studies the political process to determine the likelihood of governments' pursuing policies that are optimal or that at least improve the public's welfare according to economic norms.

MICROECONOMICS AND MACROECONOMICS

Economists have traditionally divided their analysis of economic problems into two broad categories: microeconomics and macroeconomics. Microeconomics, or *price theory*, is concerned mainly with the analysis of the factors determining the prices of individual commodities and productive resources in the economy and thus is useful in understanding the role of prices in allocating resources to alternative uses and distributing income among factor owners (for example, laborers, capitalists, landlords).

Macroeconomics, in contrast, is concerned with *aggregate* analysis. Rather than the analysis of the allocation of resources between alternative uses, it is the analysis of the forces that determine the general levels and fluctuations of economic activity. For this reason macroeconomics has often been referred to as the "theory of national income determination." Macroeconomics deals with aggregate economic analysis as opposed to individual economic analysis (and hence the "macro" "micro" distinction).

An analysis of the economics of governmental activity has both microeconomic and macroeconomic aspects. It is, in fact, customary to analyze the role and impact of government in the economy in relationship to three criteria: allocation of resources, distribution of income, and stabilization of the level

[3] Readers interested in the development of thought in public finance and the contributions of Lindahl and Wicksell may wish to consult R. A. Musgrave and A. Peacock (eds.), *Classics in the Theory of Public Finance*, International Economic Association, Macmillan, London. 1958, pp. ix–xix.

[4] Howard R. Bowen, *Toward Social Economy*, Holt, Rinehart and Winston, New York, 1948; Richard A. Musgrave, *The Theory of Public Finance*, McGraw-Hill, New York, 1959; Paul A. Samuelson, "The Pure Theory of Public Expenditure," *Review of Economics and Statistics*, November 1954, and "Diagrammatic Exposition of a Theory of Public Expenditure," *Review of Economics and Statistics*, November 1955; James M. Buchanan, *The Demand and Supply of Public Goods*, Rand McNally, Chicago, 1968.

of economic activity. A fourth possible criterion is economic growth. Studying allocation and distribution problems in relationship to governmental activity requires the use of microeconomic analysis, while a study of stabilization problems (maintaining full employment and a stable price level) will entail the use of macroeconomic analysis.

This text concentrates on microeconomic aspects of governmental activity. Throughout much of the discussion to follow it will be assumed that the economy is at full employment and that the price level is reasonably stable. There will be no discussion of *fiscal policy*—the role of government in using the budget to stabilize the economy. This is not to say that stabilization is an unimportant governmental activity. In fact, it might be argued that it is important precisely because, in part, it affects the allocation and distribution of income. Unemployed resources, particularly labor resources, can adversely affect the distribution of income. The same may be said for rampant inflation. Similarly, unemployment wastes resources by keeping them idle; and inflation can distort the pattern of investment from its most efficient allocation. In any event, the macroeconomic aspects are usually discussed in texts and courses in macroeconomic and monetary theory. Students interested in stabilization aspects of governmental activity may wish to consult any one of a number of texts available in that field.

SCOPE AND ORGANIZATION

This text is divided into four parts. Part I establishes a theoretical framework for analyzing the role of government in a market economy. Embodied in this analysis are a number of value judgments that reflect an individualistic ethic. This establishes certain *norms* concerning which results are desirable based on the underlying values. A model of a simple market economy is constructed and the basis for governmental activity in such an economy is studied. Much of the analysis of Part I comes under the heading of "welfare economics," which is an attempt to provide a basis for comparing alternative resource allocations. With the aid of welfare economics, the role of government in reallocating resources and redistributing wealth and income can be defined to some extent.

Utilizing the foundation of Part I, Part II develops principles that may help determine the optimal mix and level of governmental expenditure. A definition of a *public good* is offered that, in part, makes clear *why* the activities usually undertaken by government are not undertaken by private enterprise. With this definition in mind, principles are developed to answer the question: "What activities should government undertake?" Also included in Part II is an analysis of social decision-making. This answers the question: "How do citizens of a nation collectively make choices among issues of common interest to all of them?" Here the text departs somewhat from its strictly economic orientation. Political institutions must be studied to determine the principles by which a social consensus is reached on political issues. Voting systems and institutional processes by which social conflicts are compromised and resolved are considered here.

Finally, Part II considers the process by which the government itself establishes priorities among alternative projects. This is, of course, related to problems of social decision-making. However, the budgeting process *within* government has many unique characteristics that are worthwhile studying in isolation. In particular, the role of bureaucrats in determining expenditure programs must be carefully considered. In addition, there is a discussion of cost-benefit analysis, a tool designed to help bureaucrats rank alternative expenditure programs according to certain economic criteria. Cost-benefit analysis attempts to answer the question: "What effects do alternative governmental policies have on social objectives?"

In Part III methods of financing governmental expenditure programs are considered. Alternative taxing schemes are discussed and illustrated with reference mainly to tax policy in the United States. The text will again draw on the principles developed in Part I to evaluate alternative tax structures. The goal here is to answer the question: "What effect does the financing of governmental activity have on social objectives?" The effects of alternative taxes on the allocation of resources, distribution of wealth and income, economic growth, and other social variables will be detailed.

Finally, Part IV analyzes some of the problems faced by urban areas within the context of our federalist structure. The problems of local finance and expenditure in the United States are studied. In addition, there is a discussion of revenue-sharing plans and urban problems.

SUMMARY

This text deals with the microeconomic aspects of the complex interrelationships among individuals, their society, and their government. An analysis of governmental activity in a market economy must include the basis for such activities and the effect of alternative revenue and expenditure policies on social objectives. Economic criteria may be used to determine an optimal government budget. But the political process must be studied as well to ascertain how effective it is in inducing governments and politicians to pursue policies that approximate the hypothetically "optimal" budget. To accomplish this task, the text includes an analysis of both public expenditure and tax policies as well as alternative methods of social decision-making.

PART I

A Theoretical Background

1

Efficient Allocation of Resources, Human Welfare, and the Market Economy

Economics is often referred to as "the science of scarcity." Among other things, it analyzes the choices made by households and businesses in allocating scarce resources to alternative uses. While human wants and desires may be limitless, resources available to satisfy those wants are not. Thus, households operate under budget constraints, and businesses operate under technology and re-source constraints. It is this scarcity of resources that gives rise to prices for commodities and factors of production.

There are alternative forms of economic organization for the production and distribution of goods and services. These include the free-market economy, where all productive resources are privately owned and prices are determined competitively in the market places where the various buyers and sellers meet. Alternatively, in a socialist-planned economy, productive resources are publicly owned and economic activity and decisions are determined by a planning board that directs resources to those alternative uses that are in accord with the board's goals. The institutions of the United States in the 1970s are such that the economic organization falls somewhere between the two alternative forms. The United States system is a "mixed economy" in the sense that, while the bulk of productive resources is privately owned, there is a signifi-cant amount of governmental intervention in the market. Governmental units regulate competition, redistribute income, and absorb resources from the private sector to provide such services as national defense, the postal system, education, police and fire protection.

There are two approaches to analyzing economic policy: normative and positive. The normative approach sets criteria, or *norms*, based on underlying

11

value judgments and then proceeds to make policy recommendations designed to satisfy the criteria. The positive approach makes behavioral assumptions relating to the actions of individuals and seeks to predict economic outcomes.[1] Under the latter approach, the observed behavior of individuals is compared to the economist's predictions, and his hypotheses are accepted or rejected. While the normative approach includes the assumption of values, the positive approach seeks to predict the actions of individuals when they are presented with a choice among alternative policies. The positive approach poses testable hypotheses designed to determine, among other things, the identity of individually held values. Thus, the normative approach might recommend that government undertake given activities, such as the regulation of monopolies or the provision of roads and national defense, because they will lead to achievement of predetermined criteria. The positive approach would predict that individuals would choose governmental activities over private activities because there would be mutual gains accruing to individuals when, say, government withdraws resources from private use to supply national defense services or regulates monopolies. The economist's predictions could then be verified by observing the political behavior of individuals. If his prediction is incorrect, then his theory is rejected. In short, normative theory seeks to prescribe "what ought to be," while positive theory studies or explains "what is." Both the normative and positive approaches have been used to provide an economic rationale for governmental activity. The text reviews both these methodologies.

THE NORMATIVE APPROACH

Human Welfare

An assessment of human welfare requires value judgments concerning that which is "desirable" in a moral or ethical sense. There are essentially three such judgments necessary for the standard normative approach, but before stating them it will first be necessary to define some terms.

A *household* represents a private decision-making unit. Households make choices among alternative consumption possibilities and alternative uses of resources. They sell their productive resources to firms and thereby obtain the income to finance the households' consumption of goods and services. *Firms* are private economic units that make choices to combine productive resources in various ways to produce different kinds of goods and services.

A *community* is a group of households and firms existing together under a generally accepted system of economic and political rules or "institutions."

---

[1] For a detailed discussion of the positive approach see James M. Buchanan, "Positive Economics, Welfare Economics, and Political Economy," *Journal of Law and Economics*, October 1959.

The term "community" may be used as synonymous with "society," "nation," or "country."

The value judgments may now be set forth:

VALUE JUDGMENT 1: Welfare in a community *should* be defined in terms of the welfare of each and every household comprising the community.

VALUE JUDGMENT 2: Any household *should* be considered the best judge of its own welfare.

VALUE JUDGMENT 3: If any change in the allocation of resources increases the welfare of at least one household without reducing the welfare of any other household, then that change *should* be considered desirable.

The word "should" is italicized in each of the preceding three statements to emphasize that these judgments involve prescriptions concerning "what ought to be." As such they appear to embody what might be referred to as an *individualistic ethic.* The welfare in a community is viewed as dependent on the welfare of individual households comprising that community. In addition, the individual household evaluates its own welfare. It must again be emphasized that the judgments represent statements of what is "good," and as such they are not universally acceptable and one should not expect them to be. Values differ among societies and among individuals and it is rare to find two societies accepting precisely the same values. Those who shun an individualistic philosophy are likely to find the stated values unacceptable.

In addition, economists generally refrain from attempting to make any interpersonal or interhousehold comparisons of welfare.[2] If a policy benefits some households while harming others, there is no objective basis for making any statement concerning whether or not this change constitutes an improvement in the community. This is not to say that such comparisons cannot be made. It merely suggests that any such comparisons must be on a subjective basis and as such involve the observer's own particular set of ethics. Interpersonal comparisons of welfare are attempted by policy makers and individuals all the time, *but* it is highly unlikely that any two individuals would agree uniformly in comparing welfare of households. This is what economists mean when they say that such comparisons cannot be made on a "scientific" basis.

The Efficiency Criteria

The welfare of any household in an economic sense depends on the quantities of goods and services the household consumes. The total amount of commodi-

---

[2] This is one of the basic tenets of the "new" welfare economics that was developed in the early twentieth century. For example, the reader may wish to consult the classic work by Lionel Robbins, *An Essay on the Nature and Significance of Economic Science,* Macmillan, London, 1932, for a discussion of interpersonal comparisons of utility and scientific objectivity.

ties a household can consume over a given time period clearly depends on the household's real income, which in a free enterprise economy depends on the amount of productive resources the household owns and the relative prices of both outputs and inputs. If a community embraces the individualistic ethic embodied in the three value judgments discussed previously, then one would expect that the actual mix of goods and services produced by the economic system, given its endowment of resources and state of technology, will be related to consumer tastes and the distribution of income. Those households with relatively high income will have greater influence on the employment of resources to alternative output in accordance with their preferences than will low-income households. High-income households have more "dollars," representing property rights to the use of scarce resources, to bid for the output of the economic system. A shift in income distribution away from households that prefer automobiles to those that prefer books will be likely to alter production in such a way as to increase the output of books and decrease that of automobiles.

There are alternative processes available for employing resources to produce any given output combination. For example, if consumer tastes call for the production of a million automobiles, then the producers of this output are confronted with the problem of employing labor, capital, and land in such a manner as to produce this output volume at minimum costs. The concept of productive efficiency is often used to evaluate alternative uses of inputs in producing any bundle of output. In common-sense terms, productive efficiency simply means the avoidance of unnecessary waste of scarce resources.

Productive efficiency also relates to human welfare. If productive resources are used efficiently, then there presumably will be more output produced by these resources in comparison with the alternative of inefficient utilization. Insofar as the welfare of households depends on the amounts of goods and services they consume, and their wants are virtually limitless (they are not easily satiated with goods and services), more efficient utilization of productive resources is likely to increase human welfare in a community.

A somewhat more rigorous criterion for productive efficiency is offered as follows:

THE CRITERION OF PRODUCTIVE EFFICIENCY: Productive resources are efficiently allocated if and only if it is not possible to increase the production of any one good or service without reducing the production of some other good or service.

The cost of a change in the allocation of productive resources is the foregone alternative output. This is called the "opportunity cost." In simple terms, the policy recommendation based on the efficiency criterion simply says that "if a change in the utilization of inputs enables one to obtain something for nothing, then one *should* undertake that change." Thus, the normative economist recommends undertaking all reallocations of productive resources that can be made at zero opportunity cost.

The human welfare norms may be used to establish a criterion for making recommendations concerning the allocation of resources among alternative uses. Value judgment 3 implies that it is desirable to make all those policy changes that improve the welfare of at least one household while doing no harm to any others. When all such policy changes have been made, the economy is said to satisfy the Pareto efficiency criterion[3] as defined below:

THE PARETO EFFICIENCY CRITERION: The allocation of resources among alternative uses is Pareto efficient if and only if it is not possible to increase the welfare of any one household without reducing the welfare of some other household.

It is clear that an economy cannot meet the Pareto criterion unless it is also satisfying the criterion of productive efficiency. For if productive resources were not efficiently utilized, a change in their allocation would result in more output at zero opportunity cost. This would imply that at least one household could be made better off by consuming more output while no other household need suffer a reduction in consumption and therefore welfare. Thus, Pareto efficiency can prevail only if productive efficiency is also present.

There is likely to be a multitude of alternative resource allocations that will satisfy the Pareto criterion. Each one will differ in terms of the distribution of economic welfare among households. For any distribution of income it will usually be possible to find an allocation of resources among alternative uses that will satisfy the Pareto criterion. Of course, one would expect the Pareto efficient output combination to be dependent on the income distribution insofar as consumer tastes differ. The reason for this is that shifts in economic power to bid for the use of the community's scarce resources occur with changes in the distribution of income. When such economic power is shifted among households with different tastes it is likely that producers will be induced to change their output mix in favor of the goods preferred by the households enjoying the increase in relative income.

Although the Pareto criterion is useful in determining the efficient allocation of resources among alternative uses for any given distribution of income, it offers no basis to compare economic situations of efficiency that differ in terms of the distribution of income. Changes in the distribution of income imply that some household will be made better off at the expense of another's being made worse off insofar as economic welfare of a household depends only on the quantities of goods and services it consumes. Such distributional changes cannot be evaluated by efficiency criteria. Instead, some criterion of "equity,"

[3] Vilfredo Pareto (1848–1923) was an Italian economist who extensively investigated the concept of economic efficiency. Economists have come to call the efficiency criterion set forth above the "Pareto efficiency criterion" in honor of Pareto's contributions.

or "fairness," is needed, a criterion that cannot be dictated by the economist. It must in some sense represent a consensus of the ethical values held by the households comprising a community and will usually be determined through the political process.

It remains to relate the criteria of efficiency to economic policy. What recommendations and evaluations can the economist make on the basis of these criteria? Any change in the allocation of resources that satisfies the Pareto criterion will be evaluated as "desirable" by the normative economist. If all changes satisfying value judgment 3 have already been made, then the only way one can increase the welfare of any one household is by reducing the welfare of some other household in the community. When this occurs welfare is said to be redistributed among households. Since there is no objective basis for comparing the welfare of any two households, the economist can offer no recommendation as to whether the resulting redistribution is desirable. Instead, he describes as best he can the economic characteristics of the redistribution (for example, it might increase the real income of poor people at the expense of decreasing the real income of the rich) and allows the community itself to decide whether the resulting change is, in fact, desirable. If the individualistic philosophy is accepted, this will imply the necessity of some sort of political process through which collective decisions, or a "social consensus," may be reached. A discussion of such processes will be postponed to Chapter 5. Alternatively, the redistribution might be evaluated on the basis of a non-individualistic criterion, as when a dictator, on the basis of his own concept of "justice," makes interhousehold comparisons of welfare.

In summary, the economist's role in evaluating social change is to provide data concerning the effect of such change on efficiency in resource allocation and the distribution of income. Policy changes that satisfy the efficiency criteria can be endorsed as desirable provided there is no change in the distribution of income. In many cases, there will be conflicts between efficiency and notions of equity. Improvements in efficiency may be obtainable only at the expense of a redistribution of economic welfare that some members of the community might judge to be undesirable. The resulting conflict will usually be resolved through the political process.

A NO-GOVERNMENT MARKET ECONOMY

Imagine the existence of a community with no formal government. The abstraction will require that property rights to resources be well-defined and that households respect those rights. If this were not the case, one would expect the households in the community to collectively organize in a way to protect property rights. This would, of course, imply the existence of a government to provide a legal system and police-protection services. If it is assumed that individuals in this imaginary community are all considerate of the rights of others so that there is no theft or disagreements concerning the ownership of property, then the unlikely assumption of no government may be accepted.[4]

Further, assume that the households of this community have organized their economic activity on the basis of a system of free enterprise. Thus, productive resources are privately owned and households sell their resources to business firms in exchange for some monetary unit (or commodity) which may be used to purchase goods and services. Productive resources include land, labor, and capital, where capital is defined to include human as well as physical forms. Human capital consists of skills that are either a natural endowment and/or acquired over a period of time. The ownership pattern of productive resources reflects, among other things, past individual choices as well as historical "accidents" and the rules for inheritance of wealth. Thus, all the land may be owned by a small percentage of households in the community or capital may be concentrated in the hands of a very few households.

The resource-ownership pattern, along with the prices of the productive resources, determine the distribution of income at any point in time. The capacity of households to purchase goods and services depends on their incomes and the prices of the goods and services produced by business firms. Each household may bid for goods and services according to its income and preferences. This bidding process is often referred to as the principle of "consumer sovereignty." By bidding for the output of firms, consumers can "direct" business firms to produce the goods and services they desire. Motivated by the lure of profits, firms tend to use their resources to produce those commodities that are in greatest demand. Of course, the greater the income of a household, the larger the quantity of dollar bids it can offer in the market place and the greater its power to induce business firms to produce the commodities it desires.

If individual households and business firms take the prices of outputs and inputs (productive resources) respectively as given, so that no economic unit has control over prices (that is, there is perfect competition in all markets), then the allocation of resources in this economy will satisfy the efficiency criteria. Business firms will produce at prices equal to their marginal costs to maximize their profits, and resources will be directed to producing those goods and services that are most desired by households according to the principle of consumer sovereignty. That is, assuming that productive resources are mobile, the profit incentive will induce business firms to use their resources to produce

---

[4] Some "commodities" even in this imaginary economy will not be subject to property rights. For example, the moon and the stars, the sky and the beauty of physical surroundings such as trees, landscape, and so forth, would be available to all citizens of the community to behold and enjoy according to their preferences. Such commodities are said to be "collectively consumed." The text will have considerably more to say about such goods in Chapters 2 and 3, when man-made goods and services having similar properties to the "moon and the stars" in the sense that they are collectively consumed will be discussed.

commodities that are desired by households. For example, an increase in the demand for wheat by households will, other things being equal, raise the price of wheat and the profit potential of wheat production. This will induce firms to enter wheat production, thereby satisfying the increased demand. Prices are the signals for such reallocations in response to changing demand patterns. Households will have their preferences satisfied because the commodities that they wish to consume, subject to the constraint of their incomes, will be available at prices dependent on the total demand for those commodities. In such an ideal economy, Adam Smith's famous "invisible hand" would be at work, resulting in an efficient allocation of resources as each household and business firm independently pursues its own self-interests.[5]

However, the efficient solution that emerges to the problem of allocating resources in this hypothetical perfectly competitive, free-enterprise economy is only one of many possible efficient results, each one differing with respect to income distribution. Many individuals in the community may find the initial income and wealth distribution to be inequitable. Some households may feel "compassion" for the poor and would therefore have their own well-being improved if income were redistributed toward lower-income groups. Others might feel that a certain income distribution is necessary for social stability or may simply have tastes for living in a society with a certain income distribution.[6] Such judgments on the part of individual households clearly involve interpersonal comparisons of well-being. But these comparisons are made on a subjective rather than an objective basis. Thus, it is quite possible that no two households within the community will feel exactly the same concerning that which constitutes an "equitable" income distribution.

In part, the attitudes of households are likely to be conditioned by their actual position within the existing income distribution. Low-income households favor changes in income distribution that will improve their relative position. They are more likely to prefer a uniform income distribution in which all households have the same income than are households that have relatively large accumulations of wealth.

Any plan or mechanism to redistribute income has to be generally accepted by the members of the community and enforced by an appropriate authority. Political institutions are the vehicles by which individual preferences concerning income redistribution are transformed into collective decisions. After agreeing on a plan to redistribute income, the community creates a tax-transfer mechanism designed to achieve that end. Some governing authority is likely

[5] See Adam Smith, *The Wealth of Nations*, The Modern Library, Random House, New York, p. 423.

[6] This view implies that the welfare of any individual household in the community is interdependent with that of other households. An interesting and rigorous analysis of such interdependence and its consequences for income redistribution is offered by H. M. Hochman and J. D. Rodgers, "Pareto Optimal Redistribution," *American Economic Review*, September 1969, pp. 542–557.

to emerge as an agent for administering the community's political decision to transfer income among households. Thus, even though a perfectly competitive, free-enterprise economy operates efficiently, political considerations may result in governmental activity designed to redistribute income.

When the system of markets comprising the economy does *not* operate so as to satisfy the efficiency criteria, then there may be grounds for additional governmental activity. If any one household or business firm can influence the prices of the commodities or factors of production they buy or sell, then resources are likely to be used inefficiently. For example, a monopoly cannot sell all the output it wishes at a fixed price. Since the monopolist is the only firm in an industry its attempts to sell additional units of output result in a fall in output price. Profit-maximizing behavior by monopolies results in less output being supplied at higher prices relative to that which would be the case if the industry were composed of many small firms. This restriction of output resulting from the monopolist's attempts to maximize profits prevents the attainment of efficiency and causes a loss of welfare to the community. The normative economist would therefore recommend that governmental activity is desirable on efficiency grounds to regulate monopoly market power.

The economy also might be subject to fluctuations in the employment of productive resources. Since unemployment wastes productive resources, the efficiency criteria would indicate that governmental activity designed to stabilize the economy would be desirable.

The market mechanism might inefficiently supply some goods and services. This would be the case if, when such goods are either produced or consumed, third parties other than buyers and sellers are either benefited or harmed. Third parties are not likely to be charged for the benefits or compensated for the costs if excessive difficulties are involved in evaluating such benefits and costs. Such third-party benefits and costs are said to be "externalities." When such a situation exists, market behavior will lead to inefficient resource utilization, and governmental activity may be desirable to "internalize" the external effects. For example, because air pollution is partly caused by the burning of high sulfur fuels, a tax imposed by government on the sulfur content of fuel might lead to a more efficient use of resources. Externalities and resulting governmental activity will be extensively discussed in Chapter 2.

Finally, some goods and services, such as police and fire protection, cannot be consumed by individuals in units that can be priced. Such goods are said to be "collectively consumed." Since private business firms cannot usually make profits on goods they cannot sell on a per-unit basis, they may be inefficient in attempting to supply any goods that are at least partially indivisible among users. Benefits from collectively consumed goods are available to all households and firms. Thus, collectively consumed goods are called "public goods," and they are likely to be more efficiently supplied by government rather than by private enterprise. One may define the three bases for governmental activity —redistribution, regulation, and stabilization—as collectively consumed goods.

Since they are more efficiently supplied by public rather than by private economic activity, public goods will be supplied to all at zero price and their resource costs will be financed by taxation rather than by per-unit pricing. Public goods will be discussed in greater detail in Chapter 3.

Governmental activity is not a panacea for defects in the free-enterprise economy. It is quite possible that governmental intervention into markets to correct for deficiencies may, in turn, create new distortions. For example, it will be shown that the current United States income-tax structure with its myriad of complex provisions distorts (in relationship to efficiency criteria) the private decision-making of economic units. Furthermore, intervention may serve to restrict individual choice in such a way as to conflict with the individualistic value judgments underlying the normative analysis. Therefore, all implications of governmental activity must be carefully considered before any activity is undertaken. The costs of such activity must be weighed against the benefits.

THE POSITIVE APPROACH

The positive approach uses no norms or value judgments. Rather than making recommendations designed to achieve certain criteria, the positive economist makes predictions based on behavioral and other assumptions about households and business firms. His predictions, if observable, may be verified by referring to the actual political and market behavior of individuals.

The efficiency criteria are, however, still relevant in positive economics. The positive economist may construct a theory that specifies conditions under which the efficiency conditions also will be satisfied. For example, assume a society where all economic participants attempt to maximize their gains from trade. If the efficiency criteria are not satisfied, there will exist possibilities for mutual gains from trade and one would expect individuals to seek such gains until they are all achieved. Thus, the positive economist would predict that efficiency will be an outcome in a community where all individuals maximize their gains from trade. Efficiency here is a result, not a social criterion as in the normative approach. Given the preferences of households, their maximizing behavior will lead to a choice of political and economic institutions that permit mutual gains from trade.

The positive economist views his role as one of presenting alternative policies and their probable effects while allowing members of a community to choose among the alternatives through the political process. He will also study the effect of alternative political institutions on collective choices. For example, he might predict the outcome of an election decided by a simple majority and compare this with the predicted outcome under a system that requires unanimous consent.

While the normative approach recommends all those resource reallocations that are presumed to satisfy the efficiency criteria, the positive approach would have all policy changes tested against their political acceptance. As the discussion of the normative approach has hinted, that approach alone cannot be used to make recommended changes *among* efficient alternatives. Even when using the normative approach the economist must study the political process to determine the acceptability of any policy recommendation. This is the case, for example, with changes in income distribution—no objective criterion is available on the basis of the normative economist's value judgments for ranking one distribution above another.

PARETIAN WELFARE ECONOMICS[7]

It is possible to add to the discussion of economic efficiency by deriving explicit conditions for the achievement of such efficiency. The basic model is known as "welfare economics," or "Paretian welfare theory," from Vilfredo Pareto, the Italian economist who developed much of the logic of the theory in the early twentieth century.[8]

The analysis rests on a number of assumptions. It is static in the sense that time is not considered as a variable. There are no impediments to the mobility of productive resources and no uncertainty. Property rights are assumed to be well-defined so that there is no need for an enforcement authority. There are no "spillover" effects of economic activity, that is, a household's well-being depends only on the commodities it consumes directly and not on the actions of some other household or business firm. Furthermore, the production of any good or service produced by any business firm depends only on the input applied directly in its productive process and not on the inputs used in some other productive process by some other firm. There is no government and no goods are consumed collectively.

Productive relationships in the economy are such that the marginal product of any given input used in any productive process always decreases, while all other inputs are held at fixed levels. Furthermore, when all the inputs used in any productive process are increased by some proportion, then output increases either by the same proportion or less than proportionately. This rules out the possibility of increasing returns to scale. Total productive resources available for alternative uses are assumed to be fixed.

Finally, household preferences are such that they are not easily satiated and marginal rates of substitution between any pair of goods are diminishing. Households can order alternative bundles of goods and services according to preference or indifference.

[7] Students who are not interested in the more technical aspects of economic theory may skim or skip this section without significant loss in continuity.

[8] Vilfredo Pareto (1848–1923), *Manual of Political Economy*, A. M. Kelly, New York, 1971.

Derivation of the Efficiency Conditions

To simplify the analysis, consider a community that consists of exactly two households and two businesses that utilize exactly two productive resources, labor and capital, in producing two different commodities: figs and grapes. One firm specializes in the production of figs, while the other produces only grapes. Call the hypothetical economy "Eden." The two households will be referred to as "Adam" and "Eve."

Consider, first, the technological relationships within this economy. There are two production functions: one for figs and the other for grapes. Such functions by definition give the maximum attainable output from any input combination. Call the total output of figs F and the total output of grapes G. If L_F is the amount of labor used in the production of figs and K_F is the amount of capital used in the production of figs, then

$$F = F(L_F, K_F) \tag{1.1}$$

is the production function for figs.

Similarly, if G is the total output of grapes and L_G is the amount of labor used in the production of grapes while K_G is the amount of capital used in the production of grapes, then

$$G = G(L_G, K_G) \tag{1.2}$$

is the production function for grapes.

Notice that the output of figs depends *only* on the inputs used in producing figs and *not* those used in producing grapes. Similarly, the output of grapes depends *only* on the amounts of labor and capital used in the process of producing grapes.

In addition, all available labor and capital will be fully employed in the production of figs and grapes. If L is the available stock of labor and K the available stock of capital, then this condition can be written as follows:

$$L = L_F + L_G \tag{1.3}$$

$$K = K_F + K_G \tag{1.4}$$

It should be noted that L and K are parameters; that is, they represent data which are given to the economist. On the other hand, L_F, L_G, K_F, and K_G are variables whose values are to be solved in the model.

Productive Efficiency

Productive efficiency requires that it not be possible to reallocate inputs to alternative uses in such a manner as to increase the output of any one good without reducing the output of some alternative good. For a two-goods world, this criterion will be met when, for any specified output level of one good, the maximum possible amount of the alternative good is being produced, given the community's endowment of inputs and technology.

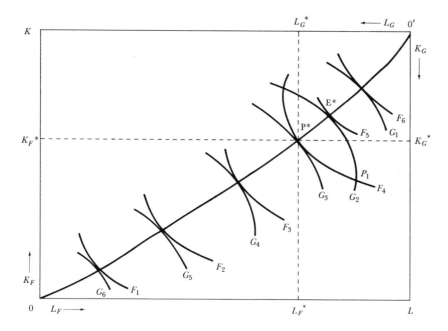

FIGURE 1.1

The next step is to determine the conditions that will lead Eden to the goal of productive efficiency in the use of its inputs. This may be accomplished by employing an "Edgeworth-Bowley box diagram." Such a diagram is constructed in the following manner: Let the length of the horizontal side of the rectangle illustrated in Figure 1.1 equal the total available stock of labor L in Eden. The length of the vertical side represents the total available stock of capital K in Eden. Now, measure the amount of capital used in the production of figs upward along the vertical side of the box $0K$ and measure the amount of labor used in production of figs along the horizontal side of the box $0L$. If productive resources are presumed to be always fully employed, then it must follow that any labor or capital not used in the production of figs *must* be used in the production of grapes. This may be seen by simply rearranging terms in equations (1.3) and (1.4) as follows:

$$L_G = L - L_F \tag{1.5}$$

$$K_G = K - K_F \tag{1.6}$$

The diagram accounts for equations (1.5) and (1.6) by measuring the amounts of labor and capital used in the production of grapes from the origin $0'$. Any point within the Edgeworth-Bowley box will therefore correspond to certain values of the four variables L_F, K_F, L_G, and K_G. For example, at point P^* the four values are:

$$L_F = 0L_F^* \qquad L_G = 0'L_G^*$$

$$K_F = 0K_F^* \qquad K_G = 0'K_G^*$$

It is a simple matter to plot the isoquants corresponding to the production functions for figs and grapes within the Edgeworth-Bowley box. Using 0 as the origin for plotting the fig isoquants (labeled F_1 to F_6), it is seen that these isoquants are convex to the origin, implying that the marginal rate of technical substitution of capital for labor diminishes as more labor is substituted for capital in the production of figs. Through any point within the box there will, of course, be an isoquant corresponding to some level of production of figs. Isoquants farther away from the origin 0 represent higher production levels for figs.

In the same fashion, isoquants corresponding to different levels of production for grapes may be plotted. However, now $0'$ is used as the origin. The isoquants for grapes (labeled G_1 to G_6) are therefore convex to $0'$ and those farther from $0'$ correspond to higher levels of production of grapes. Now it easily can be seen that each point within the Edgeworth-Bowley box corresponds to values for six variables. Referring again to point P^*, it has already been shown that it corresponds to values of L_F, K_F, L_G, and K_G. As soon as the input mix is specified, so are the production levels of the two outputs by the production functions [see equations (1.1) and (1.2)]. Thus, at point P^*, the use of $0L_F^*$ labor $0K_F^*$ capital in the production of figs implies an output level of F_4 of figs, where F_4 is the level of production of figs corresponding to the isoquant through P^*. The reader should check his understanding of this by showing that the output of grapes at P^* is G_3.

Consider the point P_1 in Figure 1.1. At that point, the implied input mix gives an output F_4 of figs and G_2 of grapes. Some thought will indicate that the input mix at P_1 is not efficient. Why? Because Adam and Eve can clearly increase their production of grapes to G_3, which represents a higher level of production for grapes, *without* decreasing their production of figs. This is accomplished by moving along the isoquant F_4 until the highest grape isoquant is reached. (Remember that even though they have not been drawn in Figure 1.1, there is a grape isoquant through every point on F_4.) The highest one that can be reached is clearly G_3, where G_3 is just tangent to F_4. How does Eden move from P_1 to P^*? Simply reallocate labor away from the production of figs while replacing it with capital. The reader may wish to measure the amount of this resource transfer in Figure 1.1 in order to test his understanding of the reasoning involved. Once point P^* is reached, it is no longer possible to increase the production of grapes while the production of figs is held at F_4.

Similarly, it may easily be shown that, at P_1, the production of figs could be increased without decreasing the production of grapes if the production of grapes is held at G_2. This is accomplished by moving along the isoquant corresponding to G_2 until the point E^* is reached.

Similar exercises may be performed for any point within the box. Only those points corresponding to tangencies between fig and grape isoquants will fulfill the requirements of productive efficiency. The line 00' has been drawn to connect all the points of tangency. Along 00' it is impossible to increase the production of any one good without decreasing the production of the other. Thus, 00' defines all values for F, G, L_F, L_G, K_F, and K_G that satisfy the requirement of productive efficiency. All the points of 00' correspond to tangencies between some fig isoquant and some grape isoquant. Now, the slope of the fig isoquant is its marginal rate of technical substitution of capital for labor in the production of figs. Writing this slope as $MRTS_{KL}{}^F$, it follows that

$$MRTS_{KL}{}^F = MRTS_{KL}{}^G \qquad (1.7)$$

where $MRTS_{KL}{}^G$ is the slope of any grape isoquant, defines *all* points on the efficiency locus 00'.

The economic information displayed in the efficiency locus may be summarized in alternative fashion. To do this, consider what the efficiency locus implies. Given the economy's resources (L and K), any point on 00' gives the maximum amount of figs that can be produced for any given level of production for grapes *and* the maximum amount of grapes that can be produced given any level of production for figs. This is precisely the definition of an economy's transformation locus. Thus, plotting the quantity of figs on the vertical axis of Figure 1.2 and the quantity of grapes on the horizontal axis, the curve TT' gives the economy's potential for producing combinations of figs and grapes efficiently, given its endowment of resources (L and K). The transformation curve has the usual shape. That is, it is concave to the origin, implying an increasing marginal rate of transformation of figs into grapes as more grapes are produced.

Each point on TT' gives a different output allocation for the economy (that is, a different combination of F and G). This serves to emphasize the fact that there is *an infinity* of output allocations that satisfy the criterion of productive efficiency. There is, however, no basis to decide whether a move from a point which is *not* efficient (a point *within* $T0T'$) to a point which *is* efficient (one *on* TT') is desirable in all cases. Referring to Figure 1.2, a movement from point A to any point on arc BC may be said to be "desirable" because it increases the output of *both* figs and grapes. However, there is no basis for saying that a movement from point A to a point off arc BC, like D, is "desirable." A movement from A to D increases the output of one good while *reducing* the output of the other. The same will hold for any movement from A to a point on TT' off the arc BC.

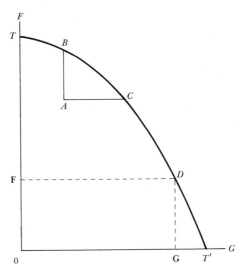

FIGURE 1.2

Pareto Efficiency

Thus far, nothing has been said about the welfare of Adam and Eve. Value judgment 3 states that any change in the allocation of resources which increases the welfare of any one household without reducing that of any other is desirable. Both Adam and Eve have utility functions that describe their preferences for figs and grapes and index their well-being. Using the subscript ♂ for Adam and ♀ for Eve, their utility functions may be written as follows:

$$U_\delta = U(F_\delta, G_\delta) \tag{1.8}$$

$$U_\circ = U(F_\circ, G_\circ) \tag{1.9}$$

where U_δ is Adam's utility level taken as a function of the amount of figs and grapes (F_δ and G_δ) that he alone consumes. Similarly, $U_\circ$ is Eve's utility level that is taken to depend only on the figs and grapes that she alone consumes. Apparently, both Adam and Eve are rather selfish individuals—the amounts of figs and grapes consumed by Eve does not affect Adam's utility and vice versa. To derive the criteria for Paretian efficiency, it is again necessary to construct an Edgeworth-Bowley box similar to that used for the case of production. There are, however, a number of differences between the box to be drawn now and that drawn for the purpose of deriving the technological optima. The first difference concerns what goes inside the box. Now, instead of production functions for figs and grapes, both Adam's and Eve's utility functions are plotted. Second, whereas the sides of the production box were taken to be fixed, the sides of the consumption box are variable. That is, it was assumed that there was a *fixed stock* of labor and capital available to produce figs and grapes. The sides of the Edgeworth-Bowley box for consumption represents the total amount of figs and grapes available for consumption. It is clear that these are variables. Referring again to Figure 1.2, it is seen that each point on the transformation locus TT' represents a different mix of F and G. It follows that there are an infinite number of Edgeworth-Bowley boxes that may be drawn—one for each point on TT'.

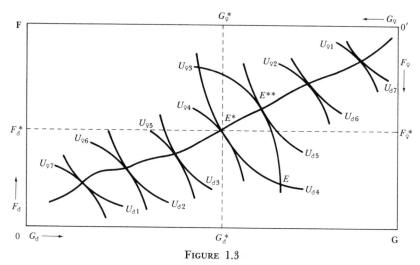

FIGURE 1.3

One of the boxes is illustrated in Figure 1.3. It corresponds to point D on the transformation curve of Figure 1.2 where $F = \mathbf{F}$ and $G = \mathbf{G}$. Adam's utility is measured from the origin 0, while Eve's utility is measured from the origin 0′. As one moves northeast from 0, Adam is successively better off as he moves to higher indifference curves. Similarly, Eve is placed on higher utility curves as one moves from 0′ toward 0. Any point within the box corresponds to values for the allocation of the total available supplies of figs and grapes between Adam and Eve—F_{δ}, F_{φ}, G_{δ}, G_{φ}—such that the total available supply of figs and grapes produced are consumed. That is,

$$\mathbf{F} = F_{\delta} + F_{\varphi} \tag{1.10}$$

$$\mathbf{G} = G_{\delta} + G_{\varphi} \tag{1.11}$$

In addition, each such point within the box implies some level of ordinal utility for both Adam and Eve [this follows from equations (1.8) and (1.9)]. Note that it is not necessary to compare the utility levels of Adam and Eve. It is required only that both Adam and Eve know when they are better or worse off.

To derive the conditions for Paretian efficiency, consider value judgment 3 once again. When a situation has been reached where it is no longer possible to make either Adam or Eve better without making one of them worse off, one can no longer recommend any reallocation of the total output of figs and grapes that satisfies the norm. First, assume that the output of figs and grapes is fixed at **F** and **G** respectively. This assumption will be lifted momentarily.

Consider point E in Figure 1.3. Is this point Pareto efficient? The answer is clearly no. Why? Because one can easily make Eve better off without harming Adam by moving along the indifference curve labeled $U_{\delta4}$ to point E^*. As one moves from E to E^*, Adam receives more figs at the expense of giving up some grapes, while Eve gains grapes and loses figs. At E^*, where the indifference curve corresponding to $U_{\delta4}$ is just tangent to that corresponding to $U_{\varphi4}$, it is no longer possible to reallocate grapes and figs between Adam and Eve so as to make one better off without making the other worse off. At point E^*, Adam consumes $0G_{\delta}^*$ of grapes and $0F_{\delta}^*$ of figs, while Eve consumes $0'G_{\varphi}^*$ of grapes and $0'F_{\varphi}^*$ of figs. To test the understanding of this, the reader may wish to show why point E^{**} is also a Pareto efficient allocation of the fixed amount of figs and grapes between Adam and Eve.

The points E^* and E^{**} are not the only positions of Paretian efficiency. Indeed, there are many such points—one for each possible tangency between the two sets of indifference curves. Each tangency represents a different distribution of goods and well-being between Adam and Eve.

Now, the slope of any indifference curve in the box is simply the marginal rate of substitution of figs for grapes. Writing the slopes of Adam's indifference curves in relationship to the origin 0 as $MRS_{FG}{}^{\delta}$ and the slopes of Eve's indifference curves in relationship to the origin $0'$ as $MRS_{FG}{}^{\varphi}$, it follows that all points of Paretian efficiency within the box must satisfy the following criterion:

$$MRS_{FG}{}^{\delta} = MRS_{FG}{}^{\varphi} \qquad (1.12)$$

Equation (1.12) merely states that, in order for an allocation of the fixed amount of goods to be Pareto efficient, the two relevant indifference curves must be tangent, implying that their slopes are equal.

Lift the assumption that the outputs of figs and grapes are fixed. One must now solve for the Pareto efficient production levels of the two outputs as well as the efficient allocation of goods among Adam and Eve. When one considers the fact that it is possible to "transform" figs into grapes according to the terms implied by the slope of the transformation curve of Figure 1.2 (the marginal rate of transformation of figs into grapes), it becomes evident that not all the points on the locus of tangencies between the two sets of indifference curves in Figure 1.3 are really efficient. To understand this, consider the following example: Suppose that at point E^* in Figure 1.3 the marginal rate of substitution of figs for grapes is one for both Adam and Eve. Thus,

$$MRS_{FG}{}^{\delta} = MRS_{FG}{}^{\varphi} = 1 \qquad (1.13)$$

Call the marginal rate of transformation of figs for grapes MRT_{FG}, and suppose that its value is two at point D in Figure 1.2. This implies that, at that particular point on Eden's transformation curve, two figs can be produced by diverting the labor and capital used to produce one grape over into fig production. But, by assumption, only one fig is necessary to replace one grape in order to keep Adam and Eve at the same level of utility at point E^* in Figure 1.3. Thus, if one fig is taken from Adam and replaced with one grape, he will not be made any worse off by this exchange. Needless to say, taking a grape from Adam has no effect on Eve's utility. Now the resources that were previously employed to produce this grape for Adam can be diverted to fig production, and by assumption, *two* figs can be produced. One of these figs must be given to Adam to compensate him for his loss of a grape. But this leaves one extra fig. The extra fig can be given either to Adam or Eve or divided between them. In any event, either both of them will be better than they were previously, or one can be made better without making the other worse off. It follows that no position can be considered Pareto efficient until all gains from trade of this kind have been exhausted. This will occur only for those points where the rates at which Adam and Eve are willing to substitute figs for grapes while retaining the same level of utility is precisely equal to the rate at which figs may be transformed into grapes at the margin by diverting resources (labor and capital) from the production of one commodity to the other. That is, the following must hold:

$$MRS_{FG}{}^{\delta} = MRS_{FG}{}^{\varphi} = MRT_{FG} \qquad (1.14)$$

There will be at least one output combination satisfying the efficiency condition. The actual number of efficient output solutions depends on the differences in tastes among households. If Adam and Eve had identical utility functions, there would be one unique point satisfying equation (1.14). In that case, a change in the distribution of income between Adam and Eve would not alter the relative demands for figs and grapes, and would therefore result in no change in the output combination produced. If, however, Adam and Eve do have different tastes, then any change in income distribution would alter relative demands and cause a change in the efficient output mix (that is, lead the economy to a new efficient point on the transformation curve).

There are, therefore, likely to be many allocations satisfying the efficiency criteria when tastes differ among households. Each one will differ in terms of the distribution of welfare. Insofar as Adam and Eve have different tastes, changes in income distribution alter the efficient-resource-use pattern. Thus, for any income distribution, the model specifies the output demands of Adam and Eve from the utility functions [equations (1.8) and (1.9)]. Given the income distribution, there is some efficient output mix (F, G) where $F = F_{\delta} + F_{\varphi}$ and $G = G_{\delta} + G_{\varphi}$ allowing Adam and Eve each to maximize his welfare within his income. The production functions [equations (1.1) and (1.2)] give the efficient allocation of inputs L_F, L_G, K_F, K_G necessary to produce that mix. Thus, for any income distribution, the model produces a solution for the variables:

$$F, G, L_F, L_G, K_F, K_G, U_{\delta}, U_{\varphi}, F_{\delta}, F_{\varphi}, G_{\delta}, G_{\varphi}$$

The model *does not*, however, provide any basis for ranking one income distribution above another.

The Social Welfare Function: A Digression

Some normative economists attempt to do more than simply specify the efficient outcomes. They try to develop criteria to rank alternative income distributions. As has been emphasized, there is no objective way to do this. Positive economists have therefore been extremely critical of attempts to rank hypothetical income distributions.[9]

The technique used by the normative economists is to postulate the existence of a "social welfare function" that permits a ranking of social welfare states dependent on individual welfare. Thus, social welfare W is taken as a function of individual welfare. For the hypothetical community of Eden, social welfare will depend on the utility levels of Adam and Eve:

$$W = W(U_\delta, U_\varphi) \tag{1.15}$$

This function embodies ethical evaluation of the importance of Adam's and Eve's relative welfare in determining social welfare. The actual form of the function depends on the weights, or coefficients, that are applied to individual utilities. The function can then be used to choose among alternative efficient income distributions. Thus, the welfare distribution that maximizes social welfare is chosen as "best." Once the social-welfare-maximizing values of U_δ and U_φ are known, the values of the other variables are easily determined from the utility and production functions giving a unique solution vector.

Where does the social welfare function come from? The normative economists seem to take it as given. The weights applied to individual utilities are apparently exogenously given through the prejudices of some "deity." But since value judgment 2 states that only a household can evaluate its own welfare, the application of arbitrary weights to individual utilities in computing social welfare is apparently inconsistent with the individualistic ethic of the entire theoretical construct. The willingness of individuals to agree to an alteration of any existing income distribution must be explained in terms of individualistic criteria.

EFFICIENCY AND ECONOMIC INSTITUTIONS

The efficiency conditions derived for the simple two-person, two-good, two-input world of Eden can easily be generalized for a world of many consumers,

---

[9] James Buchanan has argued, quite convincingly, that resorting to the social welfare function is inconsistent with the basic value judgments of Paretian welfare economics precisely because it is based on a non-individualistic ethic. See his *Demand and Supply of Public Goods*, Rand McNally, Chicago, 1968, pp. 193–197.

many goods, and many inputs. This will be done in the appendix to this chapter. The efficiency conditions for Eden are summarized in equations (1.7) and (1.14). The reader will recall that equation (1.7) states that the marginal rate of technical substitution of labor for capital must be equal in the production of figs and grapes (or any number of commodities), while equation (1.14) states that the rate at which both Adam and Eve (or any number of citizens in Eden) are willing to substitute figs for grapes (or any other pair of commodities) at some fixed level of well-being must be equal to the rate at which figs may be transformed into grapes in Eden's economy. These conditions have been derived independently of *any* assumptions about the institutional structure of the economic system. It remains now to evaluate the performance of alternative economic institutions in relationship to the efficiency criteria.

Consider a free-enterprise market economy operating under conditions of perfect competition in all markets. Under this set of institutions, productive resources are privately owned and no individual market participant has any power whatsoever to affect prices of the commodities or inputs he buys or sells. In other words, prices may be taken as data (as opposed to variables) from the point of view of individual buyers and sellers. Furthermore, the price of any given commodity must be assumed to be identical for all buyers and sellers of that particular commodity. This implies that there are no "distortions" in the market place—such as taxes—that cause the price received by sellers to differ from the price paid by buyers.

To determine the "desirability" of a perfectly competitive economy, one merely has to know if such a set of economic institutions will satisfy the efficiency criteria. Consider, first, the behavior of producers of figs and grapes in Eden. In accordance with the supposition of perfect competition in all markets, the producers of figs and grapes take the prices of labor and capital as fixed and behave such as to minimize the cost of producing any given output. If the price of labor is P_L and the price of capital is P_K, then the total cost of producing any output is

$$C = P_K K + P_L L \qquad (1.16)$$

The more labor and capital used, the greater the cost of production. If cost is held constant at **C**, equation (1.16) may be plotted on a set of axes, with labor measured on the vertical axis and capital on the horizontal axis. The resultant relationship is called an "isocost" line, and it defines all those combinations of labor and capital that cost **C** dollars. This is illustrated in Figure 1.4. There will be one isocost line through every point within the set of axes. Each isocost line corresponds to a different value of C. Lines further from the origin imply greater purchases of both L and K and therefore greater total cost.

Now, consider the combinations of labor and capital that might be used to produce a particular amount of figs, say $F = \mathbf{F}$ in Eden. This information is summarized in the isoquant corresponding to $F = \mathbf{F}$ and is illustrated in Figure 1.4. In order to produce this particular output of figs at minimum cost, the input combination corresponding to the tangency of the isoquant with some isocost line is chosen. At that point, the slope of the isocost line equals the slope of the isoquant corresponding to $F = \mathbf{F}$. The slope of the isoquant is simply the marginal rate of technical substitution of capital for labor in the production of figs, while the slope of the isocost line is the ratio of the price of capital to the price of labor. [The reader may verify this by solving equation (1.16) for K in terms of C, L, P_L, and P_K.] The cost of producing *any* output of figs will be minimized when the isoquant corresponding to that level of production is tangent to an isocost line. Thus, the conditions for minimizing the cost of production of any output of figs is

$$MRTS_{KL}{}^{F} = \frac{P_L}{P_K} \tag{1.17}$$

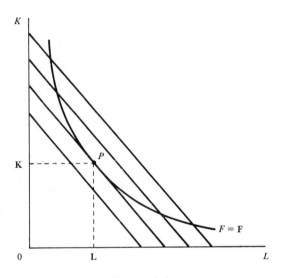

FIGURE 1.4

A similar argument may be advanced for the production of grapes. The only necessary alteration is to draw the isoquant corresponding to a particular level of grape production in Figure 1.4. This is left as an exercise for the reader. The conclusion is similar. To minimize costs of production for any output level, the grape producer must set the marginal rate of technical substitution of capital for labor in the production of grapes equal to the ratio of the price of labor to the price of capital.

$$MRTS_{KL}{}^{G} = \frac{P_L}{P_K} \tag{1.18}$$

Now, assuming no distortions (like taxes) in the market, the relative price of labor with respect to capital (P_L/P_K) will be the same for producers of figs and grapes. Since both producers adjust so as to equate their marginal rates of technical substitution equal to the same ratio of prices, it follows that they also adjust to set these rates of substitution equal to one another. Thus, combining equations (1.17) and (1.18) yields

$$MRTS_{KL}{}^F = MRTS_{KL}{}^G = \frac{P_L}{P_K} \tag{1.19}$$

But, taking equation (1.19) with the assumption of full employment of labor and capital [equations (1.3) and (1.4)] is *precisely* the condition for efficiency in production. It follows that perfect competition in the markets for labor and capital implies that the criterion of productive efficiency will be satisfied. That is, the economy will automatically be led to a point *on* as opposed to *within* its transformation frontier.

Next, consider the decisions concerning the *level* of production for figs and grapes. If P_F is the price of figs and P_G is the price of grapes, the producers can maximize profits by selecting that level of output for which the price of each commodity is equal to the marginal cost of producing that output. Thus, profits are at maximum for both fig and grape producers when they have adjusted their output to satisfy the following conditions:

$$P_F = MC_F \tag{1.20}$$

$$P_G = MC_G \tag{1.21}$$

where MC_F and MC_G are the marginal costs of figs and grapes respectively. The information represented in these two equations may be combined into one equation by dividing equation (1.21) by (1.20).

$$\frac{P_G}{P_F} = \frac{MC_G}{MC_F} \tag{1.22}$$

It may easily be shown that the ratio of marginal costs in (1.22) represents Eden's marginal rate of transformation of figs into grapes. The slope of the transformation curve may be interpreted as the amount of one commodity that must be foregone in order to produce one more unit of the other commodity. The value of the extra resources necessary to produce this one more unit is the marginal cost of producing that unit as measured by the foregone alternative commodity output that could have been produced by them. In symbolic form, if ΔF is a change in fig output and ΔG is a change in grape output,

$$MC_F = \Delta G \tag{1.23}$$

$$MC_G = \Delta F \tag{1.24}$$

Dividing (1.24) by (1.23) gives

$$\frac{\Delta F}{\Delta G} = \frac{MC_G}{MC_F} = MRT_{FG} = \frac{P_G}{P_F} \tag{1.25}$$

Note that the marginal rate of transformation is negative although the sign has not been indicated in (1.25). This is because the output of one good must be reduced to increase the output of the other along the transformation curve, given the available resources in Eden. The "bowed-out" shape of the transformation curve reflects the fact that marginal costs of production increase as the production of any good increases. To see the shape, move along the transformation curve of Figure 1.2 from T to T', thereby increasing the output of grapes at the expense of decreasing the output of figs. When this is done, the marginal cost of grapes will increase because more are produced, while the marginal cost of figs will decrease because less are produced. The ratio of the marginal cost of grapes to figs therefore increases, causing the slope of TT' to increase as point T' is approached.

Adam and Eve also take the prices of figs and grapes as given and behave accordingly. Both Adam and Eve have a certain income level dependent on the amount of labor and capital they own and on prices. This income level, together with the prices of figs and grapes, determines their budget constraint. The tangency between their budget constraint line and an indifference curve in their preference map defines the consumption pattern they choose in order to maximize their utility. This is illustrated in Figure 1.5.

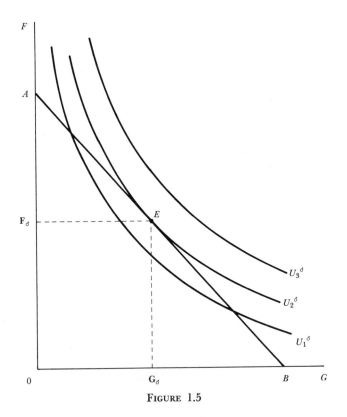

FIGURE 1.5

The budget line is AB and $\mathring{U}_1{}^\delta$, $U_2{}^\delta$, $U_3{}^\delta$ are indifference curves in Adam's preference map. A similar diagram could be drawn for Eve. Point E represents Adam's equilibrium position implying that he consumes $\mathbf{F}_\delta$ figs and $\mathbf{G}_\delta$ grapes in order to maximize his utility. At E the slope of some indifference curve is equal to the slope of the budget line. The slope of the indifference curve is simply Adam's marginal rate of substitution of figs for grapes, while the slope of the budget line is the ratio of the price of grapes to the price of figs. This may be written as follows:

$$\frac{P_G}{P_F} = MRS_{FG}{}^\delta \tag{1.26}$$

Similarly, for Eve at equilibrium,

$$\frac{P_G}{P_F} = MRS_{FG}{}^\circ \tag{1.27}$$

If both producers and consumers in Eden react to the same price ratio in Eden, it just so happens that they will behave in such a manner as to satisfy the condition for Paretian efficiency! To understand this, refer to equations (1.25), (1.26), and (1.27); the relevant slopes are all equal to the same price ratio. It follows that these slopes must be equal to each other.

That is:

$$MRS_{FG}{}^\delta = MRS_{FG}{}^\circ = MRT_{FG} = \frac{P_G}{P_F} \tag{1.28}$$

which is the condition for Paretian efficiency. A perfectly competitive economy therefore is "desirable" for Eden because it leads to Paretian efficiency.

But there are likely to be many possible efficient resource allocations if tastes differ between Adam and Eve. Which one will the market economy achieve? This depends on the initial income distribution between Adam and Eve that, in turn, depends in part on the amount of productive resources owned by each individual. Their income is the sum of payments received by them in return for the services of the productive resources they own. Call the amount of labor and capital owned by Adam L_δ and K_δ respectively. Eve's labor supply is $L_\circ$ while $K_\circ$ is her supply of capital. All the available capital and labor is distributed between Adam and Eve so that

$$L = L_\delta + L_\circ \tag{1.29}$$

and

$$K = K_\delta + K_\circ \tag{1.30}$$

Given the prices of labor and capital, Adam's and Eve's income level are I_δ and $I_\circ$ respectively and may be expressed as follows:

$$I_\delta = P_L L_\delta + P_K K_\delta \tag{1.31}$$

$$I_\circ = P_L L_\circ + P_K K_\circ \tag{1.32}$$

If Adam and Eve have differing preferences, any change in the distribution of income will shift the relative demand for figs and grapes, thereby resulting in a change to a new efficient output mix.

Under certain circumstances, Adam and Eve might agree to an alternation in the distribution of income. For example, Adam's welfare may be interdependent with that of Eve's. In this case, Adam might be able to improve his *own* welfare by making Eve better off. It would therefore be in his interest to give some of his income to Eve without asking for any service to be given in return. While such mutually benefiting transfers are easy to administer in a two-person world, they may require a more sophisticated administrative mechanism when there are many households each with different ideas about that which constitutes a desirable distribution. Under these circumstances, a government might emerge from the community's political institutions to act as an agent for redistributing income according to an agreed plan that allows mutual gains, due to interdependent utility functions, to be realized through income redistribution. This implies that some households will pay taxes while others will receive transfer payments.

The kind of taxes the government uses must be of a special type. The government must be careful not to destroy the identity of relative prices as used by producers and consumers. That is, the taxes must not be reflected in any of the relative prices of outputs or inputs that might distort them in such a way as to make the attainment of efficiency impossible. A type of tax satisfying this condition consists of *lump-sum transfers*. These are "neutral" taxes and subsidies that are not related to any economic activity by Adam and Eve. An example of such a tax is a "head tax" that is levied at a fixed amount on each individual. The only way an individual can avoid the full amount of such a tax is to cease existing (a rather drastic step). More will be said about such taxes in the following chapters.

ALTERNATIVE ECONOMIC INSTITUTIONS AND EFFICIENCY

There are alternative economic institutions that may conceivably satisfy the efficiency criteria. Productive resources may be owned by the state and may be allocated according to a central plan devised by a managerial agency. In such a socialist economy, resource allocation may be efficient if the planners succeed in calculating "shadow prices" of productive resources and commodities that correctly reflect their marginal products and marginal costs respectively. Given the shadow prices, households and plant managers would then proceed to maximize their returns from trade. In the same way as described in the market economy above, this would lead to an efficient outcome satisfying equations (1.7) and (1.14). The actual efficient resource allocation that will emerge under such a set of institutions will again depend on the income distribution. Since resources are not privately owned, the income distribution will have to be determined by the planners and stipends must be paid to all citizens to achieve that distribution and its implied resource allocation.

There is, however, reason to believe that such a planned-socialist economy will not attain efficiency in a dynamic or rapidly changing environment. In such a world, knowledge itself about productive relations and consumption possibilities is likely to be a scarce good. Prices represent an avenue for communication of such knowledge. If there is a natural disaster destroying half of the world's oil supply, this information eventually gets to the common man through an increase in the price of oil products even though, at first, its occurrence may be known only by a few. The market economy, with its allowance for rapid price changes, provides a mechanism for economizing on such scarce knowledge.[10] Each economic unit need participate only in its own specialized occupation with its own knowledge requirement, but the complex interrelationships between and among markets will permit rapid communication of occurrences in other markets.

In a planned economy, the managerial committee would require knowledge about changes in all markets simultaneously to achieve the same result and the ability to change prices rapidly. If knowledge is costly to acquire, then it may be difficult for the planners to acquire and use it to adjust prices in such a way as to accomodate shifts in supply and demand. Thus, when knowledge is a scarce "good," then a market economy may, in fact, be preferable over a planned one on the basis of the efficiency criteria.

MARKET IMPERFECTIONS

A number of conclusions may be reached concerning the desirable market structure in terms of the efficiency criteria. It has just been shown that a system of perfectly competitive markets satisfies the criteria for Paretian efficiency. Suppose that there are elements of *monopoly* present in markets. This means that producers possess a degree of market power in the sense that they may influence the price of their output by manipulating their production. Prices can no longer be taken as given for these producers. In order to maximize their profits, producers no longer set prices equal to marginal costs. Instead, they produce that amount of output corresponding to the point where marginal cost of output is less than price. Since the producers now bid the prices down as they attempt to sell more of the product (the demand curve slopes downward), the marginal revenue is always *less* than the price of the product. To reach the output levels that maximize profits, the monopolists must restrict the amount of production to a level below that which would prevail if the

[10] For a classic discussion of the knowledge problem and alternative economic institutions, see F. A. Hayek, "The Use of Knowledge in Society," *American Economic Review*, September 1945.

monopoly were organized as a perfectly competitive industry. When the monopolists equate marginal revenues with marginal costs they find that marginal revenues are less than prices because the demand curve is not infinitely elastic as is the case for firms operating under conditions of perfect competition. If the producer of, say, figs, has a monopoly in the economy of Eden, he produces that output corresponding to

$$MR_F = MC_F \tag{1.33}$$

where MR_F is the marginal revenue of figs ($P_F > MR_F$) and MC_F is the marginal cost of producing figs. If there is still perfect competition in the production of grapes, the following will be true for the profit maximizing output of grapes:

$$P_G = MC_G \tag{1.34}$$

Dividing equation (1.34) by (1.33) gives

$$\frac{P_G}{MR_F} = \frac{MC_G}{MC_F} = MRT_{FG} \tag{1.35}$$

Since consumers set their MRS_{FG} equal to the ratio of prices P_G/P_F, it follows that for any consumer

$$MRS_{FG} \neq MRT_{FG} \tag{1.36}$$

That is, the independent maximizing behavior of producers and consumers no longer acts to automatically achieve efficiency. For this reason, monopoly is viewed to be "undesirable" by many economists. To maximize his profits a monopolist produces less relative to a perfectly competitive industry producing the same good, and in doing so, he prevents the market from attaining an efficient resource allocation.

Similarly monopoly power in factor markets results in less of the factor (say labor) being offered for sale in order for the seller of that factor to maximize his return. Monopoly power in factor markets prevents the attainment of efficiency in production. This implies that under such conditions the economy operates *within* its transformation frontier. The normative economist therefore often recommends governmental regulation of competition insofar as this is necessary to attain an efficient resource allocation.

SUMMARY

Paretian efficiency is attained when it no longer is possible to increase the welfare of any one household without reducing the welfare of some other household by reallocating economic resources. While the normative approach to economic policy views efficiency as a criterion and recommends actions designed to achieve it, the positive approach predicts that efficiency is a likely outcome under economic and political institutions that allow individuals to maximize their gains from trade.

A free-enterprise market economy operating under conditions of perfect competition in all markets in which all economic participants attempt to maximize their gains from trade will automatically result in an efficient resource allocation. When tastes differ among households in the community, the actual output allocation that emerges is likely to be only one of many possible efficient outcomes. Each efficient outcome will differ in terms of the distribution of income and welfare among households. In a free-enterprise economy, the distribution of income depends largely on the pattern of ownership of productive resources and prices. Efficiency might also be attained under alternative economic institutions such as planned socialism.

Governmental activity may emerge in a free-enterprise market economy when it can improve efficiency. Governmental action may be desirable to redistribute income, regulate competition, stabilize the general level of economic activity, and provide services that are inefficiently supplied by business firms because of spillover costs or benefits. Income redistribution may be required when some households view their welfare as dependent on that of other households. The government may act as an agent to transfer income among households according to a plan collectively agreed upon by all households through political institutions. The regulation of competition by government may assure that independent maximizing activity does achieve efficiency. Unemployment wastes productive resources, and households might also agree to governmental intervention for stabilization of the general level of economic activity to attain efficiency. Finally, households may be willing to surrender part of their command over private goods to a government for the withdrawal of resources from private use to produce goods and services that business firms supply inefficiently. Components of such services are likely to be indivisible across households in such a manner that benefits cannot be easily priced. Examples of such "public goods" include national defense, police, and judicial services. To some degree, income redistribution, regulation, and stabilization may be viewed as goods whose benefits are collectively consumed by households and are therefore more efficiently supplied publicly through governmental activity rather than through private economic activity.

Mathematical Appendix to Chapter 1

The Paretian welfare analysis for the simple two-input, two-output, two-person economy of Eden can easily be generalized for a hypothetical economy that has as many inputs, outputs, and households as one cares to imagine. The conditions for efficiency may be easily derived by utilizing the method of

Lagrange.[11] This technique enables one to maximize any continuous function subject to an equality constraint.

THE MODEL

GIVEN:

1. An economy producing n outputs with m inputs for s households.

2. $Q_i = Q_i(f_{ij})$, $(i = 1, \cdots, n)$, $(j = 1, \cdots, m)$ is the production function for the ith output. The term f_{ij} represents the amount of the jth factor of production (input) used in the production of output i. Q_i is the physical quantity of output i produced. All inputs are perfectly divisible; each production function is such as to exhibit diminishing marginal rates of technical substitution between any pair of inputs; returns to scale are non-increasing for the production of every output.

3. $\mathbf{F}_j = \sum_i f_{ij}$, where $\mathbf{F}_j$ is the *fixed* amount of input j in the economy and $\sum_i f_{ij}$ is its total utilization. This is the resource constraint. It assures that no more of any input will be used than that amount that is physically available, and further that all inputs will always be fully employed.

4. $U_g = U_g(Q_{ig})$, $(g = 1, \cdots, s)$, $(i = 1, \cdots, n)$ is the utility function of the gth household. The term Q_{ig} represents the amount of output i consumed by household g. All utility functions exhibit diminishing marginal rates of substitution between any pair of outputs.

5. $Q_i = \sum_g Q_{ig}$; that is, the total output of the ith good (a *variable*) is equal to the sum of its consumption by all households.

6. $T(Q_i, \mathbf{F}_j) = 0$, $(i = 1, \cdots, n)$, $(j = 1, \cdots, m)$ is the economy's transformation function written in implicit form.

DERIVATION OF THE EFFICIENCY CONDITIONS

Productive Efficiency

PROBLEM STATED: To maximize the production of any output i given any level of some other output h, $\mathbf{Q}_h$, and the resource constraint.

Form the Lagrangean expression:

$$L = Q_i(f_{ij}) + \lambda_h[Q_h(f_{hj}) - \mathbf{Q}_h] + \mu_j[\sum_i f_{ij} - \mathbf{F}_j] \qquad (1.37)$$

---

[11] For an excellent exposition of the method of Lagrange, see William J. Baumol, *Economic Theory and Operations Analysis*, sec. ed., Prentice-Hall, Englewood Cliffs, N. J., 1965, pp. 60–65.

where $(i = 1, \cdots, n)$ $(i \neq h)$, $(j = 1, \cdots, m)$, and λ_h, μ_j are the Lagrangean multipliers.

The first-order conditions for a maximum are as follows (second-order conditions for a maximum will hold if the assumptions given above hold):

$$\frac{\partial L}{\partial f_{ij}} = \frac{\partial Q_i}{\partial f_{ij}} + \mu_j = 0 \tag{1.38}$$

$$\frac{\partial L}{\partial f_{hj}} = \frac{\partial Q_h}{\partial f_{hj}} \lambda_h + \mu_j = 0 \tag{1.39}$$

for all i, j.

For any two inputs, say j and k $(j \neq k)$, the following holds (from equations (1.38) and (1.39)):

$$\frac{\partial Q_i}{\partial f_{ij}} = \frac{\partial Q_h}{\partial f_{hj}} \cdot \lambda_h \tag{1.40}$$

$$\frac{\partial Q_i}{\partial f_{ik}} = \frac{\partial Q_h}{\partial f_{hk}} \cdot \lambda_h \tag{1.41}$$

Dividing (1.40) by (1.41) gives

$$\frac{\partial Q_i/\partial f_{ij}}{\partial Q_i/\partial f_{ik}} = \frac{\partial Q_h/\partial f_{hj}}{\partial Q_h/\partial f_{hk}} \tag{1.42}$$

But the left side of equation (1.42) is simply the marginal rate of technical substitution of input k for input j in the production of output i, while the right side is the marginal rate of technical substitution of input k for input j in the production of output h. Thus,

$$MRTS_{kj}{}^i = MRTS_{kj}{}^h \tag{1.43}$$

for all i, j, k, $(i \neq h)$, $(j \neq k)$.

The locus of points satisfying condition (1.43) will give the economy's transformation frontier where, given the resource constraints, the production of any good i is at a maximum given the production of any other good h. Any resource allocation satisfying equation (1.43) will automatically satisfy the criterion of productive efficiency.

Paretian Efficiency

PROBLEM STATED: To maximize the utility of any household g given any level of utility for some other consuming unit z, U_z, the transformation function and the requirement that total output produced must equal total output consumed.

Form the Lagrangean expression

$$L = U_g\,(Q_{ig}) + \lambda_z[U_z(Q_{iz}) - \mathbf{U}_z] + \theta[T(Q_i, \mathbf{F}_j)] + \mu_i[\textstyle\sum_g Q_{ig} - Q_i] \quad (1.44)$$

where $(g = 1, \cdots, s)$, $(z \neq g)$, $(i = 1, \cdots, n)$, $(j = 1, \cdots, m)$, and where θ, λ_z and μ_i are Lagrangean multipliers. The first-order conditions for a maximum are as follows (second-order conditions for a maximum will hold given the assumptions made above):

$$\frac{\partial L}{\partial Q_{ig}} = \frac{\partial U_g}{\partial Q_{ig}} + \mu_i = 0 \qquad\qquad (1.45)$$

$$\frac{\partial L}{\partial Q_{iz}} = \frac{\partial U_z}{\partial Q_{iz}} \cdot \lambda_z + \mu_i = 0 \qquad\qquad (1.46)$$

$$\frac{\partial L}{\partial Q_i} = \frac{\partial T}{\partial Q_i} \cdot \theta - \mu_i = 0 \qquad\qquad (1.47)$$

For any two outputs, say i and h $(i \neq h)$, the following holds [from equations (1.45), (1.46), and (1.47)]:

$$-\frac{\partial U}{\partial Q_{ig}} = -\frac{\partial U_z}{\partial Q_{iz}} \cdot \lambda_z = \frac{\partial T}{\partial Q_i} \cdot \theta \qquad\qquad (1.48)$$

$$-\frac{\partial U_g}{\partial Q_{hg}} = -\frac{\partial U_z}{\partial Q_{hz}} \cdot \lambda_z = \frac{\partial T}{\partial Q_h} \cdot \theta \qquad\qquad (1.49)$$

Dividing (1.48) by (1.49) gives

$$\frac{\partial U_g/\partial Q_{ig}}{\partial U_g/\partial Q_{hg}} = \frac{\partial U_z/\partial Q_{iz}}{\partial U_z/\partial Q_{hz}} = \frac{\partial T/\partial Q_i}{\partial T/\partial Q_h} \qquad\qquad (1.50)$$

which may be rewritten as

$$MRS_{hi}{}^g = MRS_{hi}{}^z = MRT_{hi} \qquad\qquad (1.51)$$

The locus of points satisfying the criterion gives the "utility" frontier where any one individual cannot be made better off without making some other individual worse off. Any resource allocation satisfying equation (1.51) will also satisfy the conditions for Paretian efficiency.

2

Market Failure, Externalities,
and Public Policy

A *market failure* is said to exist when independent maximizing behavior in a perfectly competitive system of markets no longer automatically leads the economy to a position of Paretian efficiency. When this happens, prices fail to give the required "signals" necessary for the market automatically to achieve a Pareto-efficient resource allocation; for example, prices may not reflect the true social costs of resources. This chapter discusses cases where the market mechanism fails as an institutional foundation for achieving efficiency. The causes for such breakdowns will be identified, and possible corrections of the resulting misallocation of resources will be suggested. As will become obvious to the reader as the argument progresses, many of the problems discussed in the Introduction are symptoms of market failure.

EXTERNALITIES

Perhaps the most prevalent form of market failure in modern industrial economies is the result of external effects in both production and consumption. External effects, or *externalities,* are said to exist when the production or consumption activities of one economic unit affect the productivity or well-being of another economic unit *and* no compensation is paid for the externally generated benefits or costs. Two conditions are therefore required for the existence of an externality:

1. Interdependence between economic units.
2. Non-compensation for the effects of interdependence.

43

Both of the conditions must be present simultaneously for an external effect.

Externalities result in market failure because their presence causes prices to give improper "signals" concerning the true scarcity of resources. The resulting inefficient resource utilization may require governmental intervention in the appropriate market to aid in the "internalization" of the external effects of production and/or consumption. An externality is said to be "internalized" when market participants are forced to recognize their interdependence by paying appropriate compensation to the externally affected parties. Note that the internalization of an externality need *not* require the elimination of the interdependence. It merely requires full compensation for the value of the external benefits and costs among the concerned households and business firms. Of course, any change in costs of conducting economic activity is likely to induce a change in behavior. Maximizing behavior will lead households and business firms to seek the least costly alternative resource allocation after the imposition of any internalization scheme.

A number of questions must be posed prior to evaluating alternative methods for internalizing the external effects in such a way as to reattain efficient resource utilization. These questions include the following:

1. What aspects of which production or consumption activities generate the external effect?
2. Who are the externally affected parties and what are their property rights?
3. Do the externally affected parties receive external benefits or bear external costs?
4. What is the valuation of the external effects by the externally affected parties?
5. What are the alternative methods of internalizing the externality?
6. Which method is most efficient?

To correct the distortions in resource allocation due to externalities, therefore, requires an enormous amount of information concerning both technology and consumer preference. Answers to the first three questions essentially require detective work to *identify* the source of the externality, the externally affected parties, property rights to scarce resources, and the external benefits or costs. The answer to the fourth question requires a technique to evaluate and *measure* the external benefits or costs based on knowledge of technology and consumer preferences. Finally, answers to the fifth and sixth questions require an analysis of the feasibility and effectiveness of alternative policies designed to achieve efficiency within the context of the answers to the previous four questions. The process of answering the questions is likely to be costly in itself when information is scarce. Such information-gathering cost will have to be considered in evaluating alternative solutions.

An efficient solution may or may not require governmental intervention. In general, as the number of externally affected parties and the number of economic units generating external effects increases, governmental intervention is likely to be efficient. However, even if all information is available to internalize the externality, there is no reason to expect that the political process will induce governing authorities to undertake an efficient policy. Alternative policies for internalizing externalities under varying conditions will be discussed. First, consider some examples of externalities.

Examples of Externalities

Suppose there are a number of oil refineries operating in a densely populated metropolitan area. Assume that in addition to producing oil they also produce, as a by-product, air pollutants. Now, these pollutants do not have any "brand name" on them in the sense that it is difficult to tell by which company they are being produced. Furthermore, there is certainly no direct incentive for the companies to "package" their pollutants and sell them because pollutants are not economic goods but economic "bads." These atmospheric pollutants have the habit of drifting over the neighboring population centers where they contribute to the impaired health and perhaps the premature death of the inhabitants, increase the rate of corrosion of various materials, cause textiles to deteriorate at a more rapid rate, and adversely affect vegetation in the surrounding areas. In this case, the oil refineries are said to be effecting an "external diseconomy." That is to say, they are inflicting harm on the inhabitants of the surrounding areas by impairing their health. They are also increasing maintenance costs to producers in the areas because of more rapid corrosion of some capital goods. And further, the victims of this pollution (which needless to say is only partly produced by the oil refineries) are receiving *no compensation* for their economic losses by the perpetrators of the external diseconomy. Alternatively, one might say that the polluters are not being charged for the damage that the external effects of their production are inflicting on surrounding producers and consumers. Their costs of production should include these charges. The only costs the oil refineries recognize when planning their productive activities are those they must incur in hiring labor, attracting capital, and purchasing raw materials. These are their *private costs*. If one were to add to the private costs the valuation of the economic harm of pollution attributable to the oil companies, one would obtain the *social costs* of their productive activity. In the case of an external diseconomy, social costs of production are greater than the private costs of production, and more of the activity generating such external costs is undertaken than is efficient.

As an example of a different type of external effect, consider the case of an individual who fireproofs his house. By undertaking such an activity, he indirectly benefits his neighbors by reducing the probability that their homes will catch fire. Assume that there is no way this individual can induce his neighbors to pay for the external benefit he bestows upon them by the act of fireproofing his own home. In this case, the homeowner is generating an *external economy* consumed by his close neighbors. The social costs of fire-proofing are greater than the homeowner's private costs (the costs of materials and labor). In this case, the true social costs are equal to the homeowner's private costs less the value of external benefits received by neighboring home-owners. An external economy may, therefore, be said to exist when private costs of a particular activity exceed social costs. When there is an external economy present, one would expect the level of the economic activity generating the external effect to be less than the efficient amount.

Externalities are common in everyday life. Every time you drive your car, believe it or not, you become a perpetrator of an external diseconomy. You contribute to pollution of the air and possibly to traffic congestion. That is, if you drive downtown one day to do some shopping, the only costs you anticipate are those for gasoline (and perhaps if you are very sophisticated, depreciation charges on your car). But on the way your car spews forth carbon monoxide into the atmosphere and possibly contributes to a traffic jam that in turn might mean the loss of valuable time to other citizens. Every citizen acting alone recognizes only the private costs of his own trip. But the inter-action of all individuals who think in this fashion acts to make the social costs of a trip considerably greater than the sum of the private costs of all individuals traveling by car on that particular day. This is an example of a *reciprocal externality*. Here individuals simultaneously impose external costs upon each other.

It is easy to find other examples. If you keep your lawn well cut and have an abundance of flora in your front yard, then your neighbors again reap an external benefit because the neighborhood is prettier. On the other hand, if you allow your house to fall into a state of disrepair to the extent that it becomes an eyesore, you may inflict an external diseconomy on your neighbors by making the neighborhood "ugly" or a less-desirable place to live. This may hurt the well-being of your neighbors in a psychological sense, but it may also inflict economic losses on them by reducing their property values. If you live in an apartment where the walls are thin and you make an excessive amount of noise, then you may be inflicting an external diseconomy on your neighbors in the adjoining apartments.

With these examples in mind, the concept of an externality can be further examined. One element common to all the examples is interdependence. The production activities of the oil companies affect the welfare of consumers and the production possibilities of other firms. The activity of the homeowner in improving his house affects the welfare of his neighbors. These interdependencies may be conceptually generalized by stating that what is involved is an interdependence of production and/or utility functions. Given the current state of technology, the production of refined oil enters into the utility functions of the residents of the surrounding area by making them worse off because of pollution. Similarly, by adversely effecting the productivity of their employees and increasing costs of maintaining machines and equipment subject to the corrosive properties of pollutants, the production of refined oil enters into the production functions of surrounding enterprises.

But interdependence alone is not sufficient for the existence of an externality. In addition, the perpetrator of the externality must not be charged for the damage he inflicts in order to qualify his action as a case of external diseconomy. Furthermore, the victims of the external diseconomy must not be receiving full compensation for their economic losses. In the case of an external economy, the perpetrator must not be receiving full compensation for the external benefits he generates, and the recipients of these benefits must not be "charged" for the benefits received.

Alternative Methods of Internalization

In many cases, it is desirable to internalize an externality through the use of charges designed to equate private costs with social costs. Through what mechanisms may charges for damages and benefits be assessed? One such mechanism is, of course, the price system. When the prices of activities that are interdependent do not reflect the valuation of that interdependence, then the prices will not reflect the true marginal costs of the economic activity. The producer of the product generating the externality bases his behavior *only* on the private costs of his activity. This being the case, even if perfect competition prevails in all markets, efficiency will not be achieved by the independent maximizing behavior of market participants. Even if a producer does in fact set prices equal to marginal costs, an inefficient output level will be selected because the producer's assessment of his marginal costs of production is incorrect. In the case of an external diseconomy, marginal costs are too low relative to society's valuation of the costs of the particular activity involved; while in the case of an external economy, marginal costs are too high relative to society's evaluation of that activity. When externalities exist, perfect competition is, therefore, no longer a desirable economic institution because it no longer leads the economy to a position of Paretian efficiency. The existence of externalities thus provides a possible rationale for governmental intervention in a market economy through the use of taxes and subsidies designed to change prices in such a manner as to make them reflect social costs and to compensate (or charge) externally affected parties. Internalization requires information on property rights and the external effects of consumption and production in order to "price" the externality. Gathering such information may be very costly.

But the price system is not the only mechanism through which charges for the costs and/or benefits of external effects can be assessed. Another possible institution through which these charges may be assessed is the legal system. If the perpetrator of an external diseconomy is clearly identifiable and if the victims of the diseconomy can prove that their damages stem from the activities of some particular producer, then a basis for litigation can easily be established.

Such litigation, if successful, is another method of increasing the perpetrator's costs so that they reflect all interdependencies with his activity. Those claiming damages can sue the perpetrator. In the case of external benefits, those generating the benefits can sue the beneficiaries in order to obtain compensation for the external economy. \\.

There is still a third mechanism by which private costs can be altered to reflect social costs. In many ways, this third method is simpler than the two already outlined. It consists solely in informal bargaining between the parties involved. Channels for such informal bargaining do not, however, always exist. As in the case of the litigation solution, the externally affected parties must know exactly who the perpetrator of the externality is and all the victims (or beneficiaries) must be cognizant of the harm (or benefits) being done to them. Such bargains may be initiated by either the perpetrator or the victim in the case of an external diseconomy. The victim may find it worthwhile to bribe the perpetrator to alter his behavior or to attempt to obtain payment from the perpetrator for damages done. Rather than pay damages, the perpetrator might find it in his interest to bribe the victim to leave the area or alter his behavior in such a way as to eliminate the source of interdependence.

The concept of an externality is vital to an understanding of many of the social problems faced by mature industrial societies. Environmental pollution, depletion of natural resources, traffic jams, and other forms of congestion due to the presence of too many people in the same place at the same time are all the result of externalities. The reader should therefore be sure that he understands the meaning of externality. To repeat, an *externality* is an uncompensated interdependence between utility and/or production functions that causes private costs (those perceived by the relevant decision-making units) to diverge from social costs (those incurred by society as a whole as a result of the activity generating the externality).

The next question that must be asked is, of course, "What role must the government assume in coping with the problems caused by externalities?" There is clearly a basis for possible government intervention into the workings of the market mechanism when externalities exist because the independent action of producers and consumers may no longer automatically lead the economy to an efficient resource allocation. But what should the government do? In principle, the answer to this question is simple. The government should attempt to provide a basis through which the costs or benefits of externalities can be internalized so as to achieve efficiency. That is, the oil producers' private costs must somehow be raised to reflect the external costs they impose on people indirectly harmed by their activities. One way of doing this is to tax the oil producers in such a way as to increase their costs according to the amount of external damage they inflict on others. When this is done, one would expect the producers to change their behavior accordingly. Since the marginal costs of producing any given output will now include the tax, one would expect the producers to alter their output level in the short run.

Suppose the external costs of oil refining vary directly with the output of refined oil. For example, each barrel of refined oil might be associated with $1 of external costs, say, in the form of total pollution damage. Further, assume that the producers of refined oil operate under conditions of perfect competition. The situation in the oil industry is illustrated in Figure 2.1.

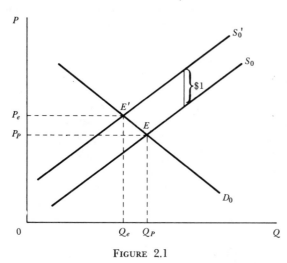

FIGURE 2.1

The demand curve D_0 represents the total demand for refined oil. The supply curve S_0 represents the marginal private cost of supplying oil as figured by the oil producers. The initial equilibrium output corresponding to point E is Q_P, which corresponds to the point of production where the oil producers' marginal private cost is equal to price P_P. This is the output level that will emerge in a perfectly competitive market. But since each unit of output is associated with external costs of $1, Q_P is not an efficient outcome. At that point, external costs of $\$Q_P$ are being generated.

The efficient output corresponds to the level of production where marginal social cost is equal to price of output. The marginal social cost of production can be incorporated into Figure 2.1 by adding $1 of external cost to marginal private costs at each level of output. This gives the curve S_0', and the efficient-output level corresponds to the level of production where marginal social cost is equal to price. This occurs at point E' where the output of oil is Q_e.

The independent maximizing behavior of oil producers and consumers, however, leads to the inefficient-output level Q_P. What alternative public policies are available to induce a cutback in refined-oil output to the efficient level? First, consider an excise tax of $1 per unit of oil. The effect of the excise tax is to increase the refiners' marginal private costs by $1 at each unit of output. In effect, this shifts the supply curve upward from S_0 to S_0' and results in a new equilibrium at E' where price rises to P_e and output falls to Q_e, its efficient level. The tax of $1 per unit will collect $\$Q_e$ in revenue.

External costs will fall from $\$Q_P$ to $\$Q_e$ as a result of the tax. The revenue collected may be used to fully compensate those bearing the remaining external costs of production provided that they are identifiable (that is, their property rights to the external effect can be defined). Note that the efficient solution is *not* one where pollution is eliminated. Efficiency merely requires that producers who are generating the externality consider its cost when making their output decisions and that compensation is paid to the victims of the externality.

One would expect the firms to behave somewhat differently in the long run. In the long run, when fixed commitments expire, the firms will weigh the tax bills they now are paying relative to the costs of changing production techniques in such a way as to reduce the external effects resulting from their activity. In the case of air pollution externalities, this might involve shifting to a new fuel source or installing a filtering device. If the annual cost of such an alteration in the firms' productive processes is less than that of the annual pollution tax bill, one would expect the firms to undertake such an innovation because the alteration will improve the firms' profit position.

Alternatively, the government could regulate the output level of the firms by requiring them to produce at Q_e while setting price P_e. Direct regulation may, however, prove difficult to administer in the short run if it moves the firms away from a position of maximum attainable profits. In addition, such a policy would provide no revenue that could be used to compensate the victims of pollution. Another solution might be to make the oil producers legally liable for damages caused by the external effects of their production. If the costs of acquiring information on damages is low enough, victims may organize to sue the oil producers for damages. If the suit is successful, the producers will adjust their output—as in the case of the excise tax—to take into account the damage costs.

These solutions seem simple enough, at least on paper. The basic principle supporting the governmental tax scheme is to have producers' behavior reflect the full social costs of their activities. The difficulties that now must be resolved are complex. First, how does one evaluate the economic losses as a result of a particular external diseconomy (or benefits in the case of an external economy)? Second, on what part of a firm's productive process should the tax be assessed? Should the tax be on each unit of output or should it be assessed on a particular input used in the productive process? Third, who will eventually pay the tax? Will the tax be absorbed out of the producer's profit, or can he raise his prices so that the tax is paid by the consumers of the product? Or can he lower the wages paid to his employees and thereby have them absorb the tax? And fourth, how can the victims and perpetrators of the externality and their property rights be identified? Unfortunately, these four questions, as vital as they are to the correct governmental action, are not easy to answer.

Consider the problem of evaluating the costs or benefits of an externality.

Many of the costs, for example, of air polution are very difficult to detect. They may consist of minute impairments to individual health that go unnoticed for years. Furthermore, some ecologists indicate that there may be long-range effects of air pollution that are not as yet fully comprehended. These may include a significant impairment in the ability of plant life to synthesize carbohydrates from solar energy. This could occur because persistent pollution can prevent some of the sun's rays from reaching the earth's surface. If this is true, the costs of air pollution may be very high to future generations because a general reduction in food supply would be attributable to the pollution.

Many effects of externalities are difficult to quantify. How does one put a value on the increasing amount of litter on the streets of cities? How does one value the displeasing aesthetic effect of billboards along our highways? How does one estimate the cost of an ugly building in an otherwise appealing neighborhood? How does one evaluate the benefits of education accruing to parties other than those being educated?

"Small-Number Externalities": The Coase Theorem

In some cases, when the number of perpetrators of external effects and externally affected parties is relatively small, it can be shown that the independent maximizing behavior of the parties involved is likely to produce an efficient resource allocation. Consider the following example, where there is only one "perpetrator" and one "victim" in an external diseconomy relationship: The two parties involved are a cattle producer and a wheat producer whose land plots lie side-by-side. There is no fence between the adjoining plots of land, and the cattle occasionally stray into the wheat fields, thus damaging the crop. As the size of the cattle producer's herd increases, it is inevitable that more steers will stray into the wheat fields and damage more wheat. Thus, an increase in the supply of cattle may be obtained only at the cost of a decrease in the supply of wheat. Assume that the law is such as to require the cattle producer to pay all damages to the wheat farmer. This forces the cattle producer to take into account the external effect of his production on the wheat production. In effect, the law acts to "internalize" the externality in such a way as to increase the cattle producer's private costs to the point where they are equal to social costs (the direct costs incurred by the cattle producer *plus* the value of the damage to the wheat crop). It is interesting now to compare the behavior of the cattle producer in the absence of a mechanism for charging for damages to the wheat producer to the behavior of the cattle producer in the presence of such a mechanism. The data for this comparison are illustrated in Table 2.1.

In the absence of any damage inflicted on the wheat farm, the cattleman will choose to have a herd of 4 cattle.

TABLE 2.1

(1)	(2)	(3)	(4)
Size of cattle herd	Annual profits based on private cost	Annual value of damage to wheat farmer	Annual profits based on social costs [col. (2) — col. (3)]
1	$100	$10	$90
2	$150	$15	$135
3	$175	$30	$145*
4	$185*	$45	$140
5	$180	$55	$125
6	$175	$70	$105

* Maximum profits.

As shown in column (2) of Table 2.1, four is the number of cattle that maximizes his profits. If, however, there are damages inflicted on the farmer for which he is liable, the cattleman's profits will be reduced accordingly at each level of output. The new profit schedule in the last column of Table 2.1 is computed on the basis of full social costs and is obtained simply by deducting damages paid by the cattleman to the wheat farmer at each level of output (that is, size of herd) for cattle production. After this calculation is performed, maximum profit now corresponds to a herd size of 3 rather than 4 cattle.

Assume now that the cattleman is *not* liable for damages. How much money will the wheat farmer be willing to give to the cattleman to "bribe" him to reduce the size of his herd? Suppose that the cattleman is contemplating adding a fourth steer to his herd of three. This fourth steer will increase the annual damage inflicted on the wheat farmer from $30 to $45. Because the marginal increase in damages will be $15 ($45 − $30), the farmer will be willing to pay the cattleman as much as $15 to bribe him to keep his herd size down to three. If the cattleman is aware of the farmer's willingness to bribe him, then he foregoes this payment if he decides to increase the herd. In other words, this $15 must be added into his marginal costs for the purpose of calculating his profits on the herd of 4 steers. Indeed, these costs are foregone at each level of output. Thus, for the first steer, the wheat farmer is willing to pay $10, the marginal value of damage done by that steer. Hence, when this foregone "bribe" is subtracted from the figures in column (1), the profit becomes $90. Similarly, the farmer is willing to pay another $5 to prevent the cattleman from adding a second steer. Hence, the profit for a herd of 2 steers is really $150 less the value of marginal damages caused by the first and second steers ($10 + $5 = $15), which is $135. If this calculation is performed for every level of cattle output, the profit schedule obtained is identical to that of column (4) and the cattleman will choose a herd size of 3 steers. Thus, even if the cattleman is *not liable* for damages, knowledge of the cost he foregoes from a possible bribe by the farmer that is equal in amount to the sum of marginal damage done at each level of production will cause him to act in exactly the same way as he would if he were liable for damage. The difference, of course, is that it is the farmer rather than the cattleman who is bearing the cost of reducing the herd size. The theory that states that the output of cattle will be the same whether or not the cattle producer is liable for damages inflicted on the wheat farmer is sometimes referred to as the "Coase theorem" from Ronald Coase, who first developed the formula.[1] Thus, allocative efficiency is achieved irrespective of assignments for damages.

Suppose the annual cost of erecting a fence between the two land plots is $35. Recall that the equilibrium (maximum profit) herd size was three when the cattleman was liable for damages inflicted upon the farmer. Consider again the cattleman's decision concerning the addition of a fourth steer to his herd. Referring to Table 2.1, it appears that his profits, inclusive of the costs of damage to the wheat, fall from $145 to $140 without the fence. With the fence, his profits *rise* from $145 to $150 ($185 − $35). Table 2.2 gives his profits at each level of output when the fence is installed.

TABLE 2.2

(1) Size of cattle herd	(2) Annual profits based on private costs	(3) Annual cost of fence	(4) Annual profits after deducting cost of fence
1	$100	$35	$65
2	$150	$35	$115
3	$175	$35	$140
4	$185*	$35	$150*
5	$180	$35	$145
6	$175	$35	$140

* Maximum profits.

It is clear that if the cost of the fence is in fact $35 per year, then the cattleman will elect to build it because by doing so he can increase his maximum profits by $5 per year. Under these conditions, he chooses a herd size of four and earns annual profits of $150. But suppose the annual cost of the fence is $50? In that case, the cattleman cannot increase his profits by building the fence and will elect to continue paying the damages to the farmer while working with a herd size of three. To understand why this is so, substitute $50 in column (3) of Table 2.2 and calculate the cattle profits for each herd size.

[1] See Ronald Coase, "The Problem of Social Cost," *Journal of Law and Economics*, October 1960. Reprinted in William Breit and Harold M. Hochman (eds.), *Readings in Microeconomics*, Holt, Rinehart and Winston, New York, 1968, pp. 423–456. The examples used in this section are similar to those used by Coase.

If the cattleman is not liable for damage and the cost of building the fence is $35, then the same result is obtained, but in this case, the cost of the fence will be borne by the farmer. This happens because the farmer will elect to build the fence when the cattle producer increases his herd size to four rather than to pay the cattleman the amount of $45. This lowers the cattleman's cost for adding the fourth steer and results in profits of $150. If he were to add a fifth steer, his profits would fall to $145, as shown in Table 2.2.

Finally, consider a situation where, in the absence of an adjoining cattle farm, the maximum annual profits attainable by the *wheat* producer are $20. When the cattle farmer enters the area, the farmer's profits become losses of $10 ($20 − $30 damage) if the cattleman is not liable for the damage done to the wheat crop. But when the cattle producer *is* liable, the farmer's profits simply remain at $20. Now the cattle producer is paying $30 a year to the farmer, while the farmer earns $20 in profits. It appears that the farmer could do better by simply ceasing production and accepting the $30 a year from the cattleman, thereby increasing his annual income by $10. There is clearly room for some bargaining to take place. The cattleman would be willing to buy out the farmer for any price up to and including $30 a year. The farmer will accept any payment of at least $20 a year. If a bargain is struck for $25 a year, the farmer can increase his annual income by $5 a year when he sells to the cattleman, and the cattleman has a new annual profit schedule as illustrated in Table 2.3. The cattleman's new maximum profits are $160 and the equilibrium herd size is four. But suppose the annual maximum profits on the wheat land are $100. In this case, there is no basis for negotiation to purchase the wheat land because neither party may increase his annual income as a result.

TABLE 2.3

(1) Size of cattle herd	(2) Annual profits based on private costs	(3) Annual cost of wheat land	(4) Annual profits after purchase of wheat land
1	$100	$25	$75
2	$150	$25	$125
3	$175	$25	$150
4	$185*	$25	$160*
5	$180	$25	$155
6	$170	$25	$145

* Maximum profits.

The Coase theorem is significant because it indicates that, in many cases, external effects may be "internalized" without government intervention in the market mechanism. But in order to apply the Coase theorem to a particular situation, it is absolutely necessary to clearly identify the two parties involved in the externality. Furthermore, the costs of organizing the externally affected parties for the purpose of either bribing the perpetrators to alter their behavior or initiating litigation against the perpetrators must be very low. In general, these costs will be low when the number of externally affected parties is small enough so that property rights to the external effects are easily defined. For example, in the case of air pollution, the number of people affected tends to be very large. The costs of organizing these people for legal action against the perpetrators include door-to-door campaigns, advertisements in newspapers, and so on. These costs may be very high. Furthermore, there are many firms responsible for air pollution in a given area. These include industrial establishments, power companies, and many firms such as automobile manufacturers not even located in the particular area involved. Once the externally affected group is organized, it faces the additional problem of deciding whom to sue or whom to bribe. Contrast the air-pollution case with the case of an industrial firm's polluting a body of water that is used by a small number of fishermen to provide their livelihood. In this case, the fishermen know exactly whom to sue or bribe (the polluter is clearly identifiable) and the costs for the fishermen to get together are likely to be low. The results of the Coase theorem will be applicable and there will not be any need for governmental intervention to internalize (say by a tax or direct regulation) the externality. That is to say, the theorem is relevant to those that may be termed "small-number externalities."[2] The theorem emphasizes the reciprocal relationship involved in small-number externalities. In the case of the wheat-cattle example, the fact that an increase in the supply of cattle can be obtained only at the cost of a reduction in the output of wheat emphasizes this reciprocity. The best solution is the one that equates social costs to private costs while foregoing the minimum amount of an output valued in terms of dollars.

The reader should note that, when private costs are made equal to social costs in an externality relationship, the ensuing change of behavior of the party involved is not necessarily such as to eliminate the damages (or benefits in the case of an external economy) completely. In the case of the small-number example of the cattle and wheat producers, when the cost of installing a fence is too high relative to the damage done by the cattle, the solution is such as not to eliminate the damage but simply to make the cattle producer take account of the damage in his cost calculations. The Pareto efficient solution is the one that maximizes the value of production when all external costs are taken into account by the party generating the externality. The selected method of "internalizing" the externality should be that which entails the minimum cost in terms of foregone income (and/or utility) to the parties

---

[2] This term has been used by James Buchanan in his *Demand and Supply of Public Goods*, Rand McNally, Chicago, 1968, chapter 9, p. 176.

involved. In order to achieve this result, policy makers must choose the method of internalization that will lead to the least loss of economic welfare in the economy. The methods may include the establishment of legal liability for damages or the elimination of legal liability, the imposition of taxes, and when the costs of organizing for the purposes of bargaining are very high, direct regulation. In each case, the cost of the scheme in terms of foregone output and utility should be estimated, and the method involving minimum opportunity cost should be selected.

Property Rights: Information and Transaction Costs

The costs of gathering information and establishing a mechanism for transactions involving property rights must be considered in evaluating alternative policies for internalizing externalities. The collection of information and provision of an exchange mechanism for external effects are likely to be a costly service that will absorb scarce resources.[3]

In the cattle-wheat example, information-gathering costs and the costs of initiating transactions for trades leading to compensation for damages and adjustment of output are tacitly presumed to be negligible. Private action is likely to lead to an efficient resolution of conflicts concerning property rights to external effects when both transaction and information costs are relatively low. Governmental action is likely to be desirable in cases where it is costly to assign property rights to the externality to victims (beneficiaries) and perpetrators of externalities. Such costs are likely to be high when there are a large number of people simultaneously affected by and perhaps generating the externality. Private negotiation is likely to internalize an externality only when the bargaining and transaction costs incurred in seeking the solution are low relative to the gains possible through private trades.

The price of any good, service, or by-product produced by economic activity is, at least in part, dependent on the property rights to its use and the extent and cost at which such property rights can be enforced.[4] The property rights over the damaged wheat in the cattle-wheat example are easily enforced. Both victim and perpetrator are easily identified and liability for damages is easily established. In the case of air pollution, property rights to the pollutants and their damages are likely to be costly to establish and enforce. How can one determine who is the perpetrator of the pollutants he breathes that impair his health? Is it the oil companies, the automobile manufacturers, the airlines, or the ordinary motorist? To identify the perpetrator and to put "brand names" on pollutants so that they can be traded might prove very costly. Who should be sued? Who should do the suing? What is the transaction cost of a

---

[3] See Harold Demsetz, "The Exchange and Enforcement of Property Rights," *Journal of Law and Economics*, October 1964.

[4] Demsetz, p. 17.

private bargain? Answers to these questions depend on the ease with which property rights can be assigned and enforced. If transaction costs are high, then one will not expect private action to be effective in internalizing the externality. In cases where these bargaining costs are high, governmental action will be desirable to internalize the externality so as to achieve an efficient solution.

Any governmental action to help internalize the externality will have to be forthcoming through the political process. The public solution has costs as well, and these must be compared to any quasi-market solution through private negotiation. The costs of the public solution include the time and effort necessary to reach a political agreement and the dissatisfaction of citizens not agreeing with the decision. These will be discussed in Chapter 4. There is no guarantee that the solution that will emerge from the political process will be efficient. Indeed, in some cases, governmental intervention may make the situation worse rather than better.

For example, if the external effects of oil refining are geographically constrained and there is only one oil refinery located in an area that has only a few inhabitants, then it might be relatively easy for low-cost private bargains for internalizing the externality to occur between the perpetrator of the external effects and the small number of victims. In such a case, governmental action, say, in the form of regulation of the oil refiner's output designed to cut back pollution by reducing the level of production, may be inefficient if no compensation is paid to the victims for their damages. The reason for this is that there still are opportunities for the victims and the perpetrator to trade away the interdependence despite the government regulation. Thus, a bargain is likely to be reached that will reduce output below the efficient output level the government regulators attempt to achieve. Thus, when low-cost channels for bargaining exist, governmental intervention may be an inefficient method for internalizing externalities.[5]

In summary, governmental action to internalize externalities is likely to be an efficient policy alternative when the transaction costs involved in reaching private agreement are high relative to the possible gains from trade. In general, such transaction costs will be high when it is difficult to assign and enforce the property rights to the externality. Under such circumstances, there will be no basis to assign any "price" to the externality and trades will be costly if not infeasible. Governmental action, when transaction costs are prohibitive, will attempt to approximate an efficient solution. There are a number of alternative policies available to government to do this. Each such policy requires the gathering of vast amounts of information for effectiveness that, in itself, may be costly in the sense that it will absorb scarce resources. The policy alterna-

---

[5] See James M. Buchanan and William Craig Stubblebein, "Externality," *Economica*, November 1962. Reprinted in Breit and Hochman, pp. 477–488.

List Policy alternatives

tives include methods to adjust resource allocation such as corrective excise taxes on outputs or inputs, regulation of output levels or input use, subsidies paid to producers or consumers to "bribe" them to curtail or increase external-ity-generating activities as well as subsidies to encourage technological im-provements that might eliminate the source of interdependence (for example, pollution control devices). In addition, some attempts may be made to simulate trades designed to approximate the compensation necessary for an efficient solution. This, of course, will be difficult if it is costly under existing technology to evaluate the external effects and identify both victims and perpetrators. For example, oil producers may be taxed, and the proceeds of the tax may be earmarked for use in paying medical expenses and other compensations to victims of lung diseases or to subsidize the replacement of corroded materials. Of course, under such a plan, it is likely that many people will receive com-pensation whose losses are not really caused by the air pollution perpetrated by the oil producers.

There is no guarantee that the political process will induce governmental authorities to choose the most efficient policy alternative. This is because it may be difficult and costly for voters to obtain information on the consequences of each alternative policy, and the final governmental decision may impose costs on some citizens (for example, the polluters) when preferences differ among citizens. Ideally, all costs including transactions costs, costs of political activity and information, and the gains from altering resource allocation should be considered in evaluating alternative internalization methods. When the costs of internalization exceed the gains, then any attempt at implementing the internalization scheme will not improve efficiency.

Externalities and Income Distribution

The resource reallocation ensuing from public policies and private actions that attempt to internalize externalities are likely to alter the distribution of income as well. Citizens are likely to evaluate any policy, therefore, partially in terms of the change in output and prices and the corresponding effect on their relative incomes. In some cases, citizens may be willing to bear external costs if they receive substantial income transfers that might be eliminated if the external costs were internalized. Residents of low-income communities with considerable unemployment are often willing to allow firms that may generate externalities, say, in the form of pollution, to locate in their area if they believe their increase in income will be greater than the external costs they will bear. Such income-distribution effects cannot be discounted in the choice of an efficient policy for internalizing externalities. Given household prefer-ences, the most efficient solution could conceivably be to take *no* public action at all to internalize the externality. Policy makers and politicians often have to consider such trade-offs between changes in resource allocation and changes in income distribution.

THE ECONOMICS OF POLLUTION

During recent years in the United States and other modern industrial nations (including the Soviet Union), pollution of the natural environment has become a serious social problem. Many households and groups of "concerned citizens" are calling for governmental intervention in the market to help internalize external pollution costs. The political concern for the effects of continued pollution of air, land, and water resources is reflected in the passage from President Nixon's State of the Union Address quoted in the Introduction. Many other politicians have hopped on the "pollution bandwagon" in the hope of attracting the votes of citizens concerned about the costs of continued pollution. Many business firms are becoming pollution conscious and are increasing their outlays for pollution control and raising their prices to reflect these increases in marginal costs. Finally, concerned citizens' groups are forming as pressure groups in order to force business and government to take measures to reduce pollution. In many instances, these pressure groups are sophisticated and have obtained the resources necessary to initiate litigation for damages perpetrated by various polluters.

Since most pollution problems are classic examples of externalities, the principles previously developed can be used to seek an efficient policy for controlling pollution. Ideally, the minimum-cost policy should be the one selected. The choice of an efficient solution will require vast amounts of information on the costs, sources, and identity of victims of pollution.

Consider the problems associated with the choice of an efficient solution to controlling air pollution. In a sense, air pollution represents the inefficient utilization of fuel resources. Air pollutants are waste particles and gases that under current technology cannot be recycled into further positively priced production or consumption. Property rights to pollutants are not easily assigned, and it is thus often infeasible to "exchange" pollutants privately. That is to say, private individuals find it difficult to control the amount of pollutants they "consume," and it may be difficult to identify the source of pollution. Since transactions between victims and perpetrators to internalize the externality are likely to be costly, there appears to be some basis for believing that governmental action may achieve an efficient solution to the problem. However, in some cases where proof of damage and identification of polluters is possible at low costs relative to the gains from successful litigation, one might expect efficient solutions to emerge from court action. In other cases, governmental action could be used to lower the costs of private transactions by establishing legal liability for pollution damages, thereby facilitating private litigation.

All the alternative policies discussed (taxes, subsidies, regulation, and so forth) are candidates for efficient solutions. In all cases, such policies require information on the portion of the productive (or consumptive) process generating the externality as well as the value of damages. If some attempt at compensation is made, then an attempt at identifying the groups bearing the costs of pollution needs to be made as well.

Consider now some of the unique aspects of environmental pollution problems. A business firm discharging solid and gaseous waste matter into the atmosphere is, in effect, using the air as an input in its productive process. Most likely it is not charged for the use of air resources since such goods as air are difficult and costly to price. Air is usually considered a "free good." However, the resource cost of using the air as a waste receptacle is not zero in an industrial community where the ability of air to disperse pollutants is limited because of already high saturation levels.

The costs of air pollution are related to the quantity and kinds of pollutants being emitted, the rate of dispersion of those pollutants, and chemical and physical reactions among the pollutants in the air. These factors differ among communities. Thus, in a densely populated, highly industrial area any given quantity and mix of pollutants may be more costly than the same quantity and mix in a sparsely populated, less-industrial area because the ability of the air to disperse pollutants may already be diminished in the industrial area. Similarly, climatic conditions such as the prevailing winds and the possibility of thermal inversions will affect the rate of dispersal of pollutants and the external costs.

Measuring Air Pollution Costs

Measurement of the external costs of air pollution can be both difficult and costly. Any such measurement depends on the current state of knowledge concerning the effects of air pollutants. Air pollution may affect human health and agricultural productivity and add to industrial costs by increasing corrosion rates of capital and building materials. There might be other incidental costs such as traffic accidents caused by reduced visibility during heavy pollution. But insofar as air is only one depository for waste matter, the sum of these costs may overestimate the true social costs of air pollution. For example, an alternative to burning rubbish is to dump it in a waterway or to bury it. In this case, any cutback in air-pollution costs may be associated with an increase in water and other types of pollution costs. These interdependencies among pollution problems will have to be considered in the choice of an efficient air-pollution control policy.[6] Thus, an estimate of alternative pollution foregone under given waste-disposal technology will have to be deducted from the computed air-pollution damage costs.

How can such cost estimates be made? One method is to obtain quantitative estimates of the damage caused by air pollution through reduction in the productivity of inputs and human welfare. Insofar as such damage is in the

[6] See Robert U. Ayres and Allen V. Kneese, "Production, Consumption, and Externalities," *American Economic Review*, June 1969.

form of lost consumer satisfaction of resources to which no property rights are defined such as the physical beauty of the natural environment, it may be difficult to obtain precise measurement if consumer tastes differ. It might also be extremely difficult to attribute the incidence of a human disease to any specific form of air pollution. In addition, part of the costs of pollution includes the resources devoted to coping with its effects such as medical care and private expenditures designed to lessen the damage of air pollution (for example, air conditioning). Insofar as air pollution impairs human health to the extent of shortening the life span of individuals and reducing their ability to work, one must put a value on human time. One method for accomplishing this is to compute the lost earnings of individuals whose life span is shortened or whose work time is debilitated by the effects of air pollution. However, such an estimate will be likely to underestimate the true value of human life because human satisfactions are not directly correlated with earning capacity.

Similarly, estimates would have to be made of lost agricultural output and plant life used for recreation (for example, shade trees) as a result of air pollution. Finally, costs incurred in coping with increased corrosion and dirt must be computed. These will include such mundane activities as increased laundry bills by households as well as increased maintenance costs for business firms.

There may, however, be an alternative method of estimating air-pollution costs. Insofar as air pollution is geographically constrained, one might expect it to affect the desirability of living or locating any activities in the polluted area. Other things being equal, this would imply that the demand for real estate in the polluted area will fall and there will be a consequent fall in the value of the real estate. If a statistical estimate of the drop in property values due to increased air pollution can be made, then this would approximate the value of air-pollution damage in the area given consumer preferences (as reflected in the demand for real estate).

Good estimates of air-pollution damage value are crucial when choosing an efficient policy of controlling pollution. Any policy will involve a reallocation of resources. Indeed, to reduce air pollution it may be necessary to forego some output and therefore consumer satisfaction as producers cutback output and invest in devices to control pollution. Prices of goods whose production and consumption generate air pollution are likely to increase, thereby reducing the quantity bought and sold. Thus, any policy for controlling pollution will be costly in the sense that some real output and consumer satisfactions will have to be foregone to obtain, say, cleaner air. An estimate of this opportunity cost is necessary in order to make the choice of an efficient policy. If the cost of controlling pollution as evaluated under existing knowledge and consumer tastes is greater than the damage done by that pollution, then it would not be efficient to attempt to control the pollution. In such a case, the "cure" will be more painful and dangerous than the "disease." Insofar as the marginal social costs of pollution control increase with the amount of pollu-

tion abated and the marginal social benefits of controlling pollution fall with
the amount of pollution abated, the efficient solution will be one for which
the marginal social benefits are equated to marginal social costs as is illustrated
in Figure 2.2 at point P.

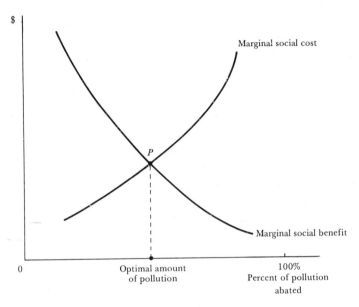

FIGURE 2.2

Identifying Victims and Perpetrators

In order to implement an efficient policy, one also requires information concerning victims and perpetrators of air pollution. Furthermore, efficiency requires that either victims receive compensation payments from the perpetrators
for their damages or alternatively that the victims bribe the perpetrators to
curtail the activity generating the air pollution (the Coase theorem). However,
when it is difficult to identify victims and perpetrators and to evaluate damages, such a quasi-market solution becomes difficult and costly, if not infeasible,
to implement. In such a case, transaction costs will outweigh the benefits from
the transactions, and private action will not achieve an efficient solution.

However, this need not always be true. Recently, lawsuits have been filed
against automobile manufacturers for pollution damages. These suits were
initiated under the antitrust laws after an important clarification by the
federal courts. The automobile companies are charged with conspiring to
prevent the development of antipollution devices. The courts have ruled that
it is no longer necessary for parties filing suits under the antitrust laws to have
a "commercial relationship" with the accused companies. The City of New

York has initiated such a suit. To be successful, the city must prove that there was such a conspiracy. It must also prove damages from the automobiles' air pollution to city-owned structures and for health benefits paid to city employees as well as city welfare clients who have been treated for air-pollution-related illnesses over the specified period. The courts denied the city permission to sue for damages incurred by all residents. This court case illustrates how governmental action may lower the costs of a quasi-market solution. In other air-pollution problems, law suits and private bargains may be infeasible if it is difficult and costly to identify victims and perpetrators and to prove damages.

Alternative Air-Pollution Control Policies

Assume that the costs of information, bargaining, and enforcement in establishing property rights to air-pollution externalities are so high as to prohibit the likelihood of efficient solutions through private action. Consider some alternative public air-pollution control policies. One set of policies concentrates only on the perpetrators of the pollution externalities. These policies attempt to achieve an efficient solution by inducing polluters to adjust their behavior in such a way as to curtail the pollution-causing activity. There is no attempt to compensate or adjust the behavior of the victims of air pollution. Such policies include taxation, subsidization, and regulation by governmental authorities of certain activities undertaken by firms and households suspected of causing pollution damages. Consider the examples given earlier in this chapter and illustrated in Figure 2.1. In this case, pollution costs are measurable and vary directly with output. An excise tax on output equal to the unit pollution costs will induce firms to cutback output to an efficient level and will provide revenue to compensate victims if they can be identified. Alternatively, the firms can be forced to produce an efficient output through regulation, or they can be "bribed" to produce an efficient output through a subsidy financed by taxes on those who will benefit from the decreased pollution, provided the victims are identified at relatively low cost.

This solution is inefficient when it is costly to identify polluters and their victims or when the "wrong" part of the productive process is taxed, regulated, or subsidized. In all cases, the governmental action will induce changes in behavior on those subject to its effects. For example, controls on air pollution might very well induce firms to change their behavior in such a way as to increase alternative forms of pollution. If pollution does not vary with output and it is output that is taxed, then the tax will not achieve a change in behavior leading to an efficient resource reallocation. The externality may be associated with use of a particular input, and a tax on output would lead to a reduction in the use of all inputs rather than a change in input combination. If it were possible to tax total pollution generated by any economic unit at a rate equal to the damage done by that pollution, then this would achieve an efficient solution. But the administrative costs involved in monitoring and evaluating pollution may make this solution infeasible.

[Ideally, any tax, subsidy, or output regulation should vary with the costs of pollution.] This would imply that the same pollution might be taxed at different rates in different geographic areas if the costs of the same pollution varies geographically with such factors as population density, industry, agriculture, and climatic conditions.

A recently proposed alternative solution to pollution problems by J. H. Dales involves the sale of "pollution rights."[7] This method takes explicit account of the fact that pollution can be considered a result of the underpricing of services yielded by scarce environmental resources. The use of air resources is usually available at zero price because of difficulties in establishing and enforcing property rights to air resources. This leads to an overuse of air resources as a waste receptacle. Dales' pollution-right scheme suggests a method for pricing scarce air resources or other natural environmental resources.

The scheme involves establishing a fee for using air resources. Since different kinds of pollution have different damage effects, all pollution has to be reduced to some common denominator. For example, 1 pound of carbon monoxide may be considered the equivalent of 5 pounds of flyash. Assuming that this measurement problem could be solved, all waste matter discharged into the atmosphere could be reduced to, say, an equivalent ton or some such measure. An authority would be established to issue "pollution rights" to discharge equivalent tons of waste into the atmosphere, assuming such pollution can be measured and polluters identified at low cost. All polluters would then be required to buy 1 pollution right, say, for each equivalent ton of wastes discharged. Furthermore, a secondary market for pollution rights could be established after the initial distribution of rights so that any firm, household, or organization could purchase them at the going price. [Organizations seeking to stop pollution could buy pollution rights to keep them from being used by polluters, thereby reducing pollution.]

Suppose the initial situation is such that the total amount of air pollution in a nation is equal to 100,000 equivalent tons, assuming that this is an accurate measure. This is the amount of pollution that occurs when the price of discharging an equivalent ton of wastes into the atmosphere is zero. This is illustrated in Figure 2.3. The curve D is the demand for services of the air in terms of equivalent tons of waste discharged into the air. Suppose the citizens of the nation through their political process agree that there should be no more than 75,000 equivalent tons of air pollution. There is no basis for knowing whether this is the efficient amount of pollution if information is scarce and the political process itself is costly. Assume, however, for the sake

---

[7] J. H. Dales, *Pollution, Property, and Prices*, University of Toronto Press, Toronto, 1970, pp. 77–100.

of argument, that this is the efficient level. A pollution-control board could then be established to issue 75,000 pollution rights—one for each equivalent ton of waste—and require each polluter to buy an appropriate amount. Given the demand for the "waste services of the air" as shown in Figure 2.3, the going price will be $1 per pollution right. Assume that the supply of pollution rights is kept fixed at 75,000, as shown in Figure 2.3. At that price, some polluters will find it cheaper to change their production techniques, reduce output, or go out of business. Thus, pollution falls immediately from 100,000 equivalent tons to 75,000 equivalent tons.

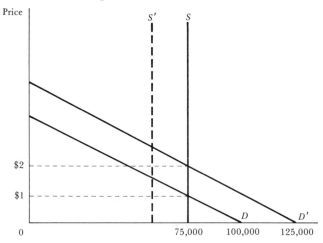

Tons of Waste in the Air
(Each ton equals one pollution right)

FIGURE 2.3

Now, the pollution-control board establishes a secondary market for the rights and allows them to be bought and sold by anyone according to certain rules. If, over time, the demand for pollution rights increases, say, from D to D', because of a population increase or a change in the demand pattern for output, the price of pollution rights would increase. But as long as the supply of pollution rights remains fixed at 75,000 and those rights can be enforced at low costs, the amount of equivalent tons of pollution will not rise above 75,000. It may, however, be less than 75,000 equivalent tons if some pollution rights are purchased by conservation groups and speculators and withdrawn from the market. This would shift the supply available to potential polluters to the left to, say, S' and further increase the price. In this manner, those who wish to control the air resources for any purpose may do so, if they are willing to pay the price.

Finally, the pollution-right quotas may be revised at any time if this appears to be desirable. Certain regions may be kept pollution free by making pollution rights unavailable for use in those areas. The board may also retain some rights for the purpose of stabilizing the market during speculative episodes.

Of course, the feasibility of the pollution-right plan depends on the costs at which those rights can be assigned and enforced, the costs of measuring pollution damage, and the costs of agreeing on a collectively acceptable level of pollution rights. These costs may be so high as to render the plan impractical. But that must be an empirical question. The efficient solution must be that which involves the minimum cost. Cost must be broadly defined to include foregone utility from goods and services including information and transaction services.

NATURAL MONOPOLY

The production of certain goods and services may be subject to economies of scale. Firms producing such goods and services can do so at lower unit costs as they expand their output. Under such conditions, competition will result in the expansion in the size of the firm until the output of the industry is supplied by only one or a few firms or until average costs begin to rise. If average costs continue to fall over the entire range of output, then one firm will emerge as a *natural monopoly*. Smaller firms will be unable to compete with the large firm because their unit costs will be much higher at their lower levels of output. Thus, under natural monopoly, one large firm tends to drive the smaller firms out of business.

It is sometimes argued that there are firms in modern industrial economies that have cost curves similar to those of the natural monopoly. One example is electric-power production. Another often cited is telephone service. The production of these services tends to proceed at greater efficiency as output levels rise. Many such "public utility" industries require a certain minimum scale of production. This rules out the possibility of perfect competition in such industries. Natural monopoly is often viewed as a market failure. In such cases, independent maximizing behavior leads to monopoly.

The cost and demand curves of a typical natural monopoly are illustrated in Figure 2.4. The firm chooses to produce output q_m, the profit maximizing output as determined by setting marginal revenue equal to marginal cost. At that particular point of production for the firm, the price of a unit of output is P_m and its average cost is AC_m. As can be seen from the diagram, price is greater than average cost for output q_m. On each unit of output the firm makes a profit of $\$(P_m - AC_m)$.

The efficient output is the one corresponding to the point where price is equal to marginal cost. This output leads to a resource allocation where the marginal rate of substitution of the natural-monopoly output for any other good or service is equal to the marginal rate of transformation of the natural-monopoly output for any other good or service, assuming that there is perfect competition in all other sectors of the economy. This implies that the firm should produce output q_c (see Figure 2.4). But at this output, the firm is incurring losses of $\$(AC_c - P_c)$ on each unit sold and has no incentive to produce q_c. Thus, private action fails to achieve efficiency. One possible solution is to publicly regulate the firm's pricing policy and to subsidize it for any losses it may incur. If average costs are interpreted to include the opportunity costs of the owners' invested capital (the "normal profit"), the firm may be induced to produce q_c if the government subsidizes each unit sold by $\$(AC_c - P_c)$. Another alternative is governmental operation at output q_c with losses once again subsidized through taxes.

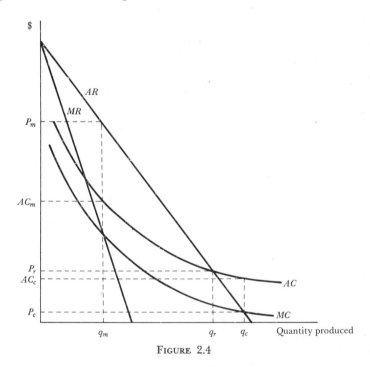

FIGURE 2.4

Suppose the government decides to use the subsidy method to achieve an efficient level of production for the natural monopoly. How is such a subsidy to be financed? Clearly the money has to come from somewhere. It means that someone has to be taxed in order for the government to pay the subsidy. The government must be very careful to raise these taxes in a manner that does not introduce any further distortion into the market mechanism's ability to automatically achieve an efficient resource allocation. If the government does accomplish this (and it is unlikely that it can, given the difficulty of imposing neutral taxes), there is still a remaining difficulty. The effect of the subsidy will be to lower the price paid by the consumers of the product that exhibits economies of scale in production. This results in an increase in their real income. At the same time, taxes have been increased to finance the subsidy, and some individuals experience a decrease in real income as a result of having to pay higher taxes. Who these people are depends on the particular tax-sharing scheme adopted by the government. In forcing an efficient resource allocation by subsidizing a particular firm, the government has altered the distribution of income. The consumers of the natural monopoly benefit by having more output at lower price, while those who bear the burden of the taxes to subsidize the monopoly are made worse off by a reduction in their real income, insofar as their tax bill is greater than any benefit they may get from consuming more of the natural-monopoly output at lower price. This policy action may not, therefore, satisfy the Pareto efficiency criterion, and there is no basis to say that it should be undertaken. Thus, governmental action to subsidize or operate natural monopolies at a loss may not always be an efficient solution.

Another alternative may be average cost pricing. Under such a policy, there will be no losses to finance through taxes. Referring to Figure 2.4, average cost pricing would result in q_r units sold at price P_r. The output produced will be somewhere between the monopoly output q_m and the competitive output q_c. The consumers of the good are receiving more output than would be forth-coming under monopoly but not as much as would be forthcoming under marginal cost pricing. Average cost pricing policy is often used by government regulatory commissions.

BALANCING DISTORTIONS: SECOND-BEST PROBLEMS

Often there are many distortions present simultaneously in a modern market economy. At any point in time, there may be monopolies, externalities, as well as other apparent inefficient behavior present in the complex of interrelated markets comprising the economy. Since it is often costly to alter resource re-allocation through private action or the political process in the sense that such changes are likely to make some households better off at the expense of making other households worse off through income redistribution, it is likely to be inefficient for policy makers to attempt to eliminate all such "distortions" simultaneously, when the costs of social change are taken into account.

Thus, at any point in time, economists must evaluate alternative policies in light of the fact that some distortions may not really be inefficiencies if the costs (through either political or private action) of eliminating them outweigh the benefits. Those remaining distortions must then be evaluated, given the fact that there are some distortions that are too costly to eliminate and there-fore are not really inefficient.

A few examples will illustrate the point. Suppose that a monopoly generates external diseconomies while producing its output. Furthermore, assume that for some reason it is too costly to breakup the monopoly and convert it into a perfectly competitive industry (for example, it might be a natural monopoly). The theory of externalities suggests that the monopoly should be induced to cutback its output while compensating the victims of its external diseconomy. But a little reflection will indicate that this is not likely to be an efficient solution to the problem. This is because the monopolist is initially producing an output level lower than the one corresponding to the equality between price and marginal cost. This is equivalent to saying that he is behaving as a perfectly competitive industry for which marginal cost has been increased to account, say, for an external diseconomy. Furthermore, in contracting his output, the monopoly imposes costs on the consumers of his product by forcing them to consume less while paying a higher price. Any policy action forcing the monopolist to further restrict his output will make consumers of his output still worse off while benefiting those who bear the external costs. This may not be an efficient solution. If transaction costs were low, there would be possibilities for a three-way bargain to be worked out concerning the output level by the monopolist, the consumers of his product, and those who bear the external costs of production. If transaction costs are prohibitive, then any governmental action would have to account for the fact that the initial monopoly-output restriction relative to that which would prevail under perfect competition might have already adjusted output to compensate for the external effects of production.[8]

Similarly, it is often asserted that real estate taxes are inefficient because they discourage production and consumption of housing. But given the reliance on real property taxes by local governments, it may be costly to eliminate this distortion. However, the federal income tax allows favorable treatment of home ownership through a variety of special provisions. This serves to encourage the production and consumption of housing. The two policies may conceivably cancel out each other's effect on the production and consumption of housing, thereby resulting in an efficient solution.

These examples illustrate applications of "the general theory of second best."[9] Essentially the theory states that if it is costly to eliminate a market distortion associated with some given economic activity, then efficiency may require that some offsetting distortion be induced in another economic activity by departing from the standard Paretian efficiency conditions in that activity. In evaluating resource reallocations, the economist has to treat each problem on an *ad hoc* basis to see if there are any "second-best" problems present.

[8] For a rigorous analysis of this case, see James M. Buchanan, "External Diseconomies, Corrective Taxes, and Market Structure," *American Economic Review*, March 1969.

[9] R. A. Lipsey and K. Lancaster, "The General Theory of Second Best," *Review of Economic Studies*, no. 1, 1956.

SUMMARY

A market failure occurs when independent maximizing behavior in a system of perfectly competitive markets does not automatically achieve efficiency. A dominant form of market failure is the externality. An externality is an uncompensated interdependence between the economic activity of at least one household or business firm and the welfare or productivity of some other household or business firm. Externalities are said to be "internalized" when market participants are made to consider the interdependence by paying appropriate compensation to (or receiving compensation from) the externally affected parties so as to achieve efficiency.

There are alternative methods to internalize externalities. In some cases, private action can be expected to achieve an efficient solution. In other cases, governmental intervention may be required. In evaluating alternative internalization schemes, all costs must be considered. These include the costs of establishing and enforcing property rights to external effects, the costs of private transactions, the costs of gathering information, and the costs of the political process as well as other resource costs (foregone output) of internalization. An internalization scheme is inefficient if its costs outweigh the benefits of eliminating the externality. Governmental action is likely to be efficient relative to private action when the cost of establishing and enforcing property rights is high. Governmental action may attempt to achieve an efficient solution through the use of taxes, subsidies, or regulation. Private action may operate through private bargains or formal litigation. The efficient internalization method is that involving minimum cost to society. Pollution is a classic example of an externality. Pollution may be viewed as the effect of underpricing the services of the natural environment, resulting in an overuse of the environment as a waste receptacle.

Another case of a market failure is a natural monopoly. A natural monopoly is a firm whose productive process is such that average costs of production fall over the entire range of output. In this case, competition leads to one firm's monopolizing the supply. If natural monopolies are regulated so as to ensure marginal cost pricing, they incur losses that must be subsidized through taxation. Governmental action may or may not be desirable in this case, depending on the income redistribution effects.

In some cases, market distortions may balance one another. A monopoly generating external diseconomies may choose an efficient output level. The theory of second best indicates that, when it is costly to eliminate one distortion, an efficient solution may be to balance that distortion with another in some other economic activity.

PART II

Public Expenditures

3

Public Expenditures: Theory and Practice

In recent years, federal, state, and local governmental expenditures in the United States have accounted for about 30 percent of annual gross national product. Slightly over two thirds of this amount has been for "exhaustive" public expenditures. Exhausive public expenditures are those that withdraw real resources from private use to provide public services such as national defense and educational facilities. The remaining one third of public expenditures has redistributed income. These "transfer payments" include federal social security and subsidy programs as well as state and local public assistance programs.

This chapter develops principles upon which one may predict when it will be efficient for government to undertake certain expenditures. Such principles can be used to explain when private action through the market mechanism is not likely to be efficient in supplying certain goods and services. An efficient allocation of resources between public and private uses will imply the existence of an optimal public budget, given the distribution of income. Since public goods are usually supplied through the political processes, one must then ask how effective that process will be in achieving an optimal public budget. The problem will be the subject of this chapter.

THE THEORY OF PUBLIC GOODS

Public goods may be defined as those goods whose production generates external benefits that are consumed by a relatively large number of households (and business firms). If such goods are produced for any one household, the benefits "spill over" to many other households. Furthermore, the nature of these spill-over effects are such that it is costly to assign property rights to them, and thus pricing of the external benefits is often infeasible. This is referred to as a "failure of the exclusion principle." The benefits of production of public goods are costly to divide into units to which prices can be assigned. As a result, it is difficult to exclude any household from consuming these benefits if they refuse to "pay" for them. The definition implies that all those goods and services whose production generates external benefits (or external costs) that are consumed by a relatively large number of households may be considered as public goods (or "bads").

The definition of public goods does not indicate the conditions under which those goods are produced and financed. The next question that must be asked, therefore, is whether such goods are more efficiently supplied by private action through market institutions or by collective action through political institutions. The answer to this question is by no means clear-cut. In point of fact, questions concerning the desirability of public versus private supply of certain goods and services are some of the most heated and emotional issues the citizens of any nation must decide. Different ideologies have developed different resolutions of the issues. The approach to the problem here will be purely economic. In a normative sense, the question may be posed in the following way: "What is the proper mix of public and private supply of alternative goods and services necessary to achieve an efficient resource allocation?" In a positive sense, the question is: "When may individual citizens acting through their political institutions be expected to choose public supply over private supply of certain goods and services?" Thus, one uses the economic criterion of efficiency to analyze which goods and services should (or can be expected to be) publicly supplied.

Pure Public Goods

Consider, first, the abstraction of a *pure public good*. Such a good, by definition, is consumed by all members of a community as soon as it is produced for any one member.[1] A pure public good is, therefore, collectively consumed by all members of a community. Each member's consumption of a pure public good does not reduce the consumption available to other members. This, in turn, implies that the marginal cost of supplying the good to additional consumers is zero. Thus, efficiency requires that pure public goods be made available at zero prices and the costs of producing these goods be financed by some means other than pricing.

[1] This definition is attributable to Paul A. Samuelson. See his "The Pure Theory of Public Expenditure," *Review of Economics and Statistics*, November 1964; also, "Diagrammatic Exposition of the Theory of Public Expenditure," *Review of Economics and Statistics*, November 1955; and "Some Aspects of Public Expenditure Theories," *Review of Economics and Statistics*, November 1958.

The definition of a pure public good may be contrasted with that of another abstraction: a pure private good. A *pure private good* is one whose benefits of consumption can be parceled among consumers such that the more that is consumed by any one individual the less there is remaining available for consumption by other individuals. A pure private good is one whose production and consumption generates no external benefits (or costs). Since additional consumption requires additional output that, in turn, absorbs scarce resources, it is efficient to price consumption of a pure private good. Efficient allocation of pure private goods requires prices to be set at the positive marginal costs of production, given the demand for such goods. Production costs are efficiently financed by the revenues obtained from pricing the outputs.

In contrast, a pure public good is one for which benefits are purely external as soon as it is produced for any one consumer. This is because the benefits of producing that good for any one consumer are presumed to spill over to all other consumers. Furthermore, it is tacitly assumed that the external benefits of producing a pure public good are such that it is so costly to assign property rights to its use that pricing is an inefficient method for financing production cost. It is too costly to efficiently apply the exclusion principle as a method of allocating the benefits of consuming pure public goods. In summary, pure public goods have two distinguishing characteristics:

1. Their benefits are *collectively consumed* by all members of the community.
2. The exclusion principle is too costly to apply so as to render pricing of the collectively consumed benefits inefficient.

It is difficult to find examples of pure public goods in the real world. Perhaps the closest approximation of a pure public good is national defense. National defense is collectively consumed by citizens of the nation, and it is costly to supply the services to consumers in units that are priced. In most nations, defense services are publicly supplied through governmental activity (or in some cases, the government acts as an agent for the community in contracting the services of private armies) at zero price. Thus, national defense services are freely consumed and supplied through governmental activity. The costs of national defense, in terms of the real resources its production requires, are usually financed through some compulsory tax-sharing scheme.

There are other goods and services that are collectively consumed as well but are supplied through private action. A good example of this is radio and television broadcasting. Services such as television programs are collectively consumed by all individuals willing to purchase a receiver and "tune in" the program. Additional viewers owning a receiver may consume any given program at no additional cost to the producer of the program or to society as a whole. Thus, the marginal cost of added consumers is zero and efficiency requires zero pricing. It is apparently costly to exclude additional viewers from enjoying the benefits of the program, although recent innovations in closed-circuit television and "pay TV" serve to indicate that these exclusion

costs may not necessarily be prohibitive in all cases. But the interesting observation to be made here is that, although television broadcasting services
apparently have characteristics similar to pure public goods, they are not
publicly supplied in the United States. Although governmental authorities do
grant licenses for the privilege of using the airways as a communication channel, television and radio broadcasting is, by and large, an activity undertaken
by private enterprise in the United States. The broadcasts themselves are
usually distributed freely (that is, at zero prices), as is true for national defense
services, but the resources necessary to finance the broadcasts are obtained from
voluntary surrender of private funds. Of course, these funds are obtained
mostly from advertisers, who receive in return the services of the broadcasts as
a medium for transmitting commercial messages. In addition, some funds are
obtained by manufacturers of television receivers, who have an interest in
encouraging the public to consume broadcast programs.

Thus, collectively consumed goods are not always supplied through governmental action. Often private action can be relied upon to undertake production of the collectively consumed good, even when it is costly to apply the
exclusion principle. It remains to determine the efficient level of collectively
consumed goods and services. The likelihood of this efficient level of output
being attained under alternative economic and political institutions may then
be assessed.

Efficient Output of Collectively Consumed Goods

Efficiency requires that economic activities be undertaken to the point where
marginal social benefits are equated with marginal social costs. Independent
maximizing behavior in a system of perfectly competitive markets by private
economic units can be expected to achieve these conditions for pure private
goods (those whose production and consumption generates no externalities).
As indicated in Chapter 1, under such conditions, marginal rates of substitution will automatically be equated with marginal rates of transformation for
any pair of pure private goods. Since the production of pure public goods
generates external benefits that are collectively consumed, such independent
action can no longer be expected to achieve an efficient outcome. Thus, an
appropriate internalization scheme is required.

First, consider the benefits of a pure public good (that is, one that is collectively consumed by all citizens in a community). Although it is conceptually
difficult to quantify the output of a pure public good such as national defense
services, it is clear that all citizens collectively consume the total amount
supplied. But it does *not* follow that all citizens place the same subjective
evaluation on this amount. In the case of a pure public good, individual consumers are not free to vary the quantity they consume. All consume the same
amount—the total amount produced. Some citizens (call them "hawks") may
value a pure public good like national defense services highly, while other
citizens (call them "doves") may feel that they receive little benefit from na-

tional defense services and may value the benefits of such services at very low or even negative values. What, then, are the social benefits of national defense services? Since all citizens collectively consume the total amount of national defense produced, it follows that the total social benefit of national defense services must be the sum of individual subjective benefits at any level of production. This differs from the social valuation of pure private goods that can be neatly parceled out among consumers in units that can be priced. The social value of a unit of a private good is reflected by its price under conditions of perfect competition. But since public goods cannot readily be divided into units that can be priced, the benefits of extensions in the output of such goods can only be measured by the sum of the marginal benefits received by such an increment in output by all citizens. Efficiency therefore requires that the production of collectively consumed goods be undertaken to the point where the sum of marginal benefits received by consumers (which reflects marginal social benefits) is equal to marginal social costs of production. Thus, efficient output of a pure public good requires that the sum of the individual marginal rates of substitution of that good for any private good be set equal to the marginal rate of transformation of the public good for any private good.

In the case of a pure private good, there are *no* spill-over effects of additional production, so that in evaluating the benefit of extra production, it is only necessary to count the benefit received by the consumer who purchases the extra output. *In the case of pure public goods, if more production is undertaken for any one consumer, then all consumers will be forced to consume more because the benefits spill over to each and every household. Thus, in evaluating extra production of pure public goods, the sum of the marginal evaluation of all households represents marginal social benefits.*

Consider an example. Suppose the production and consumption of bread generates no externalities. Thus, bread may be considered a pure private good. If the production of bread is increased by one unit, then the only extra benefits obtained by society are those accruing to the consumer who purchases and eats the bread. However, if the production of national defense services increases by one unit (assuming there are appropriate measures of this output), then all citizens of the community benefit according to their subjective evaluations of the increment in national defense. It follows that the marginal social benefits in this case are the sum of the marginal private benefits received by individual consumers.

PRIVATE ACTION, COLLECTIVE ACTION, AND EFFICIENCY

Consider the alternative sources of supply for pure public goods. Such goods may be supplied by private action through market institutions or by collective action through political institutions. Which alternative is likely to lead to an efficient output of public goods? Suppose each household in a community decides to supply its own defense against foreign enemies. If national defense is a pure public good then the defense services produced by any individual household will spill over fully to all other households as well. Thus, the defense services produced by any household will be consumed by *all* households. In other words, any household's provision of defense for itself results in external benefits consumed by *all* members of the community. Each household's provision for its own defense bestows external benefits on all other households. Private production of national defense services therefore generates reciprocal externalities among households.

There are difficulties in measuring national defense because of the problems involved in assigning units to the service produced. A rough measure of output of national defense, with no adjustment for the quality of services supplied, is the value of resources devoted to its production. Will resources be efficiently utilized in producing national defense when such services are privately supplied? A little reflection will indicate that this is not likely to be the case. Assume, initially, that each household does not consider the external benefit it receives from the defense services produced by other households. This being the case, each household, if it behaves as if it maximizes its own welfare, will employ its own resources in the production of national defense services to the point where its own marginal benefit equals its own marginal cost. However, since national defense is presumed to be a pure public good, efficiency requires that resources be employed in its production to the point where the *sum* of marginal private benefits equals marginal social costs. When households do not consider the reciprocal spill-over effects, their independent maximizing behavior will not achieve an efficient allocation of resources devoted to national defense. Instead, there will be much duplication of effort and waste of scarce resources.

Now assume that each household is cognizant of the spill-over effects it receives from the national defense activities of other households in the community. If all households behave as they did before and utilize their own resources to the point where their own marginal benefits are equal to their own marginal costs of national defense services, they will each discover that the total amount of defense services they actually consume will be considerably greater than that which they have produced themselves. This phenomenon is, of course, caused by the mutual spill-over effects of such activity. Independent maximizing behavior, however, will not produce the result noted in the preceding paragraph when households consider the mutual spill-over effects. When households are aware that they can fully consume their neighbors' national defense services, they will behave rationally if they devote none of their resources to national defense services and instead attempt to consume freely those services produced by other households. They will attempt to obtain a "free ride" from the efforts of others. Since it may be costly to price the spill-over effects of such activity, this free ride may be entirely feasible for any one household. Of course, if *all* households attempt to behave in this manner, there will be no resources devoted to the production of national defense, and consequently there will be no vehicle available for hitching free rides. In any event, unless the mutual external benefits are somehow internalized, independent maximizing behavior will result in insufficient amounts of resources devoted to national defense when some consumers attempt to be free riders.

Private action is, therefore, likely to fail in providing an efficient level of output for a pure public good such as national defense. This is because there is no feasible mechanism for establishing property rights to the use of national defense services, and it becomes impossible to price those services as a means of excluding those individuals who do not bear the costs of production in any way. Thus, the apparent inability of private action to produce an efficient outcome in the production of public goods may be viewed as another example of market failure caused by external effects in production that are too costly to internalize through some pricing mechanism. Clearly, if some sort of pricing were possible, citizens of the community would encourage one business firm to specialize in the production of national defense and to sell its "output" to citizens on a per-unit basis. But since pricing is infeasible, this is not an efficient alternative.

The efficient solution requires that resources be devoted to national defense services to the point where the sum of marginal private benefits is equal to the marginal costs, given the distribution of income. This outcome can be achieved by a scheme that has one "group" specializing in the production of national defense, distributing it freely, and charging each citizen a fee equal to his marginal benefit received from the national defense services. In effect, such a multiple-pricing scheme would serve to internalize all the external benefits of national defense production. However, this scheme may be costly to implement. It requires that each household contribute to the production of national defense forces voluntarily according to its marginal benefit. But since all households can receive the benefits of such services without such contributions, there is no incentive for them to reveal their true preferences and marginal evaluations. Instead, they may attempt to enjoy a "free ride." To be effective, this scheme requires a great deal of information on individual consumer preferences. It may be too costly or even impossible to obtain this information in view of the free-rider problem.

A remaining alternative is collective action through some set of political institutions. If citizens of the community realize that there are mutual gains to be had from specialization in national defense production accompanied by free distribution of such services, they will be likely to enter into some collective agreement through their political institutions on the output of national defense and a compulsory tax-sharing arrangement to finance production costs. While there is no guarantee that the political solution will approximate the efficient solution, it will allow specialization that may produce economies of scale through quality changes in the output produced (for example, organized armies with sophisticated weaponry are likely to produce more national defense services for the same outlay relative to private production where each citizen owns some weaponry). Furthermore, governmental supply of the pure public good also allows some compulsory cost-sharing arrangement to be achieved through the tax system.

Since the political process also will entail costs, there is no guarantee that this will, in fact, be the most efficient alternative. However, for a pure public good such as national defense, where large numbers of consumers receive external benefits, it is unlikely that private action will be efficient.

An Optimal Budget: The Lindahl Solution

Aggregate demand for a pure public good must be interpreted differently from that of the aggregate demand for any pure private good. In the case of a private good, the individual consumer is confronted with the price of the commodity and can adjust the quantity demanded of that commodity according to his preferences. This is no longer possible in the case of a pure public good such as national defense. In the first place, the concept of price is meaningless because the good is not sold on the market, and the exclusion principle does not apply. In the second place, individuals are no longer free to adjust their quantity demanded according to their preferences because all individuals must consume the same amount of the good (the total amount produced).

Assume, for the moment, that there are no compulsory taxes and that national defense services are financed by voluntary contributions of consumers. Alternatively, it may be assumed that there is perfect information on the preferences of each citizen so that they may be taxed according to the marginal benefits they receive from the pure public good. These assumptions ignore the free-rider problem and the consequent difficulties involved in inducing consumers to reveal their true valuation of the benefits of pure public goods. This will provide a basis for deriving a "true" demand for public goods.

Each individual consumer would be willing to contribute to the financing of increments in the output of a collectively supplied public good. His contribution would equal the marginal benefit he receives from an increment in national defense services, assuming that appropriate units exist to quantify the output of national defense. Thus, although individuals cannot adjust the quantity of national defense they consume according to their preferences, they *can*, in this case, adjust their voluntary cost-share bid as they wish. The total maximum voluntary contribution for an increment in output at any level of production for the community is the *sum* of individual marginal benefits received by all citizen-consumers in the community. Since all consumers must consume the same amount of national defense, it follows that the community's demand curve for national defense services is obtained by *vertically* adding the individual demand curves. Each point on this aggregate-demand curve represents the summed marginal benefits received by consumers from any quantity of national defense. Contrast this with the interpretation given to the aggregate-demand curve for any private good. The latter curve gives the sum of quantities demanded by individual consumers at any given price. The aggregate-demand curve for a private good is obtained by adding quantities demanded at alternative prices along the horizontal axis.

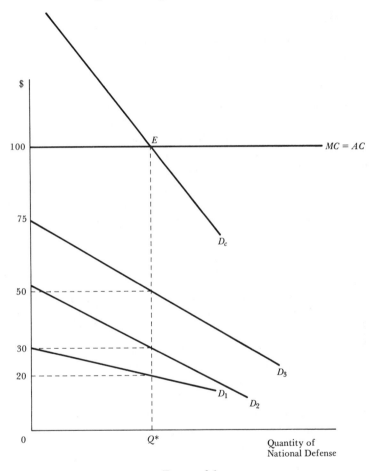

FIGURE 3.1

The derivation of a demand curve for public goods is illustrated in Figure 3.1 for a community containing three citizens. The three demand curves D_1, D_2, and D_3 reflect each of the three consumers' marginal valuation of alternative quantities of the public good. The total marginal evaluation of national defense services at any level of output is represented by the community-demand curve D_c, which is obtained by vertically summing the maximum dollar bids the three individuals would contribute to financing national defense at alternative levels of output. It is presumed that the demand curve for national defense is downward sloping, as would be the case for demand of any economic good. The curve D_c, therefore, represents the summed marginal benefits of national defense services at all levels of output.

Now consider the supply of national defense services. For simplicity, assume that average costs of production are constant and, therefore, equal to marginal costs at all levels of output. The supply of national defense services is represented as a horizontal line at, say, \$100 in Figure 3.1. This represents the unit cost of supplying an army to protect the community. The factors influencing the shape of the supply curve for a pure public good are no different from those of any other supply curve. It depends on the technology available for converting productive resources into national defense services as well as the prices of alternative inputs. Under differing circumstances, the marginal costs of national defense services might very well increase with output.

The efficient output is the one where summed marginal benefits are equal to marginal costs. This occurs at point E in Figure 3.1, where the community-demand curve D_c intersects the marginal-cost curve. This implies that the efficient output is Q^*. It must be stressed that the efficient output is likely to vary with the distribution of income in a community where tastes differ among households. This is because any change in the distribution of income will, in general, alter the demand pattern for alternative goods, and in particular, it will alter the demand pattern for public goods and the corresponding efficient level of production of such goods.

Now consider the alternatives of private action and collective action accompanied by compulsory cost sharing to achieve the efficient outcome, given the distribution of income. The unit cost of providing national defense services is assumed to be \$100. As the demand curves are drawn in Figure 3.1, it shows that this amount is in excess of the marginal evaluation of the benefits of even one unit of national defense by any one consumer. The maximum amount that any one consumer will pay for one unit of national defense is \$75 (consumer 3), which is \$25 below the required amount. Private action will therefore result in zero production of national defense services. Of course, if the costs of producing national defense services were somewhat lower (in this case, below \$75 per unit), then private action would produce some national defense services, but it is unlikely that an efficient amount would be forthcoming in a community with a large number of households because of the externality problem.

Production of a public good such as national defense can often be undertaken by private action even when the costs of public production are prohibitive for any one household. However, in such cases, the quality of the service produced by private action usually is markedly inferior to that which would prevail under collective supply, allowing for economies of specialization. National defense services may be produced by hiring the services of an army with sophisticated weaponry, or they may be provided by each individual household owning a rifle. The first alternative is likely to be beyond the financial reach of any one household (as is the case in Figure 3.1). The second alternative, however, is financially feasible for individual households, but it is likely that the quality of the service will be markedly inferior to that of a specialized army. Thus, in evaluating these two outputs of differing quality, one should reduce both to some common denominator by making a quality adjustment. This is necessary, for example, to measure the costs of alternative output levels on one set of axes in Figure 3.1. Although rifle defense seems cheaper than an army for any one household, when a quality adjustment is made, a unit of national defense supplied by households with rifles may, in fact, be much more expensive relative to the same unit supplied by a specialized army. Often, in the real world, one observes a mix of private and collective supply of public goods. Given the costs of the political process (time to gather information and voter dissatisfaction with the outcome of an election), such a mix of private and public action may be an efficient alternative.

Now consider the alternative of collective action through voluntary contributions of individuals equal to their marginal benefit from national defense services (this assumes the elimination of the free-rider and preference-revelation problems). It is assumed that individuals will desire extensions of the public-good production as long as marginal social benefits, as measured by the summed individual cost-share bids, exceed the marginal costs of production. They will desire cutbacks in national defense output when marginal costs exceed marginal social benefits, as measured again by the summed cost-share bids. With these assumptions, an equilibrium occurs at point E, resulting in the choice of the efficient output Q^*. The cost-sharing arrangements under voluntary exchange of private command over resources (in dollars) for the public good in Figure 3.1 is such that individual 3 pays \$50, while individuals 2 and 1 pay \$30 and \$20 respectively for each unit of national defense covering the unit cost of \$100. Given this cost-sharing arrangement, all three citizens demand Q^* units of the public good. This voluntary-exchange approach to determining an equilibrium volume of public goods is often called the "Lindahl solution" after Erik Lindahl, the Swedish economist who conducted a similar analysis.[2] Note that the solution simultaneously solves for the equilibrium output of the pure public good and the cost-sharing arrangements.

The implications of the foregoing analysis is that if a tax-sharing scheme that accurately reflects the marginal benefits of public goods for each individual household can be perfected, then this will lead to an equilibrium solution through unanimous collective agreement that will achieve efficiency. Of course,

[2] See Erik Lindahl, "Just Taxation: A Positive Solution," in R. A. Musgrave and A. T. Peacock (eds.), *Classics in the Theory of Public Finance,* Crowell Collier, New York, 1958, pp. 168–177. Also see R. A. Musgrave, *The Theory of Public Finance,* McGraw-Hill, New York, 1959, pp. 73–78 for a discussion of the Lindahl solution. Lindahl's model actually is somewhat different from the one presented in the text. He defines cost shares in terms of percentages of total public expenditure.

the externality problems associated with the production of pure public goods make it difficult to induce individuals to reveal their actual demands for public goods. It is rational for individuals pursuing maximizing behavior to understate their true preferences in the hope of enjoying a "free ride," while others bear the costs of financing the pure public goods' production costs.

The analysis also makes clear that the willingness of any individual household to be in favor of extensions of the public-good output collectively supplied through political institutions depends, at least in part, on his tax share of the total cost. The higher the share of the total cost, the lesser the amount that he will be willing to pay for each public good. In this sense, the individual's demand curve for public goods is the same as his demand curve for private goods; that is, it slopes downward. However, the nature of public goods is such that the individual cannot adjust the quantity consumed according to his tastes. All households collectively consume the total amount produced. The individual does, however, have the option of voting in favor of or against any particular issue depending on the quantity of public goods produced and his corresponding tax share. In this sense, the revenue and expenditure sides of the public budget are said to be interdependent. The output of public goods (and thus public expenditures) is determined jointly within the tax-sharing arrangement.

Preference Revelation, the Free-Rider Problem, and Political Institutions

The voluntary-exchange approach to determining the optimal budget requires a rather elaborate "multiple-pricing" scheme. The tax payment of each individual is contingent on the intensity of his preferences for public expenditures. Although such a scheme leads to an ideal solution in theory, practical implementation of such a tax-sharing plan is virtually impossible. If each individual knows that he pays a "tax share" dependent on his preferences, it is very likely that he understates his preferences or does not reveal his true preferences. To do this is in his interests because it conserves his scarce resources. At the same time, he does not have to forego all the benefits of governmental activity because many of the services provided by governments are not subject to the exclusion principle and his cost share might possibly be borne by others. He might, in fact, choose to contribute nothing toward the financing of governmental activity in the hope that he might enjoy a "free ride" with others bearing the cost.[3] Clearly, if all citizens behave in this way, there is no source of finance for the budget and, therefore, no benefits. But the individual who behaves in this manner assumes others will continue to contribute. Because of the lack of incentive to reveal true preferences for public

---

[3] For an interesting analysis of the free-rider problem, see James M. Buchanan, *The Demand and Supply of Public Goods*, Rand McNally, Chicago, 1968.

expenditure, it is likely that the voluntary-exchange method of finance will result in a smaller (non-optimal) budget than the theory suggests.

In view of this "free-rider problem," it is apparent that some sort of compulsion is necessary in the financing of governmental activity. This is not necessarily true for all governmental services, some of which may be subject to the exclusion principle (such as toll roads and postal services) and may, in fact, be "sold" on a per-unit basis. However, all those governmental services involving some degree of collective consumption will have to be financed through a compulsory tax scheme to avoid the possibility of "free riding."

In order to approximate the Lindahl solution for an optimal budget, some technique must be used to induce citizens to reveal their preferences for public expenditures. Such techniques are encompassed in voting rules that attempt to derive a social consensus from the individual preferences of citizens concerning public expenditures. This will be the subject matter of the following chapter.

One of the basic conclusions of the Lindahl model remains unchanged by the introduction of compulsory tax-sharing arrangements. This is the interdependence of the tax-sharing scheme with the demand for public expenditures. It is reasonable to assume that the pattern of demand for governmental services will be contingent on the financing scheme. Thus, if the United States were to change its tax structure from heavy reliance on the progressive income tax to complete reliance on sales taxes, it is likely that the resulting change in "tax-price shares" and the distribution of income would also change the demand for public goods through the voting process. This would result in a different bundle of public services and a new "optimal" budget. Insofar as the political process itself is costly, there is no guarantee that collective action through a given set of political institutions will achieve an efficient solution such as that neatly illustrated in Figure 3.1.

The problem is still further complicated when it is realized that the public budget represents a bundle of many public services and goods. The willingness of any household to vote on any budget, therefore, depends on the mix of services embodied within the budget as well as the size of the budget and the tax-sharing arrangements. Political parties often are willing to make "trades" on services included within proposed budgets in order to establish winning coalitions of voters. This enables both political parties and groups of voters to follow "strategies" that will affect the ability of the political process to achieve an optimal budget.

QUASI-PUBLIC GOODS

It may be argued that any commodity whose production or consumption generates external effects has elements of "publicness." Any activity that results in an externality has a sort of "by-product" that is consumed and positively or negatively valued by individuals not directly involved in that activity. If large numbers of individuals are externally affected by the activity, then it will often be difficult to assign property rights to the external effects and, in turn, will make infeasible the pricing of the external effects and the transactions of "trade." As a result, there is a market failure to produce an efficient output. At one extreme, the external effect is consumed by all members of a community; this is the case of a pure public good. At the other extreme, there are no external effects whatsoever generated by an economic activity; this is the case of a pure private good.

Most economic activities in the world fall somewhere between the two extremes. The alternatives of public and private supply, therefore, must be evaluated for the intermediate cases. A relevant issue now is the range of spill-over effects of any activity and the efficiency of alternative methods of internalization. In general, for external effects involving only relatively small numbers of individuals, private action may be relied on to achieve an efficient solution provided that transactions costs are not very high. For example, the costs of holding a public referendum on an issue involving the height of a fence between two adjoining properties is likely to be more costly than private bargains between the two neighbors. The spill-over effect is the concern of only one household; thus, collective action is a wasteful method of internalizing the external effects.

On the other hand, garbage collection and disposal has external effects that spill over to many members of a community. If each individual is responsible for the disposal of his own waste, he may dump it in an area where it will impose external costs on others. Furthermore, "good sanitation" is consumed by the entire community insofar as it reduces the probability of infectious diseases and improves or preserves the quality of the natural environment. Thus, although many of the benefits of garbage pickup and disposal are privately consumed, some benefits are collectively consumed. Adequate sanitation efficiency may require public supply of certain sanitation services at zero price along with compulsory tax financing. The alternative of public supply is the choice made by many communities. However, another alternative is private sanitation service through market institutions along with governmental regulation of, say, dumping practices and a system of fines for individuals not adequately disposing of their wastes through private action or the contractual services of a private sanitation firm.

In general, governmental activity is likely to be an efficient alternative when the range of spillover is relatively large and it is costly to "price" the externality. Most political debates concerning governmental activities are concerned with establishing the range of spillover and its valuation. Thus, public debates concerning the external effects of consumption and production of such goods and services as education, alcohol, drugs, fire and police protection, health services, and many others hinge on the problem of determining the source, range, and valuation of externalities and their existence. Many states run liquor stores in the belief that the consumption of alcohol, although largely a "private" activity, generates external effects that justify state administration of both sales and prices. Of course, as long as information is scarce and costly, there is no guarantee that governmental agencies will correctly assess the externality. Often, special interests will succeed in convincing legislators that an externality is associated with a particular production or consumption activity when, in fact, there is no externality. In such cases, governmental activity will move the economy away from efficiency if it produces a service to internalize a non-existent externality. Furthermore, in other cases, external effects, even those involving relatively large numbers of households, may be more efficiently internalized through private action if the costs of political action are relatively high.

James M. Buchanan, in a recent study, has generalized the theory of public goods in such a way as to depart from the extremes of pure public and private goods.[4] He accomplishes this by combining the theory of public goods with the theory of externalities. Buchanan's analysis takes explicit account of the fact that many goods and services, although collectively consumed, have characteristics of private goods in the sense that the costs of excluding individuals from their use is very low. Examples of such goods include swimming pools and motion-picture shows. On the other hand, many goods that are not strictly collectively consumed such as inoculations, fire extinguishers, and educational services generate external benefits that *are* collectively consumed.

Buchanan ranks goods along a two-dimensional spectrum on the basis of two characteristics:[5]

1. Degree of indivisibility.
2. Size of interacting group.

The first characteristic refers to the extent to which the good may be "parceled out" to individual consumers in units that can be priced. The second characteristic measures the range of the spill-over effect in terms of the subset of the community consuming it. Under this classification scheme, a pure public good is one that is perfectly indivisible among consumers while the size of the interacting group is the entire community. A private good is one for which there is no indivisibility of consumption among individuals while the size of the interacting group is limited to one individual member of the community. Buchanan's classification scheme is now flexible enough to consider goods that are neither "purely public" nor "purely private."

Three intermediate cases are delineated:

1. *Partially divisible goods consumed by a relatively small group within the community.* In such cases, an increase in the consumption of the good by one individual will reduce its availability to other members of

<hr />

[4] Buchanan, chapter 9.
[5] Buchanan, pp. 172–177.

the community by an amount *less* than one unit but greater than zero units. An example of this is individual fire protection. If there are a fixed amount of fire extinguishers available to a community, will a transfer of a fire extinguisher from citizen A to citizen B reduce citizen A's fire protection to zero? The answer is clearly, "No," because in the event of a fire, citizen A can borrow citizen B's extinguisher. In some sense, however, the quality of fire protection available to A has fallen because he must run to his neighbor to get the extinguisher in the event of a fire.

2. *Partially divisible goods consumed by a relatively large subset of the community.* Immunization programs fall into this class. By reducing the prevalence of disease in a community, such a program provides benefits that are collectively consumed by the bulk of the population. Nevertheless, the actual inoculations also provide private benefits consumed directly by individuals.

3. *Fully indivisible goods consumed by a relatively small group within the community.* Examples of this intermediate case include "clubs" of various kinds. Thus, a tennis club allows collective consumption of the facilities but keeps the membership small enough to avoid congestion. Presumably, only a small percentage of the community will belong to a given club. Also included in this category are concerts, live theater, and other performances where exclusion is possible at relatively low cost.

In all the intermediate cases, it is possible to exclude individuals from the consumption of the good in question at relatively low cost. The relevant question to ask concerning each good on the spectrum is whether collective production is relatively more efficient than private production. If a good or service can be supplied at lower cost by collectivizing its production, one expects the relevant members of the community to get together in order to organize production in this manner. Thus, the answer to the question posed earlier in this book—which goods should be public?—may be answered by weighing the costs *and* benefits of collective supply versus private supply as evaluated by the citizens of a community. All goods and services that generate external benefits and costs are potential collective goods under this approach. Even though a particular good or service may be individually consumed, it may generate external effects that are, in fact, collectively consumed by members of the community other than the buyer and seller of the commodity. These external effects are of a qualitative nature different from those of the good actually being consumed. Thus, the benefit from the production and consumption of fire extinguishers is different from the external benefit called "fire protection" that is generated by the existence of fire extinguishers in a given community.

With the preceding analysis in mind, the reader may wish to pause to consider the source of supply and characteristics of some of the commodities he consumes. Is television programing a public good? It is consumed collectively. In addition, anyone who has a receiver can pick up the signals, so that the exclusion principle does not apply. That is, at present exclusion is costly. Thus, television programing appears to be close to the definition of a pure public good. The more television one person consumes has no effect on the amount available to other members of the community. Thus television programing is relatively indivisible, and the percentage of the community consuming it is apparently rather large. But is television collectively produced? In the United States, the answer is, "No!" Television programing is provided by private enterprise and financed through revenues obtained from advertisers. However, in Great Britain, the major television programing is, in fact, collectively supplied through the British Broadcasting Company and supported through tax revenues. British citizens, in the process of weighing the costs and benefits of television programing, have apparently reached the consensus that it is more efficiently supplied collectively.

Health care provides another interesting example. The actual services of medical personnel are individually consumed. But external benefits may be generated in the production of these services if they reduce the probability of contagious diseases. There is a rationale for collective supply of such services. Thus, many states and municipalities operate clinics and hospitals financed from tax revenues. There is sometimes a charge for the services rendered to individuals by these institutions, but charges are usually below the actual unit costs of production. There are also many privately operated hospitals in this country financed through the market place. Furthermore, physicians engage in private practice and charge fees covering their full costs plus a return on their investments. Yet other countries, such as Great Britain, finance most medical and health services from tax revenues. Virtually all health services are collectively supplied in that country, even though the services are partially divisible among individuals.

Finally, consider educational services. Such services are divisible; that is to say, they are individually consumed. Furthermore, the costs of excluding individuals from the educational process are extremely low—one merely pays the tuition (the "price" for education) required. Thus, education has characteristics that closely resemble those of a pure private good. But despite the fact that much of the benefits of education accrue to the individuals directly consuming the services, it is generally agreed that the consumption of education also generates external benefits consumable by the community at large. Thus, public supply of education is believed to be an efficient alternative. Educational services to the children of the community are provided free to them, while the expenditures are financed by tax revenues. Furthermore, in many cases, higher education is heavily subsidized by tax revenues, while students pay fees that cover a small percentage of the total educational costs. Public schools, therefore, provide an example of a service that tends to be collectively supplied despite the fact that it has characteristics of private goods.

For some of these "quasi-public goods," an efficient alternative may be a mix of pricing and public subsidy. If it is possible to identify the portion of an activity that generates purely private benefits and the source of the external benefit, then consumers may be charged for their private benefit, and any remaining loss may be financed by public subsidy through compulsory tax payments. The effectiveness of such a policy depends on the ability to identify the source of the externality, so that the subsidy may be levied only on that aspect of the activity generating the externality. The difficulties involved in identifying the source of an externality as well as the recipients of the external effects have already been discussed in Chapter 2.

PUBLIC POLICY AND PUBLIC EXPENDITURES

Governments engage in activities and pursue public policies ranging from the sale of liquor and the building and maintenance of roads and schools to the establishment of national defense services and income-redistribution systems. While the theory of public goods and externalities provides a basis for understanding the conditions under which public action is efficient, there remains a huge empirical problem of actually determining and measuring externalities associated with various activities. As long as information is scarce and costly to acquire, there is no guarantee the governments will be induced through the political process to pursue efficient policies. Thus, many individuals argue that subsidies to farmers are an inefficient program. Similarly, although many tariff programs have been condemned as wasteful by a legion of economists, Congress persists in passing more legislation protecting certain industries from foreign competition. Some citizens believe that cities devote too much of their revenues to expenditures on police protection services, while others argue that not enough is being spent. Similarly, there are those who believe that educational services could be more efficiently supplied by competing private educational institutions, along with a subsidy to households with children that could be applied to the school of their choice, when compared with the alternative of publicly run and financed schools.

Rational discussion of issues concerning public policy, therefore, requires a considerable amount of scarce information. Economists can contribute to the search for an optimal budget by conducting empirical studies of the relative cost advantages of public versus private action in dealing with problems of resource allocation and income distribution. Much of this research will require empirical evidence concerning externalities. However, insofar as many external effects are subjectively evaluated, it will remain difficult to obtain data on them.

PUBLIC EXPENDITURES IN THE UNITED STATES

This section presents data on actual government expenditure in the United States. In view of the problems previously discussed, it is unlikely that the actual mix and level of public expenditure represents an "optimal" budget. It would be foolish to believe that governments always pursue efficient policies. This section is intended to give the reader some notion of the kinds of activities that governments actually pursue in the United States.

The United States has a federalistic governing structure. In addition to the national (or federal) governing authority, there are also governing authorities on the state and local levels. Local governing units range from cities, boroughs, and towns all the way to school districts. The bulk of expenditures for education, police services, sanitation services, and fire protection are undertaken by state and local governments. Expenditures for national defense, space exploration, and international affairs as well as other categories are almost exclusively the responsibility of the federal government.

The Level of Public Expenditures

The extent of governmental activity can be measured by the percentage of gross national product devoted to expenditures by governmental units. This gives a rough estimate of the amount of resources diverted from private to public use in the economy. The estimate is crude because transfer payments such as social security benefits are included in the budget data. These expenditures simply redistribute resources from some citizens to others. They do not actually divert resources from the private sector. Expenditures that do, in fact, absorb resources from the private sector (such as those for defense that utilize materials such as steel and manpower for the army) are usually referred to as "exhaustive expenditures" to distinguish them from pure transfers.

In 1969, the gross national product (GNP) was approximately $932 billion. In the same year, federal governmental expenditures were $192 billion. Thus, the federal government alone accounted for about 20 percent of GNP. In the same year, state and local government expenditures, exclusive of federal grants-in-aid, were about $101 billion, or approximately 11 percent, of GNP. Total governmental activity, therefore, accounted for about 31 percent of GNP in 1969. Furthermore, if the data are adjusted to exclude transfer payments and other "non-exhaustive" expenditures, a measure of the amount of resources diverted from private to public use can be obtained. Exhaustive expenditures (purchases of goods and services) accounted for $101.9 billion of federal government expenditures and $112.7 billion of state and local expenditures (the latter figure includes federal grants-in-aid), giving a total of $214.6 billion, or 23 percent, of GNP. Almost one quarter of all production in this country was devoted to governmental activity in 1969. If the "public sector" is defined as all governmental units, then almost one out of every four dollars earned in the United States was absorbed by the public sector to finance the production of public services.

Growth of the Public Sector in the United States

It is interesting to trace the size of the public sector as measured by the percentage of GNP devoted to governmental activity. The data for this are given in Table 3.1. In 1929, the public sector accounted for only 9.6 percent of GNP. Interestingly enough, in 1929, the bulk of governmental expenditures were undertaken by state and local governing bodies. In that year, federal government expenditures accounted for a mere 2.3 percent of GNP, while state and local governmental expenditures accounted for the remaining 7.3 percent.

TABLE 3.1

The Size of the Public Sector in the United States. Selected Years, 1929–1969
(in billions of current dollars)

Year	GNP	Federal government expenditures (F)*	State and local government expenditures (S)*†	F + S	$\frac{F}{GNP}$	$\frac{S}{GNP}$	$\frac{F + S}{GNP}$
1929	104.4	2.6	7.6	10.2	2.3	7.3	9.6
1930	91.1	2.7	8.3	11.0	3.0	9.1	12.1
1933	56.0	4.0	6.7	10.7	7.1	12.0	19.1
1939	91.1	8.9	8.6	17.5	9.8	9.4	19.2
1942	159.1	56.1	8.0	69.1	35.3	5.0	40.3
1945	213.6	84.6	8.2	92.8	39.6	3.8	43.4
1948	259.4	34.9	15.5	50.4	13.5	6.0	19.5
1951	329.0	57.8	21.2	79.0	17.6	6.4	24.0
1955	397.5	68.1	29.5	97.6	17.1	7.4	24.5
1957	440.3	79.6	35.3	114.9	18.1	8.0	26.1
1960	503.7	93.0	43.1	136.1	18.5	8.6	27.1
1963	590.5	113.9	53.1	167.0	19.3	9.0	28.3
1964	632.4	118.1	57.5	175.6	18.7	9.1	27.8
1965	683.9	123.4	62.5	185.9	18.0	9.1	27.1
1966	743.4	142.7	69.5	212.2	19.2	9.3	28.5
1967	793.5	163.8	79.1	242.9	20.6	10.0	30.6
1968	865.7	181.5	89.3	270.8	21.0	10.3	31.3
1969	932.1	192.0	101.0	293.0	20.6	10.8	31.4
1970	931.4	206.3	107.5	313.8	22.1	11.5	33.7

* Based on the National Income and Product Accounts Budget.

† Excludes federal grants-in-aid.

SOURCES: 1929–1965: U.S. Department of Commerce, Office of Business Economics, *The National Income and Product Accounts of the United States, 1929–1965*. 1965–1969: U.S. Department of Commerce, Office of Business Economics, *Survey of Current Business*.

Since 1930, the role of the federal government in the economy has expanded at a much more rapid rate than that of state and local governments. Thus, in 1960, the federal government accounted for 18.5 percent of GNP, while state and local government expenditures were only 8 percent of GNP. The sharp increases in federal expenditures for the years 1942 and 1945 to over 35 percent of GNP, of course, reflect the influence of World War II on governmental activity. From 1963 to 1969, the average rate of growth of the federal sector, as measured by its share of GNP, was 2 percent. Over the same time period, the rate of growth of state and local government expediture, as a percent of GNP, was 3.1 percent. Thus, in recent years, state and local governmental activity has been increasing at a more rapid rate than federal governmental activity.

The conclusion to be drawn from the data in Table 3.1 is that the size of the public sector, as measured by the percentage of GNP devoted to governmental activity $(F + S)/GNP$, has undergone a significant increase since 1929. In fact, the increase has been more than threefold. Total governmental expenditures have increased from 9.6 percent of GNP to 33.7 percent of GNP in the forty-one year period surveyed in Table 3.1.

The Mix of Governmental Expenditures

What is the allocation of resources within the public sector? What kinds of services do governments currently provide in the United States? This section presents data on the allocation of resources between the federal and state-local budgets.

Federal Government

The current practice of the U.S. Bureau of the Budget is to group the expenditures of the federal government into thirteen functional categories, according to the general purpose served. These categories are as follows:

1. National defense.
2. Income security.
3. Interest on debt.
4. Health.
5. Commerce and transportation.
6. Veterans benefits and services.
7. Education and manpower.
8. Agriculture and rural development.
9. General government.
10. Community development and housing.
11. International affairs.
12. Space research and technology.
13. Natural resources.

The ranking of the expenditures is on the basis of the amount of resources they absorb. Thus, the federal government expends the largest bulk of its resources on national defense expenditures. Second in importance are income security (redistribution) expenditures. The federal government spends the smallest amount of resources on natural resources programs.

Table 3.2 presents data on the mix of federal governmental expenditures for the fiscal year 1969, along with estimates for the fiscal years 1970 and 1971. These data will allow some more specific inferences to be made about the nature of governmental activity in the United States today.

TABLE 3.2

The Mix of Federal Government Expenditure
(in millions of dollars)

Function	Actual 1969	Estimate 1970	Estimate 1971*	Percentage distribution Actual 1969	Percentage distribution Estimate 1970	Percentage distribution Estimate 1971*
National defense	81,240	79,432	73,583	44.0	40.1	36.7
International affairs	3,784	4,113	3,589	2.0	2.1	1.8
Space research and technology	4,247	3,886	3,400	2.3	2.0	1.7
Agriculture	6,221	6,343	5,364	3.4	3.2	2.7
Natural resources	2,129	2,485	2,503	1.1	1.3	1.2
Commerce and transportation	7,873	9,436	8,785	4.3	4.8	4.4
Community development and housing	1,961	3,046	3,781	1.1	1.5	1.9
Education and manpower	6,825	7,538	8,129	3.7	3.8	4.0
Health	11,696	13,265	14,957	6.3	6.7	7.4
Income security	37,399	43,832	50,384	20.3	22.1	25.1
Veterans benefits	7,640	8,681	8,475	4.1	4.4	4.2
General government	2,866	3,620	4,084	1.5	1.8	2.0
Interest	15,791	17,821	17,799	8.6	9.0	8.9
[Undistributed intra-government transactions and allowances]	−5,117	−5,613	−4,064	−2.7	−2.8	−2.0]
Total expenditure	184,556	197,885	200,771			

* The estimate for 1971 is based on presidential proposals.
SOURCE: *Budget of the United States Government, 1971.*

As may be seen from the data, the two largest categories of expenditure in percentage terms are national defense and income security. In 1969, defense expenditures accounted for about 44 percent of total federal governmental expenditures. The amount of defense expenditures directly attributable to the Vietnam conflict in 1969 amounted to about 15 percent of total outlays. Expenditures on defense are projected to decline in relative importance, under the assumption that this country will gradually scale down its military commitments in Southeast Asia. In any event, the public good "national defense" apparently absorbs about 40 percent (the dominant amount) of resources available for federal use.

Income security programs include social security and public assistance payments. These programs reflect the government's role in redistributing income among citizens. In 1969, these programs accounted for 20.3 percent of total federal government outlays. This figure is projected to rise to about 25 percent on the basis of recent administrative proposals. In addition, about 8.6 percent of outlays went to pay interest on the national debt. Since the bulk of our national debt is domestically held, these payments largely represent transfers of income among citizens.

Other categories of lesser magnitude are health programs that accounted for 6.3 percent of outlays in 1969, commerce and transportation that accounted for 4.3 percent in 1969, and education and manpower that accounted for 3.7 percent in 1969.

The figures for 1970 and 1971 reflect a conscious effort on the part of the administration to reallocate funds from defense to human resources programs. Thus, on a percentage basis, expenditures on defense are projected to fall while expenditures on community development, housing, education, manpower, health, and income security are projected to rise.

State and Local Government
Table 3.3 gives the mix of state and local expenditures in both dollar and percentage terms for the year 1968. As can be seen immediately, the combined budgets of all state and local governments have a different emphasis when compared to the federal budget. There are virtually no resources devoted to defense. Instead, the dominant expenditure is education, accounting for slightly more than 40 percent of total outlays in 1968. Second in importance are highways that account for 13.2 percent of expenditures. State and local governments' redistributional activities are reflected in the public assistance and relief expenditures accounting for 10.3 percent of outlays. Health and hospitals account for 8.2 percent of expenditures, while police, fire, and sanitation services combined account for a little less than 7 percent of outlays.

The revenue-expenditure process of local governments is different in scope in many ways from that of the federal government. In some respects, these differences reflect the particular institutional arrangements in the United States, while in others, they are the result of the unique aspects of a federalistic governmental structure. The problems of state and local expenditure and financing are important enough to rate a full section in this book. Therefore, any further discussion of fiscal federalism and its implications will be deferred until Part IV.

TABLE 3.3

The Mix of State and Local Government Expenditures, 1968
(in millions of dollars)

Function	1968	Percent of total
Education	43,398	40.3
Police services	3,901	3.6
Fire protection	1,824	1.7
Prisons	1,461	1.4
Sanitation services	2,508	2.4
Health and hospitals	8,789	8.2
Public assistance and relief	11,092	10.3
Highways	14,260	13.2
Natural resources (conservation and recreation)	2,618	2.4
Public utilities	1,231	1.1
Administration	12,076	11.2
Other*	4,474	4.2
Total	107,632	100.0

* Includes regulation, agricultural support, and other miscellaneous services.
SOURCE: U.S. Department of Commerce, *National Income Accounts.*

SUMMARY

Public goods are those that are difficult to parcel out among consumers in units that can be easily priced and traded. The benefits of public goods are, at least in part, collectively consumed by a group. Such goods are usually made available to citizen consumers at zero price, while their costs of production are distributed among citizens according to some predetermined compulsory tax-sharing plan. Any good whose production or consumption generates externalities that are collectively consumed by a relatively large number of households may be considered as having characteristics of a public good. Private action through market institutions is usually inefficient in supplying public goods because of the inapplicability of the exclusion principle to benefits of public goods production. It is costly and often infeasible to assign and enforce property rights to the benefits of public goods. Thus, the market tends to fail in producing efficient amounts of such goods.

A pure public good is one that is consumed by all members of a community as soon as it is produced for any one member. The production of such a good results in externalities that spill over to all members of the community. Its benefits are, therefore, collectively consumed, and the exclusion of any one member from those benefits is infeasible. A pure private good is one whose production or consumption generates no external effects. Efficiency requires that the production of pure public goods be undertaken to the point where the *sum* of marginal private benefits is just equal to the marginal costs of production.

Private action through market institutions is likely to be inefficient in supplying pure public goods. This results from the externalities associated with the production of such goods. Independent maximizing behavior, insofar as it is cognizant of the external benefits inherent in the production of public goods, will result in individuals attempting to consume the benefits of others' efforts, while bearing no costs themselves. Attempts to obtain a "free ride" will make private action an inefficient method of production for public goods.

Collective action through political institutions may or may not achieve an efficient solution because the political process itself is costly and requires a great deal of information on consumer preferences to achieve efficiency. Ideally, an efficient solution could be achieved if each household were taxed according to the marginal benefits it received from public goods, and the public budget were expanded until the sum of extra tax revenue was just equal to marginal costs of production. This is the Lindahl solution, which solves simultaneously for the output of a pure public good and tax shares. However, problems in inducing households to reveal their true preferences for public goods resulting from free-rider effects will make this solution difficult to implement.

In actuality, many goods and services fall between the extremes of pure public and pure private goods. An economic activity that generates external effects may be considered a potential publicly supplied good. In evaluating the alternatives of public and private supply for intermediate cases, one must consider the range of spill over and the efficiency of alternative methods of internalization. In general, governmental activity is likely to be an efficient alternative when the range of spill over is relatively large and when it is costly to "price" the externality.

4

Social Choice

Much of economic theory is concerned with the problem of individual choice. The field of consumer behavior analyzes how individual households choose to allocate their scarce resources among alternative bundles of goods and services available in the market place. The field of producer behavior analyzes the choices made by business firms in determining their output level and their utilization of alternative factors of production. This chapter analyzes the process by which *communities* reach decisions. Community decisions differ from individual decisions in the sense that they are collectively made. They require agreement by more than one household. Social choice therefore requires some collective decision-making rule that will be generally acceptable to the community. One rule used in many communities is simple "majority rule." It is by no means the only possible rule.

The field of social choice analyzes the implications of alternative collective decision-making rules. It is the study of how a community composed of citizens with diverse preference patterns reaches a social choice through voting on issues relating to the level and mix of governmental activity as well as tax-sharing arrangements. All collective-decision rules, aside from "unanimity rule," imply the existence of groups of individuals who will be dissatisfied with the resulting decision. If the decision rule and process is to be viable, then it must avoid undue infringement of the rights of dissident groups. To fail on this account implies the possibility of revolution.

In a sense, the purpose of a study of collective decision-making is to show how individual preferences may be channeled into a social choice under alternative decision rules. The approach to the problem cannot be purely economic. Many "non-economic" variables enter into a determination of the choices of a society and the establishment of priorities among goals. Nevertheless, the possibility of trade-offs between goals and the votes on various issues by the citizens open the door to fruitful analysis with the aid of many of the economist's standard tools. In short, to understand collective decision-making, one must study the political process.

The political process itself is likely to have defects. Choices made through political institutions also entail costs. Governmental policies made through any voting mechanism (such as majority rule) and by political institutions may or may not be efficient. Thus, both political and market institutions may be imperfect mechanisms for achieving efficiency. In evaluating the costs and benefits of governmental activity in specific cases, one must compare the likelihood of achieving efficiency through collective action by political institutions with the alternative of private action through market institutions. Chapters 2 and 3 have outlined cases where private action is inefficient. This chapter analyzes the effectiveness of collective action as a method of achieving efficiency.

THE POLITICAL PROCESS

The United States has a representative form of government. The decisions made by such a government are not a result of direct voting by all individuals. Instead, individuals vote for representatives to participate in both executive (mayors, governors, the President) and legislative (city councilmen, state representatives, United States senators) actions of governmental decision-making. This differs from a "pure" participatory democracy in which each individual in the society participates directly in the collective decision-making process. An example of such a process is the classic New England town meeting. This method also is employed by other small units of government in this country; for example, school budgets may be approved at a public meeting by a simple majority vote.

For large groupings of individuals, representative government is more efficient than pure participatory democracy in the sense that it takes less time to reach any given decision. However, there is always the danger that the representative will not accurately reflect the preferences of his constituents in reaching decisions. When such is the case, he may impose high costs on his constitutents until the time when he seeks reelection. It is likely that he will be voted out of office in the next election if the costs are excessive.

It is also interesting to note that as most communities grow in size, they tend to develop more complex bureaucratic structures to administer collective decisions. It is apparent to many that a bureaucratic structure may develop a "mind of its own" and play an important role in proposing and initiating governmental policy. Thus, no analysis of collective choice can be complete without a discussion of bureaucracy and the role of bureaucrats in shaping policy within complex governmental organizations. Such an analysis will be provided at the end of the chapter. In addition, the following chapter will study the federal budgeting process in the United States in greater detail. Also included in that chapter will be a description of the techniques used by the bureaucratic structure to order alternative projects.

Voting Rules

Voting is a technique through which individuals can reveal their preferences for public expenditures. Since pricing is often an inefficient method of distributing public goods and other goods and services whose production generates externalities, there must be general agreement in the community concerning the level of public expenditures and the types of goods and services provided by the government as well as the compulsory tax-sharing plan. Individual households must collectively agree on the issues and accept the resulting decisions; otherwise, the outcome may euphemistically be called "chaos."

There must be some rule upon which to base collective, or group, decisions. Although the reader is undoubtedly most familiar with majority rule, where the proportion of the community necessary for agreement is approximately 51 percent, it must be emphasized that there exists a multitude of alternative decision rules. The selection of any given decision rule is complicated by the not-so-obvious fact that such a choice in itself is a collective decision! There must be general agreement on the collective decision-making rule before there can be any collective decisions.[1]

Alternative decision rules may be classified on a spectrum according to the percentage of the community required to reach the decision. On this basis, rules run the gamut from 0 percent to 100 percent of the voters. If a community has P voting citizens, then the proportion of voters required to reach a decision under a simple majority rule will be $(P/2 + 1)/P$. If unanimous consent is required, the proportion will be P/P, or 1. If some minority rule is chosen, then the required proportion of voters necessary to make a choice will be less than $\frac{1}{2}$. If a two-thirds majority is required, it will be necessary to have $2P/3$ of the voters agreeing. This is summarized in Figure 4.1.

Consider minority rule first. If the community agrees to such a decision-making rule, it runs the risk of making decisions that do not satisfy a majority of the community. In such cases, those who disagree with the decision bear external costs imposed on them by a minority of the community. When decisions are always made by a *specific* minority group, the result is called "oligarchy." The extreme form of minority rule is that in which decisions are made by only one member of the community. In the case where the decisions

---

[1] This point has been emphasized by Buchanan and Tullock in their study of constitutional choice. See James Buchanan and Gordon Tullock, *The Calculus of Consent*, University of Michigan Press, Ann Arbor, 1962, p. 5.

are always made by one specific individual, the result is monarchy (or dictatorship). It is even possible to conceive of a voting rule where decisions are made by 0 percent of the population! In such a case, the community would be ruled by some external power such as a deity or a set of traditions. In these limiting cases, there is no *collective* decision-making at all because the decisions are the result of the whims of one individual or some external force that commands the obedience of the community.

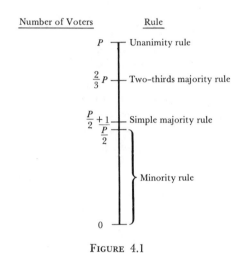

FIGURE 4.1

It is rather unlikely that a community accepting the individualistic value judgments of Chapter 1 will choose a minority rule as its criterion for social choice. If such a rule were chosen, it would mean that there would be a distinct possibility that the resulting decision would ignore the preferences of a majority of the individuals comprising the community. In terms of external effects, minority-rule decisions are likely to be very costly. On the other hand, in some ways, such decisions might be considered more efficient since less resources (especially time) would have to be devoted to making the actual decision.

Simple majority rule merely requires agreement among approximately 51 percent of the community. This is a rule commonly used to elect representatives in the United States and other countries. However, the constitutional structure of the federal government is such that other rules (such as two-thirds majority rule) are used as well. For example, confirmation of certain presidential appointees by the Senate requires a two-thirds majority.

As one moves on the scale of Figure 4.1 from zero to P, the number of voters who are likely to be dissatisfied with the collective decision declines. For simple majority rule, it is quite possible that slightly less than one half of the community will be dissatisfied with the resultant decision. For the case of the two-thirds majority rule, the maximum possible amount of dissatisfied voters declines to about 33 percent of the voting population. At point P on the scale, the decision rule requires agreement among all voters in the community. This is called "unanimity rule." In this case, the maximum amount of potentially dissatisfied participants falls to zero.

Choice of the Decision Rule

An analysis of the factors influencing the choice of collective decision-making rules has been offered by James Buchanan and Gordon Tullock.[2] Their technique is to concentrate on the factors from the point of view of the individual voting member of the community. Each individual weighs the costs and benefits of alternative decision rules in relation to his own particular interests. Decision rules that rank below the point $P/2$ on the scale of Figure 4.1 are likely to impose high external costs on individuals who do not agree with the minority consensus. They will be forced to pay taxes for activities from which they receive little or no benefit. On the other hand, decision rules requiring agreement among a very high proportion of the population also are likely to be very costly because they imply that a great deal of time might be necessary to work out a compromise agreeable to all factions within the community. Buchanan and Tullock refer to these as "decision-making costs."

Most nations actually employ a multitude of decision-making rules. Indeed it is the essence of a constitution to embody a set of diverse decision rules.[3] That is to say, there is a generally agreed procedure through which decisions are made. Citizens in the United States elect a President once every four years. Between presidential elections, the chief executive has a considerable amount of power to make decisions within the framework of the Constitution, subject to the constraint of legislative action and judicial review. It is possible that presidential decision-making power in the interval between elections might impose high costs on a significant portion of the population who find his policies repugnant. For example, many citizens apparently believe that the Gulf of Tonkin Resolution that was used by the chief executive to expand the military involvement of the United States in Southeast Asia was a mistake precisely because it resulted in a decision-making rule under which the President imposed extremely high external costs on many citizens.

The benefits of collective action may be measured by the efficiency gains obtained from the internalization of any external effects of private action. The costs of collective action are the sum of newly generated external costs of the political process and the decision-making costs of collective choices. The political process can be expected to generate externalities for all decision-making rules aside from unanimity. The actions of the citizens' voting positively on any issue passed according to some decision rule results in external costs imposed on those citizens who voted negatively on the issue and are

2 Buchanan and Tullock, especially chapter 6.
3 Buchanan and Tullock, p. 81.

therefore dissatisfied with the resulting decision. For example, the individual who is forced by majority rule to bear an increase in taxes to finance increased public services from which he receives no benefits is bearing external costs of the political process. For any single individual, the *external costs* of the political process associated with any one particular activity may be defined as the present value of the costs he expects to bear as a result of the actions of others through the political process.

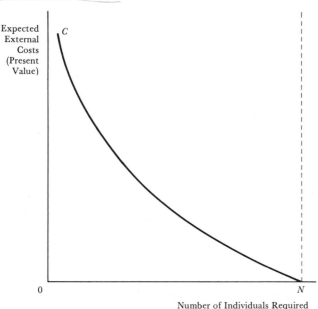

FIGURE 4.2

SOURCE: James M. Buchanan and Gordon Tullock, *The Calculus of Consent*, University of Michigan Press, Ann Arbor, 1962. Copyright © 1962 by the University of Michigan Press.

On any issue, external costs of the decision are likely to decrease as the number of individual voters required for action to take place increases. This relation is called the "external-costs function" by Buchanan and Tullock, and it is plotted in Figure 4.2.[4] The external-cost function is likely to differ among individuals. Furthermore, for different issues, the costs will differ for the same individuals. For example, the external costs of the decision to wage war are likely to be considerably higher than those corresponding to the number of limousines to be made available to government officials. For all issues and individuals, external costs will be zero when unanimous approval is required for action (point N in Figure 4.2).

---

[4] Buchanan and Tullock, p. 65.

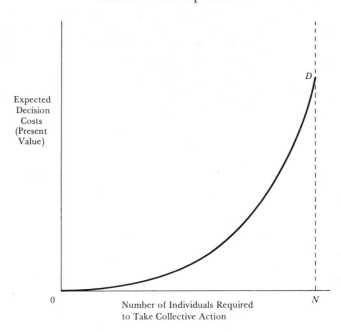

Expected
Decision
Costs
(Present
Value)

D

0

Number of Individuals Required
to Take Collective Action

N

FIGURE 4.3

SOURCE: James M. Buchanan and Gordon Tullock, *The Calculus of Consent*, University of Michigan Press, Ann Arbor, 1962. Copyright © 1962 by the University of Michigan Press.

There is also a "decision-making costs" function. Decision-making costs are likely to increase as a larger proportion of the population is required to reach a decision. This is because more time and effort will be required to reach a consensus for the group. If the decisions are made by one specific individual (say, the President) the decision-making costs are likely to be very low, since no consensus whatsoever will be required. If unanimous consent is required for action, decision-making costs may be extremely high, not only because of the time required to reach agreement, but also because the knowledge by any one individual that he can prevent action by being obstinate leads to the possibility of strategic behavior by individuals. They may withhold their consent until they succeed in extorting "bribes" from those individuals who strongly desire action on the issue. Figure 4.3 plots decision-making costs against the number of voters in the community required for positive action on an issue. The decision-making costs represent those incurred by the individual voter during the decision-making process. Once again, the costs are likely to differ among voters and between issues.

The rational individual, when asked which decision rule he prefers on each possible issue, will choose the one that minimizes the sum of the present value of the expected external and decision-making costs he must incur in the social-choice process. Figure 4.4 plots a relation representing the sum of expected external costs and decision costs on one particular issue for a given voter. For the particular issue represented in Figure 4.4, the voter will choose the voting rule represented by K in the diagram. Such a rule implies that at least K/N of the population must agree before positive action on the issue can be undertaken. This is the voting rule that minimizes the costs for this particular voter.

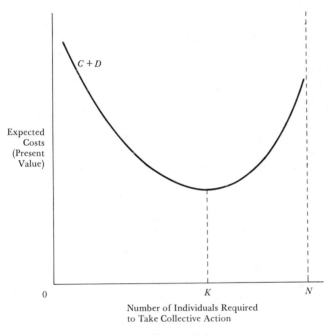

FIGURE 4.4

SOURCE: James M. Buchanan and Gordon Tullock, *The Calculus of Consent*, University of Michigan Press, Ann Arbor, 1962. Copyright © 1962 by the University of Michigan Press.

A constitution represents a set of decision rules concerning the conduct of particular activities. As such, it embodies the preferences of the citizens of a community concerning costs of different decision rules at the time of its actual writing. Most constitutions can be amended to correct for changing preferences of individuals in the community. Those activities not involving excessive external costs are likely to have decision rules falling close to the zero point on the scale of Figure 4.1. For example, most constitutions of modern nations do not state the amount of bread each individual must consume or the kind of occupation he must choose. These activities are left as private rather than collective decisions. Declaring war is usually made as a collective decision. In the United States, war can be declared only by a majority vote of the Senate.

The President is elected by a simple majority of votes in the electoral college. Senators are usually elected by a simple majority of the popular vote in the states they represent. As an exercise, the reader may wish to study the United States Constitution or the constitution of a state or local government to see how many decision rules are embodied in it. One will undoubtedly discover that some powers (that is, the sanctioned right to make collective decisions embodying external costs) are vested in the executive, while others reside with the legislature or with the community as a whole.

The following sections will discuss the advantages and disadvantages of some specific collective decision-making rules.

Unanimous Consent
The rule of unanimity requires the unanimous consent of the households comprising a community before positive action can be undertaken. As has been suggested, the external costs of unanimous consent will be zero, but decision-making costs are likely to be quite high for a community composed of individuals with diverse preferences.

It is interesting to relate the rule of unanimous consent to the economist's concept of efficiency. The reader will recall that Paretian efficiency is attained when no one household can be made better off without making some other household worse off. Using this criterion, the only policy actions that can be endorsed are those that harm no individual member of the community. Since an individual who believes that he may be harmed by a particular action can be expected to withhold his consent to such action (that is, vote against it), the rule of unanimity can assure that only those actions that satisfy the Pareto criterion will be approved, unless individual citizens play "strategies" to remain "holdouts" so that they may extort bribes from their fellow citizens to agree.

Aside from implying very high decision-making costs, the unanimity rule may make agreement on collective issues virtually impossible. This may well be a very high price to pay for the reduction of external costs of collective action to zero. It is, however, likely that "trades" would develop to compensate for the possibility of inaction. Under such arrangements, individuals who strongly favor action on particular issues will attempt to "buy" the votes of other individuals who may bear external costs as a result of positive action on the issue. These "bribes" may take the form of pecuniary compensation or the guarantee to vote positively on some other issue desired by the individuals' bearing the external cost of this particular issue. This vote trading is quite common in legislatures and has been referred to as "log-rolling." Essentially what is involved is the payment of compensation in one form or another to those who will be harmed as a result of the proposed action. Such compensation payments, although they do facilitate collective action, must, of course, be added into the decision-making costs of the unanimity rule.

Concern for the rights of minorities led Knut Wicksell, the famous nineteenth-century Swedish economist, to favor a rule of "relative unanimity."[5] Under such a rule, referendums on the extension of governmental activity, combined with specific tax-sharing plans, must pass by margins close to unanimity, such as seven eighths of the voters, for positive action. The rule still has the drawbacks of unanimous consent in the sense that it is likely to involve excessive decision-making costs as the "price" paid for protecting the rights of minority groups. An advantage of the relative unanimity rule is that the resulting distribution of tax shares is contingent on the induced "bribes." It is likely that those who most strongly prefer the particular action will finance the bulk of it after bribes are paid. If preferences are truthfully revealed, this approximates the Lindahl solution in the sense that equilibrium tax shares are close to individual marginal benefits of governmental activity.

Majority Consent
Simple majority rule has higher external costs, when compared with the rule of unanimity, but lower decision-making costs. One additional complication presents itself when simple majority rule is utilized to rank three or more alternatives. This is the possibility of "inconsistent" rankings, where the particular action undertaken as a result of the simple majority rule may depend on the order in which the alternatives are presented in pairs to the electorate. This problem has been extensively studied by a number of economists, most notably Kenneth Arrow.[6]

The possibility of inconsistency under simple majority rule has often been referred to as the "paradox of voting." For example, it is well-recognized that the outcome of an election between two political candidates may be changed drastically if a "third-party candidate" enters the race. The third-party candidate may act as a "spoiler," by splitting the support for one of the two candidates who may otherwise win the election.

One requirement of consistency is transitive rankings. This means that if the community decides on the basis of a given decision rule that it prefers A to B and it prefers B to C, then it must also prefer A to C. If A is run against C and a majority supports C over A, then the community is behaving inconsistently.

If there are three candidates running for political office, then social choices will be transitive if the elimination of any one of the three does not affect the outcome. Consider a case where three voters must decide between three candidates. To add a touch of realism to the analysis, call the three candidates

---

[5] See Knut Wicksell, "A New Principle of Just Taxation," reprinted in R. A. Musgrave and A. T. Peacock (eds.), *Classics in the Theory of Public Finance*, Macmillan, London, 1958, pp. 72–118.

[6] Kenneth Arrow, *Social Choice and Individual Values*, sec. ed., Wiley, New York, 1963.

"Humphrey," "Nixon," and "Wallace." The three voters are Schwartz, O'Brien, and Lee. Table 4.1 gives each voter's preferences for the three candidates.

TABLE 4.1

Voter	First choice	Second choice	Third choice
Schwartz	Humphrey	Nixon	Wallace
Lee	Wallace	Humphrey	Nixon
O'Brien	Nixon	Wallace	Humphrey

Now consider the result of the election if any one of the candidates is removed from the ballot. First, assume that Humphrey drops out of the race so that the contest is between Wallace and Nixon only. Referring to Table 4.1, it is seen that Schwartz will choose Nixon over Wallace (Nixon is ranked over Wallace according to Schwartz's preferences). Similarly, O'Brien chooses Nixon over Wallace. Lee, however, will clearly vote for Wallace because Wallace is ranked first according to Lee's preferences. The tally sheet for this election is shown in Table 4.2.

TABLE 4.2

	Nixon	Wallace
Schwartz	√	
Lee		√
O'Brien	√	
Total votes	2	1
Result of election: Nixon wins		

Now suppose Nixon drops out of the race (for some inexplicable reason) and the election is held for Wallace and Humphrey. Table 4.3 gives the tally sheet for such an election based on the preference of the three voters as summarized in Table 4.1.

TABLE 4.3

	Humphrey	Wallace
Schwartz	√	
Lee		√
O'Brien		√
Total votes	1	2
Result of election: Wallace wins		

This community of three voters has revealed that it prefers Nixon to Wallace and Wallace to Humphrey. If social choices are transitive, then Nixon should be preferred to Humphrey if an election were to be held with only these two candidates in the running. If this does not hold, then the community will be behaving in an inconsistent manner.

Let the election between Nixon and Humphrey be held with Wallace removed from the race. Table 4.4 presents the tally sheet for this election based on the preference of three voters.

TABLE 4.4

	Humphrey	*Nixon*
Schwartz	√	
Lee	√	
O'Brien		√
Total votes	2	1
Result of election: Humphrey wins		

The community chooses Humphrey over Nixon in this case! This community of three voters is therefore behaving in an inconsistent manner in the sense that its social choices exhibit intransitivity.

To summarize the results, the community of three voters has indicated that they prefer Nixon to Wallace and Wallace to Humphrey. Using the letter "P" to symbolize preferred, this may be written as follows:

$$\text{Nixon P Wallace} \tag{4.1}$$

$$\text{Wallace P Humphrey} \tag{4.2}$$

If choices are transitive, then equations (4.1) and (4.2) may be written as follows:

$$\text{Nixon P Wallace P Humphrey} \tag{4.3}$$

Therefore,

$$\text{Nixon P Humphrey} \tag{4.4}$$

But an election actually held between Nixon and Humphrey results in Humphrey's being chosen over Nixon by the three-citizen electorate (Humphrey P Nixon) that indicates that the community's choices are *intransitive*.

It may also be shown that the results of elections based on simple majority rule may be contingent on the order in which candidates are presented. Suppose that only two candidates at a time are to be considered. The winner of the election between the first two candidates is then run against the third candidate to determine the final results of the election. Table 4.5 presents the tally sheets for three such elections based on the preferences of Schwartz, Lee, and O'Brien.

TABLE 4.5

Election 1: Humphrey vs. Nixon, with the winner facing Wallace

Tally sheet 1			Tally sheet 2		
	Humphrey	Nixon		Humphrey	Wallace
Schwartz	V		Schwartz	V	
Lee	V		Lee		V
O'Brien		V	O'Brien		V
Total votes	2	1	Total votes	1	2
Result of election: Humphrey wins			Result of Election: Wallace wins		

RESULT OF ELECTION 1: *Wallace is the victor.*

Election 2: Humphrey vs. Wallace, with the winner facing Nixon

Tally sheet 1			Tally sheet 2		
	Humphrey	Wallace		Wallace	Nixon
Schwartz	V		Schwartz		V
Lee		V	Lee	V	
O'Brien		V	O'Brien		V
Total votes	1	2	Total votes	1	2
Result of election: Wallace wins			Result of election: Nixon wins		

RESULT OF ELECTION 2: *Nixon is the victor.*

Election 3: Nixon vs. Wallace, with the winner facing Humphrey

Tally sheet 1			Tally sheet 2		
	Nixon	Wallace		Nixon	Humphrey
Schwartz	V		Schwartz		V
Lee		V	Lee		V
O'Brien	V		O'Brien	V	
Total votes	2	1	Total votes	1	2
Result of election: Nixon wins			Result of election: Humphrey wins		

RESULT OF ELECTION 3: *Humphrey is the victor.*

The results of these three elections are most disconcerting. Depending on the order of voting in pairs, any one of the three candidates can win! One can hardly call the choices of the community "consistent" in such a case.

The examples illustrate Arrow's "general possibility theorem." The theorem states that, given a set of conditions for "collective rationality," it is not, in general, possible to devise a social-choice relation (or "function") that exhibits transitive (or consistent) preferences.[7] Arrow's conditions are summarized as follows:

1. Voters have free choices among alternatives in the election.
2. If all voters change their preference rankings in a particular way, the social ranking must not change in the opposite direction.
3. The elimination of any one alternative (or "candidate") must not affect the ranking of the other remaining alternatives (and hence the result of the election).
4. The social-choice function must be unique in the sense that the ranking should not depend on the order of presentation of the alternatives. Furthermore, the choices must exhibit transitivity.
5. The social choice function cannot be dictated by any one individual independently of the preferences of other individuals.

According to these conditions, the preferences of the three voters presented in Table 4.1 are legitimate, since voters are free to choose among alternatives without constraint. But it has been shown that when one alternative is removed, the result of the election is, in fact, changed; and furthermore, the choices as a result of the simple-majority decision rule are intransitive. Hence, conditions 3 and 4 cannot be met. From this, Arrow concludes that a simple-majority rule cannot, in general, result in a social-choice function that exhibits collective rationality.

It may be shown, however, that if individual preferences exhibit a certain pattern, then a simple-majority rule can result in consistent social preferences. This was first pointed out by Duncan Black.[8] Suppose that citizen Lee in the hypothetical three-voter community changes his preferences in such a fashion as to make Nixon his second choice and Humphrey his third choice. The preferences of the individuals in the community are now shown in Table 4.6.

TABLE 4.6

Voter	First choice	Second choice	Third choice
Schwartz	Humphrey	Nixon	Wallace
Lee	Wallace	Nixon	Humphrey
O'Brien	Nixon	Wallace	Humphrey

It can now be shown that this alteration in Lee's preferences, given the preferences of the other members of the community, produces a *consistent* social-choice relation. To understand this, conduct a test for consistency

[7] See Arrow, chapter 3.

[8] Duncan Black, "On the Rationale of Group Decision-Making," *Journal of Political Economy*, vol. 55, February 1948, pp. 23–34.

similar to that done previously. First, eliminate Humphrey and run Nixon against Wallace. The tally sheet for this election is presented in Table 4.7.

TABLE 4.7

	Nixon	Wallace
Schwartz	∨	
Lee		∨
O'Brien	∨	
Total votes	2	1
Result of election: Nixon wins		

Now eliminate Nixon and run Humphrey against Wallace. That tally sheet for this election is shown in Table 4.8.

TABLE 4.8

	Humphrey	Wallace
Schwartz	∨	
Lee		∨
O'Brien		∨
Total votes	1	2
Result of election: Wallace wins		

If the social-choice function is to be consistent, the results must imply that Nixon will defeat Humphrey if Wallace is eliminated. This follows from the requirement of transitivity. The result is shown in Table 4.9.

TABLE 4.9

	Humphrey	Nixon
Schwartz	∨	
Lee		∨
O'Brien		∨
Total votes	1	2
Result of election: Nixon wins		

Nixon does, in fact, win. Thus, social choice is consistent in this case. As an exercise, the reader may wish to conduct "run-off" elections as before but using the data in Table 4.6. He will find that, in this case, the result will be independent of the order of voting.

What causes the result to change when Lee's preferences are altered? To answer this question, it will first be necessary to arbitrarily rank the candidates according to the "extremes" they might represent. Assume Humphrey is a "leftist" relative to the other two candidates while Wallace is a "rightist." Nixon represents the "moderate" position. This scale of ranking is summarized in Figure 4.5. Using this scale, Humphrey and Wallace represent "extremes." Now examine the individual preferences exhibited in Tables 4.1 and 4.6 in relation to this scale. Schwartz and O'Brien have the same preferences in both cases, so consider them first. Schwartz apparently ranks candidates according to some index of "leftness," because his rankings are such as to correspond to an index that decreases in intensity as it moves rightward on the scale of Figure 4.5. O'Brien is a man who prefers the moderate to either extreme. His utility apparently decreases as it moves from the mid-point of the scale in Figure 4.5.

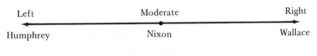

Left   Moderate   Right

Humphrey   Nixon   Wallace

FIGURE 4.5

Now consider Lee's preferences as exhibited in Table 4.1. Lee ranks Nixon, the "moderate," last. He prefers the two extremes to the moderate. He may be referred to as an "extremist." His preferences are said to be "multiple-peaked," because his utility apparently falls as it moves away from the end points of the scale in Figure 4.5. In Table 4.6, Lee's preferences are such as to make him a "rightist"; his utility apparently falls on the basis of his revealed choices as it moves away from the right end of the scale.

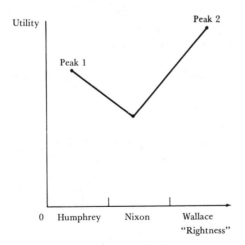

Multiple-Peaked Preference

FIGURE 4.6

NOTE: Data from Table 4.1 for Lee.

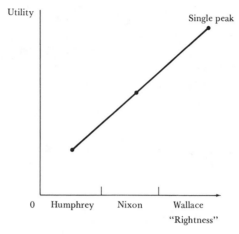

Single–Peaked Preference

FIGURE 4.7

NOTE: Data from Table 4.6 for Lee.

Plotting Lee's utility against "rightness," his preferences as exhibited in Table 4.1 have two peaks, while his preferences as exhibited in Table 4.6 have only one peak. This is shown in Figures 4.6 and 4.7. Figures 4.8 and 4.9 plot Schwartz's and O'Brien's preference functions against the degree of "rightness" of the candidates. Their preference functions apparently have single peaks.

When Lee's preferences are changed from multiple-peaked to single-peaked, the results of the election become unambiguously determinate irrespective of the order in which the candidates are considered. With this in mind, Arrow qualifies his general possibility theorem to state that the simple-majority rule for more than two alternatives does give rise to consistent social choice provided that all individuals comprising the electorate have single-peaked preferences.[9] In such a case, the "moderate" alternative is always collectively chosen over the two "extreme" alternatives.

The next question that must be asked concerns the likelihood of multiple-peaked preferences on the part of individual citizens. The reader will recall that one of Arrow's conditions specifies that individuals have complete freedom to form their preferences as they wish. There is, therefore, no a priori basis to rule out the possibility of multiple-peaked preferences. In fact, it is quite likely that such preferences will exist. Consider the well-known attitude of many individuals in this country toward the Vietnam conflict and United States involvement in Southeast Asia. Statements such as this are often heard: "If we are going to fight a war, then we should not fight it halfheartedly—we must bomb harbors and other strategic targets using all available weapons in our arsenal. If we can't fight the war like that, we should not fight at all."

[9] Arrow, p. 78. This conclusion holds only if the number of voters is odd.

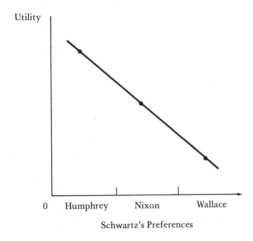

Schwartz's Preferences

FIGURE 4.8

Individuals who make such statements have multiple-peaked preferences. They prefer the two extremes of fighting an "all-out" war or not fighting at all to the "moderate" solution of fighting a limited war on the basis of a scale that ranks the war according to the intensity of military action. Thus, multiple-peaked preferences can be quite common. This being the case, Arrow's conclusion concerning the inconsistency of social choices under a simple-majority rule remains a distinct possibility. Given the widespread use of the simple-majority voting rule, this conclusion is somewhat disturbing. It must, however, be emphasized that this result occurs only when there are more than two alternatives to choose from. The predominance of the two-party system in most Western nations tends to make the specter of collective inconsistency less threatening.

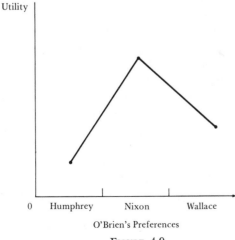

O'Brien's Preferences

FIGURE 4.9

OTHER VOTING SYSTEMS AND INTENSITY
OF FEELING

Plurality rule is a commonly used, collective decision-making rule when at least three alternatives are available to the electorate. Under plurality rule, the alternative that receives the highest percentage of the total votes cast is declared the winner. In effect, such a voting rule often allows a minority to decide. For example, if there are three issues or candidates and the vote is split so that alternative 1 receives 32 percent of all the votes, alternative 2 receives 32 percent, and alternative 3 receives 36 percent, then alternative 3 is declared the winner. In this case, the winner is favored by only a minority of the population of voters.

Plurality rule suffers from defects similar to those that are present in the case of majority rule. In particular, the addition or removal of any one alternative can change the result of the election. Thus, collective choices under plurality rule are sensitive to the number of alternatives and cannot be expected to exhibit transitivity. This is illustrated by the results of a recent election decided by plurality rule for the United States Senate from the State of New York. There were three candidates: Goodell (Republican), Ottinger (Democrat), and Buckley (Conservative). Goodell and Ottinger are generally considered "liberals," while Buckley's political persuasion is "conservative." The liberal vote was split between Ottinger and Goodell, and Buckley emerged as the victor under the plurality rule, even though the majority of voters in the State of New York favored liberal candidates. It was generally agreed that if one of the liberal candidates had withdrawn from the race, Buckley could not have won. Each liberal candidate, in effect, acted as a "spoiler" for the other.

The voting rules considered thus far offer no direct opportunity for citizens to express their intensity of feeling on particular issues. Expression of intensity of feeling serves as a safeguard against undue exploitation of minority rights by the majority. However, such systems also serve to provide an incentive for voters to reveal false preferences as part of a strategic plan to get a particular action approved.

Point-count voting allows a refined expression of intensity of feeling. Under this system, each voter is assigned a number of "points" (for example, 100) that he is free to allocate in any manner he wishes among the possible alternatives. For example, if there are three alternatives and the voter is given 100 points, he may assign 50 points to one alternative and 25 points each to the other two. If he has a very strong preference for one alternative versus the other two, he may choose to put all his 100 points on that alternative and allocate 0 points to each of the other two. The outcome is determined by adding the points assigned by all voters to each alternative. The alternative that earns the greatest number of points is declared the winner.

Point-count voting affords the opportunity for a greater revelation of preferences. As such, it may serve to protect the rights of minorities who have strong feeling on particular issues. It also greatly increases the possibility of strategic behavior on the part of voters and the possibility of high decision-making costs. It is conceivable that a "market" for points will develop as individual voters make trades on different issues. It is also possible that each voter may attempt to guess how other voters will allocate their points and base their own behavior, in part, on such guesses. For example, suppose on the basis of a 100-point system, the individuals composing the electorate have true preferences as shown in Table 4.10.

TABLE 4.10

Voter	Humphrey	Nixon	Wallace
Schwartz	60	40	0
Lee	6	4	90
O'Brien	25	40	35
Point count	91	84	125

On the basis of a point count, Wallace wins the election, even though he ranks first in the preferences of only one voter (Lee). If Schwartz has a good "gues-timate" of how the other two voters will allocate their points, he may change the outcome of the election in such a way as to get his first choice (Humphrey) elected. He can do this by giving all of his 100 points to Humphrey. This gives Humphrey 131 points compared with Wallace's 125 points and Nixon's 44. This, of course, assumes that Lee and O'Brien do not change their prefer-ences by trying to "guess" Schwartz's and each other's point allocations. Stra-tegic behavior on the part of individual voters determines the outcome of the election. Thus, although point-count voting does provide an opportunity for voters to express their intensity of feeling, it also provides an incentive for them *not* to reveal their true feelings. This could lead to inconsistent social choices on the basis of the decision rule.

Recently, it has been argued that simple majority rule itself allows voters to express their intensity of preference on issues. James Coleman has disputed Arrow's contention that the elimination of any alternative should not affect the ranking of the remaining alternatives in the social-choice function.[10] He argues that this should not be a requirement for "collective rationality." Coleman believes that such eliminations are quite likely to change the be-havior patterns of rational individuals comprising the electorate. His analysis explicitly considers the uncertainty that surrounds the outcome of any voting decision by individual citizens. Intensity of preference can be expressed through the willingness to make vote trades on particular issues. Since elimina-

[10] James S. Coleman, "The Possibility of a Social Welfare Function," *American Economic Review*, December 1966, pp. 1105–1122.

tion of any alternative limits the gains to be made by such trades, Coleman argues that such eliminations should be expected to change individual behavior and the resultant collective decision. The individual tends to trade votes on those issues he least prefers (low-intensity preference) in exchange for those he most prefers (high-intensity preference). The more issues considered in an election, the greater the possibility of trades to take place and intensity of feeling to be expressed.

IMPERFECTIONS IN THE POLITICAL PROCESS

Political institutions, like market institutions, suffer from imperfections. Market failure merely indicates that private action will be inefficient in supplying a certain good or service. It does *not* necessarily follow that collective action in supplying activities for which private action is inefficient will improve resource allocation.

The institution of majority rule, as shown, is often unable to reach consistent choices. When more than two issues or candidates are presented, the elimination of any one alternative may change the results of the election when some voters have multiple-peaked preferences. Even more important is the costly process of keeping the electorate informed on all issues. Since information gathering is costly for any one citizen, there is no reason to expect that voters are always adequately informed concerning the effects of any proposed program on themselves and others.

The problem is further complicated by the fact that issues are not usually voted on one at a time. Instead, an election often embodies a multitude of issues and proposed governmental activities. This enables political parties to employ strategies that are designed to form winning coalitions of voters, often obtained by including favors to special interest groups. A voter is often forced to accept a bundle that includes many expenditures and taxes only some of which are in his own interests. To gain favorable action on issues in his own interests, a voter often must accept external costs associated with other programs from which he obtains little or no benefit. This limits the opportunities for voters to express their preferences on individual governmental activities and political issues. He must either accept or reject the package. He cannot cut the bundle so that it includes only the programs he desires. Furthermore, a one-man, one-vote system cannot take into account the intensity of feeling on particular issues and alternative public budgets.

Political parties take advantage of the imperfections by attempting to achieve winning coalitions through a sort of "implicit logrolling." They often put together a political platform that includes services that appeal to diverse minority groups in the hope of attracting their votes. In effect, by doing so, they force voters to accept "trades" in order to achieve positive action on programs that the voters strongly prefer. This results in governmental activities being undertaken that could not achieve majority consent if voted on as single issues. Furthermore, explicit trades of this sort are made by logrolling legislators in a representative form of government in order to ensure action on programs of special interest to their constituents. If the sum of external costs and decision-making costs of collective action exceed external costs associated with private action, then governmental activity will be inefficient.

POLITICAL PARTIES, BUREAUCRATS, AND EFFICIENCY

Thus far, little has been said about the role of political parties and governmental bureaucrats in formulating the alternatives presented to the electorate. It is clear that political parties play an important role in defining issues and attempting to influence the results of elections. Recently, a number of economists have attempted to determine the influence of "party politics" on a budget. The reader will recall that an "optimal" budget in the Pareto sense is that which corresponds to the level of expenditures where marginal social benefits (equal to the sum of marginal private benefits) of governmental activity is just equal to marginal social costs (measured by the value of foregone private output when resources are directed to the public sector). Marginal benefits of any particular budget for the individual voter will depend not only on the level of expenditures but also the mix of types of expenditures within the budget. The willingness of any citizen to vote favorably on any given budget will also be dependent on the particular tax-sharing plan recommended to finance the expenditures.

Anthony Downs has concluded that the actual budget is likely to be "too small" in nations with a two-party political system.[11] Downs' conclusion is derived from an interesting model that applies some standard economic analysis to the political process. Downs characterizes political parties as "vote maximizers." An election is viewed as a contest between two alternative budgets, each embodying a flow of benefits to citizens and implying certain tax-sharing arrangements to finance the governmental activity. Each party proposes the budget it believes will maximize its chances of winning the election.

Voters, in Downs' model, are presumed to vote for the party whose policies provide them with greatest personal net benefits. Political parties rank potential expenditure policies according to their "vote-gain potential," while tax-sharing schemes are arranged according to their "vote-loss potential." The behavior of political parties is, at least in part, conditioned by their estimates of how "informed" the electorate actually is on the programs embodied in proposed budgets. If information is costly and uncertainty exists, Downs

[11] Anthony Downs, "Why the Government Budget Is Too Small in a Democracy," *World Politics*, July 1960; also, *An Economic Theory of Democracy*, Harper & Row, New York, 1957.

argues that this causes political parties to alter their proposed programs in such a manner as to result in budgets of smaller size than that which prevails if information to voters is not scarce.

In particular, if voters have better information on the costs (for example, taxes) associated with governmental activity as compared with the benefits, then it is likely that political parties will propose budgets that are smaller than those they will propose under perfect information. The reason for this stems from the character of many of the goods actually supplied collectively. Downs points out that the benefits flowing from many of the services in the budgets tend to be "remote" and "uncertain" for most voters. For example, the benefit of foreign aid to any particular citizen is likely to be questionable for him. If foreign-aid expenditures are reduced, then his tax burden is likely to fall (or inflation reduced), while there is no obvious loss of benefit to the voter. Thus, he is more likely to give his vote to the party that slashes foreign aid simply because he may increase his real income if that party wins. Other voters may feel that other expenditures in the budgets do not benefit them and would also prefer a curtailment of expenditures for those programs. Their assessments may or may not be correct because of the existence of uncertainty. Information is costly, and it is simply not worth the effort for voters to study the issues in such a way as to discover whether or not a particular program such as foreign aid really does benefit them. As a result of this "rational ignorance," political parties have an incentive to eliminate from their proposed budgets all those expenditures that produce "hidden" benefits. Furthermore, the parties are also hesitant to include programs that have uncertain benefits because these are likely to be undervalued by voters. On the other hand, Downs asserts, voters will be much better informed on the costs of governmental activity because these tend to directly reduce their real incomes. The result: a chronic tendency for political parties to propose budgets that are "too small."

Buchanan and Tullock conclude that governmental budgets are likely to be "too large" relative to the Pareto efficient size of the public sector. Their argument is based on the belief that the vote-trading processes that are inherent in majority rule cause more programs to be enacted than may be expected when each individual citizen is taxed according to the benefits he derives from the budgets (the Pareto efficient solution). In effect, Buchanan and Tullock believe that implicit logrolling processes emerge as political parties seek to form majority coalitions designed to win elections. The winning coalition will allow the individual voter to "reap benefits from collective action without bearing the full marginal costs attributable to him."[12] The results are budgets in which marginal social costs are greater than marginal social benefits. This implies that the budgets will be "too large."

Downs argues that a tendency toward "excessive" governmental expenditures can only arise under conditions of "preponderant ignorance." This

---

[12] Buchanan and Tullock, p. 201.

occurs when voters are actually ignorant of the items comprising the budgets. When this assumption is combined with the assertion by Downs that citizens are much more aware of governmental policies that affect them as income earners than those that affect them as consumers, it can be shown that governmental spending tends to be excessive. This is because political parties can win votes of various "minority" groups by proposing policies that provide such groups with direct and obvious benefits, while spreading the costs of these programs to the majority through general taxes. As a result, none of the minority groups bear the full marginal cost of the programs benefiting it. Members of particular minority groups feel that they are reaping windfall gains by not bearing the full costs of the benefits imputable to them only because they remain ignorant of the fact that there are other items in the budget that benefit other minority groups, aside from themselves, at their expense. The result is a logrolling process similar to that envisioned by Buchanan and Tullock and the same tendency toward overspending: "The government placates the majority who are exploited by allowing them to be part of exploiting minorities in other fields."[13] Downs emphasizes that this tendency toward an excessive budget size is solely a result of the citizens' being unaware that there are items in the budget that benefit minority groups to which they do not belong and the assumption that taxation to provide benefits to *all* minority groups can be concealed from the majority. He concludes that this is unlikely.

It is undoubtedly true that implicit "vote-trading" on issues does exist. But it must also be admitted that information concerning the benefits and costs of governmental activity is costly. There is no a priori basis to conclude that budgets are either "too small" or "too large," for this must be an empirical proposition. The results depend on the degree of "rational ignorance" prevalent among the electorate and the willingness of political parties to engage in logrolling.

Another problem is the determination of the effect of any imperfections in the political process on the *mix* of activities embodied in collectively chosen, public budgets. If the bargaining powers of coalitions representing various special interests differ, then one expects the proposed programs of vote-maximizing political parties to reflect such differences. The groups that have organized effectively to represent special interests are able to threaten political parties with the loss of entire voting blocs if the party does not endorse programs favorable to the members of the special-interest groups. Groups that have not organized effectively into such "lobby groups" because of, say, high transactions and information costs involved in forming groups, are not likely to have enough power to "threaten" politicians. As the power of special-interest groups changes over time, one may expect shifts in governmental poli-

[13] Anthony Downs, "Why the Government Budget Is Too Small in a Democracy," reprinted in E. S. Phelps (ed.), *Private Wants and Public Needs* (rev. ed.), Norton, New York, 1965, p. 91.

cies. For example, in recent years, anti-pollution lobby groups have grown both in size and effectiveness. The increased anti-pollution programs of political parties may, at least in part, reflect this shift. Differences in power among lobby groups can result in an inefficient mix of governmental activities being collectively chosen through political institutions.

Still another interesting approach to the study of the political process is offered by Roland McKean.[14] McKean ascribes utility functions to all those individuals directly involved in governmental activities—politicians, executives, and bureaucrats. McKean argues that all such participants bear the costs of their actions through various "complaints" from the people harmed by policy decisions. He further argues that the bearing of such costs results in a "bargaining mechanism." The public official has to

> bargain with many people who are affected and, in one way or another, encounter costs if he makes decisions that impose sacrifices on others. From those who are benefitted, on the other hand, he can bargain for compensation. The reward may be support in connection with other matters, reduced enmity, increased friendship or convenience, or some other kind of *quid pro quo*. The size and completeness of the compensations for both costs inflicted and gains bestowed depend upon bargaining strengths and circumstances (as they do in the private economy). And again the greater the extent to which these compensations are made, the less the extent to which the costs and gains felt by an official will diverge from total costs and gains.[15]

McKean argues that the existence of this implicit "bargaining system" serves to internalize the external costs and benefits generated by public officials. In the spirit of Adam Smith, he asserts that the constraints that affect public officials result in an "invisible hand" to guide their actions as they seek to maximize their utility subject to their constraints. While there is no guarantee that "optimal budgets" emerge from this bargaining process, McKean believes that the process, although imperfect, serves to prevent governmental activities from deviating very far from efficient amounts. The "invisible hand" tends to "harness individual interests within government to carry out broader objectives."[16] The process suffers when any one minority group lacks an effective channel of communication with governmental authorities.

Interesting insights into the utility functions of bureaucrats have been offered by Louis De Alessi.[17] He argues that bureaucrats maximize their utility by attempting to expand the resources under their supervision. By doing so, the bureaucrat can increase his marginal product and probably his salary as

---

[14] Roland McKean, "The Unseen Hand in Government," *American Economic Review*, June 1965, pp. 496–505.

[15] McKean, pp. 498–499.

[16] McKean, p. 504.

[17] Louis De Alessi, "Implications of Property Rights for Government Investment Choices," *American Economic Review*, March 1969.

well.[18] In order to increase their "prestige," bureaucrats tend to favor projects that involve expenditures in the present rather than the future if their stay in office is likely to be short. Furthermore, De Alessi argues that bureaucrats favor capital-intensive projects that enable them to expand the size of their present budgets. Although De Alessi's analysis makes clear that there is a tendency for bureaucrats to "overspend" and, hence, to make the budgets larger than optimal, he does not attempt to study the competition among bureaucrats. Whether bureaucrats are, in fact, adequately constrained to prevent the tendency to overspend remains an unanswered question. This problem will be studied in greater detail in the following chapter, which describes the budgeting process in the United States and some of the tools used by bureaucrats in establishing the desirability of their alternative projects.

SUMMARY

While market decisions require agreement between only two parties (buyers and sellers), collective decisions require the consent of many parties. There are alternative rules for making social choices within a community. These range from minority rule to unanimous consent. Majority rule is a popular collective decision-making mechanism, but it is by no means the only available rule.

The choice of a collective decision-making rule for any issue is, in fact, a collective decision in itself. A constitution represents a set of collective-choice rules on various issues. The costs and benefits of any collective decision rule are likely to vary with issues to be decided and individual preferences. The benefits of any collective-choice rule are the reductions in external costs that would prevail if the issue were to be decided through private action. The costs of collective action include decision-making costs and newly introduced, external costs of the political process. Decision-making costs include the time and effort necessary to reach a decision, while external costs of collective action include the dissatisfaction of voters who do not agree with the resulting collective decision. They often have to pay taxes for programs from which they receive zero benefits.

Unanimity rule has zero external costs, since all must agree before collective action can be undertaken. However, decision-making costs are likely to be quite high for unanimous consent. An optimal decision-making rule for any voter on any issue is the one that minimizes the sum of his expected external and decision-making costs.

Majority consent is often incapable of reaching consistent choices when three or more alternatives are available. If some individual preferences are "multiple-peaked," then intransitive choices are possible. This implies that

[18] De Alessi, p. 18.

the outcome of an election may be contingent on the order in which issues are presented in a run-off vote following the elimination of one alternative. In addition, majority rule offers no opportunity for voters to express their intensity of feeling.

Collective action through political processes suffers from defects that may prevent the attainment of efficiency. Information is costly and voters may not be fully aware of alternatives available to them and the costs and benefits associated with each alternative. Alternatives often contain many proposed governmental activities only some of which the voters favor. To obtain favorable action on desired programs, voters often agree to programs from which they obtain no benefits. The "package" presented to voters by political parties is often a result of an implicit "logrolling," or vote-trading, process designed to achieve winning coalitions of diverse minority groups. The programs offered by political parties may depend on the bargaining powers of minority groups, as evidenced by their ability to control voting blocs. Inefficient mixes of public goods may be proposed by political parties if there are sharp differences in the bargaining powers of alternative special-interest groups.

5

Governmental Budgeting Techniques
and Cost-Benefit Analysis

A government's budget represents a summarization of the public-expenditure plans for a given year. It is a comprehensive listing of the costs of governmental activity and the revenue sources financing that activity. In its various stages of preparation, the budget provides a tool for the planning and control of governmental activity by the executive and legislative branches of government. The budgetary process itself comprises a system through which the wishes of the electorate are translated into concrete projects and programs designed to satisfy the demand for public goods. However, it must be recognized that bureaucrats, who are involved in the budgeting process, possess a considerable degree of power to determine the particular mix of public expenditures presented to the legislative branch for discussion. Furthermore, the particular budgeting techniques used by the bureaucrats can be decisive in determining how efficiently the government utilizes resources withdrawn from the private sector of the economy.

The budgetary process is, therefore, of considerable importance in determining the actual size of the public sector. In view of its importance, it is worthwhile to study the process and the various budgeting techniques utilized by bureaucrats of the executive branch of the government for the purpose of formulating expenditure plans.

THE BUDGET

The Budget and the Budgetary Process

One must distinguish between the budget itself and the budgetary process. Strictly speaking, the *Budget of the United States Government* represents the recommendations of the executive branch of the federal government for public expenditures during the coming fiscal year. The fiscal year begins on July 1 and ends on June 30. The budget represents the culmination of over a year of planning, discussion, and review by a small army of bureaucrats, economists, and politicians. It must be emphasized that the budget as presented to the Congress in January by the President is only a list of recommendations. A considerable amount of debate ensues in both houses of the Congress before any fiscal expenditures are approved. In the process of such debate, the President's original proposals are often changed substantially.

The *budgetary process* comprises all stages of planning for the budget and the procedures by which proposed expenditures are approved and executed. This includes executive preparation and submission of the actual document to the Congress, authorization of expenditures by the Congress, and finally, execution of expenditure authorizations by the agencies. The final record of expenditures made by the federal government at the end of any fiscal year is likely to differ from the original budget submitted to the Congress as a result of modifications made in the original document during the course of the legislative session.

The Unified Budget

The size of the deficit or surplus of a given budget is often of considerable political importance because of its impact on the level of economic activity and the price level. In recent years, there has been a controversy concerning the best way to report planned expenditures in the federal budget so as to properly gauge the size of the anticipated surplus or deficit and the probable impact of the budget on the level of employment and the price level in the nation. This controversy concerns the *level* as opposed to the *mix* of public expenditures. But since restraints on the size of the federal budget mean that some federal programs may have to be curtailed or eliminated, there is, in fact, a feedback effect between the size of the budget and the mix of programs within the budget. If the size of the budget must be reduced, then the next question is, "Which programs must be cut?" Should it be education or defense expenditures or should it be something else? These are important questions that are resolved during the budgetary process.

Until recently, a number of budget concepts were utilized by the government in reporting planned expenditures.[1] These alternative concepts created a great deal of confusion in the public debate prior to budget approval. To correct these difficulties, a Presidential Commission on Budget Concepts was appointed in March 1967 for the purpose of formulating plans for a new budget concept to be used consistently by the government. The commission's recommendations resulted in the "unified budget" concept that was first implemented in the fiscal year 1969 budget. The new budget format is designed to give a more realistic picture of the impact of federal governmental spending on economic activity. It represents an improvement over the old "administrative budget" that previously was used by the executive branch to plan expenditures.

The new unified budget is considerably more comprehensive than the administrative budget because it includes the receipts and expenditures of the government trust funds and various government-sponsored organizations. These trust funds include the social security trust fund and the highway trust fund and represent a considerable amount of resources. For example, in 1969, the sum total of receipts collected by the social security and highway trust funds were over $50 billion. Thus, the trust funds amount to nearly 30 percent of total federal government revenues. The omission of these funds from the old administrative budget, therefore, resulted in an understatement of the level of governmental activity.

In addition to including the receipts and expenditures of the trust funds, the unified budget also introduced a number of innovations in the method of reporting expenditures. The new budget divides planned expenditures into two categories. The first includes *new* authorizations requested of the Congress by the President. The second indicates those expenditures that have already been authorized by the Congress in previous legislative sessions. This distinc-

---

[1] There were three alternative budgets: (1) the administrative budget, (2) the cash budget, (3) the national income accounts (NIA) budgets.

The new "unified budget" more or less replaced the administrative budget as a planning tool. Although the text here highlights the difference between the unified and administrative budget, it must also be noted that the cash and NIA budgets are still occasionally used as tools of analysis.

The cash budget is similar to the unified budget. It includes the trust fund accounts. It differs from the unified budget in certain minor ways. First of all, it is on a cash basis rather than an accrual basis. Thus, there is a difference in the timing of receipts and expenditures. In addition, some transactions such as those of enterprise-type agencies (for example, the Post Office) that are included in the cash budget are excluded from the uniform budget, while other items such as federal-employee retirement contributions are included in the unified budget but not the cash budget. Receipts from sale of existing assets are included in the cash budget but not in the unified budget.

The NIA budget represents the economic activity of the federal sector in the National Income Accounts of the U.S. Department of Commerce. It differs from the unified budget in the timing of receipts and expenditures, the treatment of net lending, and the treatment of certain items as "gross" rather than "net" terms.

tion is useful in providing information concerning ability of the Congress to control new expenditures. In addition, the unified budget provides information on the ways by which the government deficit or surplus is to be financed. It indicates the amount of new borrowing from the public as well as other financing methods such as reduction in cash balances. This information is useful in determining the impact of federal debt policy on the levels of economic activity. The unified budget has a separate accounting of expenditures financed by loans. This is useful because it is generally agreed that expenditures financed by governmental borrowing are likely to have a different economic impact compared to direct governmental purchases and transfer payments.

The unified budget also shifted the government to an accrual method of accounting. In accrual accounting, expenditures are counted at the time liabilities are incurred as opposed to being totaled at the later time when actual cash payments are made. It is argued that this accounting method provides a more realistic estimation of the economic impact of federal expenditures and tax policies.

The unified budget also provides some technical innovations for the reporting of government loans such as adding subsidies to loans made at interest rates below current market levels and including the subsidies in expenditures. In addition, federal governmental sales of participation certificates are considered as issues of new debt. A final innovation is the treatment of receipts from government enterprises (such as the Post Office) as offsets against the expenditures of those agencies rather than as revenue items.

Table 5.1 presents data on the unified budget proposed by the Nixon administration for fiscal year 1971.

It must be emphasized that the administration's estimates of revenues and expenditures are based, in part, on estimates of the general level of economic activity. These estimates of gross national product, personal income, and corporate profits are of considerable importance in planning the budget. This stems from the fact that the level of economic activity has a feedback effect on the budget itself through the "built-in stabilizers." If the administration's estimates of the indicators of the level of economic activity are inaccurate (as they quite often are), then the estimate of the budget surplus or deficit may be off the mark. The built-in stabilizers include the progressive income-tax structure, the corporation income tax, and unemployment insurance. These stabilizers cause tax collections to fall in greater proportion than the level of economic activity and cause expenditures to rise through increased transfer payments to the unemployed as their ranks increase with decreases in GNP and vice versa. If, for example, the administration overestimates the level of economic activity, then revenues are likely to be considerably less than expected, while expenditures are likely to be somewhat higher because of increased unemployment benefits paid. This would have an adverse effect on the planned surplus of $1.3 billion in the budget for fiscal year 1971. If the administration's estimates are inaccurate enough, the planned surplus might even be transformed into a deficit. The reader may wish to check the actual figures for 1971 against the administration's estimates. The expected surplus for 1971 actually became a substantial deficit!

TABLE 5.1
The Unified Budget and Financial Plan, Fiscal Year 1971

Description	*1971 estimate*
Budget authority (largely appropriations):	
Previously enacted	
Proposed for current action by Congress	$148.1
Becoming available without current action by Congress	86.7
Deductions for offsetting receipts	−16.8
Total budget authority	218.0
Receipts, expenditures, and net lending:	
Expenditure account:	
Receipts	202.1
Expenditures (excluding net lending)	200.1
Expenditure account surplus	2.0
Loan account:	
Loan disbursements	8.6
Loan repayments	7.9
Net lending	0.7
Total budget:	
Receipts	202.1
Outlays (expenditures and net lending)	200.8
Budget surplus	1.3
Federal debt held by the public (at end of fiscal year)	277.3
Plus: debt held by federal agencies and trust funds	105.2
Equals: gross federal debt	382.5
Of which:	
Treasury debt (excludes notes issued to International Monetary Fund)	370.3
Other agency debt	12.2
Budget financing:	
Net repayment of borrowing (−)	−1.2
Other means of financing	−0.1
Total budget financing	−1.3
Total budget surplus	1.3

SOURCE: U.S. Bureau of the Budget, *The Budget of the United States Government,* Fiscal Year 1971.

The administration usually plans the size of the budget with the intention of achieving a given impact on the level of employment and the rate of inflation. This stabilization aspect of the budget is usually reflected in the size of the planned budget surplus or deficit. This, in turn, may act as a constraint on the level of expenditures by the federal government. However, some expenditures represent previous commitments on the part of the federal government and are not subject to such constraints. These "uncontrollable" expenditures include social security transfer payments and interest on the national debt. If it is necessary to constrain expenditures in order to dampen economic activity, the "controllable" expenditures curtailed will depend on the priorities established through the political process. These priorities depend on the attitudes of both the executive and legislative branches of government by virtue of the powers vested in them by the Constitution and the electorate. In recent years, estimates of relatively uncontrollable expenditures indicate that they comprise between 65 and 70 percent of total federal governmental outlays.

THE BUDGETARY PROCESS

The Budget Cycle

The budgetary process establishes priorities for public expenditures through interaction among the President, executive agencies, and Congress. The *budget cycle* is the name given to the continuous process through which expenditures for various governmental projects are proposed, approved, and ultimately executed. The budget cycle has four distinct phases:

1. Executive formulation and submission.
2. Congressional authorization and appropriation.
3. Budget execution and control.
4. Audit.

Phase 1: Executive Formulation and Submission
The budget, which the President submits to the Congress early in January each year, represents the culmination of approximately a year of planning and discussion between government agencies and the U.S. Office of Management and Budget (OMB—formerly called the "Bureau of the Budget"). During this period of formulating outlays, the various governmental agencies, in effect, compete with one another for approval of their expenditure programs. The first stage of this phase is the agency's own evaluation of its requirements for resources to accomplish its mission. Agencies may propose new long-range programs or simply request the necessary resources to continue existing proj-

ects. Each agency's proposals are reviewed by personnel in the Office of Management and Budget. In the process of planning its expenditures, an agency usually consults with a "budget examiner" on the staff of OMB. The next step is a more formal review of each agency's proposals by the directors of OMB.

While this process is taking place, the President and his economic advisors interpret data on the general economic outlook for the economy and begin to formulate the particular fiscal-policy stance to be taken for the coming year. As has been indicated, their decisions may act as a constraint on the general level of expenditures if a budget surplus is required. With this formulation in mind, the President and his advisors further review priorities for public expenditures and make adjustments in individual-agency requests in accordance with the particular policies the administration wishes to pursue. This first phase of budget preparation, therefore, involves interaction among bureaucrats, economists, and the President himself to formulate plans for total budget outlays and receipts and a mix of public expenditures to reflect the priorities established by the administration. The tools used by bureaucrats and economists during this formative stage of budget preparation will be studied later in the section on program budgeting.

Phase 2: Congressional Authorization and Appropriation
The second phase of the budgetary process begins in January, when the President sends the budget to Congress. During this stage, debate on the planned expenditure programs is conducted in a "piecemeal" fashion. Different congressional committees consider approval of the various expenditure proposals. In addition, the Congress considers methods of raising revenues to finance new governmental expenditures. The problems of taxation are usually discussed separately from the problems of expenditure approval.

Congress has the power to change the mix of public expenditures as well as the size of the President's proposed budget. When an expenditure program of a particular governmental agency is approved, the Congress enacts an "authorization." Some programs are authorized for a number of years, but most programs require annual authorization by the legislature. Authorization of particular programs such as "operation head start" or the construction of a new federal building is distinct from the actual funding of these activities. The authorizing legislation usually sets a ceiling on the amount of funds that can be allocated to the particular programs in question.

Permission to incur liabilities for a new program requires additional action by the legislature. This second step permits "appropriations" to be made available to the agency. The appropriation allows the agency to enter into obligations (for example, hire labor, buy supplies) to accomplish its new objective. The appropriation of funds is called the granting of "new obligational authority (NOA)." In many cases, agencies may build "inventories" of NOA's if they do not spend all of their obligational authorities in one year. Inventory buildup makes it difficult for the Congress to control the timing of federal expenditures.

In the case of expenditures financed through trust funds, such as the social security programs and highway expenditures, the Congress has, in effect, voted permanent budget authority. This means that congressional action is unnecessary to provide annual appropriations for these expenditures.

Appropriation bills must be initiated in the House of Representatives. All appropriations first are approved by the House Appropriations Committee, while all new revenue measures are approved by the House Ways and Means Committee. After appropriation bills pass the House, they are sent to the Senate for approval. Any differences between the bills passed by the two houses of Congress are resolved by a conference committee and voted on again by both houses. Finally, all appropriation and revenue bills are sent to the President for his signature. The President does, of course, have the option to veto any bill, but his veto can be overridden by a two-thirds vote of both houses of Congress.

Phase 3: Budget Execution and Control

After budget authorities are granted, the U.S. Office of Management and Budget distributes new obligational authorities to individual agencies on a quarterly basis. In the event that an agency does not require all the new obligational authority granted to it, the Office of Management and Budget will establish reserves. These reserves may be released at a later time but only for the purpose of the original appropriation. The quarterly apportionment of NOA's affords the Office of Management and Budget a degree of control over the timing of expenditures by the agencies. When an agency actually makes a payment, it draws a check on the U.S. Treasury deposits at one of the twelve Federal Reserve Banks or at various commercial banks throughout the United States.

Phase 4: Audit

It is the individual agency's responsibility to assure that the obligations incurred during the course of the fiscal year do not exceed the limits authorized by Congress. Furthermore, expenditures must only encompass those specifically authorized by the legislature. As an additional check on the spending patterns of governmental agencies, the General Accounting Office (GAO) conducts an audit of the financial records of individual agencies and reports its findings to the Congress.

PROGRAM BUDGETING

The test of efficiency must be applied to activities within the public sector of the economy as well as those within the private sector. The resources withdrawn from private use to finance public expenditures must not be wasted through duplications of effort and/or programs that do not really accomplish their missions. In many ways, the goal of efficiency is more difficult to attain in the public sector than it is in the private sector. The reason for this stems from the fact that most governmental agencies do not operate in markets. They need not withstand the test of survival in the market place. The concept of "profits" is not applicable to the "outputs" of most agencies because their products usually have public-good attributes and, therefore, are not sold on unit bases in markets. Indeed, the concept of "outputs" for many governmental agencies is rather elusive. How does one define the output of the Office of Economic Opportunity or the Federal Bureau of Investigation? In recent years, a number of techniques have been developed to aid in achieving efficiency within the public sector. The technique of *program budgeting* has been developed to help bureaucrats plan their expenditures in order to avoid waste.

Planning-Programing-Budgeting System

A major change in the federal approach to budgeting expenditures occurred in 1965 with the introduction of the "planning-programing-budgeting system (PPBS)" by President Lyndon Johnson. This system of planning represents an attempt to introduce program budgeting as a consistent tool of analysis at all levels of federal expenditures. A distinguishing feature of program budgeting is its focus on the "output," or "mission," of an agency. A *program* can be defined as a combination of governmental activities that produces distinguishable outputs.

PPBS may be described by five steps:

1. Identify national goals.
2. Establish priorities among these goals.
3. Compute the costs of alternative programs over time.
4. Measure the benefits of alternative programs over time.
5. Choose those programs that effectively reach the selected goals at least cost.

In order to aid the implementation of PPBS, governmental activities are reclassified to reflect the types of programs undertaken by the government. The new classification scheme cuts across agency lines in such a way as to reflect more faithfully the goals of governmental activities. There are six categories of programs now used to plan federal expenditures.

1. National security programs.
2. International programs.
3. Natural resource programs.

4. Human resource programs.
5. Science, technology, and economic programs.
6. General government-management programs.

Agency Outputs

A key step in PPBS is the definition of outputs for particular programs. In many ways, this is the most difficult part of the analysis. It is often necessary to define outputs of government agencies in an arbitrary fashion because of the difficulty in obtaining a quantifiable index of the services performed by many agencies. Once the outputs are defined, PPBS attempts to seek alternative programs to produce the outputs. The program or combination of programs that achieves the desired output level at minimum cost is, in theory, the alternative selected by the governmental decision makers. PPBS requires each agency to write a "program memorandum" as part of its planning process. The program memorandum states the objectives (outputs) of the agency and lists alternative programs to achieve those objectives. Each agency is thereby forced to enumerate at least two programs and to define its outputs. The program memorandum also contains analysis resulting in the choice of the particular program that most efficiently achieves the stated objectives. In addition, agencies prepare a "program and financial plan" that gives data on the implications of current decisions on outputs and costs over a five-year period. Thus, an important element of PPBS is the responsibility of individual agencies to define their missions and seek the most efficient methods of accomplishing them. The intra-agency aspect of PPBS is often called "suboptimization."

The definition of outputs is relatively easy for some governmental agencies. The Bureau of Engraving and Printing produces, among other things, currency, stamps, and certificates. There is no insurmountable problem in measuring the outputs of this particular agency. One merely has to define units —such as the production figure of one-color stamps or the production figure of Federal Reserve notes—and add each output category to determine actual levels of output. Similarly, the Post Office produces "postal services" of various kinds. To measure its output, one might define "first-class mail" as an output category and measure it by the amount of letters sent through the system per year or month. Once the output categories of these two agencies are defined, the next step is to examine alternative programs (analogous to the concept of a productive process in the private sector) to produce target levels of output. The alternative programs then are analyzed for "cost effectiveness." The program that produces target output levels at minimum costs is selected. For the Post Office, alternative programs might embody different methods of sorting and distributing first-class mail, including automated techniques versus hand-labor techniques, and so on.

In many cases, the outputs of agencies must be considered "intermediate" as opposed to "final outputs."[2] It is generally agreed that the function of military organizations is to provide for national defense. That is, national defense is the final output of the military arm of government. But to provide national defense, a multitude of intermediate outputs is produced by military organizations. These intermediate outputs include "resupply capability," "guerrilla-war capability," "strategic-defense forces," and so on. These output categories cut across agency lines and cover the activities of the Army, Navy, Marines, and Air Force. The alternative programs represent different input mixes for providing intermediate outputs. For example, strategic defense forces might be provided by land missiles, bombers, submarine missile carriers, or some combination of these alternatives. Similarly, for agencies whose final output is improving national health—such as the Public Health Service— intermediate outputs must be defined. These outputs might include the reduction in mortality from particular diseases, the institution of new health standards for a particular industry, and so forth. Outputs usually are measured in terms of physical units. The output of a health program designed to reduce mortality is measured by the number of lives saved. For some governmental activities—such as military research and development, welfare payments, and education—the definition of outputs may be extremely difficult or even impossible. This hard fact makes it difficult to apply the techniques of PPBS uniformly to all governmental agencies.

The output and program-definition phase of PPBS essentially represents the establishment of an information system to generate data useful in achieving efficiency within the public sector. The responsibility for generating the data for this phase of PPBS lies with the individual agencies. Often the agencies will receive aid from the Office of Management and Budget and outside consultants in formulating their program memorandums. But during this stage of planning, no attempt is made to measure the benefits derived from the alternative outputs produced in the public sector.

Since there are resource constraints on the public sector, it is necessary to choose among alternative outputs. In a sense, the individual agencies are in competition with one another for approval of their programs and the outputs produced by those programs. During the stage of executive formulation of the budget, priorities must be established for the alternative outputs of the public sector. To do this, additional data must be generated concerning the benefits of alternative outputs and the programs designed to produce those outputs. In addition, data on the costs of alternative programs over time must also be available to policy makers. Once these data are generated, the officers of OMB, the President, and his advisors can make decisions concerning the relative merits of alternative programs in relation to their estimates of needs of the

[2] This point was made by Roland McKean. See his *Public Spending*, McGraw-Hill, New York, 1968, p. 132.

nation. This phase of PPBS concentrates on the choice of an *output mix* for the public sector. A useful tool for choosing among alternative government outputs is cost-benefit analysis.

Although PPBS may improve resource allocations within the public sector, it suffers from a fundamental flaw. This is the impossibility of applying its techniques consistently to all agencies within the public sector. The agencies whose projects are amenable to easy quantification will undoubtedly become more efficient in the choice of inputs and outputs. But some of the vital information that must be generated by PPBS involves the comparison of the social yield from the alternative outputs of different agencies. Those agencies whose outputs can easily be quantified will provide good information, while those agencies whose outputs are difficult to quantify will provide poor information. It is difficult to compare the data generated from the project evaluation of an irrigation project with that of an anti-poverty project. The project evaluation of the anti-poverty program is likely to be based on many arbitrary decisions because of the inherent difficulty in quantifying its output, while the data generated by the irrigation project is likely to be more precise. Comparing good data with bad data is somewhat similar to comparing apples with oranges. The two sets of data are of different species, and hence, a quantitative comparison is likely to be of questionable value. This would lead one to believe that the chief benefit of PPBS probably lies in its intra-agency phase —the phase of suboptimization—rather than in its interagency phase where alternative projects are ranked.

COST-BENEFIT ANALYSIS

Cost-benefit analysis represents a practical technique for determining the relative merits of alternative governmental projects over time. Although cost-benefit analyses are often conducted by individual agencies themselves as a method to evaluate their own outputs, such analyses represent the interagency aspect of PPBS. That is, cost-benefit analysis provides essential information to the Office of Management and Budget, the President, and the electorate to be used in making choices among alternative public outputs. It must be emphasized, however, that the quality of information to be obtained from such analysis naturally will vary with the degree of sophistication of those undertaking the study. In particular, when cost-benefit analyses of projects are conducted by the agencies who will have the responsibility of executing the approved project, there is always the danger that the bureaucrats involved will attempt to manipulate the data in such a way as to obtain a favorable relation between costs and benefits.

Cost-benefit analysis is not a new tool. It has been used in the United States since 1900 by the Army Corps of Engineers to evaluate the desirability of alternative water-resource projects. In common-sense terms, cost-benefit analysis is nothing more than a statement of the "pro's and con's" of a particular activity over a period of time. It is a very systematic way of gathering information.

There are essentially three steps involved in a cost-benefit analysis:

1. Enumerate all costs and benefits of the proposed project.
2. Evaluate all costs and benefits in dollar terms.
3. Discount future net benefits.

Although the steps may seem simple, an adequate analysis demands a great deal of ingenuity. It may require the combined talents of economists, engineers, and scientists to correctly enumerate and evaluate costs and benefits. Benefits must include all indirect effects (externalities) generated by the project. Costs must be defined correctly as alternative benefits foregone if the project is adopted (the opportunity cost). An appropriate discount rate must be chosen to compare present and future returns from alternative projects. Unfortunately, no uniform techniques have as yet been developed to insure that all cost-benefit analyses use the same procedures. This is reflected, in part, by the fact that a wide range of discount rates has been used in evaluating projects. The discussion that follows will highlight some of the still-unresolved issues in cost-benefit analysis.

Enumeration of Benefits and Costs

The preliminary step is to define the project under consideration and its output. Once this is done, the analysts can proceed to enumerate the costs incurred and benefits generated over the life of the project. Consider the enumeration of benefits first. Benefits can be divided into two categories: direct and indirect. Direct benefits are those increases in output or productivity attributable to the purpose of the project. For example, in the case of an irrigation project, the purpose is to increase the fertility of a particular tract of land. The direct benefits, in this case, will be the net increase in agricultural output on the tract of land being irrigated over time. Indirect, or "spill-over," benefits are those accruing to individuals not directly associated with the purpose of the project. In the case of an irrigation project, spill-over benefits might include the improved fertility of adjoining land that is not actually irrigated by the scheme, resulting from changes in the height of the water table in the area.

In enumerating benefits, only real increases in output and welfare are considered. Any increases in the value of existing assets are not considered a benefit of a particular project. For example, the increase in land values as a result of an irrigation project is not considered a benefit of the project itself, because such appreciation merely reflects the increased output potential of the land. Counting the increase in land value, along with the increase in output of land, results in double counting the benefits of the project. Unfortunately, this is not always understood by those undertaking cost-benefit analyses, and on occasion, double counting does occur.[3]

Another problem is the definition of indirect, or "spill-over," effects of a project. In some cases, analysts include as a benefit the extra profits of third parties not directly affected by a project. Only those effects that result in actual increases of output should be considered. Extra profits do not come under this heading.[4] In a full-employment economy, extra profits merely reflect changes in the distribution of income as a result of the project. They reflect the returns to resources attracted from alternative uses rather than increases in output. The practice of counting extra profits of third parties has been common in some cost-benefit analyses of irrigation projects.[5] In these cases, the profits of businesses that process the increased agricultural outputs as well as the profits of firms that supply goods to farmers have been included in the enumeration of benefits.

For some projects, enumeration of benefits is difficult. How does one define the benefits of an educational program or a health program? Again, the answer must give a quantifiable result that avoids double counting. In the case of a particular vocational-education program, benefits might include the increased output as reflected in higher earnings of those attaining new skills as a result of the program. In the case of an accident-prevention project, benefits might include the increased output resulting from reduced injuries and fatalities.

In enumerating costs of a project, one must be careful to reflect truly the foregone alternatives. Listing direct resource costs gives only a partial account of real costs. In addition, all external costs (those not reflected through the price system) must be included. Thus, if a new project in a given area will have the effect of attracting water resources from nearby agricultural land, the corresponding reduction in agricultural output must be included as a cost of the project.

Evaluation of Benefits and Costs

After all costs and benefits have been satisfactorily enumerated, the next step is to evaluate these costs and benefits in dollar terms. When the outputs of particular programs are not sold in markets, the problem of valuation is difficult. It is often necessary to *impute* values to outputs that are not sold. This is often done in an arbitrary fashion, because of the preference-revelation problems inherent in the nature of collective goods. A better technique is to attempt to find some surrogate measure of the value of any benefits. For

[3] Examples of double counting are offered by A. R. Prest and R. Turvey, "Cost-Benefit Analysis: A Survey," in *Surveys of Economic Theory*, volume 3, St. Martin's, New York, 1966, pp. 155–207.

[4] This has been emphasized by Roland McKean, *Efficiency in Government through Systems Analysis*, Wiley, New York, 1958, chapter 8. Also, see Prest and Turvey, p. 161.

[5] See Prest and Turvey, p. 181.

example, although the benefits of many public-health programs are collectively consumed, the value of these benefits may be reflected in the increased earnings of those whose health is improved by the project. An estimate of such increased earnings over time may be a good reflection of value of the benefits for the project. Similarly, the benefits of an educational program may be measured by an estimate of the increased earnings accruing over time to former students.

An additional problem occurs with outputs and inputs that are marketable but whose prices do not reflect their true valuation by society. This results when any output attributable to a project is sold in monopolistic markets, when external effects are generated by production of the output, or when distortions due to subsidies or taxes are present. Under such conditions, prices must be adjusted to reflect the true marginal costs to society. For example, if the prices of increased agricultural outputs of an irrigation project reflect the price supports of United States' agricultural policy, then the prices must be adjusted downward to reflect the true valuation of the outputs. If the prices of labor input reflect the monopoly power of labor unions, then a downward adjustment must be made in the wage bills to be incurred by the project. Whenever inputs are suspected of earning returns above their opportunity costs (such a differential is called "economic rent"), the returns must be adjusted to reflect opportunity costs only. Thus, all rents must be eliminated from the prices of all inputs. The elimination of such price distortions may require some arbitrary estimating decisions by the analysts.

Discounting Future Net Benefits

The next step after enumeration and evaluation of costs and benefits is to discount all future net benefits. The choice of an appropriate discount rate is of crucial importance here. The need to discount stems from the existence of positive interest rates in the economy. Positive interest rates imply that $1 of benefits in the future will be worth less than an equivalent dollar of present benefits. The reason for this is that it takes less than a dollar of resources invested "today" to produce a dollar of resources "tomorrow" (say, one year from today) when interest rates are positive. For example, if the interest rate is 5 percent per year, then to obtain $1 one year from today requires that only 95.24 cents be invested today. That is to say, $1 received one year from today is worth only 95.24 cents today. The 95.24 cents is called the "present value" of $1 to be received in one year. At the end of one year, the 95.24 cents will be equal to $1 [95.24 + (0.05) (95.24) = 100]. In general, the present value PV of X dollars to be received n years from now at simple interest rate of r is obtained by solving the equation $X = PV(1 + r)^n$.

$$PV = \frac{X}{(1 + r)^n} \tag{5.1}$$

If a particular project yields benefits over a number of years, the net benefits X_i must be discounted in each year as follows:

$$PV = \sum_i \frac{X_i}{(1 + r)^i} \qquad (5.2)$$

For example, if a project yields X_1 dollars in net benefits after the first year and X_2 dollars after the second year, its present value is:

$$PV = \frac{X_1}{(1 + r)^1} + \frac{X_2}{(1 + r)^2} \qquad (5.3)$$

The value of r will influence the present value of the dollar amount of benefits stemming from a project that yields future benefits (as most do). The choice of an appropriate discount rate is complicated by the fact that there exists a spectrum of such rates in the economy. The rates vary with the maturities of securities, risks, and other factors. Discount rates actually used in cost-benefit analyses have varied between 0 and 15 percent.[6]

What should determine the magnitude of the discount rate? First of all, it should reflect the return that can be earned on resources employed in alternative private use. This is the opportunity cost of capital invested in the public sector. Theoretically, one should not transfer resources from the private sector to the public sector if those resources can earn a higher social return in the private sector. Setting the discount rate equal to the "social opportunity cost of capital" will assure that misallocations do not occur. The opportunity cost depends on the marginal product of capital in the private sector.

Second, the discount rate should also reflect the willingness of the community to forego current consumption in exchange for future consumption. If the public project requires funds out of current consumption, then the rate at which the community sacrifices this consumption must equal the discount rate, to avoid any misallocation of resources. The rate of exchange between current and future consumption is called the "community's marginal rate of time preference."

Difficulties occur because the marginal rate of time preference is likely to diverge from the marginal product of capital. This would not occur if all capital markets were perfect, in the sense of no taxes distorting market behavior. Because of the existence of distortions, such as the corporation income tax, the community's marginal rate of time preference does not equal the marginal productivity of capital at one clear-cut interest rate. The reason for this is that the rate of return on savings as seen by those who forego consumption is different from the rate of return on investments as seen by investors. For example, if there is a 50 percent tax on corporate profits, then

---

[6] See Joint Economic Committee, Congress of the United States, *Hearings, July 30, 31, and August 1, 1968*, document 98–940, GPO, Washington, 1968.

the return to investments in the corporate sector of the economy is only one half of the actual gross percentage rate of return. If the return to savings is 10 percent, then investors who borrow capital at that rate will require a return in excess of 20 percent to undertake any project. The existence of such taxes causes investors and consumers to adjust to different interest rates and, hence, the divergence between the marginal rate of time preference and the marginal product of capital at equilibrium.

An ideal technique for determining the social rate of discount is to ascertain the kind of private expenditures that are displaced by a governmental activity and to use a weighted average of the returns that could have been earned on such expenditures as an estimate of the social rate of discount.[7] However, to obtain such an estimate of the distribution of expenditure displaced may be exceedingly difficult and costly.

As a result of the difficulties in measuring the community's marginal rate of time preference and the distribution of expenditures displaced, many economists favor the opportunity-cost approach to give a rough estimate of the social rate of discount. Such estimates of social opportunity cost consider a variety of factors, including risk premiums, taxes, and inflation.[8] For example, if risk and other complications are ignored, and the riskless market rate of interest is 5 percent, while there is a 50 percent tax on business profits, then it can be shown that the opportunity cost of capital will be 10 percent. This follows because business would require at least 10 percent to undertake investments, for their real return would be 5 percent (10 percent less 50 percent of that 10 percent, which represents the tax bill). If their return is less than 10 percent, they can do better by buying securities yielding 5 percent but not subject to business taxes.

Estimates of the social-opportunity cost of capital for the United States in the early 1970s have ranged from 7 to about 13 percent.[9] The economists making these estimates have taken account of a variety of market distortions, including taxes, risk, and inflation. The general conclusion reached is that the discount rates used by most agencies in the 1960s—3 to 5 percent—were much too low, and that this has probably resulted in a misallocation of capital resources. Many economists and legislators are beginning to realize the importance of consistent discounting procedures for cost-benefit analyses and the need for consistent discounting procedures in such studies.

Why is the choice of an appropriate discount rate so important? To begin to answer this question, one must first emphasize that it is no more important

---

[7] For an analysis yielding such an estimate, see Arnold C. Harberger, "On the Opportunity Cost of Public Borrowing," in Joint Economic Committee, *Hearings*, 1968.

[8] For an analysis using the opportunity-cost approach, see William J. Baumol, "On the Social Rate of Discount," *American Economic Review*, September 1968.

[9] See the studies done by Eckstein and Harberger in the Joint Economic Committee, *Hearings*, 1968. Also, see J. A. Seagraves, "More on the Social Rate of Discount," *Quarterly Journal of Economics*, August 1970.

than properly enumerating and evaluating costs and benefits. An analysis that uses the correct discount rate but seriously miscalculates costs and benefits will give results as misleading as a study that uses a zero discount rate. All phases of cost-benefit analysis are equally important if such studies are to yield useful information. However, the choice of the discount rate can be shown to affect the relative ranking of alternative projects and the level of efficient public expenditures. A low discount rate tends to favor projects yielding benefits further into the future relative to projects yielding current benefits. That is, low discount rates favor capital-intensive projects.

An arithmetical example illustrates this effect. Consider two alternative projects. Project 1 yields $90 in net benefits immediately, while project 2 yields $100 two years after it is undertaken and nothing at present or after one year. Project 2 is the more capital-intensive of the two. The present value of net benefits from these two projects may be calculated with a variety of discount rates and ranked according to their present values. Consider three alternative discount rates: 0, 5, and 10 percent. The present value of project 1 is always $90 because it yields only present benefits. The present value of project 2 will vary with the discount rate. Table 5.2 gives the present value of net benefits for project 2 under the alternative discount rates.

TABLE 5.2

Discount rate (in percent)	Present value of project 2	Present value of project 1
0	$\dfrac{100}{(1 + 0)^2} = 100$	90
5	$\dfrac{100}{(1 + 0.05)^2} = 90.9$	90
10	$\dfrac{100}{(1 + 0.1)^2} = 82.6$	90

As is shown in the table, the present value of project 2 is greater than that of project 1 under a discount rate of 0 and 5 percent. But if a discount rate of 10 percent is chosen, the result is such that project 1 is ranked above project 2. In general, the higher the discount rate, the less the weight given to the value of future benefits.

In addition, higher discount rates mean that fewer governmental projects can be approved. Insofar as the discount rate reflects the return to private consumption and investment, a higher rate implies that the opportunity costs of governmental activities in terms of private satisfactions foregone are greater. This, in turn, implies that efficiency requires a relatively smaller amount of public expenditures as a percentage of GNP. Some projects that previously yielded a positive value for the present value of net benefits will now show negative returns. Thus, an increase in the discount rate implies curtailment of public expenditures for efficiency.

SUMMARY

The public budget represents a summary of governmental expenditure plans and sources of finance. The size of the public sector can be influenced by the budgetary process through which bureaucrats compete for funding of projects.

The production of public goods must meet the test of efficiency. Since the outputs of many governmental agencies are difficult to quantify and cannot be sold in markets, the test of competition through profit making is not applicable to governmental bureaucrats. Program budgeting represents an attempt to achieve efficiency within the public sector. A program is a combination of activities designed to produce distinguishable public outputs. While the "outputs" of an agency are often difficult to define, they are a part of its mission. Insofar as there are alternative programs available to achieve any mission, a governmental agency must choose the alternative program that achieves its mission at minimum costs. Where many agencies are charged with missions that produce intermediate outputs which substitute for one another, program budgeting seeks the most efficient mix of such intermediate outputs. The choice of alternative programs to accomplish a given objective is the intra-agency aspect of program budgeting. It is analogous to the business firm's choice of the minimum-cost input mix to produce a given amount of output.

Cost-benefit analysis is useful in the choice of alternative public projects. A cost-benefit analysis lists and evaluates all benefits and costs of a public project and then discounts all future net benefits. This discount rate should reflect the foregone satisfactions on displaced private expenditure. Public projects yielding a social return below the social rate of discount should not be approved because, under such circumstances, displaced private expenditures would earn higher returns.

The budgetary process suffers from a number of flaws. The most serious flaw stems from the difficulties involved in defining and quantifying the outputs of governmental agencies. For some agencies, output definition is relatively easy, while for others, it is impossible because of the externalities associated with production of public goods. This makes it difficult to compare data on benefits and costs among agencies.

PART III

Taxation

6

Introduction to the Theory of Taxation

Governmental activity may be financed through various taxing schemes. Taxes represent compulsory payments by citizens to finance public expenditures. Alternatively, when feasible, government raises revenues from fees or user charges, such as tolls and admission charges to national parks, or through the issuance of public debts. Each particular method of raising revenues is likely to affect allocative decisions by private decision-making units and the distribution of income within the community. Such changes in the distribution of income, in turn, are likely to affect the demand for public expenditures by citizens of the community. The theory of taxation attempts to trace the allocative and redistributive effects of alternative taxes.

THE TAX BASE

Taxes may be levied on different bases. The *tax base* is the particular item upon which taxes are levied. Tax bases most commonly used are income, consumption, and wealth. These are economic bases. Taxes may also be applied to non-economic bases, such as, for example, "existence." A tax on existence is called a "head," or "poll," tax, and it usually is levied annually as a lump-sum payment on all adult individuals in a community. It might be $2 per head. This is a non-economic base in the sense that the amount of taxes collected does not vary with economic capacity. Income, consumption, and wealth are economic bases because they reflect the capacity of individuals to command resources. A tax on any economic base yields varying amounts of revenue depending on the size of the base. Revenue from a head tax varies only with the size of the adult population in a community.

All three economic bases are taxed in the United States. In addition, some states and localities still use poll taxes, although such taxes are only a minor source of revenue and cannot be a requirement for voting. In addition, many states and localities obtain significant amounts of revenue from non-tax sources, such as fees.

Taxes on income constitute the chief source of revenues for the federal government. The income tax base includes both individual income and the income of business corporations. In fiscal year 1971, it was estimated that individual income taxes accounted for 45 percent of federal revenues, while corporate income taxes yielded 17 percent. In addition, taxes collected from incomes by the federal government for the various social insurance programs (such as social security) yielded about 24 percent of total revenues. Thus, income taxes provide about 85 percent of the revenues for financing the activities of the federal government.

The income tax base is also utilized by state and local governments as a source of revenues but not nearly to the extent to which it is exploited by the federal government. State governments collect slightly over 20 percent of their revenues from income taxes, while the aggregate of local governments collect only about 3 percent of their revenues from this source.

The picture is different for the consumption base. Consumption taxes may be levied on retail sales in general or on the consumption of particular commodities. Taxes on the consumption of specific goods are called "excise taxes." The federal government collects only about 9 percent of its total revenues from taxes on consumption. Virtually all of this revenue is from excise taxes, the bulk of which comes from the federal tax on gasoline.

State governments obtain most of their revenues from taxes on consumption. Such taxes account for nearly 60 percent of their revenues. About half the revenues collected from taxes on consumption by the states are obtained from general retail sales taxes, while the other half is collected from a variety of excise taxes on commodities, such as gasoline, alcoholic beverages, tobacco, insurance, amusements, and so forth. Local governments make only sparse use of the consumption base, with taxes on consumption accounting for only about 7 percent of their revenues.

Property taxes, which are levied on a wealth base, are the major source of revenues for local governments in this country. The federal government, in a sense, taps the wealth base through estate and gift taxes, but it collects little revenue from wealth taxes. Similarly, property taxes constitute only a minor source of revenues for state governments (less than 3 percent of total receipts). However, property taxes account for over 80 percent of revenues collected by local governments.

Hence, although all three economic tax bases are used in the United States, the different levels of government currently utilize these bases to varying degrees. The federal government relies primarily on the income base. The states obtain the bulk of their revenues by tapping the consumption and income bases, and the local governments rely heavily on the property base. Tables 6.1 and 6.2 summarize the information.

TABLE 6.1

Federal Tax Structure, Fiscal Year 1971 Estimates
(percent distribution of tax revenue by source)

Source	Percent of revenues
Individual income taxes	45
Corporation income taxes	17
Social insurance taxes and contributions	24
Excise taxes	9
Other taxes	5
Total	100

SOURCE: U.S. Bureau of the Budget, *The Budget of the United States Government*, 1971.

TABLE 6.2

State and Local Tax Structure, Fiscal Year 1967
(percent distribution of tax revenue by source)

Source	Percent of revenues	
	States	Local governments
Property taxes	2.7	86.0
Sales and gross receipts taxes	58.2	6.7
Income taxes (individual and corporation)	22.4	3.2
Other	16.7	3.5
Total	100.0	100.0

SOURCE: U.S. Bureau of the Census, *Census of Governments*, vol. 4, 1967.

In addition to using a variety of tax bases, governments apply a variety of tax rate structures to those bases to compute the liability of the taxpayer. Three common rate structures are proportional, progressive, and regressive. Under a proportional tax, the rate applied to the base *does not vary* with the value of the base. For example, a general retail sales tax at 5 percent is a proportional tax on consumption. In the case of a progressive tax, the rate applied to the base *increases* with the value of the base. The rate structure of the federal income tax is progressive. Under a regressive rate structure, the rate of taxation *decreases* with the value of the base.

TAX SHARES

How should the burden of financing governmental activities be distributed among the citizens of a community? The answer to this question involves the choice of some optimal tax structure. This, in turn, implies the selection of appropriate tax bases and the tax rate schedules to apply to these bases. There are two basic approaches, or "philosophies," designed to determine the optimal tax structure. One is usually referred to as the "benefit approach," while the other is called the "ability-to-pay approach" to taxation.

Under the benefit approach to taxation, each citizen is taxed according to the marginal benefits he receives from governmental activities. This solution to the problem of the distribution of the burden of taxation is similar, therefore, to the Lindahl solution for simultaneously determining the optimal volume of public expenditures and tax shares (see Chapter 3). That is, the compulsory tax-sharing scheme, under the benefit approach, is identical to that in which each household makes a voluntary contribution to support governmental activities. The benefit approach has the advantage of linking the revenue and expenditure sides of the budget. However, this approach has some obvious implementation problems. When individuals know that their compulsory tax bill is on the basis of the marginal benefits they receive from governmental activities, then there is a definite incentive for them not to reveal their true preferences for public expenditures (see Chapter 3). Furthermore, to impute marginal benefits from governmental activities to individual citizens or groups of citizens may be a hopelessly difficult task. Finally, full reliance on the benefit approach may result in conflicts among the individuals concerning different conceptions of the appropriate distribution of income. The benefit approach makes no attempt to relate the tax bill to any particular economic base. To establish such a relation, it is necessary to show that the benefits of governmental activities vary with some base (say, positively with wealth).

This is not to say that the benefit approach is infeasible. The approach is often used when imputation of benefits is relatively easy. For example, it is reasonable to assume that the bulk of the benefits from governmental expenditures for roads accrue to motorists. Accordingly, the benefit principle dictates that expenditures for roads should be financed by motorists. Furthermore, if it is agreed that the relative contribution of each motorist should vary directly with his usage of public roads, it seems sensible to finance expenditures for roads through a tax on the motorist's consumption of gasoline. This, indeed, is the particular financing technique used today in the United States. A proportional tax is levied on the consumption of gasoline by various governmental units, and the proceeds from this tax are placed in a highway trust fund and earmarked for expenditures on roads. Similarly, the reliance on various user charges, such as tolls for bridges, represent application of the benefit principle to government finances.

The ability-to-pay approach attempts to relate tax shares to economic capacity. Those with greater economic capacity presumably bear higher tax burdens. Under this approach, the problem of distributing tax shares is viewed as independent of individual marginal benefits received from governmental activities. The implementation of a tax system based on "ability to pay" requires some collective agreement concerning an "equitable" distribution of the tax burden among the citizens. Individual evaluations of "equity," or "fairness," are likely to diverge among citizens whose preferences differ.

Differences in individual notions of equity make it difficult to define economic capacity. In some sense, economic capacity must measure the ability to command economic resources. Presumably, the greater the economic capacity, the greater the personal utility, insofar as utility increases material goods and services. But how does one measure economic capacity? Does it vary with income? Does it vary with consumption? Or does it vary with wealth? No objective answer can be given to these questions. A collective agreement on an index of economic capacity is required. Once this is done, a further collective choice is necessary to determine how tax shares vary with ability to pay. Since this separates decision-making on the revenue and expenditure aspects of governmental activities, it may lead to an inefficient allocation of resources between public and private uses.

Related to the ability-to-pay approach are the notions of horizontal and vertical equity. *Horizontal equity* is achieved when individuals of the same economic capacity (assuming this can be measured and collectively accepted) pay the same tax shares. *Vertical equity* is achieved when individuals of differing economic capacity pay tax shares that differ according to some collectively chosen notion of "fairness." Both these concepts are subjective and are difficult to administer. Insofar as individual assessments of economic capacity differ, one expects differing views concerning the construction of horizontal equity. Vertical equity requires even further subjective judgments on income distribution. Since subjective judgments differ among individuals, it is difficult to implement the concept except through the political process. This does not mean that the resulting collective choice is equitable in any objective sense.

CRITERIA FOR EVALUATION OF TAXES

Taxes are usually evaluated on the basis of the following economic criteria: efficiency and equity. To evaluate a tax on the basis of the efficiency criteria, one must gauge its effect on private economic decisions. If a tax introduces distortions into economic behavior, the distortions must be related to a Pareto-efficient resource allocation. For example, income taxes might distort economic choices between work and leisure. Excise taxes might reduce the consumption of the taxed goods relative to untaxed goods and, therefore, cause a misallocation of resources relative to that which might prevail in the absence of excise taxation. The distortions introduced by taxes can be roughly measured by computing the "efficiency loss" attributable to any tax. Taxes that result in no distortions in private economic behavior are said to have zero efficiency loss and are called "neutral taxes."

In addition to distorting private choices concerning resource allocation, taxes may also distort collective choices, thereby preventing the attainment of an optimal budget. The distribution of tax shares can affect the outcome of collective choices, say, under majority rule. If tax shares do not reflect the true marginal costs of governmental activities to particular citizens, the efficiency of the political process can be impaired. Political parties, in seeking to assemble winning coalitions of voters, may propose a package of public expenditures that appeals to certain special-interest groups, while also proposing that members of these groups pay taxes below their marginal benefits from the budget. Under majority rule, this may result in the electorate's approving a budget that is non-optimal. The reader may wish to refer to the discussion in Chapter 4 for elaboration of these points.

The economist cannot evaluate taxes on the basis of equity, or fairness. Equity remains a subjective concept, and the economist's judgments are no better than anybody else's. The economist can, however, generate information on how taxes affect the distribution of income in a community. Quite often taxes have rather subtle effects on relative prices that may not be immediately obvious to citizens when they are considering the impact of a proposed tax. The economist's estimates of effects that alternative taxes have on relative prices and incomes will be useful for citizens in evaluating any particular tax in relation to his own concept of equity, or fairness. Such estimates permit more-informed collective choices by participating citizens.

Most taxes alter the distribution of income. The economist's task of tracing the particular transfers of income attributable to any given tax is complicated by the fact that a tax is not always paid by the economic unit from which it is collected. Taxes on any economic base can be *shifted* from one economic unit to another through changes in the relative prices of outputs and inputs induced by movements in relative supplies and demands. Furthermore, public expenditures, as well as taxes, are likely to result in alterations in the distribution of income. The economist must, therefore, determine the effect of alternative public *budgets* on the distribution of income. The problem of determining the redistributive effects of alternative taxes and budgets is referred to as *incidence* analysis.

Taxes must also be administratively feasible to collect.[1] The cost of collection (including enforcement) must not be excessive relative to the amount of revenue actually collected. If any tax encourages evasion and if excessive resources must be devoted to detecting and punishing those evading the tax, then

---

[1] This has long been recognized by economists. Adam Smith included economy in collection as one of his four "canons" of taxation. See Adam Smith, *The Wealth of Nations*, Modern Library, Random House, New York, 1937, pp. 777–779.

an alternative revenue source should be considered. The federal income tax satisfies the requirement of administrative feasibility. Its cost of collection has been estimated at less than 1 percent of total revenue collected. On the other hand, personal property taxes, which prevail in many states, are relatively difficult to administer. There is an incentive for individual taxpayers to undervalue their real wealth or not to report valuable items that are easily concealed, such as jewelry. At the same time, the cost of checking each property listing by the individual taxpayer is prohibitive. The result is often the placement of unfair relative tax burdens on the honest citizens who list their properties correctly and inclusively. Similarly, in many communities, corruption or inadequate standards for assessment often result in real-estate assessments that do not correlate well with actual market values of the properties. Such taxes are weak on administrative grounds.

Ideally, taxes should fall on a base that is easy to measure. Any changes in the base should be accompanied by information readily available or, better yet, automatically supplied to the tax authorities. For example, most income earned in the United States is reported automatically to the federal government. In fact, in the case of wages and salaries, employers themselves act as the tax-collection agency for the government by withholding taxes from their employees and turning these funds over to the federal government. Compare this with taxes on real estate. Increases in the value of existing properties constitute increases in the wealth of their owners (other things being equal). If properties are not sold, the only way to estimate the increments of wealth is through a formal appraisal. New appraisals are costly, and the additional taxes may be difficult to impose on the property owners.

Taxes on consumption are fairly easy to administer. Often the tax is levied on the manufacturer of the commodity, as is the case for excise taxes on automobiles. Such taxes are almost impossible to evade. Retail sales taxes are simply added onto the sales bill by the retailer. In these cases, the manufacturers and retailers are used as tax collectors, and the administrative costs of collection to the government are very low.

ALTERNATIVES TO TAXATION

Taxes are compulsory payments that force citizens to surrender their command over private uses of economic resources (in terms of dollars) so as to divert such resources to public use. Taxpayers are forced to reduce their consumption of automobiles, television sets, and other private goods so that the resources necessary to produce these goods can be released to produce public goods, such as schools, roads, and armed forces. In addition, taxes are used to finance transfers of purchasing power among households.

One alternative to taxation is direct governmental appropriations of resources. The government simply orders that productive resources be used in a certain way. There are some instances when citizens will agree to such a method of finance. Perhaps the best example of this governmental direct appropriation of resources is the military draft. In this case, the government requires labor services to be performed by certain young persons for a certain period of time. The opportunity cost of the draft is the lost private output that these people would have produced had they been permitted to remain civilians. A rough estimate of this cost can be provided by the foregone earnings of drafted persons. In most cases, draftees are paid wages below their opportunity cost of earnings in civilian life. If military labor resources are financed through taxation instead of compulsory military service, then the government has to attract labor out of private uses by offering wages for military service that are competitive with those available for alternative occupations. This wage is likely to be considerably higher than that paid to draftees. Furthermore, under taxation, the cost of military labor input is spread to all taxpayers rather than mostly on the draftees. Another example of such a method of finance is the requirement (enforced by fines) that property owners keep the sidewalks in front of their homes clear and clean. This substitutes the use of private labor for the alternative of increased taxes to finance the wages of street-cleaning public employees.

Direct governmental appropriations of productive resources may disguise the true costs of governmental activities. Citizens may be less-informed of the opportunity cost of such compulsion in terms of lost private output than they are of tax shares. This, in turn, may lead to distortions in collective decisions. It is often argued that if military labor input for the Vietnam war had been financed through taxes raised to attract a volunteer army, the collective choices made by this nation and implemented by the Congress and President might have been very different.

There are other methods of financing governmental activities that also entail no compulsion. When goods subject to the exclusion principle are supplied by public authorities, pricing becomes a feasible method of finance. Examples of publicly supplied goods coming under this category are parks, museums, bridges, schools, and postal services. The costs of exclusion are very low for such goods and it is feasible to attach prices to their consumption. Under such circumstances, the application of the benefit principle is relatively easy.

In other cases, governmental activity may be financed through public borrowing. Public borrowing implies that taxation to repay the principal and interest on the debt is postponed. Thus, one often finds public buildings, public transportation systems, and dams financed through public-debt issues. Such projects typically are capital intensive; that is, they require considerable outlays of productive resources at the present but yield a steady stream of benefits, through time, when completed. It seems reasonable, therefore, not to tax the current tax base for the full amount of initial capital expenses. Instead, the funds are borrowed and repaid with interest by taxing future taxpayers, who receive the benefits flowing from, say, the new public building. Debt finance is particularly appealing to local governments. The reason for this stems from the fact that there is constant inmigration and outmigration of inhabitants subject to taxes in such localities. If tax finance is used for local capital projects, many residents who expect to leave the area soon are unlikely to vote for the project, while future residents have no vote. This could lead to inefficient collective choices. Debt finance is likely to be efficient for capital-intensive public projects.

Public Pricing

When it is possible to "sell" services produced in the public sector, decisions must be made concerning the appropriate pricing policy. A question that precedes pricing is: "Why do communities choose to supply goods that are essentially 'private' in such circumstances?" The answer is that the citizens in the community are apparently convinced that private production will not result in the appropriate amount of output being supplied to the public. In particular, if there are external economies associated with the production of such services as educational facilities, museums, and libraries, too little is likely to be produced and consumed under private production. One economist has called private goods whose consumption generates external benefits "merit goods."[2] These goods tend to be publicly supplied because it is believed that the price mechanism alone would provide inadequate incentive for an efficient level of output to be produced.

In other cases, governments supply private goods whose production is subject to decreasing long-run-average costs. Examples of such goods are drinking water, electric power, natural gas, and other goods commonly designated as "public utilities." As was shown in Chapter 2, marginal cost pricing, as is required for efficiency, will result in losses being incurred by private units operating such natural monopolies. The alternative is either public supply of such goods or public subsidy of the private units supplying such goods. If public supply is chosen, the community must also choose the method of finance. Since goods such as drinking water are generally subject to the exclusion principle (the cost of installing metering devices is low relative to the amount of revenue that can be collected from metered sale of water) pricing is a feasible alternative but the production of drinking water could, of course, also be financed out of general taxation revenues. Since it is so easy to apply the benefit principle in this case, the alternative of pricing is usually chosen.

In cases where public supply of goods subject to the exclusion principle is considered efficient, the authorities must choose appropriate prices to charge the individual consumers for services rendered. What is an "appropriate" price?

[2] Richard A. Musgrave, *The Theory of Public Finance*, McGraw-Hill, New York, 1959, p. 13.

Again, on the basis of efficiency, prices should be set equal to marginal costs of production so that supply is equal to demand (that is, the market must clear—there must be no shortages or excesses in production). But such a policy, although it might seem relatively easy to apply, is, in actuality, complex. First of all, in the case where external benefits are generated, marginal cost must be adjusted downward to reflect the value of the external benefit to society. That is, in such cases where marginal social cost differs from marginal private cost, the appropriate cost function is the marginal social cost that includes the value of the externality.

Second, in cases where the average cost of the good or service decreases with output, marginal cost pricing results in a deficit for the now governmentally owned and operated activity just as surely as it does if the activity is still privately owned. The same dilemma has to be faced in either case of public ownership or private ownership. Either the price has to rise to cover the full average cost of production, or the deficit has to be financed from general revenues. Recourse to general taxation means that those who do not neces-sarily receive direct benefit from the activity are forced to bear some of the costs. On the other hand, if the price is raised to cover average cost of produc-tion, the quantity of output demanded falls relative to the efficient amount of output, and users of the service pay a price above the marginal cost of the output. Both policies may have adverse effects on the distribution of income, but the second policy, that of pricing above marginal cost, also distorts re-source allocation. There is still no objective basis for choosing between the two alternative policies, and the choice of a policy must be considered a political question.

The choice of an appropriate price for some public services is further complicated if one considers the possibility of congestion costs. Congestion is a problem that may result when the government supplies a certain good that can be consumed collectively by only a small subset of the community at any time, but for which the cost of exclusion is low enough to make pricing feasible. Examples of goods coming under this category are public parks, zoos, recreation facilities, roads, and bridges. It is relatively inexpensive to block all entrances to parks and establish an admission charge or to put up a toll booth on a bridge. Assuming that the benefits of bridges, zoos, parks, and the like accrue mainly to those directly consuming the services flowing from such facilities, the benefit principle indicates that pricing should be used to ration and finance the consumption of these services. Once again, on the basis of the Pareto criterion, prices should be set equal to marginal costs of production.

What is the marginal cost of production for a park or a bridge? Consider the case of the bridge. The bulk of the cost incurred in building a bridge is a fixed capital expenditure that does not vary with the number of cars utilizing the bridge per unit of time. The marginal cost for such a facility is likely to be very low. The total will comprise only the costs that vary with car crossings and will include such items as maintenance and depreciation. Thus, marginal cost for accommodating additional traffic on a bridge is likely to be close to zero. Marginal cost pricing indicates that the appropriate toll to be levied is zero or some nominal charge very close to zero to cover incremental maintenance cost.

But there is another problem that must be considered in this case. This is the possibility of traffic congestion on the bridge. Congestion costs are external costs mutually inflicted on citizens by their own behavior and are comprised of loss of time and comfort by the various users of the bridge. Congestion costs represent real losses of output and welfare for society and, therefore, should be included in the marginal cost of bridge production. Congestion costs are likely to vary over time. For example, such costs are likely to be higher during "rush hours" relative to "off-peak" use times (say midnight). This suggests that tolls based on marginal cost, including marginal congestion costs, should vary with the time of the day. This introduction of congestion costs indicates that even though marginal direct resource cost for the production of bridge services may be zero, positive tolls are justified on the bridge to internalize the external congestion costs. Furthermore, the fact that congestion costs may vary with time indicates that differential tolls may be established to ration scarce bridge services at times of peak usage, a method called "peak-load pricing" that is often applied to the pricing of recreation facilities, power production, telephone services, and public transportation facilities.

User Charges

Publicly produced services having characteristics of private goods generating externalities, while not "priced" directly on a unit basis, may, nevertheless, be financed according to the benefit principle. So-called user charges may be levied on the recipients of such public services. This is the typical method of financing highway services in the United States. Under the assumption that the user benefit from roads vary directly with the amount of gasoline consumption, the federal and state excise taxes on gasoline represent user charges for the services of roads.[3] Similarly, automobile registration fees represent a flat-rate charge for the use of public road facilities. The difference between user charges and direct pricing lies in the compulsory element inherent in user charges (they are very much like taxes in this respect) and the fact that the consumption of the good or service financed by user charges is not directly linked on a per-unit basis to an actual "unit price." It is often argued that user charges represent a second-best alternative to actual pricing of publicly supplied goods

---

[3] Such a tax as utilized in the United States does not take into account the fact that cars with different types of engines get different mileage per gallon of gas. Thus, the individual who drives a small car may pay less for road services than the individual's driving the same amount of miles per year in a large car.

and services when the administrative costs of applying the exclusion principle are too high. For example, to establish tollbooths on all city streets is extremely impractical and costly. Similarly, given current technology, other methods of "metering" street usage are equally infeasible because of high costs. City tolls not only are expensive in nominal terms, but they also would contribute to congestion costs by unnecessarily inhibiting the movement of traffic. Instead, the city may decide to finance its road expenditures through a local tax on gasoline, automobile user fees, and revenue collected from parking meters.

Debt Finance

Governmental authorities also finance public expenditures through the issuance of interest-yielding public debt. Debt finance implies the sale of a security bearing the promise to pay interest over a given number of years and to return the principal loaned at the end of the given time period. There is no compulsion involved in the sale of such securities. Instead, the government competes with other borrowers in the market for scarce capital funds. The government pays the going market rate of interest, adjusted for risk and maturity characteristics of the obligation it issues. Thus, the issuance of public debt is similar in some ways to the sale of services having the regular characteristics of private goods. The government "sells" securities of various types and maturities (for example, Series E savings bonds, U.S. Treasury bills, Treasury notes, long-term governmental bonds, municipal bonds) that compete with various private securities, such as commercial-bank savings deposits, savings and loan shares, bank acceptances, and corporate bonds. In effect, the governments that issue debts are supplying "investments" for the public's portfolio.

There has been a great deal of controversy concerning the appropriateness of utilization of public debt by the various levels of government in the United States. One often hears dire predictions by politicians and news commentators concerning the inevitable "bankruptcy" of the country because of the onerous burden of a huge public debt. There is talk of the burden we are inflicting on future generations—our "grandchildren"—as a result of our current "overspending," or profligacy. On the other hand, many argue that since the public debt is largely held by citizens of this country, rather than by foreigners, there is no burden because the debt is "internal." That is to say, because we owe the debt to ourselves, payment of interest and principal of the debt merely transfers income from taxpayers to debt-holders. What is the "burden" of the debt and what are the relative advantages of debt finance when compared to tax finance?

There is no general agreement among economists concerning the "burden" of the debt. For the purposes of this discussion, the term "burden" should be thought of as the redistributive effect of debt finance. Consider the impact of debt finance in elementary terms. When governmental units obtain funds to finance public expenditures by issuing public debt, there is no compulsion involved, as there is in tax finance. Instead, securities issued by governmental authorities are purchased voluntarily by individual citizens, financial institutions, and other private economic units. The individuals who purchase such securities surrender present consumption opportunities for future consumption opportunities or substitute public debt for private securities in their portfolio. They make such a voluntary sacrifice because the return they expect to receive on their foregone consumption (their "investment") exceeds their subjective estimate of the "cost" of sacrificing current consumption opportunities. At the same time, debt finance makes it unnecessary to increase current taxes. This avoids the need to *force* citizens to curtail current consumption and saving. Under debt finance, private investment is "choked off" only to the extent to which increased governmental borrowing causes the general level of interest rates to rise by increasing the demand for credit.

It is important to distinguish "true" public borrowing from borrowing that merely represents disguised money creation. When the federal government sells securities, say, to the Federal Reserve System, and receives a payment in the form of a "created" deposit, the sale does not represent "true" borrowing. Instead, the money supply is increased, and if the economy is operating under conditions of full employment, the money creation undoubtedly increases the general price level. The resulting inflation implies that those individuals who have fixed incomes or who hold cash balances will experience a reduction in real income and/or wealth. For such individuals, the inflation is a *tax* that results in curtailment of consumption or saving. With true debt finance, there is no corresponding increase in the money supply and no induced increase in the general level of prices.

In order to pay interest on the debt and return the principal, the government usually increases taxes. If so, taxpayers in the *future* undergo reductions in consumption or saving. The increased tax revenues necessary to pay interest on the debt redistribute income from taxpayers to the holders of public debt. Since the bulk of the national (federal) debt in the United States is owed to United States citizens (it is an "internal" debt—only a very small percentage of it is owed to foreigners), its retirement would not represent a drain of resources from the country, and therefore, the effect of such retirement would be to redistribute income among citizens. The predictions of "bankruptcy" of the federal government are, therefore, without much relevance.

But is there a "burden" of the debt, and if so, is it borne by current or future generations? James Buchanan has pointed out that, to some extent, the answer to this question depends on how the term "burden" is defined.[4] There has been a great deal of confusion in discussions concerning the public debt because of inconsistent definitions of the term. Some economists argue

---

[4] See James M. Buchanan, "The Italian Tradition in Fiscal Theory," reprinted in James M. Ferguson (ed.), *Public Debt and Future Generations*, University of North Carolina Press, Chapel Hill, 1964, pp. 48–49.

that the burden of the debt cannot be transferred to future generations, but must be borne by the present generation, because resources are withdrawn from the private sector at the time the debt is created. This definition of burden merely implies that debt creation involves foregone private consumption in the current period. It neglects the fact that this sacrifice of consumption is completely *voluntary* on the part of the private economic units and is compensated by greater opportunities for future consumption as a result of interest payments on the public securities. Under the assumption that the future generation must be taxed to pay the interest burden on the debt, it is clear that they must undergo a real reduction of income (without the compensation of increased future consumption). In this sense, the burden of the debt does fall on the future generation—they bear the brunt of compulsory taxes. The burden of the debt is, therefore, a reduction in welfare of future taxpayers.[5]

Insofar as the revenue obtained from the issuance of public debt is used to finance projects that yield future benefits, one must consider the possibility that the benefits will reduce the burden of the debt. On the basis of the benefit principle, it might, in fact, be viewed as efficient to transfer the burden of present expenditures to future generations if it can be demonstrated that particular expenditures will benefit future generations. For example, it is reasonable to postpone to the future the burden of taxes for financing war, since the benefits of a successfully completed (that is, "won") war will accrue to those living in the country in the future.

The transference of the burden of finance to the future has particular relevance for capital expenditures undertaken by state and local governments within a federalist context. The reason for this stems from the fact that the make-up of the population in these areas changes over time. Such changes are not due solely to the life cycle of individuals but also to the fact that individual citizens move in and out of the area over a period of time. This implies that the population who receives the benefits of current capital expenditures (say, a new sewer system or a new school) in the future may be a completely different aggregation of people compared to those who currently live in the area. Thus, on the basis of the benefit principle, it is legitimate to finance projects that yield the bulk of their benefits in the future and in a particular local area through the issuance of public debts. The taxes levied to pay the interest and principal on the debts may, more or less, coincide with the benefits flowing from the project. Those actually receiving the benefits—the individuals comprising the future tax base—will, therefore, also bear the tax cost of financing the projects. The postponement of taxes as a result of debt issue is often referred to as "pay-as-you-use" finance. Citizens are taxed for capital expenditures at the time the expenditures yield benefits and *not* at the time

---

[5] The interpretation has been emphasized by James M. Buchanan in *Public Principles of Public Debt*, Irwin, Homewood, Ill., 1958.

the capital expenditures are initiated. The principle underlying this method of finance is similar to that of financing an automobile or a home through a loan. Many local governments have special "capital budgets" that list expenditures to be financed by the issuance of public debts.

It must be pointed out that there are some very important conceptual differences between debt finance on the federal and local levels. The market for public securities is a national one. This implies that when local governments sell public debt obligations (such as municipal general-obligation bonds) it is quite possible that the bulk of the obligations are purchased by non-residents or residents who will have moved from the locality by the time the obligation matures. Thus, when the debt is retired, resources are, in fact, "drained" from the locality, and the payments of interest and principal on the debts are not a mere redistribution of welfare within the community. On the other hand, it also means that the municipality can "import" real resources from other areas of the nation to finance capital expenditures. Thus, for local and state governments, the public debt is not an "internal" debt, but instead, it is largely an external debt. The possibility of "bankruptcy" is, therefore, a real threat to such governmental units and indicates that they should be more judicious in their issuance of public debt than the federal government. This fact is reflected in the capital markets insofar as state and local debt obligations are viewed as being more "risky" than federal obligations. Furthermore, the credit ratings of different states and municipalities depend on the history of debt servicing in the particular locality. It also should be pointed out that local governments, in general, cannot sell their securities directly to the Federal Reserve Banks in exchange for a "created" deposit. Thus, the option of "bogus" debt through money creation and inflation is not available to local governments.

In some special cases, local governments can service their debts *without* increasing taxes. This occurs when the governmental units issue public debts for the purpose of financing projects that yield future benefits in the form of services that can be sold to the public on a per-unit basis. In effect, the debts are paid from revenue obtained from sales of the projects. In such cases, the issuance of debts by local governmental units is exactly similar to issuance of debts by private corporations. Obligations of local governmental units whose retirement is dependent on sales of services are usually called municipal "revenue bonds." They differ from municipal general-obligation bonds that are retired by general taxes.

Revenue bonds usually are issued to finance expenditures on public transportation facilities and recreation facilities. General-obligation bonds are used to finance public education facilities and other capital expenditures for, say, police and fire protection, that usually are not sold on a per-unit basis. In some cases, the governmental authorities create quasi-private corporations to administer the financing and operation of particular projects. Examples of such agencies are the Tennessee Valley Authority, the New Jersey Turnpike

Authority, and the Port of New York Authority. The use of debt finance for such projects follows the "pay-as-you-use" principle. The public is not required to bear large tax increases to finance the initial capital expenditures for such projects, and the burdens of finance to pay the interest and principal on the debts is borne by the actual users of the facilities through the collection of user charges in one form or another.

Other Revenue Sources

In addition to pricing and debt finance, there are a number of miscellaneous financing techniques utilized by governments. One technique is the operation of a lottery. This method of obtaining revenues is quite popular in Latin America and is also used in a number of states in this country (New York, New Jersey, New Hampshire). By operating a lottery, the government sells gambling services to the citizenry. It competes directly with private sales of such services (either legal or illegal). Public lotteries differ from taxation in that they do not involve any compulsion, since purchases of lottery tickets are voluntary. Of course, the government must provide prizes and "odds" that are attractive enough to compete with the private supply of gambling. In addition, the amount of net revenues that the governmental unit collects from the lottery is limited by the demand for gambling services in the area.

Many governmental units also engage in retail sales of private goods, and some actually produce the private goods offered for sale. An example of this is the liquor stores run by many states in the Union. The profits of such stores often provide a significant amount of revenue to local governing units. Of course, the reasoning underlying governmental operation of such stores involves the external costs believed to be associated with consumption of alcoholic beverages. Whether public control of the distribution of hard liquor helps to internalize these costs is another question. The fact remains that, in such cases, the government is in the retail-trade business, and the profits from such business substitute for taxes.

SUMMARY

Taxes are compulsory payments by citizens to finance public expenditure. Taxes force individual citizens to surrender their command over private goods and services so that the resources used to produce these goods and services may be released for public use. Any governmental activity may be financed through alternative means. In addition to taxes of varying rates on varying bases—the activity subject to taxation—public expenditures may be financed by direct appropriation of private resources under compulsion, pricing or user charges applied to public services that are partially divisible into units, and public borrowing.

A collective choice is necessary to determine tax shares of citizens under tax finance. Since the willingness of citizens to vote affirmatively on proposed public expenditures is, at least in part, contingent on their tax shares, the choice of a tax-sharing plan is interdependent with the choice of the expenditure plan. The benefit approach to taxation would tax individuals according to the marginal benefits they receive from public expenditures. The ability-to-pay approach attempts to relate tax shares to some measure of economic capacity. Both these approaches to determining tax shares are difficult to implement. The benefit approach requires that individuals reveal their evaluations of marginal benefits they receive from governmental activities. If their tax shares are contingent on such revealed marginal benefits, then there is no incentive for them to reveal their true evaluations for public expenditures generating externalities. On the other hand, differences in individual subjective notions of "equity" make difficult the implementation of the ability-to-pay approach.

Taxes may alter private economic decisions in such a way as to result in efficiency losses for the economy. Taxes that result in no efficiency losses are called "neutral" taxes. Taxes also affect income distribution by altering relative prices of outputs and inputs. Detailed discussions of the allocative and distributive effects of taxation will be provided in the following two chapters.

7

Taxation and the Allocation of Resources

Taxes levied on economic bases usually affect the behavior of private decision-making units. Since the amount of taxes the decision-making unit pays is a function of the *size* of its economic base, the unit can reduce its taxes by regulating the size of its taxable base (say, income or consumption in a particular locality). In other words, taxpayers can, to some extent, by altering their behavior, control the burden of taxation. Pigou refers to such alterations in behavior as the "announcement aspects" of taxation: "The announcement of a tax as a rule causes people to modify their conduct with a view, in some measure, to avoiding the pressures of the tax."[1]

In the absence of other market distortions (such as externalities), taxes are likely to induce changes in economic behavior that move the economy from an efficient resource allocation. The reallocations occur as households and business firms alter their utilization pattern for the scarce resources at their command in such a manner as to avoid or lessen the burden of taxation. In particular, taxes are likely to affect the relative prices of various outputs as seen by buyers and sellers. For example, an excise tax on tobacco causes the equilibrium price of tobacco to be different for buyers and sellers of tobacco. An income tax causes the wages paid by employers to diverge from the wages actually received by workers. The withholding of income taxes from wages and salaries makes the divergence obvious to most of us.

The impairment in efficiency attributable to taxation represents a real

[1] A. C. Pigou, *A Study in Public Finance*, (third. ed.), Macmillan, London, 1947, p. 55.

164

loss in outputs and welfare for the community at large. If the efficiency gain from tax-financed governmental expenditure (internalization of externalities) does not outweigh the efficiency loss from taxation, then governmental activity may be undesirable. Although there are other criteria involved in evaluating taxes, especially distributional criteria, the effects of taxes on efficiency in resource allocation must be understood to evaluate alternative taxes and tax structures. To understand the allocative effects of taxes, the economist must analyze the effect they have on the willingness of both households and business firms to supply and purchase goods and services. Since taxes levied on economic bases affect the terms at which outputs and inputs are traded, taxes affect both the market equilibrium prices and quantities of taxed commodities and factors of production.

In this chapter we develop some general techniques to analyze and measure the allocative effects of alternative taxes and tax structures. In the following chapter we will study techniques to analyze the redistributive effects of taxation. It must be emphasized that, while this chapter ignores the distributive aspects, a study of *both* aspects is vital to evaluate alternative tax structures.

The reader must also be warned that a number of simplifying abstractions are utilized to analyze the allocative effects of taxation. A common technique is to assume that the tax being evaluated is the only one being utilized by the government. This ignores the fact that there are other taxes and market distortions present simultaneously with any tax and that the distortion introduced by any one particular tax may serve merely to counterbalance some existing distortion (recall the "theory of second best"). An analysis that ignores possible "feedback" effects is called a "partial equilibrium" analysis. A *general equilibrium analysis* attempts to consider all possible feedback effects of any given economic change. Of the two kinds of analysis, the general equilibrium approach is, at the same time, more realistic and complex. It considers more possible variables than the partial equilibrium approach and traces repercussions in other markets, aside from the one being taxed, that might affect the distortion introduced by taxation.

TAX NEUTRALITY

A tax that does not distort economic decision-making is said to be "neutral." Neutral taxes are those that do not prevent attainment of efficiency. Economists usually divide the economic impact of a given tax into two components: an allocative effect and a redistributive effect. The *allocative effect* measures the loss in welfare attributable to the inefficiency, or distortions in resource allocation, attributable to a tax (the allocative effect is sometimes referred to as the "excess burden" or "welfare cost" of a tax). The *redistributive effect* traces the transfers of income among citizens as a result of the change in relative prices of outputs and inputs induced by the tax. A neutral tax has no allocative effect (that is, the loss in efficiency is zero) but some redistributive effect (that is, it changes relative prices).

A head tax is an example of a neutral tax. Since such a tax is levied on the basis of mere existence and not on an economic base, an individual cannot alter the amount of tax he pays by altering his economic behavior. It follows that there is no distortion attributable to the head tax in the allocation of resources. Other examples of neutral taxes are taxes on the consumption of commodities for which no substitutes are available. The price elasticity of demand for such commodities is zero, and taxes on their consumption do not change resource allocations because there is no change in quantity demanded. Similarly, taxes on goods or inputs that are in fixed supply (price elasticity of supply equals zero) also are neutral because there is no opportunity for private decision-making units to change their behavior in response to the taxes. Thus, a tax is neutral if and only if there are no opportunities available to tax-payers to change their economic behavior in such a manner as to vary the amount of taxes they pay.

Tax neutrality is an ideal that is not likely to be attainable by most nations. There are many opportunities for households and business firms to control, to some extent, their aggregate tax bills by altering their economic behavior in response to most taxes. Most taxed items (including work effort) are in neither perfectly inelastic supply nor perfectly inelastic demand. It follows that most tax structures are likely to distort private economic decision-making and induce a corresponding loss in efficiency. In other words, the tax structure is not neutral.

Given the rather disheartening observation that neutrality with respect to resource allocation is not likely to be attainable, the next question that must be asked is, "What causes the loss in efficiency attributable to taxation, and how can this loss be measured?"

THE ALLOCATIVE EFFECTS OF TAXATION

Consider the effect of taxation in a particular market. For simplicity, assume that the tax under consideration is an excise tax on the production of some commodity X. Assume that this is the only tax used by the government to obtain revenue. The repercussions in other markets as a result of the effect of the tax in the market for good X are negligible, and any "feedback" effects of changes in other markets on the market for X also are negligible. This is called a "partial equilibrium analysis." Furthermore, for simplicity, assume that perfect competition prevails in all markets. There are no externalities in the consumption or production of good X or any other good.

The analysis to be undertaken here, although dealing with a specific type of tax, is completely general in the sense that it can be applied to all kinds of taxes. An excise tax is a tax levied on the sale of a particular commodity. But most taxes are taxes on the sale of particular outputs or inputs. For example, an income tax can be considered, in part, an excise tax on the sale of work effort. Any tax results in a change in the terms at which decision-making units either supply or demand resources. The resulting changes in market behavior can be used to gauge the allocative effect of any tax.

Allocative Effects of a Single Tax

Now consider the impact of the excise tax on X in the market for X under the assumptions made. Good X may be considered to be any output or input. Figure 7.1 illustrates both the pre-tax and the post-tax market conditions. Curves D and S are the demand and supply curves respectively for X. The initial pre-tax market equilibrium is at point B, implying that Q_0 units of X are sold at price P_0. When the tax is imposed, suppliers of X treat it as an increase in their marginal costs of production (alternatively, it might be considered as a deduction from average revenue—the result is the same). Thus, if a tax of t per unit is levied on every unit of X sold, the result is an increase in marginal costs of t at all levels of output, and a consequent upward shift in the supply curve (which is the marginal cost curve under perfect competition) of t at all levels of output. The effect of the tax may, therefore, be thought of as a decrease in supply.

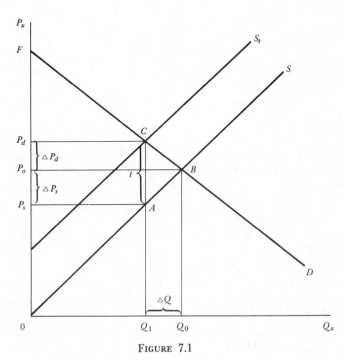

FIGURE 7.1

The decrease in supply results in a new post-tax equilibrium at C, implying that the quantity sold decreases to Q_1, and the equilibrium price rises to P_d. The price P_d is the new market price paid by the demanders (buyers) of X. But the suppliers (sellers) of X do not receive this price, for they must surrender t to the government on each unit of X sold.

The price sellers receive is, therefore, $P_d - t = P_s$. The amount of revenue collected from the tax by the government is the amount of X sold multiplied by the tax per unit, tQ_1. This is represented by the shaded rectangle P_sP_dCA in Figure 7.1. The total revenue of producers is simply P_sQ_1.

Does the excise tax introduce any distortion into the economy? Since it was assumed that perfect competition prevails in all markets and that no other distortions, such as externalities, were present, it follows that the efficiency criteria were satisfied prior to introduction of the tax (see Chapter 1 for proof of this proposition). In the pre-tax situation, consider some other good Y whose equilibrium price is P_y. In the process of maximizing their utility, consumers will adjust the relative consumption of X and Y in such a manner as to equate their marginal rates of substitution of X for Y to the ratio of the price of Y to the price of X, P_0. Producers, in the process of maximizing their profits, adjust their production so as to set prices equal to marginal costs. This results in adjustments in output until the marginal rate of transformation of X for Y is equal to the ratio of the price of Y to the price of X. This information is summarized in Table 7.1.

TABLE 7.1

Pre-tax Equilibrium

Consumers	Producers	Equilibrium
$MRS_{XY} = \dfrac{P_y}{P_0}$	$MRT_{XY} = \dfrac{P_y}{P_0}$	$MRS_{XY} = MRT_{XY}$

As Table 7.1 indicates, both producers and consumers adjust to the same relative prices, thereby automatically equating marginal rates of substitution with marginal rates of transformation and achieving a position of efficiency for the economy. Now consider the post-tax equilibrium. The price of X as seen by consumers, P_d, diverges from the price of X as seen by sellers, P_s. The tax acts as a sort of "wedge" between the consumer and seller prices: $P_d = P_s + t$. The ratio of prices as seen by consumers is now P_y/P_d, while the ratio of prices as seen by sellers is P_y/P_s. The resulting adjustment of consumption and production by buyers and sellers, as the equilibrium quantity produced decreases to Q_1, is summarized in Table 7.2. The efficiency condition is no longer satisfied because $P_y/P_d < P_y/P_s$. The independent maximizing behavior of producers and consumers no longer achieves an efficient resource allocation. There is, therefore, an efficiency loss to the economy as a result of the tax.

TABLE 7.2

Post-tax Equilibrium

Consumers	Producers	Equilibrium
$MRS_{XY} = \dfrac{P_y}{P_d}$	$MRT_{XY} = \dfrac{P_y}{P_s}$	$MRS_{XY} < MRT_{XY}$

Measurement of Efficiency Loss

Under certain restrictive assumptions, it is possible to obtain a measurement that approximates the efficiency loss attributable to the allocative effects of a tax. The measure so obtained indicates the factors that affect the magnitude of the efficiency loss and, further, is measurable empirically.

To obtain the measure of efficiency loss (sometimes referred to as the "excess burden" of taxation), consider once again the effect of a tax on the sale of some output or input X. The tax may be an excise tax on commodity X or a tax on the sale of work effort (that is, an income tax). The tax of t per unit sold disrupts the market for X by shifting the supply curve from S to S_t, decreasing the quantity sold from Q_0 to Q_1, and raising the price paid by consumers from P_0 to P_d, while lowering the price actually received by sellers after payment of the tax to P_s.

The tax has a two-pronged effect. First, the reduction in consumption of X from Q_0 to Q_1 presumably involves a loss in welfare to consumers. Second, the reduction in production of X presumably frees productive resources for alternative uses. The tax revenue obtained by the government (the area P_sP_dCA in Figure 7.1) undoubtedly will be used to bid for some of these freed productive resources in order to provide public services. The net loss in welfare to society attributable to the allocative effect of the tax may be approximated by the excess of lost consumption utility over the value of freed productive resources as a result of the reduction in output of X from Q_0 to Q_1.

If it is assumed that the taxed commodity represents only a small portion of total consumer budget outlays so that the income effects of price changes may be considered negligible, then the loss in consumer utility ΔU may be approximated by the area under the demand curve between Q_0 and Q_1.[2] The saved cost to society ΔC, as a result of productive resources made available for alternative uses, can be approximated by the area under the supply curve between Q_0 and Q_1, under the assumption of perfect competition to assure that the supply curve represents the true marginal costs of productive resources to society.

---

[2] When there is no income effect, the demand curve may be thought of as a marginal utility curve, with utility measured in terms of dollars. The area under any portion of that demand curve can, therefore, be thought of as the utility in dollar terms of the consumption included in that portion.

The net loss in welfare is, therefore, $W = \Delta U - \Delta C$. The lost utility ΔU is the area Q_1CBQ_0 in Figure 7.1, while ΔC is the area Q_1ABQ_0. It follows that the net loss in welfare to society as a result of the allocative effect of the excise tax can be approximated by the area of the triangle ABC in Figure 7.1.[3]

A little algebraic manipulation gives a more meaningful measure of efficiency loss. Call the area of ABC "W." The area W is

$$W = \tfrac{1}{2}t\Delta Q \tag{7.1}$$

where t, the tax per unit, is the base of triangle ABC, and ΔQ is its height. The tax per unit can also be expressed as the difference between the price paid by buyers P_d and the price received by sellers P_s.

$$t = P_d - P_s \tag{7.2}$$

Furthermore, the changes in price for buyers and sellers are

$$\Delta P_d = P_d - P_0 \tag{7.3}$$

and

$$\Delta P_s = P_0 - P_s \tag{7.4}$$

where P_0 is the pre-tax equilibrium price.

Now the elasticities of demand and supply at any price and quantity P, Q are

$$E_d = \frac{\Delta Q/Q}{\Delta P_d/P} \tag{7.5}$$

and

$$E_s = \frac{\Delta Q/Q}{\Delta P_s/P} \tag{7.6}$$

Substituting equations (7.3) and (7.4) in (7.5) and (7.6) gives the following:

$$E_d = \left(\frac{\Delta Q}{Q}\right)\left(\frac{P}{P_d - P_0}\right) \tag{7.7}$$

and

$$E_s = \left(\frac{\Delta Q}{Q}\right)\left(\frac{P}{P_0 - P_s}\right) \tag{7.8}$$

Solving for P_d and P_s,

$$P_d = \frac{\Delta QP}{QE_0} + P_0 \tag{7.9}$$

$$P_s = -\frac{\Delta QP}{QE_s} + P_0 \tag{7.10}$$

---

[3] The area ABC can also be thought of as the *sum* of the loss in consumer and producer surplus less the value of resources transferred to the public sector (the total revenue collected).

Substituting (7.9) and (7.10) in (7.2) yields

$$t = \frac{\Delta QP}{Q} \left(\frac{E_s + E_d}{E_s E_d} \right) \tag{7.11}$$

Solving (7.11) for ΔQ gives

$$\Delta Q = t \frac{Q}{P} \left(\frac{E_s E_d}{E_s + E_d} \right) \tag{7.12}$$

Finally, substituting (7.12) in the expression for W gives

$$W = \tfrac{1}{2} t^2 \left(\frac{Q}{P} \right) \left(\frac{E_s E_d}{E_s + E_d} \right) \tag{7.13}$$

Thus, the value of the efficiency loss due to taxation varies positively with the elasticities of supply and demand. Any commodity for which either $E_s = 0$ or $E_d = 0$ will have a zero efficiency loss. The most efficient taxes are, therefore, those levied on commodities or inputs in inelastic supply and/or demand.[4]

The algebraic result accords with commonsense reasoning. The less the opportunity to alter behavior as a result of taxation, the less the distortion introduced into the economy with respect to resource allocation. On efficiency grounds, the best taxes are those levied on goods that have few substitutes in either production or consumption.

GENERAL VERSUS SPECIFIC TAXES

The analysis in the preceding section seems to indicate that "general" taxes are more desirable on efficiency grounds than "specific" taxes. *General taxes* are those that cover a wide array of economic activities so that substitution of an untaxed activity for a taxed activity is difficult, if not impossible. Since the efficiency loss attributable to the allocative effect of a tax varies with the degree to which substitution is possible, the less the opportunity to substitute one activity for another, the less the efficiency loss. *Specific taxes* are those levied on a particular activity for which the opportunities of substitution are consider-

---

[4] It must be stressed that this conclusion rests on the assumption of zero income effects of price changes. A zero income effect implies a zero income elasticity of demand at all prices. Musgrave points out that this conclusion must be modified for commodities having either positive or negative income elasticity. "A general statement in terms of elasticities is difficult, however, if the product is elastic to both income and price. No simple rule can be given regarding the effects on excess burden either of varying degrees of income elasticity, with any given price elasticity greater than zero, or for varying degrees of price elasticity, with any given income elasticity greater than zero. Here the problem is stated better in terms of possible substitution than elasticity, the general rule being that excess burden varies positively with the degree of possible substitution." Richard A. Musgrave, *The Theory of Public Finance*, McGraw-Hill, New York, 1959, p. 147.

able. An excise tax on the consumption of some particular commodity is a specific tax, while a retail-sales tax on the national level would be a general tax on consumption.

While the distinction between general and specific taxes is useful, blanket conclusions concerning the efficiency loss attributable to such alternative taxing schemes are not. General taxes cannot unambiguously be preferred to a system of specific taxes. Instead, an economist analyzing the impact of alternative tax structures on resource allocation must examine each case separately. The efficiency loss attributable to alternative tax structures should be measured empirically.

It is tempting to argue that, on efficiency grounds, a general income tax (say, at a proportional rate) or a general sales tax is superior to a system of specific excise taxes on selected commodities or inputs. This conclusion, however, need not be true. To understand why this is so, one must examine the effects that the alternative taxing methods have on economic decision-making. Recall that an excise tax on a commodity with price elasticity of demand and/or supply of zero tends to have no efficiency loss attributable to it. It follows that such taxes, although they are on the consumption of specific commodities, have a zero efficiency loss. For example, excise taxes on the consumption of cigarettes or liquor, although they are specific taxes, tend to have non-distorting allocative effects because the price elasticity of demand for these commodities tends to be close to zero.

Although general sales taxes and general income taxes do not distort the relative prices of specific outputs in such a manner as to cause them to differ for consumers and producers, they introduce other distortions. So long as the supply of work effort and the supply of savings are not fixed, such general taxes result in an efficiency loss to the economy. Although many economists view general sales and income taxes to be superior to a system of selective excise taxes yielding the same amount of revenue for the government, such a conclusion cannot unambiguously be reached.[5] With a variable supply of work effort and savings, an income tax distorts household choices concerning the allocation of time between work and leisure and the allocation of income between consumption and saving. A general sales tax does not affect the choice between consumption and saving but does distort the choice between work and leisure. (This will be discussed in greater detail in Chapters 9 and 10.)

An efficiency loss is induced by such general taxes because they cause relative prices as seen by suppliers and purchasers of work effort and savings to diverge. A general income tax causes net wages and other income payments to diverge from gross payments. The wages paid by employers are not the same as those received by employees. The income tax acts as a wedge between gross payments by employers and net receipts from work effort to households. This

---

[5] This was first pointed out by Little, "Direct versus Indirect Taxes," *Economic Journal*, September 1951, pp. 577–584.

results in an efficiency loss as suppliers and purchasers adjust to divergent prices for work effort. Similarly, an income tax causes interest rates to differ for savers and investors. The interest rate to savers is net of tax paid on interest income, while purchasers of savings (investors) base their behavior on gross interest rates. This results in savers and investors adjusting their behavior to divergent interest rates and a corresponding efficiency loss to the economy as the marginal rate of time preference diverges from the marginal productivity of capital. A general sales tax does not affect interest rates because interest is not taxable. There is no "wedge" driven between rates paid for loanable funds by investors and those actually received by suppliers of loanable funds (savers). But general sales taxes do drive a wedge between gross income payments by producers and net receipts by households by reducing the real income of households. It follows that general sales taxes distort household choices between work and leisure.

There is, therefore, no a priori basis to prefer general taxes to a tax structure of specific taxes yielding an equivalent amount of revenues to finance governmental activities. Although specific taxes result in efficiency losses to the economy because of the distortion of choices among taxed and untaxed commodities, general taxes can result in efficiency losses to the economy as well because of the distortion of private choices between work and leisure and consumption and saving. Which loss is greater remains an empirical question to be answered by appropriate research.

The situation is further complicated when it is realized that so-called "general" taxes can have various exemptions and special deductions (tax preferences) incorporated in them that cause individuals to change their behavior in such a manner as to avoid the tax payments. Also, various market imperfections and distortions already existing in the economy can be neutralized by the allocative effects of taxation. The first complication is common in the United States income tax structure. It is almost a national avocation to play the game of searching for tax preferences and adjusting behavior to reduce tax burdens by taking advantage of exemptions. The income tax laws are extremely complex, and this serves to make such a "general" tax considerably more distorting with respect to resource allocation than a simple proportional income tax with no exemptions or exceptions. The United States tax code allows deductions from income for various expenditures and activities and also taxes income from alternative sources (for example, wages, interest, dividends, capital gains) at varying rates. A considerable amount of resources are expended in legal fees alone by taxpayers seeking to legally reduce their tax burdens by taking advantage of tax preferences embodied in the tax code. These tax preferences will be discussed later in the chapter on income taxation.

A further complication is introduced into the analysis when one considers the fact that marginal rates of taxation tend to diverge from average rates in many tax systems. In the case of the United States tax structure, this is most obvious for the income tax and it is, of course, a consequence of the progressive rate structure. The *average rate* of taxation is simply the total dollar value of taxes divided by the dollar value of the tax base upon which the taxes have been levied. The *marginal rate* of taxation is the tax rate applicable to increments to the tax base. In the case of taxes with a progressive rate structure, marginal rates of taxation are greater than the average rates. This is significant because it is the marginal rates of taxation that are crucial to the allocative effects of taxation. The decisions to alter economic behavior are a function of the marginal taxes that are leviable on that behavior. For example, a worker whose marginal tax rate is, say, 70 percent, is likely to be less willing to work overtime than is a worker whose marginal tax rate is 15 percent. Thus, the changes in behavior attributable to the tax system depend on marginal rather than average tax rates. Of course, in the case of proportional taxes, marginal rates of taxation are equivalent to average rates.

An analysis of the allocative effects of taxation is even more complicated when one considers that there are market imperfections, externalities, and other distortions likely to be present in the economy. Furthermore, changes in tax structure must be considered in the light of the taxes already present in the economy. Consideration of already existing distortions in the allocation of resources are significant, because the allocative effects of new taxes may merely serve to "balance" already existing distortions and serve to move the economy toward a "second-best" optimal resource allocation.

For example, in the case of a simple economy with two goods, one produced under conditions of monopoly and the other produced under conditions of perfect competition, an excise tax on the output of the perfectly competitive industry can actually improve resource allocation for the economy. Prior to the tax, assuming full employment of productive resources, the monopolist is restricting his output to equate marginal revenue with marginal cost. Resources not used in the production of the monopolized output must be employed in the production of the perfectly competitive output. The result is an overproduction of the perfectly competitive output and an underproduction of the monopolized output. The introduction of an excise tax on the perfectly competitive output has the effect of reducing the quantity demanded and produced of this output, thereby transferring productive resources out of the perfectly competitive industry and into the monopolized industry, assuming that the two outputs are substitutes. The distorting effect of the excise tax on the output of the perfectly competitive industry "balances out" the already-existing distortion caused by the monopoly in the economy.

Similar results are obtained when the production or consumption of some commodities in the economy generates externalities. Consider the excise taxation of the output of a commodity whose production generates an externality, say, in the form of pollution. The allocative effect of the excise tax decreases the equilibrium output of the polluter as a result of the increase in marginal costs attributable to the tax. This decrease in output adjusts production to correct for the externality. Indeed, if the tax is assessed to reflect the damage done by the pollution attributable to the production of the taxed commodity, then it will act to internalize the externality by increasing the polluter's cost to reflect the full social costs of production.

Finally, the introduction of new taxes into the system must be considered in the light of those taxes already existing. If it is politically impossible to eliminate some taxes, then it might be wise, on efficiency grounds, to consider new taxes whose allocative effects serve to "balance out" the allocative effects of existing taxes. For example, if it is believed that income tax excessively distorts the choice between work and leisure in favor of leisure, then it may be wise to consider new revenue sources that tax those commodities that are complementary with leisure. For example, excise taxes on entertainment activities and sporting equipment might serve to balance out the distorting effects of the income tax by making leisure activities more costly. In fact, a system of excise taxes designed to balance out each other's distortions and to compensate for their effects on the work-leisure choice may be more desirable on efficiency grounds than a general income tax.

The reader should keep these complications in mind when considering the allocative effects of alternative tax structures. The analysis to follow in later chapters will consider the allocative effects of both specific and general taxes on income, consumption, and wealth.

THE SOCIAL TRADE-OFF: EQUITY VERSUS EFFICIENCY

Efficiency is not the only criterion with which to evaluate the desirability of alternative taxes and tax structures. Taxes must also be rated in relation to equity definitions. Tax effects on the distribution of income must be determined. Unfortunately, the two goals, efficiency and equity, are likely to conflict. Very efficient taxes are often exceedingly inequitable by some standards, and very equitable taxes, from some points of view, may lead to large losses in efficiency for the economy.

Consider the economic effects of a head tax. Since it is levied on the non-economic base of existence, the head tax is neutral in respect to resource allocation. However, if ability to pay is believed to increase with income, such a tax is extremely inequitable from the point of view of some individuals. Consider the effect on the distribution of income if the total cost of governmental expenditures in the United States were financed simply by dividing total expenditures by total number of households and charging each household the same tax bill. Rich households would pay the same taxes as poor households. The effect would be to redistribute after-tax income away from the poor to the rich. This may be unacceptable to many citizens of the community on equity grounds. Similarly, taxes on goods with relatively inelastic demands, such as those excise taxes on cigarettes and liquor, have allocative effects that are non-distorting. At the same time, they tend to take proportionately more of the income of poor households relative to rich households and, therefore, may be undesirable under equity considerations.

On the other hand the progressive income tax is considered by some to be very equitable. The rate of taxation increases more than proportionately with income, and some citizens believe that ability to pay varies in a similar manner. However, the high marginal tax rates for high income households tend to distort choices between work and leisure, and the many tax preferences designed to promote equity result in considerable losses in efficiency for the economy as a whole as a direct allocative effect of the income tax code.

The mix of efficiency and equity in the tax structure is a political decision determined through the political process. A completely neutral tax system may not be desirable, because such a system may be inequitable by some standards. At the same time, a completely equitable tax structure may not be desirable, because it may be impossible to devise such a tax structure without distorting economic choices to such a degree that large efficiency losses are inflicted on the economy by destruction of economic incentives. Some compromise is necessary to achieve the best mix of efficiency and equity. The best mix, from the viewpoint of any citizen, depends on the individual citizen's own preferences.

SUMMARY

Taxes levied on economic bases are likely to alter private economic behavior toward reducing the burden of taxation. The resulting reallocation of resources through private action may result in an efficiency loss. If the efficiency gain from tax-financed government expenditures does not outweigh the efficiency loss attributable to taxation, then the net effect of governmental activities will impair resource allocation. Taxes that result in no efficiency loss are said to be "neutral."

The efficiency loss from taxation results from the divergence of relative prices as used by buyers and sellers. It varies with the ability of citizens to substitute untaxed for taxed activities. For goods with very low income elasticities, the efficiency loss attributable to taxation can be shown to vary positively with price elasticity of supply and demand. Taxes levied on activities that are in perfectly inelastic supply or demand with respect to price tend to be neutral or have low efficiency losses.

8

Taxation and the Distribution of Income

GOVERNMENTAL ACTIVITIES AND THE DISTRIBUTION OF INCOME

Governmental activities directly affect the distribution of real income within the private sector of the economy. Such activities withdraw resources from private use and make direct transfers of income among citizens through public assistance programs and income redistribution activities. The particular method chosen to finance the withdrawal of resources from the private sector results in direct reductions in the disposable incomes available to the economic units paying taxes. However, the net effect of the tax-expenditure process on any one household's real income depends on the benefits the household receives from governmental activities relative to the taxes the household pays.

Governmental activities have subtle effects on the distribution of income within the community. These effects may not be obvious to the casual observer. For example, it is commonly known that taxes are not always paid by the economic unit upon which they are levied. In technical terms, taxes can be *shifted* from one economic unit to another. The shifting of taxes implies that the business firm or household upon which a particular tax is levied may not, in fact, suffer a reduction in real disposable income as a result of the tax. Shifting occurs because the imposition of a tax on the sale of a particular output or input is likely to shift the supply of that output or input. In addition, there may be various intermarket movements in supply and demand affecting the prices of untaxed outputs and inputs. Thus, the effect of any given tax on the distribution of real income cannot be fully gauged until

the effect of all shifts in supply and demand on factor and commodity prices
have been ascertained.

Taxes levied on the production of some activity may be shifted "forward"
to consumers of the taxed activity or "backward" to suppliers of inputs purchased by sellers of the taxed activity. For example, a retail-sales tax is collected from merchants, but it is usually shifted forward directly to consumers.
The corporation income tax is collected from the owners of corporate business
organizations as a tax on capital invested, but it can be shown that such a tax
may conceivably alter both commodity prices and factor incomes to owners of
capital in non-corporate enterprise and, perhaps, even to wage earners. That
is, the corporation income tax may be shifted forward to consumers and/or
backward to workers.

In addition, governmental expenditure programs may alter the distribution
of income within the private sector. This is because the particular mix of
public services embodied in the budget of the public sector may not yield
benefits that accrue uniformly in the same amounts to all citizens. For example,
public education may benefit households with children relatively more than
those with retired senior citizens. Public assistance programs obviously increase the disposable income of the poor and disabled at the expense of a
reduction in the income of other groups. Government subsidies to the mortgage
market increase the real income of homeowners relative to other groups of
citizens. But the direct redistributive effects of many governmental expenditure
activities are difficult to ascertain because of the difficulties involved in imputing the direct benefits of public services to particular citizens or groups of
citizens. The difficulty stems from the fact that most public services are, at
least to some extent, collectively consumed. But even if the collective consumption component of, say, public education is ignored, it still is difficult
to estimate the increase in lifetime real income imputable to the consumption
of public education by individual citizens. Similar problems are encountered
in measuring individual benefits of such activities as national defense, police
and fire protection services, and the judicial system.

In addition, public expenditures also have subtle effects on the distribution
of income similar to those attributable to the shifting of taxes. This is because
the particular mix of governmental activities embodied in the public budget
implies a particular set of demands upon productive resources available to the
entire national community. This, in turn, implies that any particular expenditure program alters relative prices of outputs and inputs available for private
use. Furthermore, the particular demands implied by the public budget induces
secondary movements in supply and demand in the complex of markets comprising the economy, thereby introducing further changes in relative prices.
For example, if the government requires a great deal of steel for national
defense services, the price of steel is bid up. This, in turn, means that consumption goods produced with steel become more expensive, and the consumers of such goods suffer a reduction in real income. On the other hand, if

public activities involve relatively more labor input than do private economic activities, public expenditures bid up the price of labor relative to other factors of production, thereby increasing the real income of workers relative to other factor owners (capitalists and land owners). Changes in the mix of activities embodied in the budget result in changes in the distribution of income. A stinging example of this is the reduction in expenditures allocated to the space program in recent years. This has induced sharp reductions in the incomes of aerospace scientists, engineers, and specialized workers employed by the federal government and private industry through the elimination of jobs or reductions in wages and salaries.

Finally, the general *level* of governmental expenditures relative to the level of all revenues affects the distribution of income by influencing the general level of all economic activity. If the particular governmental fiscal policy induces inflation, then those individuals whose incomes are relatively fixed in monetary terms suffer a reduction in real income relative to other groups in the economy. In addition, inflation reduces the wealth of individuals holding fixed cash balances. Expected inflation may induce various shifts in supply and demand in response to efforts by individual households and firms to "hedge" against the inflation. This, in turn, induces further shifts in relative prices and the distribution of income.

On the other hand, if fiscal policy induces unemployment, then those workers who are unfortunate enough to be laid off suffer a reduction in real income relative to other groups. In addition, monetary and fiscal policy alters the return to owners of capital through its effects on interest rates and the prices of capital assets, thereby generating other shifts in supply and demand affecting the distribution of income in the private sector.

THE THEORY OF INCIDENCE

It is essential for policy makers and citizens to have reasonably accurate information concerning the effect of governmental activities on the distribution of welfare among households in the community. Insofar as a household's welfare is correlated with its real income, changes in the distribution of welfare may be approximated by measuring changes in the distribution of real income. Predictions of the effect of proposed tax and expenditure policies on the distribution of income can permit more informed collective choices on the extent and nature of governmental activities. Quantitative estimates of the redistributive effects of governmental expenditure and tax policies help voters compute their true cost shares of collectively supplied services relative to the net benefits they receive from governmental activities.

The theory of incidence analyzes the effect of governmental activities on the distribution of income. It systematically traces all direct and indirect redistributive effects of governmental activities in general or of specific revenue

and expenditure policies. The incidence of a specific governmental policy
refers to the resulting change in the distribution of income available for
private use attributable to that policy.[1] To determine the incidence of a policy,
one must take care to assure that there are no other factors attributable to,
say, other policies simultaneously affecting the distribution of income. This
implies that other variables affecting income distribution (for example, other
government policies) must be held fixed in order to obtain a meaningful
measure of the incidence of any specific policy.

With that caution in mind, one may distinguish three concepts of incidence:

1. Budget incidence.
2. Expenditure incidence.
3. Tax incidence.

Budget incidence evaluates the effects of *both* governmental expenditure
and tax policies on the distribution of income in the private sector. A comprehensive analysis of budget incidence in the United States would generate data
on the influence of the entire public sector (federal, state, and local governmental activities) on the distribution of income available to the private sector.
Alternatively, one might evaluate the incidence of a *change* in the size of the
public budget. Thus, one analyzes the effects on the distribution of income
of a particular extension of governmental activity, accompanied by increases
in taxes to finance such an extension. If one wants to rule out effects on the
general level of prices and the level of employment, one can assume that the
extra revenue obtained just finances the extension of governmental expenditure policy. This serves to abstract effects of inflation or deflation out of the
effects of the budget.[2]

A study of expenditure incidence attempts to evaluate the effects of *alternative* public expenditure projects on the distribution of income. In order to be
sure that only the expenditure project being evaluated is affecting the distribution of income, all other possible influences on the distribution of income
must be held fixed. This implies that the total level of expenditures is held
constant in real terms, and the particular project being evaluated is substituted
for some other project or group of projects. At the same time, there must be
no change in the tax structure that alters the distribution of income. This
"differential" approach to the incidence of expenditures allows the economist
to generate data concerning the relative redistributive effects of alternative
expenditure policies alone.[3] It allows policy makers and citizens to evaluate
the relative redistributive effects of alternative expenditure policies. Of course,
the determination of expenditure incidence remains difficult, because of the
inherent problems involved in imputing the collectively consumed benefits of

[1] This definition of incidence is attributable to Richard A. Musgrave. See *The Theory of
Public Finance*, McGraw-Hill, New York, 1959, pp. 207–208.

[2] Musgrave calls this "balanced-budget incidence," pp. 214–215.

[3] See Musgrave, pp. 212–215, for a more extensive discussion of differential incidence.

governmentally produced goods and services to specific households and business firms.

Differential tax incidence is the resulting change in the distribution of income when one type of tax is substituted for some alternative tax, or set of taxes, yielding an equivalent amount of revenue in real terms, while both the mix and level of government expenditures is held constant. Since any given level and mix of governmental expenditures may be financed through alternative taxing schemes, the concept of differential tax incidence enables one to determine the relative redistributive impact of alternative taxes and tax structures. An analysis of differential tax incidence attempts to delineate all direct and indirect effects of the substitution of one tax for another. This includes all secondary shifts in relative prices as a result of tax shifting as well as direct transfers of income.

It must be pointed out, however, that the concept of differential incidence ignores the interdependence between the revenue and expenditure sides of the budget. Since alternative taxing schemes, other things being equal, do have varying effects on the distribution of income in the private sector and tax shares, it follows that the assumption of holding the level and mix of government expenditures constant is questionable. The reason for this is that changes in the distribution of income and tax shares are likely to change the demand pattern for public services. The willingness to vote approval on specific projects is, in part, a function of tax shares.

THE SHIFTING AND INCIDENCE OF TAXES

The burden of a tax is not always borne fully by the economic unit that legally pays it. This is because a tax may, by shifting either supply or demand of the taxed item as well as those of untaxed items, change relative prices of outputs and inputs. The extent to which taxes can be "shifted" (that is, the burden transferred to other economic units) depends on the nature of the supply and demand functions in the particular markets affected. For example, if the seller of a good or service can raise his price with little reduction in quantity sold in response to an excise tax, then the tax burden can be shifted *forward* to consumers. If the quantity sold falls, fewer factors of production are demanded, and the tax can be shifted backward to factor owners. Of course, if both options are open to the seller, then the tax can be shifted partially backward and forward.

A completely adequate study of incidence requires a general equilibrium analysis. Markets are interdependent, and adjustments take place in response to any new tax in all markets. It is, however, still useful to employ a partial equilibrium analysis to approximate the initial effects of the introduction of a tax into the market and to gauge the extent to which shifting is possible. Such a partial equilibrium analysis does not attempt to determine the actual differential incidence of a substitution of one tax for another of equal yield. It merely analyzes the price changes induced in one particular market when a tax is introduced in it (or rescinded from it), while not tracing the repercussions in other markets and the "feedback" effects stemming from the initial price change in the taxed market.

Partial Equilibrium Analysis

The extent to which tax shifting is possible depends on a variety of factors affecting behavior in the market for the taxed activity. These include the following:

1. The structure of the market (that is, the degree of competition prevailing).
2. The length of time (that is, short-run versus long-run period).
3. The technological factors affecting long-run supply.
4. The magnitude of the elasticities of supply and demand for the taxed activity.

To illustrate how these factors influence the degree to which shifting is possible, consider the effect of an excise tax on the equilibrium price and output in some particular market. Since most taxes are levied on the sale of some output or input, the analysis for the effect of the excise tax can be considered as applicable to other kinds of taxes as well.

An excise tax is collected as a fixed amount on each unit sold. For example, an excise tax on the sale of cigarettes is set at 5 cents per pack. This is a *unit* tax. It differs from an *ad valorem* tax that is levied at some fixed percentage of the price of output. The tax affects the willingness of sellers to sell their product in the market because it affects their profits at alternative outputs. The tax is conceptualized as either an increase in average costs of production at all levels of output or a decrease in average revenues attainable by sellers at all levels of output. These two approaches to analyzing the effect of the tax are equivalent and yield the same results with respect to the effects on equilibrium price and quantity in the taxed market.

The extent to which shifting is possible depends, to some degree, on the competitive conditions in the taxed market. Consider, first, the case of perfect competition.

Shifting under Perfect Competition

Under perfect competition, no individual firm in the industry can affect the industry price of the output. Figure 8.1 gives the demand and supply curves from the industry's point of view. The curves labeled D and S are the industry's demand and supply respectively prior to the introduction of the tax.[4]

---

[4] For simplicity, it is assumed that both demand and supply curves are linear. This assumption is not necessary for the validity of the analysis in general.

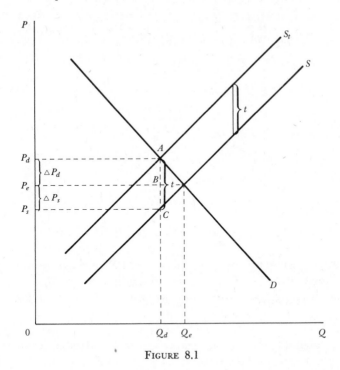

FIGURE 8.1

Consider the effects of the introduction of the tax in the short run. After the unit excise tax is introduced, there is a change in the market behavior of sellers. The tax may be thought of as an increase in average costs of production at all levels of output (or equivalently, as a decrease in average revenue attainable). This affects marginal costs of production as well. Since the tax is a fixed levy on each unit of output, marginal costs increase by the amount of the tax at all levels of output. This causes an effective decrease in supply for the industry. The new industry supply, which is simply the lateral summation of the marginal cost schedules of all firms in the industry, shifts upward by an amount t at all levels of output, where t is the unit tax.[5] The new supply curve after the imposition of the tax is, therefore, S_t in Figure 8.1. The decreased willingness to supply output on the part of sellers results in a higher equilibrium price. In Figure 8.1, price rises from P_e to P_d, while the equilibrium quantity sold falls from Q_e to Q_d.

Who pays the tax? The new equilibrium price is P_d. But producers pay t

[5] In the case of an ad valorem tax, the shift upward in supply is not a parallel one. Instead, the supply curve rotates upward. This is because, at the fixed percentage rate of taxation, increasing amounts (in dollar terms) of average revenue have to be surrendered to the government as sales increase. This is illustrated in Figure 8.2 on page 184. In the case of progressive taxation, the post-tax supply curve is non-linear, even when the original supply curve is linear. This is illustrated in Figure 8.3 on page 184.

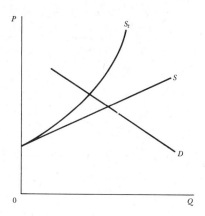

FIGURE 8.2 Ad Valorem Tax

in tax to the government on each unit sold. Their average revenue at output
Q_d is, therefore, $(P_d - t)$. The tax per unit output is equal to the difference
between the price paid by buyers and the price received by sellers. Thus,

$$P_d - P_s = t \qquad (8.1)$$

Referring to Figure 8.1, the total revenue collected by the government is equal
to tQ_d, or the area P_dACP_s. Consumers pay $(P_d - P_e)Q_d$, or ΔP_dQ_d dollars, in
taxes, while producers pay $(P_e - P_s)Q_d$, or ΔP_sQ_d dollars, in taxes. This is
summarized by the following identity:

$$(\Delta P_d + \Delta P_s)\, Q_t = tQ_d \qquad (8.2)$$

Thus, the excise tax is partially shifted to consumers by the sellers of the
taxed commodity, in this case. Furthermore, insofar as the tax reduces quantity

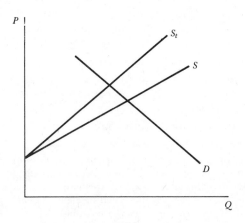

FIGURE 8.3 Progressive Tax

produced, it results in a decrease in the demand for factors of production (including labor). This can result in some backward shifting.

Given the elasticity of supply, it can be shown that the degree to which forward shifting occurs varies inversely with the elasticity of demand. The steeper the demand curve, the less the amount of tax paid by the seller. As a limiting case, when the price elasticity of demand is equal to zero, the consumers alone pay the entire tax. This is illustrated in Figure 8.4. As before, the tax can be thought of as causing the supply to move upward by a distance t. The market price rises from P_e to P_d, but in this case, there is no change in the equilibrium quantity demanded. There is no change in the average revenue received by the seller, because $P_d - t = P_e$, the initial price. The total revenue collected by the government is $(P_d - P_e)t$. This amount is paid entirely by consumers of the taxed commodity. As an exercise, the reader should show that if the price elasticity of demand is infinite, then the entire tax is paid by the seller of the taxed commodity.

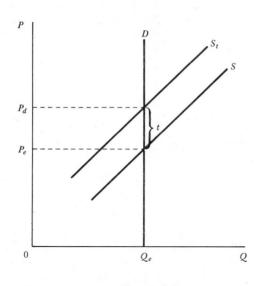

FIGURE 8.4

Given the elasticity of demand, the extent to which the tax can be shifted forward varies directly with the elasticity of supply. The elasticity of supply, in turn, depends on the nature of cost conditions in the taxed industry and the length of time allowed for adjustment. In general, supply tends to be relatively more elastic in the long run.

Consider a period of time so short that the firm cannot vary the scale of its operation within its existing plant (Marshall's "immediate" run). In this case, the supply of output is perfectly inelastic. This case is illustrated in Figure 8.5. In Figure 8.5, the tax is conceptualized as a decrease in average revenue from the point of view of sellers at all levels of output. The curve D

is the actual market demand, while D_t is the demand curve as seen by producers in the industry after the imposition of the tax of t dollars. Thus, the
imposition of the tax results in no change in the price paid by consumers.
Prior to the tax, they pay P_e, and after the imposition of the excise tax, they
still pay P_e. But producers now receive $P_s = P_e - t$. They bear the full burden
of the unit tax and cannot shift any of the tax forward to consumers. The
reason for this is that they cannot alter the quantity supplied in the immediate
run. The total revenue collected by the government is $(P_e - P_s)Q_e = tQ_e$. This
amount is paid entirely by sellers.

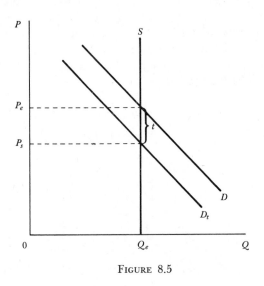

FIGURE 8.5

It is interesting to apply the case illustrated in Figure 8.5 to income taxation. If an income tax is thought of as an excise tax on the sale of work effort,
then the imposition of a unit tax of t dollars on each hour worked reduces the
average wage received at all hours by an amount t. Thus, the return to work
as seen by workers falls to amounts represented on the curve D_t at varying
levels of employment. The curve D represents the actual value of the marginal
product of labor as seen by employers (buyers of work effort) at all levels of
employment. Figure 8.5 indicates that if the supply of work effort is completely
inelastic, then the sellers of work effort (workers) bear the full burden of the
income tax, as a reduction of income equal to the full revenue collected by
the government. If, however, the supply of work effort is moderately elastic,
the case is similar to that illustrated in Figure 8.1, and workers succeed in
shifting some of the burden of the income tax forward to employers in the
form of higher wages and, therefore, lower returns on invested capital in response to the reduction of quantity of work effort supplied at all levels of
employment.

In the short run, supply tends to be more elastic relative to the immediate run. In the short run, some factors of production are held fixed while others are variable. The firm is able to vary the scale of output within its existing plant capacity. In general, one expects such variation in output in the short run to be subject to the law of diminishing returns. It follows that marginal costs rise with output for all firms in the industry, and that the industry supply curve is, therefore, upward sloping. Given a moderately elastic demand for the output of the industry, one expects some degree of forward shifting of an excise tax in the short run. The situation is similar to that illustrated in Figure 8.1. Thus, in the short run, the burden of the excise tax is likely to be shared by both buyers and sellers.

In the long run, one expects supply to be somewhat more elastic relative to the short run. This implies that the degree to which forward shifting is possible varies directly with time. Furthermore, the cost structure of the industry influences the elasticity of supply. There are three possibilities: increasing costs, constant costs, and decreasing costs.

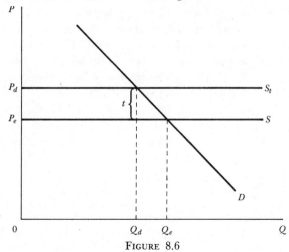

FIGURE 8.6

In the case of increasing costs, the long-run supply curve is upward sloping but somewhat more elastic than the short-run supply curve. The tax is partially shifted forward, assuming a moderately elastic demand function for the industry's output. Other things being equal, a greater share of the tax is paid by consumers in the long run, because supply tends to be more elastic.

An industry with constant costs is able to shift the tax forward fully in the long run. The long-run elasticity of supply for such an industry is infinite. This follows from the fact that the supply curve is a horizontal line, as illustrated in Figure 8.6. It follows that the effect of the tax is to shift the supply upward horizontally by an amount equal to the unit tax. The result of this is a reduction of quantity sold from Q_e to Q_d and a rise in price for consumers to P_d equal to the unit tax as shown in Figure 8.6. Thus, full forward shifting occurs in the long run for an industry of constant costs.

The long-run effect of an excise tax on an industry of decreasing costs is somewhat unusual. In this case, forward shifting in excess of 100 percent can occur! The effect of an excise tax on an industry of decreasing costs is illustrated in Figure 8.7. The tax shifts the supply upward by the amount of the unit tax causing a reduction in quantity supplied as in previous cases. But the price paid by consumers now increases by an amount *in excess* of the unit tax. Price rises from P_e to P_d, and $P_d - P_e > t$. The price received by producers *rises* from P_e to P_s, where $P_s = P_d - t$. The intuitive reason for this excessive burden placed on consumers is the fact that the tax not only increases marginal costs to producers, causing them to cut back output, it also causes them to move to a less efficient utilization of resources, thereby further increasing marginal cost. The result is a higher price due both to the tax *and* the diseconomies in production induced by the reduction in output from Q_e to Q_d assuming that the industry is forced to use marginal cost pricing.[6]

Shifting under Monopoly and Imperfect Competition

The degree to which forward shifting occurs under monopoly is somewhat less than that which prevails under perfect competition. The reason for this stems from the fact that a monopolist maximizing his profits will choose that output level corresponding to the point where marginal revenue is equal to marginal cost. In general, the marginal revenue schedule tends to be steeper than and falls below the average revenue (or demand) schedule. In the case of a linear demand function, the marginal revenue schedule is twice as steep as the demand schedule.[7] The excise tax on the monopolist increases his marginal

----

[6] This conclusion must be qualified in a number of ways. First, an industry subject to decreasing long-run average costs is not likely to be perfectly competitive. This is because there is a tendency for one or a few firms to expand output by absorbing other firms and appropriating the economies of scale. For this reason, a firm with long-run decreasing average costs is often referred to as a "natural monopoly" and tends to be regulated by the government. (See Chapter 2.) This implies that output by firms is determined by setting marginal revenue (less than price) equal to marginal cost. Thus, strictly speaking, the intersection of the demand and supply curves in Figure 8.7 does not represent any "equilibrium" under monopoly. The monopolist, if unconstrained in his pricing policy, would charge higher prices and produce less than Figure 8.7 indicates.

Second, the equilibriums in Figure 8.7 are unstable. Thus, if price rises above the equilibrium, there is excessive demand, and price does *not* return to the initial equilibrium. Similarly, price falling below any equilibrium price result in excess supply and further movement away from equilibrium.

The equilibrium is stable if the marginal cost curve is relatively steeper than the demand curve. But in this case, the conclusion of the text has to be reversed! The imposition of the tax causes price to *fall* for consumers. This is illustrated in Figure 8.8 on page 189.

The increase in marginal cost due to the tax results in an *increase* in output from Q_1 to Q_2 and a corresponding reduction in price. In this case, the tax is borne in excess of 100 percent by the seller. This is because demand is relatively more elastic than is the case illustrated in Figure 8.7.

[7] For proof of this, see any standard price theory text.

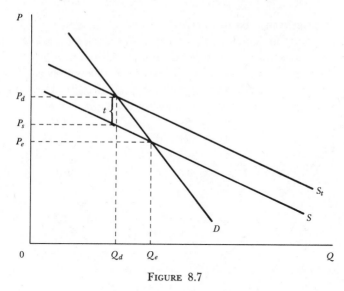

FIGURE 8.7

costs at all levels of output by an amount equal to the unit tax. However, in this case, the effect on price is somewhat more complicated.

To understand this, consider a perfectly competitive industry that has been transformed into a cartel and behaves as if it were a monopolist. This is illustrated in Figure 8.9. The demand curve for the industry's output is D, and the marginal revenue schedule corresponding to this demand is MR. The curve MC is the initial marginal cost schedule, while MC_t is the marginal cost schedule after the imposition of the excise tax. If the industry were perfectly competitive, the initial price would be P_c, and the quantity sold would be Q_c.

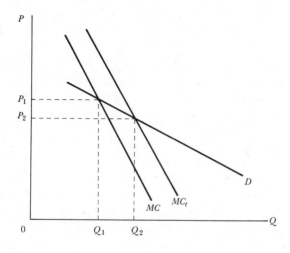

FIGURE 8.8

These are the price and quantity corresponding to the intersection of the MC curve and the demand schedule $(P = MC)$. But under monopoly, the equilibrium price and quantity correspond to the intersection of the marginal revenue and marginal cost curves $(MR = MC)$. The monopolist (or cartel) would produce $Q_0 < Q_c$ at price $P_0 > P_c$. Thus, initially the cartel produces less than the perfectly competitive industry and charges more.

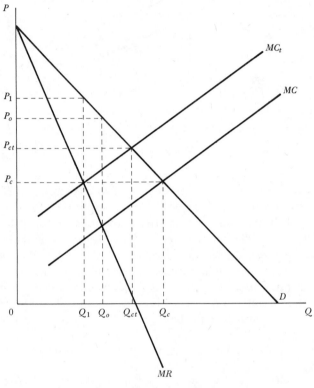

FIGURE 8.9

Now, the tax increases marginal costs from MC to MC_t at all levels of output. Under conditions of perfect competition, the effect of the tax would be to reduce quantity sold from Q_c to Q_{ct} and raise consumer prices from P_c to P_{ct}. But under monopoly, the effect of the tax is to reduce quantity sold by an amount *less* than the reduction that would prevail under perfect competition. Thus, in Figure 8.9, when the monopolist readjusts output after the tax is imposed, output falls to Q_1, and price rises to P_1. The distance Q_1Q_0 is less than the distance $Q_{ct}Q_c$. This is because the marginal revenue schedule is steeper than the demand schedule. It follows that the price rise to consumers as a result of the tax is less than that which would occur under perfect competition, because the reduction in quantity supplied as a result of the tax is less.[8] Thus, in Figure 8.6, $(P_1 - P_0) < (P_{ct} - P_c)$. Thus, there is less forward shifting under monopoly than under perfect competition. This, however, is not really very good news for consumers, because they pay a higher price for the commodity under monopoly in the first place! As can be seen in Figure 8.6, consumers still pay a higher price for the commodity in the taxed monopoly relative to the taxed perfectly competitive industry $(P_1 > P_{ct})$.

Under monopoly, the degree to which taxes are shifted in the long run also varies with the cost structure of the monopolistic firm. The conclusions of the previous analysis are still applicable for the case of monopoly. Thus, the greatest forward shifting is likely to occur under conditions of decreasing long-run average costs, while the least shifting occurs under conditions of increasing long-run average costs. Under natural monopoly, where long-run average costs decrease, it is again possible that the price can rise by an amount greater than the tax, depending on how steeply average costs fall with output and the corresponding diseconomies of scale resulting from the reduction in output caused by the tax.

It is more difficult to predict the degree to which forward shifting is possible in the case of taxes levied on commodities produced under conditions of monopolistic competition and oligopoly. The reasons for this stem from the fact that there are more relevant variables to be considered under these competitive structures. Under monopolistic competition, there are no barriers to entry in the industry, and presumably, despite product differentiation, the industry does attain an equilibrium where prices are equal to average costs including the "normal" profit. The imposition of an excise tax on such an industry is likely to result in some firms leaving the industry in the long run. As such marginal firms leave, the demand as seen by the remaining firms increases. Under these circumstances, it is quite possible that taxes may be shifted forward in excess of 100 percent (that is, the consumer price rises by more than the unit tax) even under conditions of long-run increasing average costs if demand becomes more inelastic for the remaining firms, making it profitable for them to increase prices by an amount greater than the tax.

Under oligopoly, the effect of an excise tax on commodity prices is still more difficult to predict. One reason for this is that the demand curve cannot be specified prior to specifying the beliefs that a firm holds concerning the reactions of its competitors to its own price, output, and advertising decisions. Often firms operating under oligopoly use "rules of thumb" to price their output and do not actually maximize profits. Average cost, or "mark-up" pricing, is an example of such a pricing rule. Under such circumstances, if sellers believe that the demand for their output is relatively inelastic and that competing producers of substitutes will use similar pricing rules, the tax is

---

[8] When both the demand and marginal cost curves are linear, the rise in consumer price under monopoly is precisely one half of the rise that occurs under perfect competition. For proof of this statement, see Musgrave, p. 292.

likely to be reflected solely in higher consumer prices. For example, it is generally agreed that United States excise taxes on such commodities as automobiles and tires are shifted forward to buyers fully by sellers.

General Equilibrium Analysis

It must be emphasized that the analysis of the preceding section only attempts to trace the *initial* impact of a tax on the prices of the taxed activity alone. An economy is, however, composed of a complex of interrelated markets. This implies that the effect of a disturbance in the equilibrium in any one market is not likely to be confined to that market alone. Instead, there are likely to be repercussions in other related markets and possible "feedback" effects in the market initially taxed. For example, a tax on the consumption of electric power does not only affect the price of electricity. It is also likely to have effects on the demand for various electrical appliances and the demand for natural gas for cooking and heating. These secondary shifts in demand will, of course, affect the prices of these substitutable and complementary activities. This, in turn, might result in feedback effects on both the demand and supply of electricity. Since electricity is used as an input in most productive processes, one also expects those goods whose production requires proportionately more electricity than others to rise in price relative to the others. As the reader can imagine, tracing the full general equilibrium effect of a tax on electricity is extremely difficult because of the number of markets likely to be affected. The same complexity is involved in the analysis of the effects of almost any tax.

In order to determine, say, the differential incidence of the substitution of one tax for another, all such intermarket effects have to be considered. Any individual household is affected in two ways by the distributive effects of the substitution of one tax for another tax (or group of taxes) of equal yield. First, the household is confronted with changed prices for the productive services (inputs) it owns and sells in the appropriate markets. These include changes in wages, interest rates, rents, and profits. This, in turn, is likely to lead to changes in the equilibrium quantities of productive resources the household is willing to supply to the relevant markets. Second, the household may find itself confronted with a new set of relative prices for the outputs it consumes. Given any household's preference pattern, such changes in the relative prices of outputs, in turn, alter the equilibrium quantities demanded of those outputs.

Thus, the substitution of one tax for another is likely to affect any given household by changing its money income from the sale of productive resources it owns and by changing the prices of the outputs it consumes. The net differential incidence of the substitution of one tax for another of equal yield is measured by the relative changes in *real income* of all households as a result of the policy change. This change in real income depends not only on the changes in prices in outputs and inputs but *also* in changes in quantities of outputs and inputs purchased and sold by each household.

The data generated by such a general equilibrium analysis of the distributive effects (incidence) of any governmental policy (for example, the substitution of one tax for another of equal yield) can be partially tabulated by using Lorenz curves. A Lorenz curve gives information on the distribution of income by size brackets. A hypothetical Lorenz curve is plotted in Figure 8.10. The horizontal axis gives the percent of households ranked in terms of size of income, while the vertical axis measures the percent of real income. The line 0*E* is called the "line of equal distribution." An economy whose income distribution is measured along line 0*E* has a perfectly uniform distribution of real income. To understand why this is so, consider the percent of income going to the lowest 10 percent of households (the bottom decile) for an economy whose Lorenz curve is 0*E*. Since 0*E* is at a 45-degree angle with respect to the horizontal axis, it follows that the lowest decile of households ranked in terms of income size has 10 percent of the nation's real income. Similarly, the lowest 90 percent of households has 90 percent of the nation's income. It follows that the top 10 percent of households ranked in terms of income (the top decile) also has 10 percent of the nation's real income. Any decile rank chosen has 10 percent of the nation's total real income. It follows that the distribution of income for the economy whose Lorenz curve is 0*E* is completely uniform. Every household has the same real income.

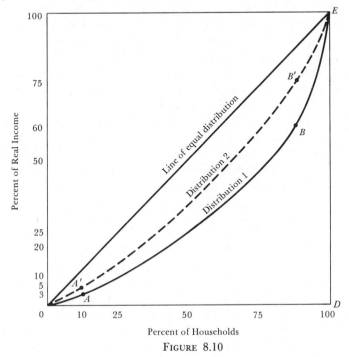

FIGURE 8.10

Most nations do not have a Lorenz curve such as $0E$. Significant degrees of income inequality exist in most societies. For example, the income distribution may be measured by the Lorenz curve $0ABE$ in Figure 8.10 (distribution 1). Such an income distribution implies that the bottom decile of households ranked in terms of income has only 3 percent of the nation's real income (point A), while the top decile of households has 40 percent of the nation's real income (point B).

Now, consider the effect of some particular governmental policy change on the distribution of income. The policy change might be the substitution of one tax for another of equal yield (differential incidence). After all changes in factor and commodity prices have been determined along with changes in quantities purchased and sold by households, the new data can be tabulated by income size brackets and plotted in Figure 8.10 as a new Lorenz curve. This permits one to compare the new income distribution by size classes with the previous income distribution before the policy change. However, insofar as households trade places within the income distribution with no change in the degree of income inequality, the Lorenz curve does not reflect the change in the distribution.

Suppose one tax is substituted for another of equal yield (all other things being equal) and the resulting new income distribution becomes $0A'B'E$ (distribution 2). Distribution 2 is relatively closer to the line of equal income distribution than is distribution 1. For example, the change in tax policy has increased the share of real national income going to the first decile of households, ranked in terms of size of income from 3 to 5 percent (point A'). Furthermore, it has apparently reduced the share of real national income going to the top decile from 40 to 25 percent (point B'). (Note that there is no way of knowing if households have changed places in the rankings along the horizontal axis.) It may be concluded that the differential incidence of this particular tax policy change is *progressive*, in the sense that it redistributes income away from the relatively "rich" toward the relatively "poor."

A rough measure of the incidence of any policy change can be obtained by comparing the area under two Lorenz curves before and after the policy change.[9] Thus, an index of incidence may be obtained for the two Lorenz curves in Figure 8.10 by computing the ratio

$$I = \frac{0A'B'ED}{0ABD} = \frac{\text{area under distribution 2}}{\text{area under distribution 1}}$$

If I exceeds unity, then the incidence of the policy change is said to be "progressive." The particular policy change illustrated in Figure 8.10 results in a progressive incidence because $I > 1$. If the ratio I is less than unity, then incidence is said to be "regressive," in the sense that it redistributes income away from the relatively poor toward the relatively rich. Finally, if the ratio I

[9] This measure was suggested by Musgrave, pp. 224–225.

is equal to unity, then the incidence is said to be "proportional," in the sense that it leaves the relative income distribution unchanged. The ratio I is, of course, only a rough measure of incidence. It is of limited usefulness when the policy change results in a new Lorenz curve that intersects the initial Lorenz curve and when the ranking of households in terms of income changes as a result of a given policy.

Differential Tax Incidence: An Example

Consider a hypothetical policy change that substitutes a national retail-sales tax for a proportional income tax of equal yield, while holding both the level and mix of public expenditures constant. The income tax base includes all wages, rents, and interest on investments, while the consumption tax base is final expenditure by all households. When a tax on consumer expenditure is substituted for an equal-yield proportional income tax, the immediate effect can be thought of as a transference of a "wedge." Business firms now have to surrender a certain proportion of the total value of their sales to the governments as payment of the sales tax. This drives a "wedge" between total receipts by all firms and payments to all factors of production (land, labor, and capital). This replaces the wedge between the gross earnings of all factors of production and disposable income resulting from the previous income tax. But the sales tax is levied *only* on consumption goods. It follows that the prices of consumption goods tend to rise relative to the prices of tax-free capital goods. This implies that the incomes of savers tend to rise relative to the incomes of consumers. The sales tax removes some of the burden of taxation from savers, because interest income escapes direct taxation when the sales tax is substituted for the proportional income tax.

However, the gain to a saver depends on his time pattern of saving. When he dissaves he will, of course, pay the sales tax. His gain, in this case, is the interest he earns on his saving while postponing the payment of the sales tax. Of course, if the saver never dissaves, he avoids paying the sales taxes completely.

The differential incidence of the substitution of a sales tax for an equal-yield proportional income tax depends on the relationship between the average propensity to save and income classes. If the proportion of income saved and the average holding period of saving rises with income, then the differential incidence of the sales tax is likely to be regressive. If, however, saving falls with income, then the differential incidence is progressive. If saving is more or less proportional to income for all income classes, the differential incidence of the sales tax is proportional.

Since most empirical studies show that saving and the holding period for saving rises with income, it may be concluded that the differential incidence of sales taxation is regressive. That is to say, substitution of a sales tax for an equal-yield income tax tends to redistribute income away from the "poor" toward the "rich." Such a substitution moves the nation's Lorenz curve further away from the line of equal income distribution. This is because the higher income classes tend to save relatively more of their income than lower income classes, and their saving tends to be more "permanent" in the sense that it does not merely represent postponed consumption but capital accumulation (that is, the massing of wealth and fortunes).

SUMMARY

Governmental tax and expenditure policies affect the distribution of income by withdrawing resources for private use, transferring income among households, and altering the relative prices of outputs and inputs. Quantitative estimates of the redistributive effects of governmental activities can permit more informed collective choices by aiding voters to compute their true cost shares of publicly supplied services relative to the benefits they receive.

The theory of incidence analyzes the effect of governmental activities on the distribution of income. The concept of differential tax incidence is useful in assessing the relative redistributive effects of alternative tax policies. It measures the resulting change in the distribution of income when one tax is substituted for another yielding an equivalent amount of revenue in real terms, while the level and mix of government expenditures is held constant.

The burden of a tax is not always borne by the economic unit upon which it is assessed, because introduction of any tax will alter relative prices. Tax burdens may, therefore, be shifted among taxpayers in subtle ways through movements in supply and demand as a result of the tax. The degree to which tax shifting is possible depends on market structure, time, technological factors affecting long-run supply, and the elasticities of demand and supply.

Analytical techniques have now been developed for determining both the allocative and distributive effects of taxation. The following chapters will analyze the economic effects of taxes on income, consumption, and wealth.

9

Taxes on Income

Taxes on income currently represent the major source of revenue to the federal government. State governments as well rely on income taxes for significant amounts of revenue. Budget estimates for fiscal year 1971 indicate that the federal government obtains approximately 45 percent of its revenue from personal income taxes, 16 percent from corporation income taxes, while an additional 24 percent comes from employment taxes (social security, unemployment compensation, and so forth). Since employment taxes are levied on both personal and business incomes, they are essentially taxes on income. Thus, the federal government obtains approximately *85 percent* of its revenue from taxes on personal and business incomes. On the average, state governments rely on taxes on income for approximately 23 percent of their total revenues. It is vital to understand the economic effects of this form of taxation precisely because of the heavy reliance on it in this country.

Income taxation is a relatively new phenomenon in the United States. Prior to 1913, the federal government's major source of revenue was the customs duty (tariffs). Although an income tax was utilized briefly (1861–1872) on the national level as an emergency measure during the Civil War, it did not become a permanent feature of the federal tax structure until the year 1913. An attempt by President Grover Cleveland in 1894 to introduce the income tax on the national level failed when the United States Supreme Court declared the enacted law unconstitutional. In 1913, a constitutional amendment was adopted that empowered Congress to levy taxes on both personal and business incomes. The initial income tax passed under the new amendment exempted the first $3000 of income from taxation for a single person and the first $4000 for a married person. All income above this exemption to $20,000 was taxed at the proportional rate of 1 percent with surcharges ranging to 7 percent for higher levels of income. The highest rate was applied to taxable income in excess of $500,000. The newly enacted income tax provided a significant amount of revenue to finance World War I. Since then, it is common knowledge that the rates of taxation applied to the income bases have increased. Currently, the top marginal rate of taxation for the federal tax structure is 70 percent.

On the state level, experience with an income tax was unfavorable prior to the early twentieth century. Although six states had experimented with income taxation in the nineteenth century, the tax proved both unpopular and difficult to administer. The first successful income tax on the state level was instituted by Wisconsin in 1911. The Wisconsin tax law featured improved administrative techniques that facilitated equitable collection of the tax. The income tax was soon adopted by other states, and currently the majority of states in the Union have taxes on personal and business incomes.

There are some fundamental conceptual problems to be grappled with before a tax on income can be introduced into any tax structure. Among the most basic of these problems is the definition of the tax base. Although this may seem to be a simple enough problem to solve, the reader will discover that there are many difficulties involved in obtaining a definition that is both consistent and operational.

This chapter is divided into two parts. Part A discusses theoretical aspects of income taxation. This includes problems of definition and administrative feasibility as well as possible economic effects of income taxation. Part B discusses income taxation as it is practiced in the United States today with respect to both personal and business incomes. Actual income taxation will be evaluated in the light of the theoretical principles developed in Part A.

A
Theory of Income Taxation

The Tax Base

Before any tax on income can be instituted, one must define a number of concepts. An essential task is, of course, to define the concept of taxable income. In addition, one must define the economic units receiving income and the time period during which such income is received.

Concepts of Income

Income concepts differ with respect to their methods of accounting. One concept measures income as a "flow" of goods and services, while another measures income as an "accrual" of property rights. Both of these concepts are meaningless unless a time period is specified. It makes no sense merely to say that an individual's income is $10,000, for this may mean $10,000 per hour, per day, per month, or per year. For tax purposes, the income of an individual economic unit is usually specified per year. Thus, income represents an annual flow, or an annual accrual.

The flow concept of income is relatively familiar. *Income* is defined as an annual flow of goods and services measured in monetary (dollar) terms. This concept measures income as the net flow of money (a measure of purchasing power) from the sale of productive services and capital assets during the year or any other relevant time period. To measure income under the flow concept, one must have data on the quantities of productive services and capital assets sold and the net prices received from the sale of these items. Thus, income for any economic unit is the total dollar value received per year from the sale of the productive services flowing from the land, labor, and capital it owns less the cost of producing or maintaining the factors of production, plus the dollar value received from the sale of existing assets less the initial cost of acquiring those assets.

The accrual concept of income, as defined by Henry Simons, views income as an indicator of "the exercise of control over the use of society's scarce resources."[1] A calculation of income under this definition implies an estimate of the extent to which an economic unit's store of property rights to control scarce resources, or its "purchasing power," has increased during a specified time period, say, a year. Such property rights can be exercised in the current period in which case they will be used to consume scarce resources, or they may be accumulated, or "stored," for later use. Accrued property rights may be exercised during the year, in which case they are converted to consumption, or they may be stored, in which case they become additions to the economic unit's net worth (the ownership of property rights).

The concept of income as an accrual of property rights has become known as the "Haig-Simons" definition of income.[2] *Income*, according to the Haig-Simons definition, is equal to the sum of annual consumption and the increase in net worth (savings):

$$Y = C + \Delta NW \tag{9.1}$$

[1] Henry Simons, *Personal Income Taxation*, University of Chicago Press, Chicago, 1938, p. 49.

[2] See Simons; also see Robert Murray Haig, "The Concept of Income: Economic and Legal Aspects" in Haig (ed.), *The Federal Income Tax*, Columbia University Press, New York, 1921, p. 7; reprinted in American Economic Association, R. A. Musgrave and C. S. Shoup (eds.), *Readings in the Economics of Taxation*, Irwin, Homewood, Ill., 1959, p. 59.

where Y is annual income, C is annual consumption, and ΔNW is annual change in net worth. Under this definition of income, all receipts from the sale of productive services and the net change in the value of existing assets are added in order to obtain a measure of income per unit time. The expenses incurred in earning the income are netted out. The Haig-Simons definition differs from the flow concept of income chiefly in the method of treating capital gains. The flow concept of income counts as income only those net capital gains realized in the current period. The Haig-Simons definition includes *all* net capital gains whether realized or not. Realized capital gains occur during a period when an existing asset, whose value has increased above its acquisition price, is actually sold. For example, if an individual acquired some common stock in a corporation last year at a cost of $1,000 and the value of the stock in the current year has risen to $2,000, he has experienced a capital gain of $1,000. Under the flow concept of income, this gain is not included in income *unless* the stock is sold in the current year. Under the accrual of property rights, or Haig-Simons concept of income, the gain is included in current income, whether or not the asset is sold in the current year, because its accrual constitutes an increase in the individual's net worth that measures his store of property rights. Net capital gains refer to total capital gains less total capital losses in a given period.

Problems of Implementation
Irrespective of which definition of income is chosen, a number of secondary questions must be answered before any income tax can be implemented. First, the economic unit upon which taxes are to be levied must be defined. Two candidates immediately present themselves: households and business firms. Thus, in the United States, taxes are levied on the net incomes of households and corporate business firms. Next, the period of time over which income is measured must be defined. The period chosen is usually a calendar year.

In addition, one must delineate the portion of income that actually will be taxable. The concept of *taxable income* implies that there are certain justifiable deductions that may be made from actual gross income per year. Thus, in the case of both concepts of income discussed, adjustments usually are made to reflect the expenses incurred in earning income. In order to maintain jobs, most people incur expenses for transportation to and from work, for lunches, for work clothes, and so on. The concept of "personal exemption," or "standard deduction," in the United States income tax code is designed to take into account those minimum living expenses necessary to maintain one's livelihood. In addition, other adjustments are also often made to reflect expenses incurred in earning income. The concept of "adjusted gross income" in the United States income tax code includes such deductions. Annual expenditures on education designed to improve vocational or professional skills and to retain one's job are deducted from gross income as expenses. Similarly, certain transportation expenses incurred in the course of regular business are considered "inputs" necessary to produce income, and they are deducted from gross income. Expenditures for child care by working mothers is another example of tax-deductible expenses. Books purchased by professional men for their work also come under this category. A home office used by a salesman or a writer can be considered an "input" in the production of income, and its cost is also deductible. Needless to say, the introduction of such "reasonable" deductions from gross income can open a Pandora's box of difficulties for the administration of the income tax. For example, deductions for business expenses incurred in "entertaining" clients may result in abuses. If such expenses are not really essential to a business, the result is unintended governmental subsidy of expenditures on luxury entertainment goods. Court decisions are often necessary to determine what constitutes "reasonable" deductions for expenses incurred in the course of earning income.

Finally, there are very difficult problems encountered in attempting to measure income either as a flow or as an accrual of property rights. Some of these difficulties stem from conceptual and administrative problems in measuring and tracing income in kind, gifts, "imputed" incomes, and capital gains. In addition, there are problems involved in treating households whose annual incomes fluctuate widely.

The United States income tax code levies taxes on the following major sources of income:

1. Wages and salaries.
2. Tips.
3. Interest.
4. Dividends and other corporate distributions.
5. Rent.
6. Royalties.
7. Certain pensions and annuities.
8. Capital gains.
9. Alimony.

This is only a partial list. There are other minor categories of income that are taxed as well. Records are usually kept of the listed categories of income, and as a result, they are easy to trace and measure. Other kinds of income that qualify as that designation under either the flow or Haig-Simons definitions prove more difficult to trace and measure. Thus, goods and services produced by individuals for their own uses are often administratively difficult to measure and, thereby, are not subject to taxation. Examples of such goods and services are homegrown food and flowers, various kinds of housework, do-it-yourself repair and maintenance of cars and homes, and so on. All such self-produced goods and services are undertaken in lieu of the expenditure of one's property rights to resources (dollars) in the market. While they constitute income, they are, nevertheless, not subject to tax. Other examples of untaxed income include certain fringe benefits of a job, such as secretarial services, transportation, subsidized food, plush office facilities, and so forth.

Similarly, homeowners receive services flowing to them from their homes in lieu of rental payments. For example, an individual who invests $20,000 in a home receives a return in the form of housing services of, say, $1,000 per year for which no rent is paid. An individual with the same money income who invests $20,000 in government bonds at 5 percent interest and who lives in rental housing expends resources for rental payments, while the $1,000 a year interest he receives from investment in bonds is subject to taxes. The after-tax income of the homeowner is greater than that of the renter, even though they have the same income and wealth ($20,000). The reason for this is that the homeowner pays no taxes on the return from his investment.[3] Of course, it could prove difficult in administrative terms to actually impute rental incomes to homeowners. Partially as a result of the measurement problem, most income tax codes make no attempt to include imputed rental incomes in taxable income. Similar consumption services are yielded by all consumer durables, such as cars, washing machines, and so forth. All these are difficult to measure and are not included in taxable income. The same holds for the "psychic" incomes individuals receive from working on a particular job or living in a particular locality.

Gifts, either in the form of cash or goods and services, *do* qualify as income under both definitions. However, the United States income tax code states flatly that gifts, bequests, and inheritances are "not income."[4] Again, there are measurement and tracing problems particularly for gifts in the form of goods and services. However, there is an additional complication manifest in this case. In the United States tax structure, gifts are not viewed as a "permanent" increase in one's earning power but as irregular, or "transitory," income. Although this is inconsistent with both the flow and accrual concepts of income, the United States tax code apparently uses some underlying concept of "regular" income that excludes gifts from the income tax base.

Similar problems occur in the treatment of capital gains. Although net capital gains (capital gains less capital losses) are income according to the Haig-Simons definition, it is sometimes argued that, like gifts, they constitute "irregular," or "transitory," income. It is difficult to accept this argument. Net positive capital gains adjusted by an index of the price level do constitute an increase in one's potential purchasing power. Such gains are income, whether

---

[3] Furthermore, the homeowner can deduct property taxes on his home and mortgage interest payments from his gross income before arriving at his taxable income. This increases the tax advantages of homeownership even more. This is part of a conscious policy to subsidize homeownership in the United States.

[4] However, property transfers, such as gifts and the transfers of property at death, are taxed through the federal estate and gift taxes and state inheritance taxes. These will be discussed in Chapter 11.

"transitory" or not. If capital gains are not taxed at all, then the income tax discriminates against incomes by source. This results in a subsidy to those individuals engaging in activities resulting in capital gains. Any social justification for such a subsidy must be couched in terms of its allocative effects. For example, it may be argued that there are external benefits associated with encouraging risk taking that yield capital gains insofar as this increases the rate of economic growth.

There is, however, a measurement problem in the case of unrealized capital gains. Recall that the Haig-Simons definition of income includes *both* realized and unrealized gains. While it may be difficult to trace capital gains on all assets, it is by no means impossible. In particular, data do exist on net capital gains in the form of changes in the value of outstanding corporate equity (stocks) and residential real estate that are major assets held by the private sector. Conceptually, it does not seem as though it would be administratively prohibitive to track these net gains in real terms accruing to households and businesses, whether or not they are realized. A recent study estimates that accrued capital gains (realized and unrealized) over the period 1946–1968 averaged more than four times the mean realized capital gains over the same period.[5]

The treatment of capital gains as "transitory" and "non-taxable" income pervades the British and certain other English-speaking nations' tax structures. *Capital gains* are usually defined as real increases in the value of assets not used as "stocks-in-trade" (equities traded by securities dealers are "stocks-in-trade"). In addition, "short-term" gains are sometimes distinguished from "long-term" gains. In the United States, long-term gains are those achieved on assets held longer than six months. Until recently, in Great Britain, no tax was levied on either long- or short-term gains, whether or not they were realized. Now, short-term realized gains are taxed in that country. In the United States, net short-term realized gains are taxed as ordinary income, while net long-term realized gains are taxed at preferentially lower rates. There is no attempt to measure and tax unrealized capital gains in the United States.

The arguments favoring preferential tax treatment of "irregular" or "transitory" income from various sources merit further discussion. These arguments suggest that one year may be too short a period of time to define income. This indicates that the proper tax base is some concept of "permanent income" that may be estimated as an average of income from all sources over a number of taxable years.[6] This serves to spread transitory gains and losses from whatever source over a number of years. Such a procedure is particularly relevant for the United States income tax code with its progressive rate structure. Under

---

[5] Michael B. McElroy, "Capital Gains and the Concept and Measurement of Purchasing Power," *Proceedings of the Business and Economic Statistics Section of the American Statistical Association*, 1970.

[6] The concept of "permanent income" is attributable to Milton Friedman; see his *Theory of the Consumption Function*, Princeton University Press, Princeton, N.J., 1957.

such a structure, two individuals with the same average annual incomes over a period of, say, five years, may pay widely differing amounts of taxes depending on the time pattern of income receipts. For example, if both individuals have an average annual income of $10,000 for the five-year period, the individual who receives his income as $10,000 in each year pays much less in taxes than the individual who receives $50,000 in one of the five years and nothing in the remaining four years because of the progressive rate structure and the collection of taxes on the base of annual income. The United States tax code now has a provision for voluntary averaging of income that benefits individuals with widely fluctuating income.

If a system of compulsory income averaging over a period of, say, five years, were adopted into the tax code, the argument for special preferential treatment of "irregular" income including net capital gains and gifts would be vitiated. An averaging scheme permits such "windfall" income to be averaged over a number of years, thereby preventing inequitable tax treatment because of the annual collection of taxes under progressive tax rates. The scheme is preferred by many economists to arbitrary preferential treatment of rigidly defined "irregular" income.[7] For example, it is debatable that net long-term capital gains represent irregular income for all recipients. For some individuals, they may, in fact, comprise stable and regular sources of income. The averaging technique serves to benefit only those individuals for whom capital gains truly represent transitory income.

TAXATION OF PERSONAL INCOME

Allocative Effects

Since income is an economic base, one does not expect an income tax to be neutral with respect to resource allocation unless the supplies of all income-producing activities are perfectly inelastic. In general, since the amount of taxes paid under an income tax does vary with the size of the taxpayer's income, one does expect some changes in the behavior of the taxpayer with a view toward decreasing the burden of income taxation. To the extent that a taxpayer can control his income, he can control the amount of income tax he pays. Furthermore, when an income tax code discriminates against income from varying sources in the sense of taxing income from alternative sources at different rates and allowing deductions from the tax base for expenses incurred in certain activities, one expects additional allocative effects. This occurs because, under such circumstances, the taxpayer can control his tax bill to the extent that he can control his sources of income and the deductions he takes from his income.

---

[7] For example, see Richard Goode, *The Individual Income Tax*, The Brookings Institution, Washington, D.C., 1964, pp. 199–204.

Clearly, the allocative effects of a tax code, such as that employed in the United States, are complex, given the preferential treatment of income from certain sources and many allowable deductions from the tax base (tax preferences). To facilitate understanding of the effect of personal income taxes on resource allocations, the following analysis will be undertaken on a step-by-step basis. First, the text considers the allocative effects of a simple proportional income tax with no tax preferences. Under such a tax, all personal income—irrespective of source and with no allowable deductions—is taxed at the same percentage rate. The effects of a proportional income tax will then be compared with those of an equal-yield progressive income tax with no tax preferences. Finally, the effect of tax preferences, in the form of preferential treatment of income by source or of special deductions from income, will be analyzed with respect to their effects on the allocation of resources.

A Simple Proportional Income Tax and the Work-Leisure Choice

Under a simple proportional income tax, the return from all income sources decreases by a fixed percentage rate. There are no tax preferences under such a simple income tax code. Under such circumstances, the only way a taxpayer can avoid or control his tax bill is by altering his income. Consider the effects of such a tax on choices by households concerning allocation of time between work and leisure and allocation of present income between consumption and saving.

Individual taxpayers may be viewed as having preferences between work and leisure. Given the rate of return from work effort, the individual has an equilibrium allocation of time between work and leisure. The equilibrium allocation is a function of *both* individual preferences and the return from work effort. Since a proportional income tax reduces the return from work effort, one expects that it will influence the individual work-leisure choice, under the assumption that the supply of work effort is not completely inelastic. However, it is not possible to make any general predictions of the effect of the tax on the allocation of time between work and leisure. Some individuals may choose to work less because of the tax, while others may choose to work more after the tax is imposed. The actual result for each individual depends on his preferences for work as opposed to leisure.

An individual's preferences between work and leisure may be depicted by a preference map between income and leisure. It is assumed that the individual can trade the leisure good for income (or all other goods) by choosing an allocation of time between work and leisure. The term "work" is interpreted broadly to include all income-producing activities. The individual is presumed to be able actually to choose the amount of hours that he wishes to work during, say, each day, without restraint. He has a certain number of hours available each day that he may retain as leisure or "trade" at the average rate of return in the market for income. Assume that the return to work effort is simply r dollars per hour for this individual.

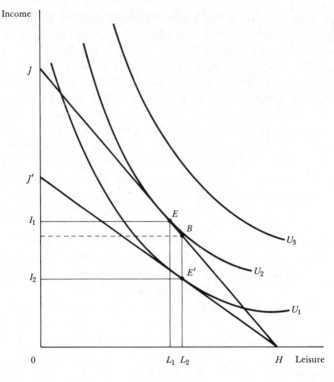

FIGURE 9.1

This information is illustrated in Figure 9.1. The curves U_1, U_2, and U_3 represent three indifference curves between income and leisure. The indifference curves exhibit diminishing marginal rate of substitution of income for leisure. On the horizontal axis, the distance $0H$ represents the number of hours per day available to allocate between work and leisure. This is less than twenty-four hours because the individual presumably has to devote some time to sleeping, eating, and so forth. The line HJ gives the opportunities for the individual to trade leisure for income. If he chooses not to work at all, his income is zero in this simple model. This is illustrated at point H in Figure 9.1. At that point, the individual is "consuming" his entire allotment of leisure and is, therefore, earning zero income. For any other point along HJ, the individual's income may be expressed as

$$I = r(H - L) \tag{9.2}$$

where L is the amount of hours of leisure per day (a variable), r is the average return to work effort (a parameter), and H is the total available hours per day. The maximum income the individual can earn, in this case, is $0J$ dollars per day. This is his income when he "consumes" no leisure and works H hours per day. If $L = 0$, then from equation (9.2), $I = rH$ dollars.

Under the assumption of a diminishing marginal rate of substitution between income and leisure, neither the extreme J (no leisure) nor H (no work) is a likely choice. Instead, the individual will maximize his utility at some intermediate point on the line HJ. In Figure 9.1, this occurs at point E, where the indifference curve U_2 is just tangent to the wage line HJ. At that point, the slope of the indifference curve MRS_{IL} is equal to the slope of the line HJ. But from equation (9.2), the slope of HJ is simply $(-r)$, the rate of return from work effort. Since both slopes are negative, the equilibrium condition for the optimal (that is, utility maximizing) allocation of time between work and leisure is

$$r = MRS_{IL} \tag{9.3}$$

Now, consider the effect of the introduction of a simple proportional income tax on the individual's work-leisure choice. A proportional income tax of t percent reduces the return to work effort by t percent at all levels of work. The effect of this is to rotate the line that depicts the market possibilities for transforming the leisure into income through work effort from HJ down to HJ'. The equation for this transformation line now becomes

$$I = r(1 - t)\,(H - L) \tag{9.4}$$

The new equilibrium for the individual now occurs where the new transformation curve is tangent to some indifference curve. This occurs at E' in Figure 9.1. The new equilibrium condition is as follows:

$$r(1 - t) = MRS_{IL} \tag{9.5}$$

For the individual whose indifference curves are depicted in Figure 9.1, the proportional income tax has the following effects:

1. A reduction in utility from U_2 to U_1. (This ignores any benefits from governmental expenditure accruing to the individual.)
2. An increase in the "consumption" of leisure from L_1 to L_2.
3. A consequent reduction in disposable income from I_1 to I_2.

The government collects $E'B$ dollars of this individual's income in taxes. In this case, the tax has been detrimental to work effort. The individual reduces his hours worked per day by L_1L_2 as a result of the income tax. Other individuals with different tastes react differently to the imposition of an income tax. Some choose to work the same number of hours, while others conceivably choose to work more hours. The aggregate effect on work supplied, therefore, cannot be predicted without knowledge of the preferences of all taxpayers.

The proportional income tax results in an efficiency loss for the economy. With introduction of the tax, individual workers adjust their work-leisure choices until the marginal rate of substitution of income for leisure is equal to their *net wage* $r(1 - t)$. However, employers still make their hiring choices on the basis of the gross wage r. In equilibrium, employers set the value of the marginal product of labor equal to the gross wage. The "tax wedge" between the net and gross wages prevents the attainment of Paretian efficiency, as workers and employers independently adjust to equilibrium positions where the marginal benefit of labor (the value of its marginal product) no longer equals its marginal cost to the worker (the marginal rate of substitution of income for leisure).

Consider the effect of the proportional income tax on work effort in more general terms. The introduction of the tax may be represented in the same terms as the change in price of any commodity. The tax lowers the "price" of leisure by reducing the return from work effort. The effect of a price change on quantity consumed can be evaluated with the aid of reference to the income and substitution effects induced by that change.

The income tax results in a substitution effect that is unfavorable to work effort. The tax reduces the return from work effort, thereby making work less remunerative. This, in turn, makes leisure more attractive. There is an incentive to substitute leisure for work effort, because the per-hour opportunity cost (the hourly return from work effort) has fallen as a result of the introduction of the income tax. The same holds for the case of an increase in income tax rates. Thus, the substitution effect induced by the income tax is such as to increase the consumption of leisure by the individual. This substitution effect represents a potential loss of output of goods and services due to the reduction in the incentive to work.

But there is also an income effect induced by the introduction of the tax. The income effect tends to be favorable to work effort provided that leisure is a "normal" good. The income tax reduces income at all levels of work. Even if the individual chooses to work the same number of hours as he did prior to the imposition of the tax, he earns less income than he did previously. The effective reduction in income results in a decrease in the consumption of all goods with positive income elasticity (normal goods) and an increase in the consumption of all goods with negative income elasticity (inferior goods). If leisure is not an inferior good, then the income tax results in a decrease in its consumption by the individual. If he reduces his consumption of leisure, then it follows that he works more. Thus, the income effect of taxation provides an incentive to increase work effort when leisure is a normal good. In a sense, the individual tends to work harder in order to maintain his previous income level.

The actual effect on individual work effort depends on the relative magnitudes of the income and substitution effects. If the substitution effect outweighs the income effect, the individual tends to consume more leisure and, consequently, works less as a result of the tax. This is evidently the case for the individual whose indifference curves are depicted in Figure 9.1. If, however, the individual's preferences are such that the income effect outweighs the substitution effect, the result is a reduction in the consumption of leisure and consequent increase in work effort. Figure 9.2 illustrates this case. Here, after the imposition of the proportional income tax at rate t, the consumption of leisure *falls* from L_1' to L_2' as the individual moves from his initial equilibrium E to his post-tax equilibrium E'. Similarly, it is possible to envision a case where the income and substitution effects are equal in magnitude and, thus, cancel each other. In such a case, the tax has no effect on work effort. There may, however, be an efficiency loss for the economy even when the introduction of the income tax results in no change in the quantity of labor supplied. If there is no substitution effect and leisure is a normal good, then the introduction of the income tax results in an increase in work effort. When a substitution effect exists to cancel the income effect, then the individual is adjusting the quantity of labor supplied in response to the tax. As long as such an adjustment takes place for which the individual alters his marginal rate of substitution of income for leisure in response to the tax, the "tax wedge" prevents independent action from achieving the efficiency condition (equality of the value of the marginal product of labor and MRS_{IL}). The efficiency loss attributable to a simple proportional income tax varies directly with the willingness of individuals to adjust their marginal rates of substitution of income for leisure in response to the tax. The income tax is neutral if and only if its introduction results in no change in the equilibrium MRS_{IL}. Under such circumstances, the tax wedge does not prevent the independent action of workers and employers from achieving the efficiency conditions. The efficiency loss tends to vary with both the income and price elasticities of the supply of work effort.

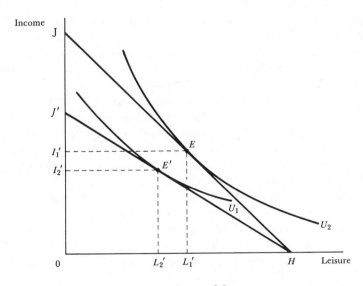

FIGURE 9.2

The Supply of Work Effort

In the previous examples, one assumes that the individual chooses without restraint the number of hours per day he wishes to work. In reality, this often is not the case. There tends to be some indivisibility, or "lumpiness," in the extent to which the individual can regulate his working hours. Thus, a "blue-collar" worker may have to work at least a forty-hour week. He may not be able to adjust his work week to thirty-six hours. The only alternative may be a part-time job of, say, twenty hours a week. He cannot vary his work week smoothly on an hour-per-hour basis.

However, the fact that there are constraints on the individual's ability to vary work effort does not imply that the supply of work effort is completely inelastic with respect to income or price. Income taxes, by reducing the return from work effort, can affect the willingness of blue-collar workers to undertake overtime work. It can affect the willingness of spouses to take part-time or full-time jobs. In addition, it can affect the willingness of individuals to engage in any sort of work effort to supplement wages and salary incomes.

Thus, although there are constraints on the ability of individuals to vary their work effort, it is highly unlikely that the supply of work effort is perfectly inelastic for any individual. Thus, a proportional income tax is likely to result in some adjustment of the work-leisure choice and in an efficiency loss to the economy as a result of the tax. A general proportional income tax with no deductions or exemptions is, therefore, not neutral with respect to resource allocation.

Progressive Taxation

The United States income tax code utilizes a progressive rate structure. Consider the effects on the equilibrium amount of work effort supplied to the market by an individual when a proportional income tax is replaced by a progressive income tax. Again, assume that the tax is levied on all income irrespective of source and allows no deductions from the tax base.

Suppose the individual pays the same dollar amount of his income in taxes under the alternative of progressive and proportional income taxation. Will he work more or less under the progressive rate structure? Under a proportional rate structure, both the average and marginal rates of taxation are equal and constant at the rate of taxation t. Under a progressive rate structure, the marginal rate of taxation increases with income and is greater than the average rate of taxation. Consequently, the average rate of taxation increases with income.

In Figure 9.3, the income transformation line prior to the imposition of any income taxes is HY. After the imposition of a proportional income tax, HY rotates downward to HY_t. For the individual whose indifference curves are drawn in that figure, work effort decreases by L_1L_2 hours per day as he moves from his initial equilibrium at P to his post-tax equilibrium at P'. The tax collects T dollars of this individual's income.

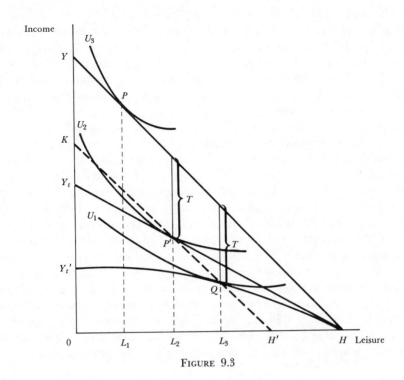

FIGURE 9.3

The line $H'K$ is called the line of "equal-tax yield." All points on that line result in tax collections of T dollars from this particular individual. The problem now becomes the choice of one progressive rate structure from an infinite number of possible rate structures that result in an equilibrium for the individual on the line $H'K$. Such a rate structure is illustrated by the curvilinear line Y_t' in Figure 9.3. This is a smoothly progressive rate structure. As income rises, the percentage of income paid in taxes continuously increases. Under the equal-yield progressive rate structure, the individual taxpayer is in equilibrium at point Q and is still paying T dollars in taxes.

It can now be demonstrated that a progressive income tax is more detrimental to individual work effort than is an equal-yield proportional income tax.[8] So long as the indifference curves exhibit a diminishing marginal rate of substitution between work and leisure, the point Q has to lie to the right of P' in Figure 9.3, implying that more leisure is consumed under the progressive rate structure. This is because the slope of the transformation curve HY_t' at point Q is less than that of the indifference curve at point P'. This follows from the fact that the marginal rate of taxation is higher at Q relative to P'.

---

[8] This is the conclusion reached by Richard A. Musgrave in a similar analysis. See his *The Theory of Public Finance*, McGraw-Hill, New York, 1959, pp. 241–243.

Since the slopes of indifference curves decrease along the line HK only as one moves to the right and below point P', any tangency along the line of equal tax yield must lie below and to the right of point P'. In Figure 9.3, the individual decreases work effort per day by L_1L_3 hours under the progressive income tax. This is greater than the reduction that prevails under a proportional tax.[9] In addition, there is a greater efficiency loss because of the reaction of this worker to the higher marginal rate of taxation.

It *cannot* be concluded from this illustration that work effort on the *national* level is less under a progressive income tax as compared with an equal-yield proportional income tax. The reason for this is that lower-income individuals tend to have both their average and marginal rates of taxation reduced by such a substitution, while relatively high-income individuals tend to have both their average and marginal rates of taxation increased. People with middle incomes may find their average rates of taxation reduced as their marginal rates increase. Lower marginal rates of taxation result in substitution effects favorable to work effort, while lower average rates of taxation result in income effects that are unfavorable to work effort (individuals tend to consume more leisure when average tax rates are reduced). Some individuals increase work effort, while others decrease work effort, depending on their preferences and their income sizes. The aggregate effect on national work effort is not generally predictable in this case. It depends on individual preferences and the distribution of taxes among income groups in the population.

Income Taxes and Savings
An income tax may also distort individual choices between consumption and saving. Interest earned on savings are subject to income taxes under both the Haig-Simons and flow definitions of income. Furthermore, most income tax codes do, in fact, tax interest on savings. As long as the interest elasticity of supply and savings to the capital markets is not zero, income taxes levied on interest incomes are likely to distort choices between current consumption and saving. Income taxes reduce the return to savings by households and are, therefore, likely to result in a reduction in the quantity of savings supplied.

The income tax drives a "wedge" between the cost of capital as seen by investors and the actual return on capital earned by savers. This "wedge" prevents the attainment of an efficient allocation of resources between present and future consumption. The resulting "efficiency loss" is in the form of a reduction in saving and a consequent fall in capital formation. The magnitude of this efficiency loss depends on, among other things, the interest elasticity of supply of savings and the rate of taxation.[10] In short, income taxes of any kind are likely to result in an intertemporal misallocation of resources between

[9] This conclusion has to be modified if the progressive rate structure is not continuously progressive. See Barlow and Sparks, "A Note on Progression and Leisure," *American Economic Review*, June 1964.

[10] Among the "other things" is the interest elasticity of investment demand.

present and future consumption, because they lower the return from savings and cause the rate to diverge from the rate seen by investors.

Furthermore, it is likely that a progressive income tax is more detrimental to saving incentives when compared to an equal-yield proportional income tax financing the same level and mix of public services. This is because the average propensity to save tends to increase with household income level. Under a completely general progressive income tax with no exceptions or deductions, households with higher incomes pay both higher average and marginal rates of taxation than do households with relatively lower incomes. Thus, a progressive income tax tends to bear most heavily on the income group with both the greatest capacity and tendency to save. These higher-income groups tend to earn lower effective interest rates on their savings after taxes relative to lower-income groups because of high marginal tax rates, and the same higher-income groups suffer greater average reductions in income because of high average rates of taxation. As a result, the aggregate effect on the quantity of saving supplied tends to be greater under a progressive rate structure when compared with the alternative of a proportional rate structure. The extent of this greater loss of saving under progressive income taxation depends in part on the degree of progression in the rate structure and the pre-tax income distribution.

The Effect of "Tax Preferences"

Most income tax codes allow for preferential taxation of income from specific sources and deductions from the tax base for individuals engaging in certain kinds of activities. Such "tax preferences" are likely to result in allocative effects that channel resources into those particular activities that are tax-preferred. The result is a distortion of private decision-making relative to that which would exist in the absence of the income tax. Tax preferences can be regarded as subsidies to particular types of economic activity. These are justified only when the tax-preferred activities generate external benefits.

The United States tax code is replete with a plethora of tax preferences. While many of these will be discussed in detail in the second part of this chapter, some of them may be listed in summary fashion now. As already indicated, the United States tax code allows for preferential tax treatment of net long-term capital gains. The first $100 of dividend income is non-taxable. Homeowners can deduct the interest paid on their mortgage loans from their taxable incomes. The interest from municipal bonds is non-taxable. Owners of capital in oil and other natural-resource extractive industries are given depletion allowances that considerably reduce their tax burdens. Contributions to charity are tax-deductible.

The listing is far from complete. In the United States, the tax code is so overladen with complicated tax preferences that a small army of lawyers, accountants, and bookkeepers are employed just to explain the complexities of the tax code to the taxpayers. The expenditure on activities designed to gain information on the tax preferences inherent in the tax code may be considered, in itself, a misallocation of resources. The result is professional expertise and skills being used for the purposes of legally avoiding taxes rather than being used in more socially productive activities. The tax preferences themselves result in allocative effects inducing resources to flow into the tax-subsidized activities.

For example, the exemption from federal taxation of interest incomes flowing from municipal bonds implies that these bonds can be issued at lower interest rates than competing securities. This, in turn, results in lower debt-service burdens to the municipalities themselves. In effect, the federal government is subsidizing the issuances of debt by municipalities. Similarly, the subtraction of interest on mortgage loans and property tax payments from taxable incomes subsidizes homeownership in the United States. More resources flow into the purchase of homes under these tax circumstances compared to that which would prevail if there were no tax advantage in home-ownership.

Whenever tax preferences exist, one expects individuals to plan their economic activities in such a manner as to take advantage of the preferences. Individuals who take advantage of tax preferences may not be responding to economic incentives but rather to artificial incentives built into the tax code if the tax preferences do not internalize externalities. In the case of activities that generate external benefits, preferential tax treatment can be justified as subsidies designed to increase the flow of resources to those activities generating the external benefits. If homeownership is viewed as generating benefits external to the homeowners, then preferential tax treatment is justified on allocative grounds. Similarly, it is often argued that preferential taxation of capital gains encourages risk-taking and saving that generates external benefits by increasing the rate of growth of the economy. Any benefits of tax preferences must be balanced against the possible distortions they cause in resource allocations.

Finally, it may be questioned whether the income tax code is a proper vehicle through which subsidies to particular activities should be made. Perhaps subsidies should be made directly to economic units engaging in activities generating external benefits, rather than "hiding" them in the tax code. This would avoid the effect of giving to the individuals who have superior information on tax laws the benefits of subsidies intended for all persons who engage in some particular activity. Furthermore, the subsidies could be debated in the Congress on their merits as subsidies rather than on dubious arguments concerning the proper definitions of income and allowable deductions.

TAXES ON BUSINESS INCOME

Income taxes are also levied on business incomes. In the case of non-incorporated businesses, the distinction between personal and business income has little significance. The return to a non-incorporated business generally is treated as personal income flowing or accruing to its owners. The corporate form of business is, however, often treated as a separate and distinct taxpaying entity. In the final analysis, taxes are paid by people, not by organizations. Thus, it is often argued that separate taxation of corporations obscures many of the real issues in tax policy by ignoring the fact that the tax ultimately must be paid by individuals located somewhere in the income distribution. While there is a great deal of merit in this criticism, there are a number of arguments in favor of separate tax treatment of corporate business incomes.

Corporate charters are privileges granted to business firms by governmental authorities. In a sense, the right of incorporation and the limited-liability provision of incorporation can be considered as an input of the productive process. It is sometimes argued that the establishment of a corporation as a legal entity gives governmental authorities the right to levy taxes on the net income of such corporations. According to this reasoning, the corporation income tax is analogous to some sort of excise tax on incorporation. However, this argument does not establish an adequate link between "incorporation" as an input and the full taxation of the net income of a corporation. In particular, it contains no reference to the individuals who pay the tax.

An argument with considerably more merit concentrates on undistributed corporate profits. If there is no tax on the net income of the corporation, undistributed corporate profits (those not paid out as dividends) escape taxation completely. This provides an incentive for a corporation to plow the profits back into the business. In effect, this provides income to owners of stock in the corporation in the form of potential capital gains in lieu of dividends and keeps a substantial portion of the income tax base free of taxation. This reduces revenue to the treasury from this source.

The tax base upon which a corporation income tax is levied is total corporate profits. This includes all receipts of the corporation less all input costs. However, the tax base does not allow a deduction for the opportunity cost of capital (the economist's concept of the "normal profit"). Thus, the corporation income tax is a tax on the sum of normal and economic profits.

The tax is levied on the corporate enterprise. Thus, if the corporate income tax is not shifted, one expects its burden to be borne by suppliers of capital to the corporate sector (stockholders). Such individuals pay taxes in the form of a lower return on their capital as well as in the form of regular personal income taxes on the dividends flowing from their capital.

The following sections will contain discussions of both the allocative and distributive effects of a corporation income tax in general terms. In particular, attention is given to effects of the tax on the return to all factors of production, capital flows, and the forms of business organization. Theoretical arguments concerning the incidence of the tax will also be discussed. Part B of this chapter will consider unique aspects of corporate income taxation in the United States.

Allocative Effects

A tax on corporate income is likely to affect economic decisions concerning the allocation of resources within the private sector of the economy. Unfortunately, one cannot determine all allocative effects of the tax until its effects on the relative prices of inputs and outputs are also known. Assume, first, that the tax is initially borne by owners of capital in the corporate sector. If this is so, one expects capital to flow from the corporate sector into investments in non-corporate businesses (for example, farming) and real assets (for example, jewelry, homes, and so forth) until the return on these alternative assets is equalized (with allowance for risk) with the post-tax returns to corporate equity. If this reallocation serves to lower the returns to all forms of investment, one expects the tax to result in a reduction in annual savings and a consequent reduction in capital formation for the economy. For example, if a proportional tax of 50 percent is levied on all corporate incomes, the net returns to capital in the corporate sector become half of the actual returns, under the assumption that the tax is, in fact, borne by capital. If the actual returns are 10 percent, holders of corporate equity receive only 5 percent after taxes. Assuming that the capital markets were initially in equilibrium prior to the imposition of the tax, capital flows from the corporate sector to the now more lucrative investments in real assets and non-corporate businesses still yielding the initial equilibrium returns of 10 percent (with adjustments for risk). This decreases the return on these alternative assets and increases the post-tax returns on corporate equity until the two are once again equal. The new equilibrium return to capital for the economy may be lower, because the tax induces a consequent reduction in capital formation.

The corporate income tax also affects the output decisions of particular firms and industries. In the short run, the tax reduces marginal revenues. But at the same time, the tax decreases marginal costs by an equivalent amount. All expenditures on inputs are reduced by the percentage rates of taxation, because the costs of inputs are deducted from the tax base. These two effects cancel each other and the profit-maximizing firms still choose the output levels at which initial marginal costs are equal to initial marginal revenues. Thus, there is no incentive for a tax on net income to induce firms to alter output choices. This argument is valid *only* in the short run. The resource flows induced by the tax in the long run are likely to affect the outputs produced by alternative industries. If resources flow out of the corporate sector into the non-corporate sector, one expects the output of the non-corporate sector to rise relative to that of the corporate sector. The tax serves to make the non-corporate business form relatively more attractive as an investment.

The corporate income tax also has more subtle effects on the allocation of resources. Relative output levels change. The incentive for firms to alter output levels is a function of their initial capital structures (the ratio of debt to equity) and the extent of competition in the markets in which they sell their outputs. If firms, for one reason or another, are concerned about their dividend rates (perhaps because of the potential effects of decreasing dividends on stock prices), there is an incentive for them to maintain the pre-tax dividends after the imposition of the tax. The incentive to do this varies with the relative amounts of stock, particularly preferred stock, compared to other financing instruments.[11] The higher the proportion of preferred stock to other equity and debt, the greater the incentive to raise prices and cut back output to maintain pre-tax dividend rates. In addition, the degree to which the tax affects output choices depends on the ability of the firms to control prices. In oligopolistic markets, where mark-up pricing is used by all competing firms in the industry, there is a greater tendency to incorporate the tax into prices in the short run, thereby reducing the quantities demanded of their output. Thus, the relative reductions in quantities produced for alternative goods and services vary with competition in output markets and the capital structures of firms producing the output.

Distributive Effects

The corporation income tax also affects the distribution of income in the community through its influence on relative output and input prices. An adequate study of the shifting and incidence of any tax requires a general equilibrium analysis. Such an analysis may be conducted in simplified terms by assuming a two-sector economy where resources are completely mobile in the long run, prices are flexible, perfect competition exists in all markets, and the total supply of factors of production available to the economy is fixed. A model built on these assumptions was used by Arnold Harberger to analyze the incidence of the corporation income tax.[12] Utilizing a general equilibrium analysis and considering long-run resource flows, Harberger shows that the effect of the tax on relative prices can be rather complex.

Assuming an initial general equilibrium, imposition of a tax on the net income of the corporate sector lowers the return to investment in the corporate sector relative to the non-corporate sector. In the long run, this induces capital to flow from the corporate sector into the non-corporate sector until the net (after-tax) return to capital is once again equalized. This tax-induced capital flow has a variety of effects on relative prices, depending on technical opportunities for substituting factors of production for each other in the two sectors and on the price elasticities of demand for the alternative outputs.

The tax can be expected to lower the return to capital in *both* the corporate and non-corporate sectors of the economy as the non-corporate sector

[11] For a discussion of this point, see C. S. Shoup, "Incidence of the Corporation Income Tax: Capital Structure and Turnover Rates," *Readings in the Economics of Taxation*, pp. 322–329.

[12] Arnold Harberger, "The Incidence of the Corporation Income Tax," *Journal of Political Economy*, June 1962.

is forced to absorb the capital input leaving the corporate sector. Thus, the real income of capital owners in general, irrespective of the use to which that capital is put, tends to fall. In addition, the output produced by the corporate sector tends to fall relative to that produced by the non-corporate sector, because of the reduction in capital input in the corporate sector and the increase in capital input in the non-corporate sector. Depending on the price elasticities of demand, these changes in supply result in an increase in the price of goods produced by the corporate sector and a decrease in the price of goods produced by the non-corporate sector. Households spending relatively large portions of their budget on goods produced by the corporate sector experience a reduction in real income relative to other households.

The tax may also conceivably affect the return to labor and other factors of production in the two sectors of the economy. For example, if labor and capital are used in fixed proportions in the corporate sector, then it follows that when capital flows out of the corporate sector in the long run, so does some amount of labor. If the non-corporate sector does not employ capital and labor in the same ratio as the corporate sector, it follows that the return to labor has to change for the economy to return to a general equilibrium. It is possible that the general level of wages in the economy may fall as a result of the tax, if the corporate sector is relatively more labor intensive than the non-corporate sector, in order to induce the non-corporate sector to absorb the labor resource flowing from the corporate sector. The extent of such changes in the prices of other inputs depends on the elasticities of substitution in production between capital and other factors in both the corporate and non-corporate sectors. Thus, the corporate income tax can also affect the real incomes of factor owners owning non-capital inputs.

The actual incidence of a corporate income tax is, of course, an empirical proposition to be determined with reference to appropriate data. Part B of this chapter discusses corporate income taxation in the United States and cites some empirical studies analyzing the incidence of the corporation income tax in this country.

B

Income Taxation in the United States

PERSONAL INCOME TAXATION

The taxation of personal income in the United States is often criticized by both economists and politicians for containing many tax preferences and "inequities." The Tax Reform Act of 1969 represents an attempt to provide a more "equitable" tax code. For example, in the tax year 1966, there were 154 individuals with adjusted gross incomes of $200,000 or more who paid *no* federal income tax. Although the recent tax reform legislation eliminates some of the tax preferences that made abuses possible, there are many who believe that there are still some fundamental weaknesses in the tax code that prevent the attainment of horizontal and vertical equity.

A major weakness in the tax code is the lack of any consistent definition of taxable income. The concept of income inherent in the tax code conforms neither to the flow nor the Haig-Simons definitions. Instead, there is discriminatory tax treatment of income by source and a multitude of allowable deductions from the tax base. Although the rate structure of the United States personal income tax is nominally progressive, the existence of tax preferences makes the real rate structure, after deductions and exemptions from the tax base, considerably less progressive than the nominal rate structure.

TAX PREFERENCES AND THE TAX REFORM ACT OF 1969[13]

The Personal Exemption

A basic deduction in the United States tax code is the "personal exemption." The 1969 tax reform increases the personal exemption allowed each taxpayer for himself and his dependents from $600 per year, in steps, to $750 per year in 1972. The philosophy of the personal exemption is that certain basic expenses are necessary for support of life, and that these basic expenses should be exempt from taxation by virtue of the fact that they are analogous to "inputs" (costs) in a productive process. While this is true, it must also be recognized that the benefits of the personal exemption to individual taxpaying households varies with both the size of the family and the marginal tax bracket. The personal exemption may have the effect of inducing households to expand their sizes, because additional children are, in fact, subsidized to some extent by the federal government. The extent of this subsidy depends on the marginal tax rate paid by the household. Using the 1972 personal exemption of $750, an additional child saves a family in the 14-percent marginal tax bracket $105 [$750(0.14)] in taxes per year, while a family in the 70-percent tax bracket saves $525 in taxes [$750(0.70)] per year.

The Low-Income Allowance

An innovation in the tax code introduced by the Tax Reform Act of 1969 is the "low-income allowance." This measure is designed specifically to provide tax relief to households whose taxable incomes are below the poverty level.

---

[13] Legislation enacted by Congress in late 1971 made some minor changes in the Tax Reform Act of 1969 and accelerated the introduction of some of its provisions into the tax code.

When fully effective in 1972, all households will be allowed a basic tax-free income allowance of $1,000, in addition to the personal exemption for each family member. This provision replaces the old minimum standard deduction that varied with family size ($200 plus $100 for each personal exemption). It provides tax relief for families whose finances are such that they cannot benefit from the standard deduction or itemized deductions. Table 9.1 shows how the low-income allowance works in the tax year 1972, when the personal exemption is $750 for households having one to four members.

TABLE 9.1

The Low-Income Allowance (LIA) and Tax-Free Income (1972)

Household size (S)	Personal exemptions (750) (S)	LIA	Tax-free income (750) (S) + LIA
1	750	1000	1750
2	1500	1000	2500
3	2250	1000	3250
4	3000	1000	4000

Thus, in 1972, a family of four with an income of $4000 or less does not have to file an income tax return. Their tax bill for federal income taxes is zero.

The Standard Deduction

The recent tax reform legislation also raises the standard deduction, in steps, to 15 percent of income to a maximum of $2000 in 1973. Individuals may elect to take either the low-income allowance (LIA) or the standard deduction or to itemize deductions. Since the LIA is fixed at $1000, households with incomes greater than $6666 (15 percent of which is $1000) will naturally elect to take the standard deduction or to itemize deductions. Thus, the standard deduction largely benefits middle-income households. Upper-income households tend to itemize their deductions, because by doing so, they can deduct amounts in excess of the maximum standard deduction $2000 (in 1973) from their taxable incomes.

Tax Preferences

Itemized deductions and tax-exempt income are called "tax preferences." While the Tax Reform Act of 1969 does not significantly curb tax preferences, it does seek to eliminate some of the abuses of the tax system by establishing a surtax of 10 percent in tax-preference income in excess of $30,000 for both individuals and corporations. Under the new system, only those who claim deductions and exemptions in excess of $30,000 are taxed on their tax preferences over that amount. This still leaves leeway for wealthy individuals to adjust their behavior to minimize their taxes.

Tax-Exempt Income

Income from a variety of sources escapes taxation completely under current federal tax regulations. Although these items are income by either the Haig-Simons or flow definition, they are not taxed for a variety of reasons. The following is an incomplete list of tax-free income sources in the United States:

1. Interest on state and municipal bonds.
2. Scholarship and fellowship grants.
3. Gifts, bequests, inheritances.
4. Social Security payments.
5. Accident, health, and casualty insurance proceeds.
6. Disability and death payments.
7. Life insurance proceeds.
8. Meals and lodgings (a form of income in kind).
9. Military allowances.
10. Rental allowances of clergymen.
11. Veterans' benefits.
12. The first $100 of dividends.

Some of these exemptions are made on legal or constitutional grounds. For example, many interpret the Constitution as prohibiting the federal government from taxing the interest on securities issued by the states and their political subdivisions. Others are made for "equity" reasons. The reader should recall that all tax preferences representing inconsistent application of the concept of income are in reality hidden subsidies to some activity. As an exercise, the reader may wish to study the preceding list and determine which groups in the population are benefiting from the exemptions. Any tax-exempt income, with the exception of interest earned on municipal securities, in excess of $30,000 in tax preferences, will be taxed at a proportional rate of 10 percent.

Deductions

The federal tax code is abundant with possibilities for itemized deductions by taxpayers. All interest on personal debt is deductible from gross income. The dominant component of this interest deduction is interest on home mortgages. While interest justifiably can be considered an expense item in running a household, its deduction results in differing tax treatment of renters and investors in assets other than homes and consumer durables relative to homeowners and individuals purchasing consumer durables on credit. The reason for this is that the homeowner or purchaser of consumer durables is not taxed on the imputed return he earns on his assets, while the investor in financial assets (stocks, bonds, and so forth) is taxed on the monetary yield of his assets. In effect, the interest rates paid by debtors who itemize their deductions are subsidized by the government. For example, a taxpayer in the 70-percent marginal tax bracket who makes a loan at an interest of 12 percent per year really pays only 3.6 percent per year, because he saves 70 cents in taxes for each dollar of interest he pays. In effect, the federal government pays the remaining 8.4 percent [12(0.7)] of his loan through reduced tax collections. This subsidy to borrowing is likely to result in an overallocation of resources to consumer credit.

Many taxes paid to state and local governments are also deductible from gross income for individuals who choose to itemize their deductions. These include state and local income taxes, retail-sales taxes, and local property taxes. Individuals who itemize deductions and who live in areas with high local tax rates receive the benefits of this provision at the expense of other taxpayers. The allowance of such deductions undoubtedly stems from the belief that individuals should not be excessively burdened by taxation, irrespective of the level of the government that does the taxing. This argument neglects the fact that taxes paid to local governments "buy" a different "package" of public services than do taxes paid to the federal government. Those who live in high-tax localities conceivably receive better schools, roads, sanitation services, and so forth than do those living in low-tax localities. Thus, the deduction of local taxes ignores the benefits received by the individuals who pay those taxes. To allow deduction for the costs of local public services, while not attempting to impute the benefits flowing from those services, results in an inconsistent definition of income. Since the measurement of benefits flowing to individuals from local public services is difficult, many argue that the deduction of state and local taxes should not be allowed.

Deductions also are allowed for charitable contributions up to 50 percent of adjusted gross income. The effect of this provision is to subsidize philanthropy. If the expenditures of the philanthropic and other non-profit (for example, educational) institutions substitute for public expenditures, then the effect of this provision may be to reduce taxes in the aggregate as public spending is reduced.

In addition, individuals are allowed to deduct medical expenditures in excess of 3 percent of gross income within certain limits. This deduction is allowed under the assumption that medical expenses constitute "irregular" and uncertain burdens that can seriously impair tax-paying ability. Individuals are also allowed to deduct payments for health insurance on a limited basis, even when these payments do not exceed 3 percent of gross income.

Other less-important deductions from gross income are allowed for depreciation, bad debts, depletion in natural resource investments, moving expenses, and so on. Deductions for taxes, interests, contributions, and medical expenses are the four major tax-preference deductions. In the tax year 1968, there were over 32 million tax returns with itemized deductions accounting for adjusted gross income to approximately $369 billion. These returns made total deductions of about $69 billion. The largest category of deductions was taxes, which accounted for over $24 billion. Interest is the second largest category, with $18.5 billion deducted. Contributions accounted for about $11 billion, while medical expenses totaled about $8.5 billion. Table 9.2 shows itemized deductions by income class in the tax year 1968.

TABLE 9.2

Individual Income Tax Returns with Itemized Deductions (by adjusted gross income classes, 1968)

[Money figures in millions of dollars. Preliminary. Includes returns of resident aliens. Based on a sample of returns as filed, unaudited except to insure proper execution.]

Adjusted gross income classes	Returns with itemized deductions (1,000)	Adjusted gross income	Itemized deductions					
			Total	Taxes	Interests	Contributions	Medical expenses	Other
Total	32,066	368,983	69,202	24,386	18,526	11,157	8,485	6,650
Taxable returns	30,409	363,136	65,872	23,696	17,826	10,682	7,391	6,280
Under $2000	285	462	149	42	12	27	48	19
$2000–$2999	774	1,970	544	153	60	99	172	60
$3000–$3999	1,248	4,406	1,100	328	157	192	297	127
$4000–$4999	1,659	7,485	1,812	540	335	284	443	211
$5000–$9999	11,963	91,093	18,755	5,979	5,142	2,644	2,996	1,993
$10,000–$14,999	8,739	106,236	18,994	6,905	5,878	2,654	1,889	1,669
$15,000–$49,999	5,367	115,589	18,431	7,514	4,965	3,020	1,378	1,554
$50,000 and over	373	35,894	6,087	2,234	1,276	1,760	168	647
Nontaxable returns	1,657	5,847	3,329	690	700	475	1,093	371

SOURCE: U.S. Treasury Department, Internal Revenue Service, *Preliminary Statistics of Income, 1968: Individual Income Tax Returns.*

Capital Gains and Personal Incomes

Long-term net capital gains are taxed at preferential rates. *Long-term gains* are defined as those realized on assets held longer than six months, provided that they are not "stocks-in-trade." Short-term gains are taxed as regular income. An individual who realizes net long-term gains can include half the gain in regular income and have half taxed as regular income. The long-term net capital gains are, in effect, taxed at one half the taxpayer's marginal rate of taxation. However, the maximum rate of taxation on such gains is 25 percent. Individuals who are above the 50-percent marginal tax bracket benefit from this provision. Taxpayers may also deduct 50 percent of net long-term capital losses from regular income under current rules.

The recent tax legislation retains the six-month holding period definition of long-term gains but stipulates that those taxpayers earning capital gains in excess of $50,000 per year are no longer eligible for the 25 percent maximum rate on the excess over $50,000. Instead, they have to pay one half of their marginal rate of taxation on the net long-term gains above $50,000, when the new legislation is fully effective in 1972. Since the maximum marginal tax rate is 70 percent, this means that the rate of taxation on excess gains will be 35 percent. Furthermore, under the new legislation, individuals with tax preferences in excess of $30,000 are subject to a surtax of 10 percent on the 50 percent of net long-term gains deducted from gross incomes. For these individuals, the effective rate of taxation on long-term gains will increase somewhat.

The fact that, despite the reforms of the 1969 legislation, capital gains are still taxed at preferentially lower rates than is other income implies that there is still an incentive to convert ordinary income into capital gains (for example, executives receive salary compensation in the form of corporate stock to achieve capital gains). However, the moderate increases in tax rates applied to capital gains earned by very wealthy individuals will tend to diminish this incentive. The new legislation also introduces a maximum tax on earned income of 50 percent for individuals with less than $30,000 in tax preferences in 1972. Earned income consists largely of wages, salaries, and other compensation from the sale of personal services. The new provision narrows the gap between effective tax rates on capital gains and earned income for wealthy taxpayers. This is likely to further diminish the incentive to convert ordinary income into capital gains.

OTHER ASPECTS OF PERSONAL INCOME TAXATION IN THE UNITED STATES

In addition to the tax preferences discussed, the tax code allows numerous deductions for costs incurred in earning income. These costs have already been discussed in Part A. Among the costs that the United States tax code allows as deductions are child care payments, certain educational expenses, union dues, dues to professional associations, home office expenses, expenses for work clothes, and expenses incurred in seeking work.

The tax laws also allow income averaging on a voluntary basis. An individual may average his income under the new tax laws if his current year's income is $3,000 greater than 120 percent of the average of taxable income in the preceding four years. In addition, a taxpayer must be a citizen of the United States and have provided at least 50 percent of his own support throughout the five-year averaging period. Averageable income is the difference between the current year's income and 120 percent of the previous four years' average income. An individual who averages his income applies a special formula to averageable income to compute his tax bill. The effect of this formula is to spread the tax burden over five years and compute an average rate of annual taxation. By doing this, the taxpayer escapes the burden of sharply progressive rates on his current year's income. For an individual who experiences a substantial increase in taxable income in the current year, the tax saving achieved by averaging can be considerable.

ALLOCATIVE EFFECTS OF INCOME TAXATION IN THE UNITED STATES

As indicated in Part A of this chapter, income taxation affects choices concerning the allocation of resources within the private sector. Taxes on income affect choices concerning the allocation of time between work and leisure and the allocation of current income between consumption and savings. In addition, the existence of tax preferences has rather subtle effects on the allocation of resources among particular uses. Tax preferences can result in individuals basing their economic choices, in part, on tax incentives rather than on true economic incentives.

A number of early studies on the effect of the progressive rate structure on the work-leisure choice indicated that the effect on the work-leisure choice may be negligible for higher-income taxpayers.[14] However, these studies based their conclusions on interviews with executives. The executives interviewed apparently responded to sociological incentives, such as prestige and other indicators of success in their careers, rather than to monetary rewards. The results of these studies were criticized on many grounds. The interview method was suspect as a reliable indicator of true attitudes, and it was argued that executives are not representative of other taxpaying groups in the population.

[14] For example, see Thomas H. Sanders, *Effects of Taxation on Executives*, Harvard University, Graduate School of Business Administration, Boston, 1951; or George F. Break, "Income Taxes and Incentives to Work: An Empirical Study," *American Economic Review*, September 1957.

A more recent study by Arnold Harberger of the effect of taxes on the work-leisure choices, using 1961 data, indicates that the distortion in the work-leisure choice as a result of the progressive rate structure in the United States income tax may be about $1 billion per year in lost output[15] when compared to an equal-yield neutral tax (say, a head tax). His method involves a rough estimation of the elasticity of supply of work effort and the wage income earned in each tax bracket. Harberger points out that reductions in work effort may come in the following principal forms:[16]

1. Longer vacations.
2. Increased early retirement.
3. Less labor force participation of women.
4. Less supplemental labor income from sources other than main employment.

Harberger's analysis leads him to believe that the income tax results in a 5-percent reduction in work effort in the $25,000–$50,000 bracket and an 11-percent reduction in the highest tax brackets relative to an equal-yield, lump-sum tax. He concludes that this distortion reduced GNP by about $1 billion in 1961. Harberger further argues that this efficiency loss can be reduced by lowering marginal tax rates and eliminating or reducing many tax preferences. Such a move would reduce the distortion in the work-leisure choice and collect approximately the same amount of revenue.

DISTRIBUTIVE EFFECTS OF INCOME TAXATION IN THE UNITED STATES

The progressive rate structure of the United States income tax is designed to redistribute income from the relatively rich to the relatively poor. The marginal rates of taxation vary from 14 percent on the first $500 of taxable income to 70 percent on taxable income in excess of $100,000. However, the degree of progression in the rate structure is markedly reduced by the existence of the multitude of tax preferences present in the tax code. Simple calculations of the average rate of taxation by income class for the year 1960 indicated that the lowest income classes paid approximately 3.5 percent of their income in income taxes, while the highest income classes paid about 25.9 percent. This data led Richard Goode to conclude that the income tax does serve to reduce income concentration.[17]

---

[15] Arnold Harberger, "Taxation, Resource Allocation, and Welfare," in National Bureau of Economic Research and the Brookings Institution, *The Role of Direct and Indirect Taxes in the Federal Revenue System*, Princeton University Press, Princeton, N.J., 1964, pp. 25–80.

[16] Harberger, p. 50.

[17] Goode, p. 263.

But his conclusions are based on personal income statistics rather than on the Haig-Simons or flow concepts of income. A recent study by Benjamin Okner indicates that, despite the high nominal marginal rate structure, the federal income tax does not significantly alter the distribution of income in the United States.[18] Using 1965 data, Okner concludes that the existence of tax preferences comes close to canceling the effect of the progressive rate structure.[19]

A somewhat more comprehensive study of the effect of taxes on the distribution of income by a tax foundation, using 1958 data, discovered that when all federal, state, and local taxes are considered (including property and sales taxes), the tax rate structure proves to be proportional in all but the highest-income class.[20] Furthermore, using tax-foundation data, Michael McElroy shows that, when income is broadly defined to include both realized and unrealized capital gains, the overall tax rate structure may even be somewhat regressive.[21] Table 9.3 gives the results of the tax-foundation study and the modified results when capital gains are considered income as in the Haig-Simons definition of income.

TABLE 9.3
The Burden of Federal, State, and Local Taxes by Income Class

1958 income	Taxes as a percent of total income	Taxes as a percent of total income and capital gains
Less than $4,000	27.5	26.6
$4000–$5999	26.0	25.4
$6000–$7999	25.8	24.5
$8000–$14,999	24.2	21.9
$15,000 and over	38.1	26.0

SOURCE: M. B. McElroy, "Capital Gains and the Concept and Measurement of Income," *Proceedings of the Business and Economic Statistics Section of the American Statistical Association*, 1970, p. 138. Copyright © 1970 by American Statistical Association.

The revenue raised by the 14–70-percent progressive income tax could be obtained alternatively from approximately a 20-percent proportional income tax with no tax preferences. While substituting a proportional income tax for the current progressive levy is likely to increase the tax rates for some low-income households somewhat (incomes less than $5,000 per year), it is also likely that such a substitution would increase the rate of taxation for many

[18] Benjamin A. Okner, *Income Distribution and the Federal Income Tax*, Institute of Public Administration, University of Michigan, Ann Arbor, 1966, p. 6.

[19] Okner, p. 7.

[20] Tax Foundation, Inc., *Allocation of the Tax Burden by Income Class*, New York, May 1960.

[21] McElroy, p. 138.

upper-income households (say, those with incomes in excess of $25,000 per year) who currently benefit from many tax preferences. Thus, a substitution need not necessarily redistribute income in favor of the "rich." The "rich" currently pay low effective rates of taxation anyway.

THE CORPORATION INCOME TAX

The corporate income tax in the United States taxes the net revenues of corporate business organizations above $25,000 per year at a proportional rate of 48 percent. A lower rate of 22 percent is applied to the first $25,000 of net revenues. *Net revenue* is defined as the total revenue earned by a corporation less all input costs, including depreciation and interest on loans. Capital gains earned by corporations are taxed at a rate of 30 percent. In addition, there is an averaging provision in the law that allows corporations to carry losses backward for three years or forward for five years. The revenue collected from the corporation income tax accounts for about 20 percent of total federal tax collections.

Among the controversial features of the corporation income tax are certain provisions that allow preferential tax treatment of specific industries. Perhaps the most controversial of these provisions is the depletion allowance given many extractive industries. The depletion allowances permit such industries to deduct a percentage of their profits from the tax base before computing taxable incomes. This allowance subsidizes the operations of such industries. Many have argued that such a subsidy is not justified on allocative grounds, while others argue that it is necessary to cover risks involved in searching for scarce deposits of natural resources.

Among the industries that receive the benefits of depletion allowances are oil and gas producers. Depletion allowances are also given to producers of timber, clay, sand, gravel, and other resources. The Tax Reform Act of 1969 reduced the depletion allowance available to the oil industry from 27½ percent to 22 percent. By exempting a portion of net incomes from taxation, the depletion allowances serve to induce capital to flow into those extractive industries receiving the benefits in excess of that which would be invested in the absence of such allowances.

Other industries receiving preferential tax treatment include financial institutions and real estate dealers. Financial institutions are allowed deductions for "bad debt" reserves that lower their tax burdens, and there are special real estate depreciation rules that benefit the real estate industry.

As the discussion in Part A of this chapter seems to indicate, one of the chief policy issues concerning the corporation income tax is its incidence. While the tax is levied on the corporate sector, there is good reason to suspect that the tax is shifted to factor owners in non-incorporated businesses and to consumers through higher prices. A number of empirical studies have been conducted on the incidence of the corporation income tax. Unfortunately, there is not, as yet, any general agreement concerning who actually pays the tax.

An econometric study by Krzyzaniak and Musgrave concludes that the corporation income tax has no effect on the return to capital and is, in fact, fully reflected in higher prices to consumers.[22] A more recent study by Cragg, Harberger, and Mieszkowski[23] criticizes the Krzyzaniak-Musgrave model for not adequately accounting for cyclical effects on the data (the return to capital 1935–1959). This more recent study concludes that the tax is fully borne by capital owners and is not reflected in higher prices. The burden of the corporate income tax is apparently well concealed. Economists have not as yet discovered who pays this tax.

INCOME TAXATION AND INCOME MAINTENANCE

Negative Income Taxation

In recent years, a number of economists have recommended using the personal income tax as a tool for alleviating poverty. Such plans for "negative income taxation" of poverty incomes have received a great deal of attention as a method for reforming the welfare payment system in the United States. Although a detailed discussion of the current income maintenance system in the United States is beyond the scope of this work, one may note that many persons argue that such payments serve to perpetuate poverty by dampening the work incentive of the welfare recipients. The reason for this stems from the fact that benefits are often terminated when poor households begin to earn incomes. Their welfare payments are sometimes reduced almost on a dollar-for-dollar earned basis. This, in effect, subjects the poor to a 100-percent marginal tax rate. In addition, it is argued that many aspects of income maintenance in this country subject the poor to degrading investigations and qualifying tests. One program of public assistance, Aid to Families of Dependent Children (AFDC), has been extensively criticized. This program mainly aids fatherless households with one or more children. The AFDC program has apparently created an artificial incentive for fathers to leave their families so as to render them eligible for welfare payments.

A negative income tax plan could replace the existing income maintenance system. One such possible plan has been proposed by Milton Friedman.[24] His

[22] Marion Krzyzaniak and R. A. Musgrave, *The Shifting of the Corporation Income Tax*, Johns Hopkins Press, Baltimore, 1963.

[23] Cragg, Harberger, Mieszkowski, "Empirical Evidence on the Incidence of the Corporation Income Tax," *Journal of Political Economy*, December 1967.

[24] See Milton Friedman, "The Case for the Negative Income Tax," in M. R. Laird (ed.), *Republican Papers*, Praeger, New York, 1968.

plan would establish an income guarantee that would vary with family size and a negative tax rate of 50 percent while abolishing all other governmental programs designed to redistribute income, including social security, minimum wage legislation, tariffs, rent controls, progressive income taxation, and others. Such a plan would have to be integrated with the income tax rate structure. The rate structure would be modified in such a manner so that households below the poverty income line (defined as $3,968 for a family of four by the U.S. Department of Health, Education, and Welfare for the year 1970) would receive negative tax stipends, while households with income substantially above the poverty level would have their tax rates increased to finance payments to the poor. This, in effect, would substantially increase the progressiveness of the tax rate structure. To properly gauge the effects of any negative income tax plan, one must view it as an income redistribution plan. As such, it must increase the real incomes of some households while decreasing the real incomes of other households. A relevant policy question thus becomes, "which households in the income distribution will pay for the plan, and which households will receive its direct benefits?"

Direct income redistribution can be justified on efficiency grounds when there are externalities associated with the transfer of income among households. Utility functions among households may be interdependent when the upper-income groups feel "compassion" for the poor or fear that low-income individuals may riot or turn to crime if their income levels are below some poverty level. Under such circumstances, income transfers provide indirect benefits to those households financing the plan as well as to those low-income households receiving direct benefits.

Often individuals get benefits from low-income groups engaging in particular consumption activities, such as the consumption of food, housing, and education. In many cases, transfer payments are made "in kind" to assure that the poor engage in consumption activities that generate external benefits. This is the rationale for subsidized public housing, food distribution, and education programs for the poor. Of course, any such programs restrict the range of choices available to poor households, and for this reason, many prefer direct cash stipends to transfers "in kind."

Consider the Friedman version of the negative income tax plan. Friedman points out that "the present welfare programs that provide [an income transfer] are . . . a mess. They are costly, inefficient, destructive of the pride, self-reliance, and incentive of the people helped, and interfere seriously with the effective operation of the economic system."[25] Friedman recommends scrapping the "present grab-bag" of redistributive programs for a minimum income guarantee through negative income taxation.

All negative income tax plans have two basic parameters: an income guarantee Y_g and a negative tax rate t_n. Under the Friedman plan, the income

[25] Friedman, in *Republican Papers*, pp. 203–204.

guarantee varies with family size. For a family of four, the income guarantee is, say, $1500 per year. The negative tax rate applied to earned income is 50 percent. This means that for each dollar the household earns by its own work efforts, the welfare stipend is reduced by 50 cents. The tax rate is considerably lower than the 100-percent rate implicit in many of the existing welfare programs and is, therefore, believed to be more conducive to work effort relative to the existing income maintenance programs. But the Tax Reform Act of 1969 introduced a maximum marginal tax rate on earned income of 50 percent. This means that poor families, according to the Friedman plan, will be paying the highest marginal tax rate on earned income in the income tax rate schedule. They will pay the same marginal tax rate as the richest families. The 50-percent tax rate may still be too inhibiting to work incentive.

Under the Friedman plan, a family of four has an income guarantee of about $1500.[26] This means that if their earned income is zero, the transfer T they receive from the government (their negative taxes) is $1500. For each dollar of income earned, the transfer payment is reduced by the negative tax rate of 50 percent applied to that dollar of earning, or by 50 cents. This implies that eventually the transfer payment will be reduced to zero and the family will begin paying positive taxes. The level of income at which this occurs is called the "break-even income."

The transfer received by the family can be expressed algebraically as follows:

$$T = Y_g - t_n Y_e \tag{9.6}$$

where T is the dollar value of the transfer payment, Y_g is the income guarantee, t_n is the negative tax rate, and Y_e is earned income. The break-even level of income Y_B can be computed by setting the value of transfer payments T equal to zero.

$$0 = Y_g - t_n Y_B \tag{9.7}$$

$$Y_B = \frac{Y_g}{t_n} \tag{9.8}$$

Y_B is the level of earned income at which the family is neither receiving negative tax payments nor paying positive taxes. Under the Friedman plan, a family of four reaches the break-even level of income when earned income becomes $3000 per year ($Y_g = 1500$; $t_n = 50$ percent; thus, $Y_B = 1500/0.5 = 3000).

A family's disposable income Y_d may be computed by summing earned income and negative tax payments.

$$Y_d = Y_e + T \tag{9.9}$$

[26] Friedman, in *Republican Papers*, p. 209.

For example, suppose a family of four has earned income of $2000 per year. Its disposable income is $2000 plus 1500 minus [(0.5) (2000)], or $2500 per year.

A crucial, but difficult, step in implementing a negative income tax plan comes after the break-even level of income is reached. After that point, the family begins paying positive taxes. Since the lowest marginal tax rate in the current federal income tax rate structure is 14 percent, the family experiences a sharp reduction in its marginal tax rate after it reaches the break-even level of earned income. The method through which the relatively high, negative tax rates are merged into the relatively low, positive rates can substantially affect the cost of the plan and its effect on work incentive.

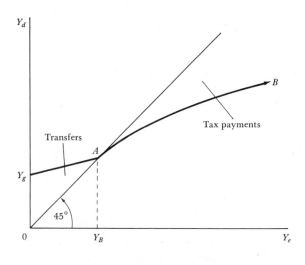

FIGURE 9.4

One method would simply let the marginal tax rate fall sharply after the break-even level of income is reached. This technique is illustrated in Figure 9.4, where disposable income Y_d is plotted against earned income. After the break-even level of income Y_B is reached, the family begins paying positive tax rates that increase with income. The curvilinear shape of the tax line AB, after B, reflects the progressive rate schedule.

Another technique, recommended by James Tobin, Joseph Pechman, and Peter Mieszkowski involves a gradual merging of the negative tax rate into the positive tax rates.[27] This technique benefits a substantial number of taxpayers not receiving actual negative tax payments by reducing their tax payments relative to their taxes in the absence of the plan. The effect of this plan is illustrated in Figure 9.5. The calculations are based on a $2600-income guarantee for a family of four, a 50-percent negative tax rate, and the 1967

[27] See James Tobin, Joseph Pechman, and Peter Mieszkowski, "Is a Negative Income Tax Practical?" *Yale Law Journal*, November 1967.

marginal tax rate schedule.[28] Families with incomes between points *A* and *D* ($3000 to $6144) experience tax reductions relative to the current tax schedule, while all households with incomes below the break-even level of income of $5200 are paid negative taxes. Such a merging of the two rate structures greatly increases the cost of the plan. To finance this added cost, all households not experiencing tax reductions have to undergo sharp increases in taxes, thereby shifting the line *DB* (the 1967 tax rate schedule) downward.

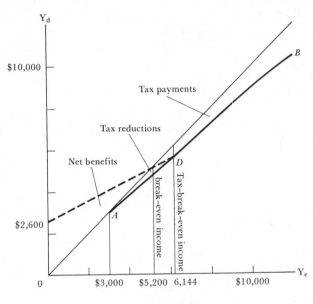

FIGURE 9.5

NOTE: t_n applies up to the point where $t_n Y_e = t Y_e$ where t is the rate in present tax system, that is, where tax liability is equal to that which would have been paid under the regular tax structure.

SOURCE: James Tobin, J. A. Pechman, and Peter M. Mieszkowski, "Is a Negative Income Tax Practical?" *The Yale Law Journal*, November 1967. Reprinted by permission of the Yale Law Journal Company and Fred B. Rothman & Company from *The Yale Law Journal*, 77, p. 7.

Negative Income Taxation, Work Incentive, and Financing Cost

It has been argued that the lower marginal tax rate associated with the negative income tax plans compared to existing income maintenance programs will be more favorable to work effort by welfare recipients. Nevertheless, economic analysis leads one to expect that the negative tax plan still inhibits work incentive relative to work incentive in the absence of any income main-

[28] Tobin considers alternative plans as well with differing income guarantees and negative tax rates. Figure 9.5 appears on p. 7 of Tobin, Pechman, and Mieszkowski.

tenance scheme. Individuals who receive negative income tax transfers experience an increase in real incomes. This leads to an income effect that is unfavorable to work effort as individuals have an incentive to increase consumption of leisure. In addition, families subject to higher marginal tax rates as a result of the high negative tax rate experience a substitution effect unfavorable to work effort. The 50-percent tax rate cuts wages in half. Both the income and substitution effects introduced by the plan, assuming tastes are fixed, are unfavorable to work effort. However, these effects are likely to be much less inhibiting than those stemming from an income maintenance system with an implicit marginal tax rate of 100 percent.

But the negative income tax plan is properly viewed as an income redistribution mechanism. This implies that some households must experience a reduction in real incomes in order to finance the transfer payments accruing to lower-income families. Although some of the cost of the program can undoubtedly be financed out of resources currently devoted to existing income maintenance programs, the cost of a new plan may be considerably higher than the cost of existing programs if the income guarantee is set at a relatively higher level and the number of households eligible for transfers is increased. In addition, the particular scheme chosen to merge the negative tax rates with lower positive tax rates also affects the cost. If the real income of the poor is increased relative to existing programs, it follows that higher-income households have to experience a reduction in real incomes. The only realistic way to finance such an income redistribution plan is to use the income tax. Any other financing arrangements (such as consumption taxes or inflation) are likely to vitiate the effects of the income redistribution plan because their regressiveness may decrease the real income of the poor. Thus, it may be necessary to sharply increase the marginal and average tax rates of households not benefiting from the plan. This may be severely inhibiting to the work incentive of these households. The net effect on work effort depends on the possible increase in work effort by the poor and the possible decrease in work effort due to higher average tax rates for the income groups not receiving negative tax benefits.

SUMMARY

Taxes on income are a major source of revenue to federal and state governments. A fundamental problem in implementing an income tax is defining the tax base. Income is usually measured as an annual flow or an annual accrual. The flow concept defines income as an annual flow of goods and services measured in monetary units. The accrual concept views income as an annual increase in purchasing power. Both households and corporations pay income taxes in the United States. Deductions are allowed from gross income to arrive at *taxable income*. Tax-exempt income and special deductions from gross income are called "tax preferences." The many tax preferences inherent in the United States income tax code make the concept of taxable income conform to neither the flow nor accrual concepts. Tax preferences are justified on efficiency grounds only when they serve to internalize externalities.

To the extent that taxpayers can control their incomes, they can control the amount of income taxes they pay. In addition, when tax preferences exist, taxpayers can control their tax burdens by varying the sources of their income and their economic activities. Income taxes can affect choices concerning the allocation of time between work and leisure, consumption versus saving, and the flow of resources to certain tax-preferred activities relative to other activities. The allocative effects of income taxation are likely to result in efficiency losses for the community. The efficiency loss due to the impact of income taxation on the work-leisure choice depends, at least in part, on the elasticity of supply of labor.

Taxes on corporate income can affect the return to capital and other inputs and/or can serve to raise prices. Corporate income taxes may cause resources to flow from the corporate sector to alternative uses. This reduces the return to savings and induces a consequent reduction in capital formation. The incidence of the corporation income tax remains an empirical problem that has yet to be resolved.

A major weakness in the current United States tax code is the lack of any consistent definition of taxable income. Although the rate schedule of the federal income tax is nominally progressive, the existence of many tax preferences tends to result in a considerable moderation of such progression. The Tax Reform Act of 1969 sought to provide some relief to low-income taxpayers, while moderating some of the tax preferences used by upper-income households. It is, however, doubtful that these innovations will result in any significant redistribution of the income tax burden. Recently, a number of plans to redistribute income through "negative income taxation" have been proposed. It should be kept in mind that the revenue raised by the current 14–70-percent progressive income tax could alternatively be obtained from approximately a 20-percent proportional income tax with no tax preferences.

10

Taxes on Consumption

Taxes on consumption represent the major source of revenues for state governments in the United States. For example, in the fiscal year 1967, consumption taxes that usually are levied on retail sales accounted for nearly 60 percent of total state revenues. In this country, the consumption base is tapped as a revenue source, as well, by the federal and local governments. In fact, prior to 1913 the major federal source of tax revenues was the customs duty which is a tax on the consumption of imported goods. Today, the federal government relies on excise taxes—those levied on the consumption of specific goods and services, such as tires or telephone use—for about 9 percent of its revenues, while local governments rely on retail-sales taxes for about 7 percent of their revenues.

While the choice of an index of ability to pay necessarily involves a value judgment, some economists have argued that consumption is a better index of "ability to pay" than is income.[1] General consumption taxes do not directly tax savings or investment incomes. But insofar as lifetime consumption and disposable incomes are equal for most households, substitution of a consumption tax for an equal-yield income tax merely results in a temporal redistribution of tax payments for most households. The consumption tax does, however, encourage individual households to accumulate estates to transfer to the next generation relative to the income tax and in the absence of any wealth-transfer taxes.

Taxes on consumption can be *general* or *specific*. Specific consumption taxes are levied on certain types of consumption activities. They are, in other words,

---

[1] See Nicholas Kaldor, *An Expenditure Tax*, Allen and Unwin, London, 1955, chapter 1.

discriminatory taxes. Specific consumption taxes usually are called "excise taxes" and may be levied either as a unit tax or an ad valorem tax. For example, federal taxes on automobiles and telephone services are excise taxes. In cases where the tax is designed to internalize the externalities associated with particular consumption activities, excises are called "sumptuary taxes." Federal and state taxes on alcoholic beverages, tobacco, and certain types of amusements are examples of sumptuary taxes.

General consumption taxes are, at least in theory, levied on all forms of consumption expenditures without discrimination. The most widely used general consumption tax in the United States is the retail-sales tax that provides the bulk of revenues to state governments. Retail-sales taxes usually are levied as a fixed percentage of most expenditures on the retail level.

Other forms of general consumption taxation include expenditure taxes, turnover taxes, and value-added taxes. An *expenditure tax* differs from other forms of consumption taxes in that it is a *direct*, rather than an *indirect*, tax. That is to say, it is levied on households rather than on the items they consume. Under expenditure taxation, each household files an annual return on which it lists its consumption expenditure, similar to the form used to collect personal income taxes. This type of tax makes personal exemptions and deductions from the tax base administratively feasible. A *turnover* tax is levied on consumption at every stage of production. Thus, turnover taxes are levied on the consumption of intermediate goods as well as final goods. A *value-added tax* (VAT) is also a multi-stage levy, but it allows deductions from the tax base for the purchase of intermediate goods at each level of production. This latter form of taxation is used widely in Western European nations. The relative merits of these alternative forms of general consumption taxation will be discussed in detail.

THE TAX BASE

General Consumption Taxation

In theory, a general consumption tax is levied on the final consumption of all goods and services. Under the foregoing definition of the tax base, the purchase of inputs and intermediate goods used to produce more goods and services is exempt from taxation. Furthermore, under a precise definition of the consumption base, all capital expenditures are exempt from taxation. This includes the consumption of consumer durables, such as homes and automobiles, that yield service flows over a long period of time as well as the consumption of producer durables, such as machinery. The service flows emanating from these capital assets (that is, depreciation) are, however, included in the tax base. An administrative problem develops in attempting to find an acceptable guideline to determine those expenditures for consumption and those for capital assets.

Of course, savings and interest are exempt from taxation until the time they are converted into final consumption. As has been indicated, the general consumption tax taxes the same base as a general personal income tax for households consuming all their income over their lifetimes. The difference lies solely in the timing of tax payments and the consequent interest saving to households under the consumption tax.

In practice, few "general" consumption taxes are implemented in such a way as to conform to this precise definition of the tax base. This is attributable to both administrative problems and political constraints. For example, many retail-sales taxes are levied only on the consumption of tangible goods. The consumption of personal services, such as haircuts, entertainment and transportation services are usually exempt from the tax. In addition, many states that levy retail-sales taxes exempt the consumption of certain "basic" goods from taxation in order to achieve a more "equitable" distribution of the tax burden. Thus, the consumption of food and grocery items as well as medicine and drugs are often exempt from taxation. Finally, many consumption taxes are levied on the purchase of capital goods rather than on the depreciation of such goods. For example, most retail-sales taxes in the United States are levied on the purchases of automobiles and other consumer durables. In the case where these durable goods subject to consumption taxes are purchased by business firms, they increase the marginal costs of production and are reflected in higher retail prices that are then used as the base to apply the consumption tax again. This results in "pyramiding" of taxes and a consequent higher tax rate to be borne by final consumers.

To the extent that actual "general" consumption taxes allow exemptions and tax capital expenditures, they can no longer be considered "general" taxes. Instead, they are specific taxes that are likely to distort consumption patterns among goods and services relative to the pattern in the absence of taxation. For example, if personal services are exempt from taxation under a retail-sales tax, one expects more consumption of these services relative to the taxed consumption goods than consumption in the absence of taxation. A sales tax levied on the consumption of certain capital goods purchased by business firms results in relatively higher rates of taxation for the consumption of goods whose productive process makes intensive uses of the taxed capital goods. This, in turn, is likely to distort economic choices.

The Tax Rate

A truly general consumption tax taxes all consumption activities at the same rate. Usually, this is some fixed percentage rate. Thus, a general retail-sales tax is a proportional tax on all final consumption activities. If the rates of taxation vary with the consumption activities, the tax likely is discriminatory and distorts resource allocation among consumption goods and services. At the extreme, a specific excise tax on one commodity applies differential tax rates.

The rate is positive on the consumption of the specific good upon which the excise is levied and zero for the consumption of all other goods and services.

In practice, it may be deemed desirable to apply tax rates that vary with the types and amounts of consumption activities. For example, the consumption of "luxury" goods may be taxed at a higher rate than ordinary consumption, while the consumption of necessities, such as food, may be taxed at lower rates to achieve a collectively chosen equity objective. Progressive rates of taxation on consumption expenditures can be implemented as well through machinery designed to administer an expenditure tax. Both the definition of the tax base and the choice of the rate structure are properly regarded as collective decisions to be made according to some collective decision rule.

Specific Consumption Taxation

As the discussion of general consumption taxation has suggested, *specific taxation* is present whenever exemptions are allowed from the tax base and/or different consumption activities are subject to differential tax rates. This may be considered desirable on either equity or efficiency grounds. Differential taxation of consumption alters the tax incidence and may be used to help achieve a certain equity goal. Furthermore, when the consumption of a particular good or service is believed to generate externalities (for example, liquor consumption), relatively high tax rates on that consumption can serve to internalize the external costs. In any event, the tax base under specific consumption taxation is some subset of the general consumption base.

ALLOCATIVE EFFECTS

Consider the allocative effects of a truly general proportional consumption tax. A general consumption tax lowers the return to work effort in a fashion similar to that of income taxation. Rather than suffering a decrease in wages at the source level, workers now find that, assuming the consumption tax is fully reflected in retail prices, each dollar of wages purchases fewer goods and services. Thus, the general sales tax is likely to distort individual choices between work and leisure. Provided that the supply of work effort is not completely inelastic, a proportional consumption tax either increases or decreases the quantity of work effort supplied by the individual, depending on the relative strengths of the income and substitution effects (see Chapter 9).

On the other hand, the general consumption tax does not introduce any efficiency loss for the economy in the choice between consumption and saving. The reason for this is that interest income is not taxed under the consumption levy. As a result, the interest paid by investors is the same as the interest earned by savers. This implies that, in the absence of any other taxes or distortions in the economy, the independent maximizing behavior of investors and savers achieves an efficient allocation of resources between present and future consumption under a proportional consumption tax. The marginal productivity of capital is equated with the community's marginal rate of time preference at one clear-cut interest rate.

Specific consumption taxes are likely to cause efficiency losses for the economy by distorting choices among various goods and services. The reasons for this, as well as a method for measuring the efficiency loss due to excise taxation, were discussed in detail in Chapter 7. Specific excise taxes may, however, be desirable on allocative grounds when they serve to internalize external costs associated with particular consumption activities. Furthermore, such taxes can be used to counteract undesirable effects on the work-leisure choices causing a reduction in work effort in favor of leisure. This can be accomplished by levying excise taxes on the consumption of those activities believed to be complementary with leisure, such as hobby equipment, amusements, and sports shows and sports equipment.

DISTRIBUTIVE EFFECTS

General consumption taxes often are accused of being extremely "regressive." Strictly speaking, most general sales taxes are proportional taxes in the sense that they tax *all* consumption, the tax base, at the same rate. However, insofar as saving as a percent of income tends to rise as income rises, such taxes are likely to have regressive redistributive effects when compared to the income base. Since lower-income households tend to spend high percentages of their incomes on current consumption, they tend to pay higher percentages of their current incomes in taxes relative to higher-income households under proportional consumption taxation without any exemptions, or deductions, from the tax base. But this argument is based on a short-time definition of the tax base. Its validity depends, in part, on the motives for saving by households. If all saving is simply deferred consumption, then defining the tax base as lifetime consumption per household results in a proportional consumption tax that attacks the same tax base as an equal-yield proportional income tax. The only benefit to savers under this comparison of a general consumption tax with an income tax is the interest the savers can earn on the amounts of their savings instead of the consumption taxes they would have paid had they chosen to consume the income in the current period rather than in the future. The general consumption tax is not as regressive with respect to income as one expects when saving is defined simply as deferred consumption. Thus, the redistributive effects of consumption taxation are partially contingent on the chosen time interval.

The situation becomes more complex when some savings are assumed to accrue in perpetuity, and there are no taxes on the transfers of such accrued wealth between generations. Provided that there are no wealth or wealth transfer taxes, the portion of savings that is never spent escapes taxation completely. To the extent that households accumulate fortunes in this manner, a general consumption tax tends to redistribute income in their favor.

To the extent that exemptions and deductions are allowed under general consumption taxation, the distributive effects of the tax are modified accordingly. In general, the tax burden is distributed according to household-expenditure patterns. Those households that spend proportionally more of their incomes on exempted consumption activities pay lower rates of taxation with respect to either the income or total consumption base. For example, if personal services are exempted from taxation under a retail-sales tax, then households that tend to spend higher proportions of their budgets on such services pay proportionately less in taxes. Furthermore, such exemption introduces allocative effects serving to induce all households to substitute services for goods in order to escape the burdens of taxation. In order to determine the actual redistributive effects of such an exemption, one has to empirically determine the manner in which expenditures on personal services varies with household-income levels.

The alleged "regressiveness" of retail-sales taxes can be alleviated, if not eliminated entirely, by judicious exemption of consumption goods and services upon which low-income households spend proportionately large amounts of their incomes. For example, assuming that low-income households spend large percentages of their incomes on basic foods and groceries, as well as on work clothes and medicines, the burden of sales taxation on low-income households can be significantly reduced by eliminating the consumption of these items from the tax base. The precise effect such exemptions have on the distribution of income remains an empirical question to be determined by appropriate research.

Similarly, the distributive effects of specific consumption taxes, such as excise taxes, customs duties, and sumptuary taxes, depend on household-expenditure patterns. An excise tax placed on the consumption of items used largely by high-income households is likely to have "progressive" redistributive effects. For example, provided that it is mainly the rich that consume jewelry, so-called luxury taxes levied on jewelry can serve to redistribute income away from the relatively "rich" and toward the relatively "poor."

FORMS OF GENERAL CONSUMPTION TAXATION

There are essentially four methods of general consumption taxation: single-stage sales taxation, turnover taxation (a multistage sales tax), value-added taxation, and the expenditure tax, which is levied directly on households rather than the items they consume. Although there are many forms of single-stage sales taxation (including manufacturer's sales taxes and wholesale-sales taxes), the text will only consider the retail-sales tax, the dominant form of general consumption taxation in the United States.

Retail-Sales Taxes

A *retail-sales tax* is usually an ad valorem tax of a fixed percent levied on the dollar value of retail purchases made by consumers. It usually is shifted forward 100 percent to consumers, depending on market conditions, thereby resulting in an increase in prices equal to the tax rate. The tax on retail sales is levied only on final-stage consumption and is collected from business establishments making retail sales. However, as previous discussion has indicated, in many instances, the tax exempts personal services and basic food items from the tax base. Furthermore, the tax sometimes is applied to purchases made by business firms to be used for further production, such as office furniture, automobiles, fuel, and other equipment. Thus, as a matter of practicality, the retail-sales tax cannot be considered either a general tax or one that is levied solely on final consumption.

Although there has been some controversy concerning whether or not a national retail-sales tax would be reflected in higher prices, the general consensus appears to be that prices will rise unless monetary authorities refuse to expand the money supply in response to the introduction of the tax.[2] If monetary authorities refuse to expand the money supply, the result could be unemployment or a reduction in factor income, depending on whether or not the returns to factors are inflexible downward. Under such circumstances (which would be unlikely), the tax can be borne by factor owners rather than by consumers. It can be safely assumed that a national retail-sales tax will result in an increase in consumer goods' prices relative to other prices when such a tax is substituted for, say, an equal-yield proportional income tax.

But as it is implemented in the United States, the retail-sales tax is primarily a state and local rather than a national fiscal instrument. Its merits must, therefore, be discussed as a locally administered tax within the framework of the federal system. Sales taxes are utilized as a major revenue source in forty-five states. In addition, many local governments use retail-sales taxes as revenue sources. Sales taxes were first enacted on the state level in the 1930s in response to the need for a more stable revenue source in the face of falling incomes and property values. The first local sales tax was enacted by the City of New York in 1934. Currently, over 3000 local governments utilize retail sales as a tax base. Most state and local retail-sales taxes are collected from retailers, and much of the administrative costs of the tax is, therefore, borne by retail firms. Some states compensate retailers for bearing the administrative costs.

A possible allocative effect of local sales taxation is a loss of retail trade to neighboring jurisdictions where the sales tax is either absent or applied at a lower rate. The migration of retail sales to another taxing jurisdiction can have the effect of reducing employment and/or business profits in the taxing jurisdiction. This, in turn, decreases the actual amount of taxes collected. To

---

[2] For a discussion of the controversy, see John F. Due, "Sales Taxation and the Consumer," *American Economic Review*, December 1963.

the extent that the demand for local retail goods is not perfectly inelastic, one expects only partial shifting of the retail-sales tax. That is, retail prices necessarily need not rise by the full amount of the tax if the tax causes sales to migrate. If the consumption tax base is elastic with respect to the rate of taxation, then increases in the rate of sales taxation result in less, not more, revenue collected.

In some cases, it is possible to apply a local sales tax on items purchased in neighboring jurisdictions but used in the taxing jurisdiction. This is accomplished through "use taxes." For example, in the case of an automobile purchased outside the taxing jurisdiction, the state or locality levying the tax can require the tax to be paid before the automobile can be registered in that area. Of course, use taxes are difficult to enforce in the case of consumption goods that are not required to be registered. Recent empirical evidence has indicated that sales tax-rate differentials among neighboring taxing jurisdictions (for example, the central city and the suburbs) do have significant effects on per-capita retail-sales distribution among the taxing jurisdictions.[3]

Perhaps the most frequent complaint made by some citizens against state and local sales taxes is the assertion that they are "regressive" with respect to income. Empirical research has, however, shown that the degree of regression tends to be rather mild. Research by the University of Wisconsin Tax Study Committee in 1959 indicates that a typical 2-percent sales tax levied on all goods including food but exempting most services accounts for about 4½ percent of the incomes of households with incomes of less than $1000 per year, while amounting to less than 1 percent of the incomes of households with incomes over $10,000. However, for families with incomes between $1000 and $9000, the degree of regression ranges from a little over 2 percent of income of the poorest families to a little over 1 percent of income for families with incomes close to $10,000. The committee further concludes that exempting food purchases, while increasing the rate of taxation to 3 percent of retail sales, makes little difference in the pattern of regression.[4] A more recent study of the New Jersey sales tax concludes that exempting food used for home consumption changes the sales tax into a tax that is proportional with respect to incomes for most New Jersey households.[5] This is because of low-income elasticity of the demand for food purchases and the fact that food expenditures are large relative to total spending for low-income families. This study also concludes that exempting clothing purchases from the tax base tends to increase the regressiveness of the tax, while exempting utilities (gas, electric,

[3] John L. Mikesell, "Central Cities and Sales-Tax Differentials," *National Tax Journal*, June 1970, p. 213.

[4] University of Wisconsin Tax Study Committee, *Wisconsin's State and Local Tax Burden*, 1959. Also, see James A. Maxwell, *Financing State and Local Governments*, rev. ed., Brookings Institution, Washington, D.C., 1969, pp. 96–100.

[5] Jeffrey M. Schaefer, "Sales Tax Regressivity under Alternative Tax Bases and Income Concepts," *National Tax Journal*, December 1969, pp. 524–527.

telephone, and so forth) decreases regressivity. Thus, although sales taxes do appear to be regressive, the degree of regressiveness does not seem to be as pronounced as some critics would like the public to believe and may be moderated, and even eliminated, through use of food and utility exemptions.

There are alternative methods for reducing the regressiveness of sales taxes aside from exempting food and medicines. Fifteen of the forty-five states utilizing retail-sales taxes do exempt food from the tax base. This is believed to be particularly beneficial to low-income families with many dependents. Other states utilize tax credits against state income-tax liability. Under this plan, households are allowed to deduct certain amounts from their income taxes, depending on the size of their families.

A final "virtue" of the retail-sales tax is its revenue stability. Consumption expenditures are more stable than incomes. Thus, a state income tax provides a less-stable tax base over time than does the consumption tax. One study estimates that a "typical" 2-percent retail-sales tax yields more revenue than a "typical" state progressive income tax with rates running from 1 to 7 percent.[6]

Turnover Taxes

Turnover taxes are multi-stage sales taxes that are levied at some fixed rate on transactions at all levels of production. The effective tax rate on alternative goods and services is, therefore, conditioned by the number of stages of production. The turnover tax has been utilized in Germany and other European countries as a major revenue source. Germany replaced its turnover tax with a value-added tax in early 1968. Of course, the turnover tax provides an artificial incentive to vertical integration among firms in order to reduce the number of production stages and interfirm transactions and, consequently, reduce the tax liability. The tax usually is reflected in higher final consumption prices. However, the rates of taxation vary with the number of stages of production. The distributive effects of the tax, therefore, depend on consumer preferences for and among multi-stage produced goods and services.

The turnover tax is an extremely productive levy. It produces high stable yields at very low rates. The relatively low rate employed at any level of transaction is believed to discourage tax evasion. Of course, the reason for the high yield is the "pyramiding" of the tax rates on multi-stage production that considerably increases the final effective rate of taxation. The pyramiding occurs when firms apply percentage markups to purchase prices to include the tax.

The turnover tax, as utilized in Germany, was criticized by some as being regressive. However, empirical studies have shown that the tax actually was somewhat progressive.[7] This is due to the fact that the effective rates on many food items were lower than those on clothing and other manufactured goods.

---

[6] See Maxwell, p. 100.

[7] See John F. Due, *Sales Taxation*, University of Illinois Press, Urbana, 1957, p. 59.

Any changes in production techniques that alter the number of processing stages could influence the final effective tax rates. It is administratively difficult to grant specific exemptions under turnover taxation relative to retail-sales taxation. The turnover tax is not a truly general tax because it applies discriminatory rates on alternative goods and services dependent on the number of productive stages.

Value-Added Taxes

The value-added tax (VAT) currently is utilized as a major revenue source by all members of the European Economic Community (West Germany, France, Italy, Belgium, the Netherlands, and Luxembourg). The tax was first adopted in 1954 by the French National Government (*tax sur la valeur ajoutee*), and in addition to the EEC countries, the tax currently is used by Denmark, Norway, and Sweden as well as by Finland, Greece, Mexico, and Brazil.

In essence, the *value-added tax* is simply a multi-stage sales tax that exempts the purchase of intermediate goods and services from the tax base. In recent years, there has been increased interest among economists and politicians in introducing the VAT into the federal tax structure. The tax has been considered both as a partial substitute for the corporation income tax and as a source of new revenue. It has also been advocated as a means of improving the United States balance-of-payments position. As an indirect tax, VAT is eligible under the General Agreement on Tariffs and Trade (GATT) for rebate to domestic exporters and for imposition on imports as a border tax. Since the structure of United States taxes is now heavily weighted toward direct (for example, income) taxes that are not eligible for export-rebate and border-tax imposition, while the rate structure of taxes in most European countries is largely indirect, introduction of a value-added tax seems to permit an improvement in the terms of United States trade relative to some of its major competitors.

Meaning of Value Added

Value added by a business firm is simply the difference between the firm's collections in sales proceeds and its expenditures in purchasing intermediate goods from other firms. For all firms in the national economy, the aggregate value added is the national product. Value added, for the firm or the nation, can be measured in one of two ways: First, it is the value of total transactions minus the value of all intermediate transactions, where an intermediate transaction is one involving the purchase of goods to be further processed by a firm into a final product; second, it equals the sum of all factor payments—wages, rents, interest, and profits.

Types of Value-Added Taxes

It is customary to classify different types of value-added taxes according to the manner in which they apply to a firm's purchase of capital goods. One approach is to allow no deduction from the tax base either for a firm's initial outlays on capital goods or for amortized deductions on such outlays. This is known as a "product-type" value-added tax. A second alternative, known as an "income-type" tax, allows no deduction for the costs of capital equipment in the year of purchase but permits a deduction for annual depreciation over the life of the equipment. A third alternative, known as the "consumption-type" tax, allows the full cost of capital equipment to be deducted in the year of purchase and increases the tax base by an appropriate amount in the years the equipment is being "consumed" in the process of production. In short, the base for the consumption-type tax is the same as that for a general retail-sales tax on consumer goods, while that for the income-type is the same as for a proportional income tax.

The variant of the tax used in France and other EEC member states is the "consumption type." The French have promoted this type of value-added tax because of its alleged stimulus to investment expenditures. By exempting capital outlays at the time of purchase, the "consumption-type" tax provides a kind of "investment-tax-credit" incentive. Thus, as it is commonly administered in most countries, the tax base for the VAT is equivalent to that of any general consumption tax. In principle, one expects the allocative and distributive effects of the VAT to be similar to those of any equal-yield general consumption tax.

Administration of the VAT

A value-added tax is not simple to administer. Its application gives rise to difficult problems in defining the tax base when there are unrealized capital gains or losses on real property. Decisions must be made about imputed rental of owner-occupied dwellings and the definition of depreciation and depletion. Moreover, there are problems in defining value added for certain labor-intensive service industries, such as financial institutions.

Notwithstanding these administrative problems, the tax apparently has proved to be an effective revenue instrument in France and other member states of the European Economic Community. It currently produces 24–40 percent of national governmental revenues in most EEC nations.[8] The basic document for administering the tax in these countries is the sales invoice. The tax liability of each taxpayer at each stage of production is a percentage of gross sales less the value-added tax already included in the invoices representing payments for intermediate goods and services. This technique embodies a sort of built-in "anti-evasion" mechanism.[9] If any firm fails to pay its tax liability at some stage of production, it then becomes the tax liability of the producer in the following production stage. This, in effect, results in automatic

---

[8] Richard W. Lindholm, "The Value Added Tax: A Short Review of the Literature," *Journal of Economic Literature*, December 1970, p. 1179.

[9] Lindholm, p. 1180.

enforcement of tax compliance by the business firms themselves. The tax is payable monthly. At the end of each month, business firms submit returns summarizing taxable sales and tax credits. The "invoice method" has produced very good results in France and might be considered as an appropriate administrative mechanism should the tax be introduced in the United States.

Allocative and Distributive Effects

The economic effects of introducing a VAT into the federal tax structure depend, in part, on the type of VAT chosen and the method by which it is introduced. The VAT can serve as a complete or partial substitute for any one of a number of existing federal taxes, including excise taxes, the corporation income tax, or the personal income tax. Furthermore, VAT can be introduced as a wholly new revenue source. Most frequently, it has been recommended as a partial substitute for the corporation income tax.

It has been estimated that an income-type value-added tax of approximately 7–9 percent would be needed to provide the same amount of revenue now yielded by the corporate profits tax of 48 percent. Alternatively, a 7-percent value-added tax could permit a substantial reduction in the existing corporation and individual income tax rates, while yielding the same revenue. Other specific estimates indicate that each 2 percent of value-added tax could replace 10–12 percentage points of the federal corporate income tax.[10]

A value-added tax strikes *all* factor incomes (rents, wages, and so on, in addition to corporate profits). It is often argued that a corporation income tax (provided that it is not shifted) distorts the "true" market return to capital and, thereby, hampers investment. Since the VAT applies to all kinds of income, this artificial barrier to investment choices can be eased if the value-added tax is substituted, in full or in part, for the profits tax.

One common argument in favor of the VAT over the profits tax is that the former is neutral between efficient versus inefficient producers. It often is claimed that the corporate profits tax provides a sort of "subsidy" to inefficient producers. A firm that makes no profits simply does not pay any tax. In this sense, efficient producers (those with high profit rates) are discriminated against relative to the inefficient producers. A value-added tax falls on all producers at the same percentage rate, thereby eliminating the "subsidy effect" of the corporation income tax. This may, however, make it difficult for new firms, whose profits tend to be relatively low in initial years, to start successful operations.

In order to study the possible economic effects of a substitution of the value-added tax for the corporate profits tax, it, first, is necessary to know the economic effects of the existing corporate tax structure. In particular, it is interesting to know *who* actually pays the corporate profits tax. Unfortunately,

[10] See Richard A. Musgrave and P. B. Richman, "Allocation Aspects: Domestic and International" in Conference Report of the National Bureau of Economic Research and The Brookings Institution, *The Role of Direct and Indirect Taxes in the Federal Revenue System*, Princeton University Press, Princeton, N.J., 1964, p. 91.

as has been discussed in Chapter 9, there is no general agreement among economists as to the incidence of the corporation income tax.

If it is assumed that the corporate profits tax is *not* shifted (that is, it falls solely on the return to capital), then it follows that a full or partial substitution of an "income-type" value-added tax for the existing corporate profits tax *reduces* the tax burden on profits, while increasing the burden on other types of income (rent, wages, and so forth). There is a redistribution of disposable income *away* from wage earners to capital owners that tends to be regressive, a probable decrease in consumption relative to savings, and possibly favorable effects on investment incentives because of the decreased taxation of profits. As indicated, the removal of the tax on profits also alleviates the distortion of the return to capital. This is undoubtedly true, but a new distortion is introduced between income and leisure because the tax on wage incomes is increased, and this tends to distort the workers' choice between work and leisure.

The conclusions are markedly different if the corporation income tax is, at least, partially shifted. In such a case, the introduction of the "income-type" value-added tax does not substantially ease the burden on profits because these were not depressed in the first instance. Thus, there is no substantial redistribution of income in favor of capital. However, since the degree of shifting varies from industry to industry and firm to firm, the substitution of the value-added tax alleviates the capriciousness of the effect on factor incomes resulting from inter-firm differences. That is to say, since a value-added tax is more general than the profits tax and falls clearly on total product, there is less discrimination between wage workers in different industries than under the profits tax.

If the complications of a progressive rate scale and personal exemptions are ignored, the effect of the substitution of an "income-type" value-added tax for an equal-yield proportional income tax can be sketched easily. Such a substitution simply can be viewed as a change in the source of withholding of an income tax imposed on factor income. The "tax wedge" between factor payments (wages, rents, and so on) and disposable incomes is removed and replaced by a new "wedge" between sales proceeds and factor payments. If product prices remain unchanged, factor payments fall and disposable incomes remain unchanged in money terms; if product prices rise, factor payments remain unchanged and disposable incomes rise in money terms but remain constant in real terms. Both employees and firm owners find that the real income calculated after tax is the same for both types of taxes.

The difference between an "income-type" and a "consumption-type" value-added tax is precisely the same as that between an equal-yield income and a sales tax. And just as a retail-sales tax favors the saver relative to the consumer, the "consumption-type" value-added tax relative to the "income type" benefits the saver and, therefore, tends to increase the supply of investible funds. Also, because savers tend to be in upper-income brackets, the "consumption-type" value-added tax is regressive relative to the "income-type" levy.

The value-added tax is amenable to rate discrimination in order to alleviate regressive effects. Although rate discrimination undoubtedly introduces additional distortions in resource allocations among alternative goods and services, the nation can collectively agree to discrimination on equity grounds. France has applied rate discrimination with rather good results. That country applies a "basic" tax rate to most transactions. However, a "low rate" is applied to the production of most foodstuffs and educational supplies, while an "intermediate rate" is applied to certain food products not benefiting from the "low rate" and to various utilities, non-educational books, and passenger transport. Both the low and intermediate rates are below the basic rate. Finally, there is an "increased rate" above the basic rate applied to a variety of luxury items. Such rate discrimination conceivably can turn the VAT into a progressive tax.

Expenditure Taxes

The expenditure tax is a direct tax. It is levied on households rather than on consumption transactions. The tax liability of each household is a function of its taxable consumption over a given period of time. Such a tax can be administered in a fashion similar to that which currently is used for income taxation. That is, each household is required to file an annual return on which it lists its consumption expenditures and computed tax liability. However, in addition to data on income, data on saving is required to measure total annual consumption. The expenditure tax has been used by only two countries: India and Ceylon. It is often argued that an expenditure tax encounters problems of both administration and compliance that limit its effectiveness.

Expenditure taxation permits rate discrimination on the basis of household economic circumstances to an extent not possible through indirect forms of consumption taxation. In particular, it permits progressive tax rates according to total expenditures, personal deductions, and exemptions as well as the exemption of particular types of expenditures for taxation. It also permits taxation of the depreciation of consumer durables and other capital goods.

The substitution of an expenditure tax for an equal-yield income tax does not tend to have much effect on the work-leisure choice. However, such a substitution removes downward distortions in the interest rates received by savers under the income tax. As a result, it is likely to increase the amount of savings. Furthermore, partial use of an expenditure tax at the federal level might serve to compensate for some of the tax preferences in the income tax code that result in some high-income households paying little or no taxes relative to their incomes.

When instituting an expenditure tax, a collective definition of "taxable consumption" has to be chosen. Expenditure is calculated simply as income less the net increase in saving. This, in turn, means a satisfactory definition of both income and saving is required. If this definition of consumption is acquired, detailed accounting of consumption expenditures by each household is not required in order to administer the tax. However, data on transactions that represent changes in household net wealth are needed in order to measure consumption. Such data can prove costly to obtain if it is relatively easy to conceal assets and liabilities.[11] However, if the expenditure tax is used in conjunction with an income tax, the extra data generated can serve to increase compliance rates under existing income taxation.

The expenditure tax is believed to be more conducive to capital formation, and this might serve to increase economic growth if it is substituted in full for an income tax. However, its chief merit as a consumption tax is its ability to provide households with exemptions and deductions so as to more readily comply with collectively accepted notions of equity while tapping the consumption base.

SPECIFIC CONSUMPTION TAXES

Specific consumption taxes are levied on certain types of consumption activities. As such, they distort choices among goods and services and result in efficiency losses to the economy stemming from the tax wedge inserted between relative prices as seen by consumers and producers (see Chapter 7). The incidence of specific consumption taxes is contingent upon demand and supply conditions.

Some specific consumption taxes are designed to raise revenues, while others (sumptuary taxes) are intended to discourage particular consumption activities. For example, excise taxes on tires are primarily designed to raise revenues, while taxes on liquor consumption, although they do raise considerable revenues, are intended to discourage liquor consumption. Some types of tariffs are designed to discourage consumption of foreign merchandise. Insofar as such tariffs increase the prices consumers pay for particular merchandise, they serve to redistribute income from the domestic consumers of the merchandise toward the owners and workers of the protected domestic industries.

The federal government has decreased its use of excise taxes in recent years. There are still excise taxes on some automotive products, but these revenues usually are earmarked for highway expenditures and can be considered user charges. There is still a federal excise tax on telephone service. In the past, luggage, jewelry, and restaurant services were also taxed by the federal government. Both federal and state governments tax liquor and cigarette consumption. In many cases, the consumption activities singled out for taxation either are alleged to generate externalities or can be considered "luxury" goods or services.

---

[11] For a discussion of pragmatic problems involved in implementing an expenditure tax, see Patrick L. Kelley, "Is an Expenditure Tax Feasible?" *National Tax Journal*, September 1970.

Prior to 1913, the federal government relied extensively on customs duties as a revenue source. Today, tariffs represent less than 1 percent of revenues collected by the federal government. The rates applied to many items are high and clearly are designed to discourage importation of foreign merchandise rather than to raise revenue. In a sense, tariffs that are successful revenue instruments cannot fulfill their function as protective devices for domestic industries, simply because the high revenue capability implies that they are ineffective in discouraging domestic consumption of foreign merchandise. Some United States customs duties currently amount to 25–50 percent of the dollar value of imported goods. Very high rates are applied to wool items, wearing apparel, and china tableware.

The incidence of a tariff depends on the income elasticity of the protected merchandise. In cases where the tariff succeeds in inducing domestic consumers to substitute domestic merchandise for the cheaper foreign goods, the effect is to redistribute income from the consumers toward the high-cost producers of the domestic goods. In cases where the protected commodities are consumed largely by high-income households and produced by low-income households, the resulting redistribution of income can be progressive. However, there is a net efficiency loss to the economy as a result of the indirect subsidization of the relatively inefficient domestic producers.

If the tariff is ineffective in reducing the consumption of foreign goods, then the effect is to reduce the real income of the consumers of these goods, while increasing government revenues and not affecting the domestic production of the protected goods. The overall incidence of the tariff, in this case, depends on the income class of consumers of the good upon which the duty is levied and on the disposition of the additional federal revenue.

Although tariffs impair free trade and prevent global efficiency in production, they persist in many countries as a redistributive device. While most economists abhor the use of inefficient policies to attain a given redistributive goal, it remains a fact of life that the political process continues to result in some legislation that does sacrifice efficiency to attain an equity goal. This being the case, the economist attempts to sketch both the allocative and distributive effects of specific tariffs so as to generate information that will permit reasoned collective decisions on such specific consumption taxes.

SUMMARY

Taxes on consumption represent the major source of revenues for state governments in this country. Taxes on consumption are *general* or *specific*. General consumption taxes are levied on all consumption activity without exception, while specific consumption taxes are levied only on some consumption activities. General consumption taxes include retail-sales, turnover, value-added, and expenditure taxes. Consumption taxes levied on specific goods are called "excise taxes." Exemptions from the tax base serve to render most "general" consumption taxes into specific taxes that distort economic choices among consumption alternatives. Retail-sales taxes often exempt food and personal services from the tax base, thereby inducing consumers to purchase relatively more of these exempted items than they would in the absence of the tax.

General consumption taxation lowers the return to work effort in a fashion similar to that of income taxation. A general consumption tax is, therefore, likely to distort individual choices between work and leisure and result in efficiency losses for the economy. However, since consumption taxes are not levied on interest incomes, they do not distort choices between present and future consumption.

The redistributive effects of general consumption taxes are contingent partially on the time horizon used in defining the tax base. If all saving is simply deferred consumption, then defining the tax base as lifetime consumption results in a proportional consumption tax attacking roughly the same tax base as an equal-yield proportional income tax. If the tax base is defined as annual consumption, then a general consumption tax, such as one levied on retail sales, tends to have regressive redistributive effects insofar as saving as a percent of income increases as household income increases. These regressive effects can be moderated by exempting certain basic consumption items, such as food and medicines, from the tax base.

11

Taxes on Wealth

A general tax on wealth, or property, is levied on the assets owned by households and corporations in the private sector. General taxes on wealth are more difficult to administer than general taxes on income or consumption, because the wealth base is more difficult to measure accurately. Despite the problems of implementation, the general wealth tax has a long history of utilization by governmental authorities.[1] A general property tax was used in England during the medieval period to finance the Crusades. Such taxes were levied on rents and movable property. Evidence also exists that the tax was utilized in ancient Rome. In the colonial period of the United States, wealth taxes were utilized by many of the colonial governments. While colonies initially relied on poll taxes to finance their modest requirements for public expenditures, they switched to taxes on real and personal property as wealth differences developed among the colonists.

It has been observed by many economists that the utilization of the wealth base for taxation purposes appears to run a cyclical course. This "property-tax cycle" is correlated with the economic development of a society.[2] The tax first appears as a per-unit levy on land alone. As income and wealth differentials become more pronounced during economic development, it becomes a proportional tax on the holding of all wealth—land, other real assets, and personal

---

[1] For a good discussion of the historical development of property taxation, see Arthur D. Lynn, Jr., "Property-Tax Development: Selected Historical Perspectives," in Richard W. Lindholm (ed.), *Property Taxation: U.S.A.*, University of Wisconsin Press, Madison, 1967.

[2] Lynn, in Lindholm, p. 16.

property. Finally, as the society reaches economic maturity and wealth takes on new and heterogenous forms, the general property tax becomes difficult to administer effectively, and it becomes essentially a tax on land and improvements thereon, that is, real estate. In point of fact, there is a movement in the United States today to reform the property tax in such a way as to transform it into a tax on land alone. This would complete the cycle once again.

Although both intangible and tangible personal property are taxed in some states, the bulk of the revenues currently raised by property taxes in the United States comes from taxes on real estate. The wealth base is not tapped at all by the federal government but is utilized mainly by local governing units. It accounts for approximately 86 percent of the general revenues collected by the local governments.

Many argue that it is necessary to tax wealth in addition to income and consumption in order to achieve "equity" within the tax structure. Quite often individual households with relatively low incomes have substantial holdings of wealth in the form of real assets. In the case of homes and consumer durables that yield non-monetary returns, households may escape taxation completely under an income tax, because of problems associated with measuring imputed rent and service flows. Insofar as economic capacity varies with wealth as well as income, equity, on the basis of the ability-to-pay principle, cannot be achieved in the tax structure by taxing only one economic base. Thus, taxes must be levied on wealth in addition to those levied on income and consumption. A diversified tax structure, if properly constructed, is unlikely to have any tax "shelters" where taxpayers can escape taxation in accordance with their economic capacities.

THE TAX BASE

A General Property Tax

A general property tax is levied on all forms of wealth in the economy. In order to determine the wealth base, all forms of property owned by taxpayers must be listed and its value must be assessed. In listing property, care must be taken to avoid double-counting of assets. Assessing the value of wealth that is not often sold on the market is one of the most difficult aspects of property taxation.

There are two approaches to listing the wealth of taxpayers. The first considers *only* the net assets of households, while the second considers *both* the net assets of households and corporations. Both methods yield the same results. The first approach merely takes into account the fact that corporations are ultimately owned by households, and the net assets of such corporations are reflected in the value of outstanding corporate stock.

Using the first approach, total wealth may be considered to have the following three components:

1. All real property (that is, land and improvements thereon) owned by households.
2. All tangible personal property owned by households. This includes all movable assets, such as cars, furniture, clothing, jewelry, and so forth.
3. All intangible personal property owned by households. This includes stocks, bonds, cash, and other "paper" assets reflecting assets owned by corporations and governments.

Furthermore, to obtain a measure of net wealth and to avoid double-counting of assets, all debt incurred by households and firms (for example, mortgages, loans, and so on) has to be subtracted from the tax base. A fourth possible form of wealth that might be included in the tax base is human capital. This includes special skills owned or acquired through educational investments. However, it is difficult to assess the value of human capital, and its taxation may dampen incentives to acquire special skills through education.

The second approach includes the assets of corporations but excludes intangible property representing claims on the assets of such corporations. Thus, this approach does not tax outstanding corporate stock, for to do so involves double-taxation of corporate assets. In addition, this approach deducts all debt incurred by the private sector from the tax base to obtain a measure of net wealth.

Needless to say, there are some rather severe administrative problems encountered in implementing a general property tax in an economically mature society. This stems, in part, from problems encountered in attempting to list all forms of property, particularly tangible personal property and intangible property. Many forms of movable personal property (such as jewelry) are easy to conceal, and this encourages tax evasion. Taxes on personal property often place a disproportionate share of the burden on honest taxpayers who list all their movable personal assets, even though they realize that the costs of checking the validity of their listings are so prohibitive as to prevent governments from enforcing honest listings. Except for the case of movable personal property that must be registered with local governments, such as automobiles, taxes on this form of wealth prove both easy to evade and difficult to enforce. The same holds for intangible personal property. In the case of unregistered securities, concealment is relatively easy and, again, enforcement of tax laws can prove costly to governing authorities. Although many local governments in the United States do tax personal property and some tax intangible personal property, the tax rates applying to these forms of wealth are typically very low so as to discourage tax evasion.

The administrative problems encountered in taxing both tangible and intangible personal property has led to a wealth tax that falls mainly on real estate and exempts other forms of wealth. This is in accordance with the "property-tax cycle" previously discussed. Taxes on real estate are difficult to evade, for the simple reason that it is virtually impossible to conceal such assets. Real estate is registered with local authorities, and the structures on land are open to view by all. The problem now becomes to determine which real estate is taxable and to assess the value of such real estate. In the United States, all localities exempt from the tax base most property owned by religious and charitable institutions. For example, in Boston, approximately 42 percent of all real estate is exempt from taxation. This is largely land owned by churches and educational institutions. In addition, constitutional law prohibits local governments from levying taxes on real estate owned by the federal government. However, the federal government often makes payments in lieu of taxes to localities in which it owns property.

Assessment of Property Value

After all property subject to taxation has been listed, it is necessary to estimate, or assess, the value of the property before the tax can be implemented. Assessment of property values can be extremely difficult in instances of assets for which markets do not exist and assets that are traded infrequently. Assessment practices are often criticized as being too subjective. It is asserted that political power exercised by particular property holders in some communities results in relatively lower assessments compared to market values. Also, lags in re-assessment of older properties often results in new structures being assessed higher than older properties of equal market values.

In the case of a general property tax, assessors estimate the value of both real estate and movable personal property. If assessment is to be reasonably accurate and fair, the asset value of property should closely approximate the market value. The property tax typically is levied as a percentage rate of assessed valuation. In the initial stage of the "property-tax cycle," the tax is levied on a per-unit (for example, per-acre) basis; as differences in the value of land sites develop during maturation of an economy, the tax becomes an ad valorem levy.

The assessor's task is relatively easy for intangible personal property. Well-organized markets exist for trading stocks, bonds, mortgages, and other "paper" assets, and prices are available on a daily basis. Similarly, good markets exist for the trading of automobiles, and for this form of personal property, assessment is, again, a relatively easy task. But markets for the most prevalent form of taxable wealth, real estate, are not that well-organized. The assessor often approximates the value of such assets on a subjective basis.

One method that the economist might suggest to assess the value of real estate is to attempt to determine the capitalized value of such assets. This entails estimating the net annual rent flowing from both the land and strucure thereon in monetary terms and the life of the structure. Once estimates of these two parameters are made, it is a simple matter to compute the present value of the real estate using a discount rate reflecting the opportunity cost of capital. However, it may be difficult to estimate imputed rentals, especially for non-income producing property and vacant lots. Often the assessor projects rents into the future based on predictions of future development in the area. Assessors typically keep records of recent sales of property within an area. This enables them to follow the prices of similar competing properties within an area. They also must be acquainted with growth trends in the area to predict possible changes in property values over time. Property must be re-assessed periodically in order to reflect changing market values. In a particular community with a given demand and supply of real estate, values of particular structures are likely to vary with location, age of structure, quality of construction, size of structure, appearance, and other factors.

Thus, the assessor, or appraiser, must gather a great amount of data and effectively analyze growth trends in a community to accurately approximate the market value of both residential and business real estate. The assessor must possess many skills to do his job effectively and fairly. Unfortunately, salaries for assessors in many states are low relative to other comparable work, and it is difficult to attract competent personnel into the profession.[3] There is a need to raise professional standards and salaries for assessing personnel in order to assure that similar properties are assessed equitably and arbitrary subjective judgments by assessors are cut to a minimum. Under conditions of rising market values, only competent and well-staffed assessment offices can keep assessments current.

Fractional Assessment

A peculiar phenomenon in the administration of the property tax is the practice of fractional assessment of market value. A study conducted by the U.S. Bureau of the Census in 1961 shows that the national average for locally assessed real estate was only 29 percent of 1961 market value.[4] Although most states have legal assessment standards of 100 percent, the statutes are not enforced. Average state assessment ratios range from a low of about 6 percent to a high of about 80 percent.[5] The practice of fractional assessment by local authorities is confusing to the electorate.

Under a policy of fractional assessment, the property tax rate overstates the real rate of taxation. For example, if the property tax rate is nominally 3

---

[3] See Paul V. Corusy, "Raising the Professional Standards of Assessing Personnel" in *The Property Tax: Problems and Potentials*, Tax Institute of America, Princeton, N.J., 1967.

[4] John Shannon, "Conflict between State Assessment Law and Local Assessment Practices," in Lindholm, p. 39.

[5] Shannon, in Lindholm, pp. 40–41.

percent but the assessment ratio is only 33⅓ percent of true market value, then the effective rate of taxation is merely 1 percent. The motivation for fractional assessment apparently is political. Since World War II, property values have risen steadily, while assessments and assessment ratios have remained fairly static. By keeping assessments and assessment ratios static, assessment officials prevent expansion of the tax base and force voters to raise nominal property tax rates for expenditures on particular public services (for example, education). As pointed out by one writer, this gives the assessment officials, in many cases, virtual power as budget officers.[6] By refusing to let the property tax base grow with needs as property market values rise, the assessor can exercise a degree of control over expenditure policy by forcing referendums on tax rate increases when they otherwise are unnecessary. Furthermore, in many cases, apportionment of state-aid funds to local communities are made on the basis of assessed value of real estate, with more state-aid funds going to localities with lower assessments. This provides an incentive for communities to keep their assessments low so as to obtain more state aid than competing communities. As long as state-aid funds are tied to local assessments, there is an incentive for communities to keep assessments low, thereby attempting to "compete" state-aid funds away from other communities. Fractional assessment practices also enable local governments to tax different types of property at different rates even when proportional taxation is required by law. This is accomplished easily by applying a higher assessment ratio to certain forms of property. For example, if the legal rate of taxation is 3 percent and one-family homes are assessed at 33⅓ percent of market value, while apartment houses containing fifty or more units are assessed at 66⅔ percent of market value, then the effective rates of taxation in these alternative forms of property are 1 percent on the one-family homes and 2 percent on the apartments. The apartments are being taxed at twice the effective rate on single-family homes. In the United States, it is common to assess apartment houses at higher ratios than single-family dwellings.[7] In addition, certain forms of commercial enterprises, such as retail-sales establishments, typically are taxed at higher effective rates than one-family homes because of the application of relatively higher assessment ratios. Such policies can result in socially undesirable allocative effects for a community, such as a reduction in the supply of apartments and retail establishments. In addition, the distributive effects of such a policy may be deemed inequitable by some citizens.

Assessors and local governing authorities apparently are unwilling to stop the practice of fractional assessment and to conform with state statutes requiring 100-percent assessment. There is a need for state action to standardize assessment ratios and practices.

[6] Shannon, in Lindholm, p. 54.

[7] For data on differential assessment, see Dick Netzer, *Economics of the Property Tax*, Brookings Institution, Washington, D.C., 1966, p. 78.

ALLOCATIVE EFFECTS OF WEALTH TAXATION

General Property Tax

Consider the effects of a general property tax, that is, one levied on all forms of wealth. In principle, such a tax falls on all accumulated savings. This reduces the general return to savings and is likely to reduce the rate of savings (provided that the elasticity of supply of savings is not zero) and, therefore, the rate of growth for the economy. If the elasticity of supply of savings is equal to zero and the economy is closed so that no opportunities are available for capital to "flee" the country, then the general wealth tax is neutral with respect to resource allocations. That is, there are no opportunities to substitute an untaxed activity (for example, consumption) for the taxed activity (wealth holding), so there is no change in behavior to avoid the tax and no consequent misallocation of resources.

Compared to equal-yield general taxes levied on the alternative economic bases of income and consumption, the wealth tax appears to be relatively more detrimental to the incentive to save. The extent of any such reduction in savings rates will, of course, depend on the extent to which the aggregate propensity to save in the economy responds to changes in the rates of interest. On the other hand, a general wealth tax has little or no effect on the return to work effort. Thus, when compared to equal-yield taxes on income and consumption, the wealth tax is likely to be less distorting to the work-leisure choice.

In practice, a wealth tax is not likely to be completely general, because of administrative difficulties encountered in measuring and assessing all forms of wealth. In particular, it is reasonable to assume that human capital escapes taxation even under a "general" wealth tax. If this is, in fact, the case then the wealth tax induces a reallocation of investment choices toward human capital and away from other assets. It is also possible that, other things being equal, the tax induces business firms to substitute labor input for taxable physical assets in their productive processes. The extent of such reallocation depends, of course, on the relative elasticities of supply and demand for taxable physical capital, untaxed human capital, and labor input. Historical data show that the technological advantages of substituting capital for labor are so strong as to outweigh any detrimental effects of the property tax on capital input.[8]

Specific Property Taxes

In point of fact, as previous discussion indicates, a truly general property tax is likely to prove administratively infeasible. Most property taxes are specific taxes in the sense that they are levied on only certain forms of wealth. Taxes

[8] Netzer, p. 72.

on real assets (land and improvements thereon) account for approximately 80 percent of all revenue collected from property tax levies in the United States. Furthermore, over 50 percent of the taxes collected on real property comes from non-farm residential real estate.[9] As a tax on real estate, the property tax provides an incentive to substitute alternative inputs for real property. In addition, in states where personal property is not taxed or is taxed at lower rates than real property, the tax can, other things being equal, affect choices between real-property consumption and the consumption of consumer durables by making the latter relatively more attractive. Thus, it is possible that the property tax discourages the production and consumption of housing. The property tax, as it is utilized in the United States, is also likely to induce some rather subtle allocative effects because it is a local levy, and rates of taxation do differ among communities. The property tax can be a factor determining the location of industry. One expects real-property-intensive industries (other things being equal) to locate in areas where the property tax is relatively low, while labor-intensive industries choose to locate in areas with relatively high property tax rates. However, in order to include all factors in a firm's location decision, one also has to consider the benefits financed by property taxation in alternative location sites. Communities with low tax rates may lack essential public services or have lower quality public services to be utilized by industry.

In analyzing the allocative effects of property taxes on real estate, it is useful to divide such taxes into two components: one part falling on the land itself, while the other is assumed to fall on the structure on the land.

Taxes on Land

Since the supply of land is, in effect, perfectly inelastic, a tax on land tends to be neutral with respect to resource allocation. That is to say, a tax on land alone does not affect the quantity of land supplied to any particular area because landowners cannot withdraw their land from the market. Thus, there is no change in behavior induced by the tax that affects the quantity of land on the market. The rent earned on the land is a pure economic surplus that can be taxed without any effect on quantity supplied. However, if the tax is confined to land alone, the tax may affect the relative intensity of use of that land. The land tax reduces rents earned on the land by the full amount of the tax, and land prices fall to reflect the future tax burden. This may induce landlords to use their land more intensively so as to generate an income stream from it to partially offset the land tax. Thus, it is often argued that land taxes may produce desirable allocative effects by stimulating investments and improvements in land complementary to the development of economies.

Taxes on land alone have a long history of advocacy in the United States. Perhaps the most important name associated with land taxation is that of

---

[9] Netzer, p. 19.

Henry George (1839–1897).[10] While George's economic philosophy is beyond the scope of this book, his ideas led to an almost fanatical advocacy of the "single-tax doctrine," under which all taxes except those levied on land would be rescinded.[11] The tax on land would then be such as to appropriate all rents from landlords. In effect, such a policy would nationalize landownership. George correctly reasoned that rent was a pure economic surplus, and its full taxation would not alter the quantity of land supplied. Furthermore, he believed that such high rates of land taxation would encourage investment in the land in the form of structures of various sorts, thereby accelerating economic development. While the utilization of the land tax as a "single tax" today would scarcely yield enough revenues to finance state and local public expenditures, to say nothing concerning federal expenditures, many economists believe it would be an improvement over current taxation of real estate (both land and structures), because it would result in a more efficient land-use pattern.[12] Of course, it may be administratively difficult to separate the value of land from the value of structures thereon.

Taxes on Structures

In contrast to the portion of real estate taxes on land, one expects taxes on structures to alter the quantity of structures supplied in the long run. Such taxes discourage investments in real property and result in a reduction in supply of housing and business enterprises for particular communities. The extent of this allocative effect depends on the elasticity of supply of investments in real property. This supply schedule is not likely to be perfectly inelastic, as is the case for the supply of land. The tax on structures may also have the effect of encouraging the substitution of other inputs for real property. It may induce investments to flow from uses that are real-property intensive into alternative uses. A classic example of this effect is the railroad industry. Since railroading is a real-estate intensive industry, property taxes cut deeply into the rate of return in the railroad industry.[13] This serves to discourage investment in railroads and impede the modern development of the industry. One expects property taxes in general to distort the pattern of investments away from capital-intensive uses toward labor-intensive uses in the long run.

In areas where property tax rates are relatively high, these effects serve to

---

[10] For a discussion of George's ideas, see Reid R. Hansen, "Henry George: Economics or Theology?" in Lindholm.

[11] George qualified his "single-tax doctrine" to allow for taxes on liquor, gambling, and bequests, as well. See Hansen, in Lindholm, p. 68.

[12] For an estimate of the revenue that might be obtained by taxing all rents away, see Hansen, in Lindholm, p. 70.

[13] It has been estimated that property taxes absorb about 3.5 percent of rail operating revenues but only 0.4 percent of operating revenues for truckers and 0.2 percent for air carriers. See Netzer, p. 73.

impede development or renewal projects. In the United States, hard-pressed central cities are forced to apply high tax rates to real property that, in turn, serve to exasperate already existing financial and social problems by diminishing the supply of new housing structures, discouraging the development of new industry, and possibly causing existing industry to relocate.

The decrease in the supply of housing as a result of the property tax may, however, be offset by other policies. The favorable treatment of homeownership in the United States income tax code serves as an offsetting stimulus to investment in housing.

Local communities are aware of the detrimental effects of property taxes on investment and location decisions. To compensate for this, many communities offer property tax exemptions or abatements to attract industry and other forms of investment in land. Some states exempt industrial property from taxes for a number of years in the hope that this will influence location decisions. Other states abate a certain proportion of taxes for particular uses of land to encourage investment in, for example, apartment houses.

DISTRIBUTIVE EFFECTS

General Property Tax

A truly general property tax levied on all forms of wealth tends to be fully borne by owners of capital assets in a closed (no-foreign-trade) economy. The return to wealth falls by the full amount of the tax. This occurs because a truly general wealth tax offers no opportunity to substitute untaxed assets for taxed assets. As a result, there are no routes available for wealth holders to avoid taxation, and the stock of wealth is not altered. The rate of return on all investments, therefore, falls by the amount of the tax.

This conclusion must, however, be qualified by the extent to which opportunities exist to import and export capital assets and the extent to which the supply of savings is not perfectly inelastic. If capital is internationally mobile then one expects the tax to cause a reduction in inflow of foreign capital and an outflow of domestic capital to the now more lucrative investments in foreign capital markets. The consequent reduction in domestic investments tends to raise output prices until the return to investments rises to its pre-tax level. Under these circumstances, assuming perfect mobility of capital, the tax is shifted fully to consumers and owners of factors of production other than capital.

Similarly, if the supply of savings is not perfectly inelastic, savers substitute consumption activities for additions in net wealth. This reduces the rate of capital accumulation and raises the return to wealth holding as prices rise. The result is some shifting of the burden of wealth taxation to other groups who are not wealth holders.

Furthermore, the administrative difficulties involved in imposing a truly general wealth tax make greater the likelihood of some transference of tax burden from wealth holders. If, for example, the tax induces the shift of investments from real assets to human capital, the return on real assets rises, thereby preventing a reduction in the return to assets equal to the full amount of the tax.

Specific Property Taxes

The possibility of tax shifting is significantly greater under specific property taxation when compared to general property taxation. Under specific property taxation, only certain forms of wealth are subject to taxation. This implies that there are more opportunities available for individuals to rearrange their assets with a view toward avoiding the tax. Consequently, there are numerous movements in relative supplies and demands and a resulting change in the relative prices of alternative assets. One expects the prices of taxed forms of wealth to fall relative to the prices of untaxed forms of wealth if there is no shifting of tax burden. The process through which the prices of taxed assets fall in value relative to other assets is called "tax capitalization." Tax capitalization, in effect, concentrates the full burden of future property tax payments on the current owner of the taxed assets. If a tax is fully capitalized, then there is no shifting. That is to say, the tax is borne by owners of the taxed form of wealth at the time of tax imposition.

Consider the reasons for tax capitalization under specific property taxation. Suppose, for example, that only wealth held in the form of real estate is taxed. Assuming that capital markets are initially in equilibrium, the return on real estate is identical with the return on all other forms of wealth (adjusted for risk). Assume that the imposition of the tax reduces the return on real estate by the full amount of the tax. If the current holders of real estate wish to sell their assets, they have to do so on terms that are competitive with alternative assets. Thus, if the equilibrium return on all assets is say, 5 percent, real estate has to be sold on terms that yield investors at least a 5-percent return. But the tax reduces the annual return below 5 percent. It follows that the taxed asset has to be sold at a capital loss just great enough to raise the yield to 5 percent. The reduction in the market price of the asset caused by the tax-induced reduction in return is the tax capitalization.

The process of tax capitalization can also be illustrated algebraically. The present value of any capital asset depends on the return earned by holding the asset, the life span of the asset, and the rate of discount for the economy. The rate of discount represents the opportunity cost of holding any one particular form of wealth and may roughly be considered the average market return to investment in the economy, or the marginal product of capital. Thus, the value of any capital asset that yields an annual return of Y can be expressed as follows:

$$V = \sum_{i=0}^{n} \frac{Y}{(1 + r)^i} \tag{11.1}$$

where V is the market value of the asset, n is the number of years the asset will last, Y is the annual return, and r is the rate of discount.[14] If it is assumed that the asset has an infinite life, then $n = \infty$ and equation (11.1) reduces to

$$V = \frac{Y}{r} \tag{11.2}$$

Consider the effect of a property tax on a particular asset of infinite life. The tax at rate t, if unshifted, reduces the annual return to the asset by an amount tV_t, where V_t is the market value of the asset after the tax is imposed. The post-tax annual return on the asset is, therefore, $Y - tV_t$. The new market value of the asset can be expressed as follows:

$$V_t = \frac{Y_t}{r} = \frac{Y - tV_t}{r} \tag{11.3}$$

where Y_t is the post-tax return. Solving for V_t, equation (11.3) can be reduced to

$$V_t = \frac{Y}{r + t} \tag{11.4}$$

Equation (11.4) is the formula for full capitalization of a tax on an asset of infinite life. The expression for the effect of the tax on the market value of an asset of less than infinite life can easily be derived but is somewhat more complicated than equation (11.4). In effect, tax capitalization puts the entire burden of taxation on current property holders who are selling the assets. For assets yielding the same annual return, the magnitude of reduction in price, therefore, varies directly with the anticipated life span of the asset.

For example, suppose a wealth tax of 5 percent is levied on one specific asset of infinite life having pre-tax return of $1000 per year. If the rate of discount is 5 percent, the pre-tax market value of that asset is $1000/0.05 = $20,000 from equation (11.2). By substituting in (11.4), the effect of full capitalization of the tax on market value of the asset can easily be determined. The new value is $1000/(0.05 + 0.05), or only $10,000. Thus, full capitalization of the tax reduces the value of the asset subject to taxation by a factor of 50 percent! If the asset has a shorter life span, the reduction in market value accordingly is less. Full capitalization occurs only if the tax is not shifted initially. If the tax is shifted, then the return Y falls by less than an amount tV_t. In the case of complete shifting, there is no reduction in the annual return.

---

[14] See Chapter 5 for a discussion of the rate of discount.

Taxes on Real Estate

Can property taxes on real estate be shifted? This is a relevant question to pose, particularly since in the United States the bulk of the property tax base consists of real estate. Real estate has two component parts: the land itself and all permanent improvements erected on the land. The value of any piece of real estate is, therefore, the sum of the value of the land and the value of all structures on the land. Assuming that it is possible to separate the value of land from the value of improvements thereon, one can discuss the degree of shifting of such property taxes with reference to the portion of the tax that falls on the two component parts of the real estate.

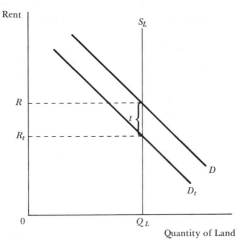

FIGURE 11.1

It is generally agreed that the portion of the tax on the land itself cannot be shifted. This is because the supply of land in any given area is perfectly inelastic. The rent on the land itself is lowered by the full amount of the tax because the supply of land is fixed. This is illustrated in Figure 11.1. S_L is the fixed supply of land, and D is the demand for land. The imposition of a tax of t on each unit of land decreases the average rent taken by landlords. Thus, the demand for land, as seen by the landlords, falls to D_T. The equilibrium rent paid by users of land remains at R in Figure 11.1, but the rent received by landlords falls to R_t. The fall in rents is exactly equal to the full amount of tax revenues collected by the government. Thus, the component of the tax on the land cannot be shifted. This implies that this portion of the tax, other things being equal, tends to be capitalized into lower land prices reflecting the increased tax burden.

The effect of the tax on the structures on the real estate varies with time. In the short run, it is likely that the return to buildings is reduced somewhat, thereby resulting in some capitalization of the tax. But in contrast to land, capital used in construction can be applied to alternative uses not subject to taxation. This suggests that the supplies of capital to construction tend to be responsive to the returns to construction. Thus, in the long run, the property tax induces a reallocation of capital to other uses and from construction. Such a reallocation continues to occur until the post-tax returns on construction are once again on par with the returns on alternative assets. Thus, the net return to structures tends to be pushed to its pre-tax level as the decreased stock of structures results in higher rents. The component of the tax that falls on structures is, therefore, shifted forward to renters or future purchasers of real estate. There is no capitalization of this portion of the tax because rents rise just enough to maintain the previous net return from the structures.

If, however, it is maintained that it is not possible to separate the value of land from the value of structures, then the theory of shifting must be modified. Under this approach, the value of land is dependent mainly on the productivity of capital applied to that land. Since the property tax on real estate discourages investment in the land, the rents on real estate rise. This approach argues that the rents on the land component of real estate rises, too, so that both the land and structure portions of the property tax are shifted to users of land in the form of higher rents.[15]

In analyzing the incidence of the property tax it is also useful to divide real estate taxes into two basic categories: those levied on residential property, and those levied on non-residential property. Non-residential property taxes are largely those levied on businesses. As is pointed out by Netzer, business property taxes (especially those on utilities and retail trade) are, in part, general consumption taxes, because they are undoubtedly shifted forward to consumers of outputs produced on those properties.[16] The extent of such shifting depends, of course, on the price elasticity of demands for outputs. Outputs sold by utilities and retail establishments tend to be relatively price inelastic, because they tend to be sold in local markets. Firms producing outputs that must compete in national or global markets are less successful in shifting property taxes by raising prices because their demands tend to be more elastic.

Property Taxes as User Prices

It is often argued that the property tax, as it is administered in the United States, is analogous to a "price" for local public services. Since the property tax is the main source of revenues for local governments, it finances the bulk of services supplied by such local governmental units. Thus, differences in property tax collections per capita among communities are likely to imply differences in quantities and qualities of local public services (for example, education, sewage facilities, police protection, and so on) supplied by local communities within the federal system. A community that increases its prop-

---

[15] This approach is attributable to F. Y. Edgeworth.
[16] Netzer, p. 40.

erty tax rates to improve public services is likely to increase the demand for real property in that area, if such improvements make it a more desirable site for housing and certain business activities.

This relationship between property tax rates and level of locally supplied public services suggests that it might be useful to apply the overall budget approach to determining the incidence of property taxation within the context of a federal system. Under this general equilibrium approach, *both* the influence of taxation and the public expenditures financed by taxation are considered in determining the effect of property taxation on the return to wealth and asset prices.

Suppose a local community increases its property tax rates to improve its educational and sanitation facilities. Consider the effect of such an increase in the local public budget on residential property values. The increase in tax rates is likely to have a depressing effect on property values, at least in the short run before the stock of housing begins to decrease as a result of the tax-induced lower returns to holding of real estate. That is to say, one expects the tax to be capitalized so that the incidence of the increase in taxation is such as to lower the values of housing owned by current residents of the community. But suppose the improved educational and sanitation facilities financed by the tax make this community a more desirable place to live relative to surrounding communities. This tends to *increase* the demands for residential housing. Thus, the expenditures financed by increased property taxation tend to result in an *increase* in property values. This tends to shift the burden of the rate increase from current to new and entering residents of the community.

Under this approach, the actual incidence of local property taxation depends on the relative magnitudes of the two forces acting on property values. If the increment in public services is valued by current and future residents in excess of the increment in the tax bill, then property values may actually rise in response to the increase in tax rates and increased supply of public goods. That is, it is possible that the increase in tax rates may be shifted in excess of 100 percent by current local residents through appreciated property values, if the increase in demand for housing in the area induced by improved public services is great enough. If on the other hand, the increased demand for housing just balances the tendency for the tax to be capitalized, there is no change in property values, and current residents suffer no reduction in rents (implicit or monetary). Finally, if the increase in demand for housing as a result of the increased budget is weak, the tendency for the tax to be capitalized is not offset and the return to housing held by current residents falls.

An Empirical Study of the Incidence of
Residential Property Taxation

A recent empirical study of the effect of property taxation on residential property values in fifty-three communities in northeastern New Jersey by Wallace E. Oates provides evidence on the extent to which property taxes are,

in fact, shifted.[17] Oates attempts to measure the effects of *both* the expenditure
and revenue sides of local public budgets on property values. The model utilized includes a variety of variables one can expect to influence property values.
These include proximity to central city and various indicators of the physical
characteristics of residences in the area. With these other factors statistically
taken into account, Oates proceeds to isolate the effects of effective property
tax rates and local public expenditures on property values. Expenditures per
pupil are used as a rough indicator of the level of public services financed by
the property tax.

The empirical analysis of the data shows that, in isolation, property values
do, in fact, vary negatively with tax rates and positively with expenditures
per pupil for the fifty-three communities in the sample. For example, the
empirical analysis suggests that an increase in local property tax rates alone
from 2 to 3 percent tends to reduce the value of a typical house with market
value of $20,000 and a forty-year expected life by $1500. Since full capitalization of this tax increase evaluated at a 5-percent discount rate reduces the value
of such a house by $2260, the analysis indicates that part (about two thirds) of
the tax is capitalized in the form of lower property values.[18] If, however, half
of this increase in property tax rates is used to finance an increase in per-pupil
educational expenditures, the analysis shows that property values tend to rise
by about $1200. If the other half of revenue collected from the property tax
is used to improve other public services not included in Oates' analysis, one
expects further increases in property values to cancel the depressing effects of
tax capitalization. Thus, the evidence indicates that the bulk of the property
tax alone is capitalized into lower property values, but when the revenues
collected from the tax are used to improve local public services, increased
benefits of such services increase the demand for housing, and rents in the
community rise so as to offset the depressive effects of increased tax rates on
the market prices of residential real estate.

PROPERTY TAXATION IN THE UNITED STATES
AND THE DISTRIBUTION OF INCOME

Some Empirical Evidence

Most empirical evidence indicates that the property tax, as it is administered
in the United States, is regressive with respect to money income. There are
good intuitive reasons to expect this result. Expenditures on housing by
households tend to rise less than proportionately with incomes. That is, rela-

---

[17] Wallace E. Oates, "The Effects of Property Taxes and Local Public Spending on
Property Values," *Journal of Political Economy*, November–December, 1969.

[18] Oates, p. 965.

tively higher-income households tend to spend a lower percentage of their income on housing compared to low-income households. This low-income elasticity of expenditures on housing is relevant to the impact of the property tax on income distribution in the United States because of the simple fact that roughly half of the revenue collected from the property tax comes from non-farm residential real estate. This implies a high likelihood of regressive effects with respect to current money incomes of such property taxation. Netzer estimates that the property tax in 1963 was equal to an equivalent excise tax on housing expenditures of 17–18 percent.[19]

In addition, current assessment policies in the United States tend to contribute to regressivity. As has been discussed, the policy of fractional assessment often results in relatively higher effective tax rates applied to apartment houses and the properties of certain local business establishments. Furthermore, in some cases, inequitable assessment practices result in relatively more expensive houses assessed at lower percentages of market value than less costly houses. Since lower-income households tend to live in apartments and spend larger proportions of their income on housing and consumption goods sold by local retailers, the higher effective tax rates applied to apartments and local retail-business property is likely to cut sharply into their disposable money income, under the presumption that such taxes are shifted forward to renters and consumers.

Studies on the actual effect of property taxes on income distribution yield varying results depending on the concept of income utilized. Using current money income, one study finds that total property taxes are markedly regressive for the income range of $1000–$8000 per year, with households of $1000 annual income paying about 7 percent of their income in property taxes compared to about 3.8 percent paid by households with $8000 annual income. The study shows some mild progression in the $8000–$25,000 income range, with households of $25,000 annual income paying slightly less than 5 percent of their income in property taxes.[20]

One obtains a different picture if taxable money income is used rather than current money income. The reason for this is that property tax payments can be deducted from gross income under current federal income-tax-code regulations. For households that itemize their deductions and own their homes, this can mean a substantial tax saving. In effect, they can transfer some of their tax burden to the national income tax base by reducing their income tax payments. For example, a household in the 50-percent income tax bracket can, in effect, have the federal government bear half its property tax bill when it deducts property tax payments from its gross income. With this in mind, it is not surprising that when deductions from gross income are taken into account for determining the impact of the property tax on income distribution, rela-

[19] Netzer, p. 168.
[20] Netzer, p. 40.

tively more regression results. There is evidence that while households with $1000 money income pay 7 percent of their income in property taxes, and households with $8000 money income pay about 3.3 percent of their income in property taxes, households with $25,000 income pay only about 3 percent of their income to local governments in the form of property taxes, when the income-tax deduction is taken into account.[21]

When only the middle-income ranges (say, $4000–$12,000 per year) are considered, the tax appears to be roughly proportional with respect to income at a rate of around 4 percent of income. However, the very poor households tend to pay almost twice this amount (5–10 percent) of their income in property taxes, while the very rich tend to pay less than 4 percent of their income in the form of local property taxes. There is evidence that these income redistribution effects vary widely among taxing jurisdictions. In particular, the tax tends to be markedly more regressive in its overall income redistribution effects in large cities in the United States. One estimate of the effect of the residential real estate tax in New York City in 1960–1961 indicated that households below the median income for the city tended to pay twice the percentage of income in property taxes that households with above-median incomes paid for that year.[22] Furthermore, evidence indicates that poorer communities tend to have higher effective property tax rates than relatively richer communities.

Some studies have evaluated the distributive effects of property taxation with respect to the concept of "permanent income."[23] Permanent income may be thought of as a household's expected annual income over its lifetime. These studies indicate that the property tax is much less regressive when evaluated with respect to permanent rather than current income. One reason for this is that housing expenditures tend to be considerably more elastic with respect to permanent income. Of course, if one compares the distributive effects of the property tax with those of alternative taxes (for example, sales taxes), the distributive effects of these alternative taxes must be determined with respect to the same concept of income.

Evaluation of Property Taxation in the United States

Despite the many administrative, allocative, and distributive problems associated with property taxation in the United States, the tax has proved popular because of its satisfactory revenue-producing performance in the post-war era. The responsiveness of property tax revenues to increases in GNP and the needs of the community have led many observers to note that the tax is apparently a better fiscal instrument than its critics have suggested. How can the property tax be improved? It is possible that undesirable allocative effects can be elimi-

[21] Netzer, p. 41.

[22] Dick Netzer, "Some Alternatives in Property Tax Reform," in *The Property Tax: Problems and Potentials*, p. 387.

[23] Netzer, *Economics of the Property Tax*, p. 42 and pp. 62–66.

nated through a shift to land taxation and the use of tax abatements, while undesirable distributive effects can be cushioned by improved assessment practices. Land taxes have been utilized for over a century in Australia and for an even longer period in Denmark. The tax on land alone has performed well in these two countries, and it is believed that such land taxes have led to a more efficient land-use pattern. As indicated, the tax on land value does not have the undesirable allocative effects attributable to real estate taxation under which the flow of capital into construction uses is discouraged. The Australian and Danish experience with the tax has indicated that the administrative problems involved in separating land values from the values of improvements thereon are not insurmountable. Data often exist on sales of unimproved lots in an area or on older structures sold with the land that are demolished after sale in order to permit new construction. These sales enable assessors to make estimates of the value of land in any given locality. It is argued that land taxes prevent underuse of land and may, therefore, be helpful in encouraging private interests to aid in the renewal of central cities by acquiring land in such areas and developing it. Such development is often discouraged by high taxes on real estate in the central cities. Since taxes on land alone cannot be shifted, the tax is capitalized into lower land values, thereby encouraging private interests to use land more intensively as an input in their productive processes. Under current real estate taxes, land improvement is penalized by higher taxes because improvements increase the values of real estate and result in substantially higher tax bills. Of course, a shift to land taxation in this country is likely to alter the distributive effects of property taxation. In particular, those landowners who are employing their land inefficiently, and those who use land-intensive productive techniques (for example, farmers) are likely to experience an increase in tax burdens. It is unlikely that political reality will permit a complete shift to land taxation in this country in the near future. However, it may be feasible to tax land at relatively higher rates than those applied to structures. This is currently the practice in the City of Pittsburgh.

Property tax abatements exempt new industries locating in a community from property taxes for a given number of years. Such exemption from property taxation for new industry is popular in many southern states in the United States. However, such exemptions are made at the expense of the other property taxpayers in the community in the sense that their tax bills must be raised accordingly to support expanding public services. Furthermore, such policies appear to be of questionable value in promoting efficient land use and actually attracting industry. Tax abatement has been used in New York to encourage private construction of apartment houses. Such construction projects are given a 50-percent tax abatement.[24] Specific abatements are likely to be subject to political manipulation that prevents the optimal land-use pattern from being attained.

[24] Netzer, *Economics of the Property Tax*, p. 85.

Some of the regressive distributive effects of property taxation in the United States can be alleviated by the introduction of more consistent assessment practices and policies. Reform of assessment practices could cure many of the current inequalities of assessment that prevent attainment of horizontal and vertical equity in taxation. Currently, property owners who possess some degree of political power often succeed in getting their properties taxed at lower effective rates compared to other property owners who lack such power. This usually is achieved through relatively favorable assessment ratios applied to such properties. In addition, better bases for estimating market value exist for properties that produce money rents, such as apartment houses. As a result of this, assessors' estimates of the value of apartment houses often are much closer to market values than those of expensive one-family residential structures that do not produce money rents and are not frequently sold. Such one-family homes typically are under-assessed. This results in higher effective tax rates on rental units. Since these taxes are probably shifted, and lower-income people tend to live in rental units, this contributes to regressivity.

Reform of current assessment practices undoubtedly will increase the costs of administering the property tax in the United States. Netzer estimates that currently, in the larger United States cities, local assessment-administration costs tend to amount to less than 1 percent of revenues collected. Netzer believes that significantly more equitable practices can be achieved in larger cities by raising administrative costs to no more than 1.5 percent of revenues collected.[25] This entails, for example, higher salaries for assessors and more education in the techniques of assessment. He does point out, however, that there are likely to be economies of scale in assessment and doubts that smaller communities will be able to hire appropriate assessment talent at correspondingly low administrative costs relative to revenue collected.[26] Improved administration may be a good investment for larger communities if it helps achieve vertical and horizontal equity. One method of improving assessment quality for small communities may be to encourage them to hire the services of private assessors under contract. Perhaps a state or federal corps of assessors could be established to help smaller communities improve their property taxes at relatively lower administrative costs.

PROPERTY TRANSFER TAXES

Property transfer taxes include estate, inheritance, and gift taxes. These taxes are levied on transfers of wealth among citizens. Property transfer taxes represent a feasible method of taxing accumulations of wealth that normally

---

[25] Netzer, *Economics of the Property Tax*, p. 174.
[26] Netzer, *Economics of the Property Tax*, p. 176.

escape other forms of taxation. In the case of wealth transferred at time of death, the state supervises the administration of the bequest, and good data exist on the accumulation of wealth. Thus, it is relatively easy for the state to levy taxes on wealth accumulations transferred from one generation to another.

Estate, Inheritance, and Gift Taxes

Estate and inheritance taxes are sometimes referred to as "death duties." They are levied essentially as excise taxes on the rights to transfer properties at time of death. The federal government levies taxes on property transfers before death as well in the form of gift taxation. While federal death taxes are levied on estates themselves, state taxes are levied on the inheritances and, therefore, represent the tax liabilities of the heirs.

The federal estate taxes account for less than 2 percent of total federal revenues. Although levied according to a fairly progressive rate scale, the tax allows many exemptions. The tax allows a basic $60,000 exemption plus other specific deductions and exemptions, and taxes the remainder according to a progressive rate structure ranging 3–77 percent. The highest rate is applied to the portion of the estate over $10,000,000. Included among the specific deductions from the tax base are legal and funeral expenses, debts, and charitable contributions. In addition, one half of the estate may be left to the surviving spouse exempt of all taxes. When the surviving spouse dies, the remainder of the estate presumably is bequeathed to the remaining heirs. In effect, this splits the tax base and permits much lower rates of taxation than would otherwise prevail.

In the absence of a federal gift tax, all estate taxes could be avoided by transferring property prior to death. The federal gift tax prevents such avoidance to some degree. Gift taxes are levied on the individual making the gifts. The rates applied to gifts are 25 percent lower than those applying to estate taxation, and the individual is allowed a $30,000 lifetime gift exemption and annual per-person exemption of $3000. This permits tax-free transfers during the life of the donor over the $60,000-estate tax exemption. There has been no substantial change in the federal statutes concerning estate and gift taxation since 1942.

Most states levy taxes on inheritances. These taxes are the liabilities of the beneficiaries of the estate. It is often argued that this is a more "equitable" property transfer tax because the effective tax rates can be correlated with the ability of the heir to pay. Furthermore, higher exemptions and lower effective tax rates are generally allowed to closer relatives of the deceased.

Property transfer taxes can be avoided by establishing trusts that are not subject to estate taxation until dissolved. Wealthy individuals apparently make intensive use of this provision. In addition, bequests to charitable foundations are deductible without limit from the tax base.

Allocative Effects

The taxation of property transfers is likely to reduce savings and affect work incentives. By consuming their wealth before death, individuals can avoid estate taxes. Furthermore, the knowledge that part of an estate will be taxed at death might affect the willingness of individuals to earn incomes in excess of their lifetime consumption requirements. While these effects have not been empirically measured, it is unlikely that estate taxes are more impairing to incentives to save and invest than equal-yield income taxes. This is because most individuals base economic decisions on current events rather than events at time of death. Income taxes directly reduce the returns from current work efforts and savings and are, therefore, more likely to dampen work and savings incentives.

States are reluctant to increase their property transfer taxes, despite the fact that accumulations of wealth represent a relatively untapped source of revenues. Recommendations by such authorities as the Advisory Commission on Intergovernmental Relations point out that such taxes should be utilized more effectively. The reason for this is that states desire to attract wealthy residents in order to expand other bases of taxation. They fear that a higher property transfer taxes would have the undesirable allocative effect of discouraging wealthy individuals from locating within their tax jurisdictions. This "competitive effect" of taxation among the states acts as a constraint on increased property transfer taxation.

Distributive Effects

There is a case for increased property transfer taxation on the grounds that it could serve to correct many of the "inequities" currently present in the overall tax structure. At current low effective rates of taxation due to numerous tax preferences, the tax probably has little effect on the distribution of income and wealth in the United States. Increased property transfer taxation could correct for shortcomings in the income tax code that prevent the attainment of horizontal equity by not fully taxing all accretions in net worth and, thus, permit lower rates of taxation for the bulk of the population. In particular, regressive real estate and sales taxation could be reduced if states and local governments relied more extensively on property transfer taxation.

SUMMARY

General property taxes are levied on all forms of wealth, while specific property taxes are levied only on certain forms of wealth. Most of the revenue collected through property taxation in the United States comes from the real estate tax that is a specific tax on the holding of real wealth. Property taxes account for approximately 86 percent of the general revenues collected by local governments in this country.

Determining the value of wealth that is infrequently traded is one of the most difficult aspects of property taxation. A truly general wealth tax is difficult to administer because of the problems involved in measuring all forms of wealth (especially human wealth). The estimation of the value of an untraded asset is called "assessment." Accurate assessment closely approximates the market value of an asset. Property must be periodically reassessed to reflect changing market values.

Compared to equal-yield general taxes levied on the alternative economic bases of income and consumption, a general wealth tax is more detrimental to saving incentive but less detrimental to work incentive. Although a tax on land cannot be shifted, taxes on structures can, because they can alter the supply of resources to construction. Differing property tax rates among communities affect the location decisions of households and business firms.

The process through which the prices of taxed assets fall in value relative to untaxed assets is called "tax capitalization." Tax capitalization concentrates the full burden of future tax payments on owners of taxed wealth at the time the tax initially is levied. If the expenditures financed by property taxation serve to increase the demand for property, then the depressing effect of the tax on asset prices may be offset.

Most empirical studies of property taxation in the United States show that the tax has regressive effects on the distribution of income. Since the tax falls heavily on residential real estate, and expenditures on housing by households tend to rise less than proportionately with income, this distributive effect is not surprising.

PART IV

Fiscal Federalism and Urban Problems

12

Fiscal Federalism

The United States has a *federal* system of government. Under such a system, there are numerous levels of government through which individuals collectively supply public services and raise revenues to finance these services. The various levels of government include the federal (or central) government, state governments, and subdivisions of the states ranging from counties and cities to school and other special districts. All these levels of government have varying degrees of political power to supply public services and raise revenues. Such a multi-level governing system raises some interesting questions in a study of the economics of governmental activities. What is the most efficient allocation of responsibilities among the alternative levels of government given the preferences of individual citizens? In general, the greater the power of the central governing authority, the more uniform the kinds of services supplied to citizens; the greater the power of local governing authorities, the greater the diversity of public services supplied within the nation. But along with diversity comes the possibility of fragmented, or non-coordinated, collective decision-making among communities and diseconomies resulting from small-scale supply of services exhibiting economies of scale.

The federal system of government has the advantage of permitting a nation to accommodate a wide range of preferences by citizens for public services. Insofar as citizens and business firms are mobile, and the jurisdiction of governing units is local, alternative governmental expenditure and revenue policies on the state and local levels can induce various "locational effects" that act as a constraint on policy decisions. For example, a state or local government may be hesitant to introduce a new tax if it fears that this tax can easily be avoided by citizens transferring the taxed economic activity to another jurisdiction where the tax does not exist. Thus, there is likely to be some degree of intergovernmental competition among jurisdictions that influences both expenditure and revenue policies of state and local governments within a federal system. The effect of such intergovernmental competition on efficient utilization of resources will be discussed.

THE ECONOMICS OF GOVERNMENTAL ACTIVITIES WITHIN A FEDERAL SYSTEM

One may utilize the efficiency criteria to determine the optimal division of responsibilities among different levels of government wthin a federal system. On the basis of these criteria, the central government undertakes those activities that it can supply most efficiently relative to other levels of governments, given the preference of citizens in the nation. In general, activities coming within this category are those that affect all citizens in the nation irrespective of their places of residence. These activities are likely to come closest to the definition of *pure* public goods in the sense that the production for any one individual in the nation makes them equally available for consumption by all other individuals in the nation. In other words, those public services whose supply generates external effects that are given non-zero values by all citizens in the nation, irrespective of their location, are most efficiently supplied and financed by the federal (that is, central) level of government. Activities in this category include national defense services, social insurance services, interstate transportation facilities, international affairs, and certain income redistribution activities.

Activities that are collectively consumed within state or local jurisdictions should be chosen collectively according to some decision rule by citizens of state or local jurisdictions. For example, police, fire, and sanitation services are likely to yield benefits consumed largely by residents within a local jurisdiction. It follows that the residents of the local jurisdiction should determine collectively the amount of resources they wish to surrender to the appropriate local governing authorities to supply police, fire, and sanitation services. Under ideal conditions, one expects them to agree collectively on an amount of such public services corresponding to the point at which the sum of marginal benefits of public services is equal to the marginal costs of production of local public services. This yields an efficient amount of public goods, presuming that the benefits and costs of the provision of these local public services are located within the community itself. Of course, there is no guarantee that the political process at the state or local level will produce the "ideal" efficient outcome.

The availability of local governing jurisdictions enables citizens within these localities to satisfy their preferences for public goods and services to an extent that might be impossible if there were only one level of government. Thus, communities whose citizens have strong preferences for recreation facilities can choose to surrender the command over private resources for the purpose of building public parks and other public recreational facilities and, say, devote little of their resources to supplying public libraries. Other communities whose citizens are relatively more interested in the arts can choose collectively to have few public parks and, instead, use significant amounts of their resources for public concerts, art exhibits, and libraries. In a sense, the political process is most efficient when individuals of relatively similar preferences congregate in local communities where they can best satisfy their preferences for public services. Under these conditions, both decision-making and external costs of political action are likely to be low. The optimal size of a local political unit depends on the range of spillover of the costs and benefits of public expenditures.

Complications develop when the benefits of public expenditures are regional in the sense that they are consumed by citizens located in more than one political jurisdiction. This occurs when the benefits of local public services produced by any one political jurisdiction "spill out" to residents of neighboring jurisdictions. Similar complications ensue when all the benefits of local public services are consumed within one political jurisdiction, but some of the costs of supplying those services are borne by residents of neighboring communities. In both these cases, one expects decision-making on the local level to result in inefficient amounts of produced public services, because the spill-over costs or benefits tend to be ignored by the local residents who make the collective decision, even when the local political processes are efficient.

This suggests that the supply of collective activities that generate regional costs and benefits needs to be determined through some form of intergovernmental cooperation that internalizes the external costs and benefits. If intergovernmental cooperation is infeasible, then it is often desirable for a higher level of government to coordinate local decisions through appropriate subsidies or taxes or by creating regional commissions.

In summary, collective choices concerning the level of outputs of public services should be made by that subset of the population who bears the costs of supply and the benefits of consumption. However, this rule achieves efficiency only when the political processes at the various levels of government are capable of achieving efficient outcomes. Public services consumed by the entire population of the nation should be supplied and financed through the central government, and all citizens should participate in the collective decisions to determine the choices of output levels. On the other hand, the outputs of public services that are consumed by only a small subset of the population should be collectively determined by that subset, and the costs of supply should be borne only by citizens within that subset. In reality, political jurisdictions are not always drawn with economic considerations in mind. This implies that the costs and benefits of local public services can extend over a subset of the population that is different from the subset which makes the collective decisions. When this occurs, there may be a misallocation of resources between public and private use.

In addition to the range of external benefits involved in the supply of public services, the efficiency criterion indicates that the productive technology involved in supplying public services must also be considered. This is relevant because the production of many public services exhibit significant economies of scale, implying that the costs of supplying given levels and qualities of public service decline as a large subset of the national population consume some outputs. Economies of scale can extend over a larger subset of the population than the subset which actually consumes the benefits of certain public services. For example, although the benefits of such local services as fire protection, hospitals, and schools are largely consumed on a local level, local supply may be undesirable for small communities because of high unit costs associated with small fire departments, schools, and hospitals. There may be economies of scale at certain minimum sizes of many local public services.[1] This implies that, although many public services do, in fact, generate benefits that are consumed on the local level, not every community should attempt to supply these services. Very small communities may be content to have some higher level of government provide their hospitals and schools, because of the cost savings achieved by that method of supply and obtain such services under contract with a larger unit of government. This implies that a diversity of preferences for public services may not be able to be accommodated completely because of high resource costs associated with low levels of scale for some public services.

Recently, however, it has been argued that economies of scale in the supply of public services need not necessarily be a significant factor in determining optimal sizes of local political governing units.[2] For public services that are moderately divisible among users, it often is possible to separate the unit of government that articulates the demand for service from the unit of government that actually produces the service. In such cases, an elected public official can act as an agent for the small community in contracting for public services produced by higher levels of government. This method has been used by a number of small municipalities in Los Angeles County, California, to provide such services as sewers, lighting, fire protection, and law enforcement.[3] By creating "special districts" for the purpose of contracting for the public services produced by higher levels of government, municipalities can achieve efficiency

---

[1] Empirical studies show that there are some scale economies for fire protection, high schools, and hospitals. For a summary of this empirical work, see Werner Z. Hirsch, *The Economics of State and Local Government*, McGraw-Hill, New York, 1970, p. 183.

[2] See Robert L. Bish, *The Public Economy of Metropolitan Areas*, Markham, Chicago, 1971, chapter 3.

[3] Bish, pp. 81–93.

within the public sector that is independent of the technology involved in producing public goods.

The Theory of Local Governmental Expenditures

Some useful insights into public-expenditure theory within federal systems are obtained from a model developed by Charles M. Tiebout.[4] Tiebout assumes that there is a difference between the supply mechanism for public services on the federal and local levels that stems from the mobility of citizens within a federal system of government. On the national level, the federal government attempts to supply public services that accord with the preferences of citizens as manifest through a particular collective decision rule (for example, majority rule and representative government). On the local level, the pattern of public expenditures and revenues is likely to be set according to the preferences of older residents. Furthermore, because of the diversity of political preferences among local jurisdictions, the level and mix of local expenditures and taxes are likely to exhibit wide variations among communities. Given this variety of revenue and expenditure patterns among communities, one expects that the citizens who make decisions concerning the locations of their residences will choose the communities whose public budget best satisfies their own preferences for public services, provided that they are not restricted in their mobility among communities. Thus, on the local level, public expenditures and revenue patterns tend to be set, and the mobile citizen maximizes his utility by choosing some particular political jurisdiction within which to locate his residence.

The Tiebout model assumes that all "consumer-voters" are fully mobile among communities and possess full knowledge of the public budgets in alternative political jurisdictions. There are many communities that offer similar employment opportunities to citizens. There are no spill-over costs or benefits of governmental activities. Finally, an *optimum* community size is defined as that which corresponds to minimum unit costs of public services. Communities above optimal size attempt to discourage new residents, while communities below optimal size attempt to attract new residents.

Under this set of restrictive assumptions, a quasi-market equilibrium is attained when all residents are located in the community that best satisfies their political preferences, subject to the constraint that all communities are providing public services at minimum unit costs. The constraint implies that some citizens may have to be content with a "second-choice" community. If all communities can supply public services at constant costs, implying that there are no economies or diseconomies of scale, then one expects the equilibrium to be completely analogous to a market equilibrium, because in the extreme case,

[4] Charles M. Tiebout, "A Pure Theory of Local Expenditures," *Journal of Political Economy*, October 1956.

an iconoclast can establish a one-man community that provides all the public services he requires, and there are an infinite number of "communities" available to satisfy every citizen's preferences. In this situation, "competition" among communities results in an efficient solution similar to that produced by a perfectly competitive market economy.

Although the basic assumptions of the Tiebout model are, of course, extremely restrictive, it does offer some insights into some of the unique problems of public-expenditure analysis within a federal context. Citizens are not completely mobile among communities and often possess only imperfect knowledge of local public budgets. Furthermore, although there are a large number of communities within the federal system, they differ in their employment opportunities and in geographical and climatic conditions. That is to say, there are many other factors aside from political preferences for public expenditures that are likely to affect the locational choices of citizens. Finally, as previous discussion indicates, there are "spill-over" costs and benefits associated with the supply of local public services. However, the Tiebout model is relevant because, at least at the margin, some households *do* respond to differences among public budgets in alternative communities.

In particular, the model appears to be useful in partially explaining the exodus of households from the central city to surrounding suburban communities that has occurred in the United States since the end of World War II. Clearly, mobility of households is not perfect. But within a constrained geographic area, it is possible for a citizen to change his place of residence to one in a neighboring political jurisdiction while maintaining his employment in his old political jurisdiction. The proliferation of the private automobile in the post-war era and generally improved transportation facilities make such moves relatively easy. In part, citizens are motivated to move to smaller political jurisdictions in the suburbs of central cities because of lower tax rates and better-quality public services (such as schools) relative to those prevailing in the central cities. This is in accord with the basic tenets of the Tiebout hypothesis. Thus, the model is useful in explaining movements within a constrained geographical area constituting one relatively large labor market. It is not very useful in explaining moves across larger geographical areas (for example, interstate) because of the impediments to mobility and the variety of other factors influencing locational choices.

The existence of spill-over costs and benefits also complicate the Tiebout model, because they cause residents of local communities to make decisions on the basis of inadequate data. The Tiebout approach implies that local taxes are analogous to "prices" for local public services. Citizens who desire high quality and quantity of public services gravitate to those communities with relatively higher tax rates. That is to say, the model suggests that citizens shop for a set of local public services in much the same manner as they shop for automobiles. Their choices of communities as residence sites depend on tax rates, local public services financed by revenues, and relative preferences for public and private expenditures. If, however, all public services are not financed through taxes on local bases, the alternative community tax rates do not accurately reflect the costs of public services and cannot be considered the full "prices" for such services. Furthermore, when local jurisdictions receive state or federal aid, the "prices" paid by residents are subsidized by higher levels of government. The deduction of state and local taxes from the federal income tax base is an example of a "cost spillover" that enables local communities to finance their public services through a reduction in federal income tax collections. Thus, when there are spill-over costs and benefits of local governmental activities, the "competition" between local governments is less likely to achieve efficiency.

In summary, the ability of households to express their preferences for alternative local public budgets by "voting on their feet" provides a partial explanation of residential choices in a constrained metropolitan area comprising a relatively large labor market. However, impediments to mobility on the regional and national levels, due chiefly to restrictions in employment opportunities, make the conclusions of the Tiebout model questionable if applied to regional residential choices. Finally, local taxes are not likely to be an accurate measure of the "prices" for local public services because of the existence of spill-over costs and benefits. All these factors result in an equilibrium residential-choice pattern that is not "optimal" in any sense. That is to say, at any point, there are households who are dissatisfied with their current political jurisdiction but who, for one reason or another are not able to move. Other residents can move either into or out of a community in response to tax rates that do not represent the true marginal costs of local public services.

The Theory of Taxation within a Federal System

The Local Tax Base

The ability of tax bases to partially "migrate" from one taxing jurisdiction to another creates problems that constrain the revenue-raising capabilities of local governing units. The possibility of induced "locational effects" of local taxation is well recognized by local governing authorities and can serve to prevent them from pursuing inefficient policies. Such recognition may account, in part, for local reliance on property taxation in the United States. Real property is relatively immobile compared to other tax bases. It is virtually impossible to relocate land from one community to another, and shifts in the supply of the structures on the land generally occur only in the long run. However, this does not suggest that local property tax policy can have no effect on the value of the property tax base. As the discussion in Chapter 11 indicated, unrestrained property taxation can result in long-run allocative effects that impede the economic development of a locality and, consequently, reduce the value of its real property tax base.

Local taxing authorities are, therefore, concerned with the elasticity of the local tax base with respect to the rate of taxation. So long as resources are mobile among political jurisdictions, the knowledge of elasticities is crucial to the implementation of effective local tax and expenditure policies. If the local tax base is elastic with respect to the rate of taxation, then increases in the rates of taxation result in a reduction rather than an increase in tax revenues collected. If B is the current dollar value of the local tax base, and t is the current rate of taxation in percentage terms for any community, and ΔB is the change in the value of the tax base induced by a change in the rate of taxation, Δt, then the elasticity of the tax base e_t is

$$e_t = \frac{\text{percentage change in value of tax base}}{\text{percentage change in rate of taxation}} = \frac{\Delta B/B}{\Delta t/t} \qquad (12.1)$$

If e_t is greater than unity, then the tax base is elastic, and an increase in the rate of taxation results in a decrease in revenues collected. If e_t is equal to unity, then any change in the rate of taxation results in no change in the amount of revenues collected. Finally, if e_t is less than unity, the tax base is inelastic with respect to the rate of taxation, and an increase in the rate of taxation results in an increase in the amount of revenues collected by the tax.

Thus, for a local taxing jurisdiction, an increase in the rate of taxation applied to any base results in an increase in revenue collections from that base if and only if the elasticity of that tax base with respect to the rate of taxation is less than unity. The next question to ask is, "What factors determine the elasticity of the tax base?"

Among the factors affecting e_t are the degree of mobility of taxed resources, the rates of taxation applied to similar tax bases in surrounding communities, the public services supplied by surrounding communities, and the initial amount of revenues collected from that base compared to, for example, local income. In addition, the services financed through the increase in tax rates affect locational choices by households and business firms that, in turn, affect the value of the local tax base. If individual economic units feel that extra taxation exceeds the benefits they obtain from increased public expenditures, they will consider relocation (other things being equal). An elastic tax base, therefore, implies that local governments are pursuing inefficient policies in the sense that the marginal costs of governmental activities exceed the marginal benefits. Thus, tax competition forces local governments to be more responsive to the needs of their citizens and, thus, improve, efficiency.

Because of mobility of resources and the presence of alternative tax jurisdictions that provide similar public services, taxes that might be neutral if imposed on the national level can have severe allocative effects when imposed on the local level. For example, the classic head tax is neutral on the national level but is likely to induce locational effects if imposed on the local level, when households are mobile and substitute communities exist. Individuals who wish to avoid the head tax simply can move to an alternative community where the tax is not used. If the local population (the tax base under a head tax) of the locality is elastic with respect to the rate of taxation, any increase in the head tax results in a decrease in revenues. Finally, taxes that account for only very small percentages of taxpayers' incomes are likely to have tax bases that are inelastic with respect to the rate of taxation. For example, a 10-percent increase in the rate of taxation applied to a tax base that currently yields revenues equal to less than 1 percent of local income results in less resource transfers among communities than does an equivalent 10-percent increase in the rate of taxation applied to a base that currently yields 15 percent of local income. In general, the greater the degree of uniformity among local tax and expenditure policies, the less elastic is the local tax base. Within local taxing jurisdictions in the federal system, no tax base is completely inelastic. Injudicious taxation of any given base eventually erodes that base as resources are reallocated among jurisdictions to avoid the burdens of local taxation. Since tax rates are often changed in discrete rather than continuous variations, one expects threshold levels of taxation beyond which any sharp increases induce economic decision-making units to relocate their economic activities. A recent example of this effect was the attempt by the City of New York to increase the stock-transfer tax that applies to transactions on the New York Stock Exchange. A threat by the exchange to relocate their operations to New Jersey induced the city to retreat and forget the tax increase.

The elasticity of tax bases often results in competition among communities for residents and business firms whose economic activities increase the values of local tax bases. Such competition often acts as a constraint on the sizes of local public budgets. Local taxing jurisdictions hesitate to increase tax rates for fear of putting themselves at competitive disadvantages relative to other jurisdictions as sites for the conduct of various kinds of economic activities. Of course, the expenditure sides of local budgets also are considered factors in the location decisions of economic units. Jurisdictions that are reluctant to raise taxes may lack public services that attract citizens as residents. However, business firms often are not major consumers of local public services, such as education, that constitute the bulk of local budget expenditures. Communities that are interested in attracting businesses of various sorts, to ultimately broaden their tax bases, may conclude that lower tax rates can be more useful in attracting economic activities than are extensive public services. The gains to be obtained from keeping tax rates and, therefore, local public budgets at low levels vary from community to community.

Property Taxes, Sales Taxes, and Local Finances
In the United States, local governments rely on property taxes and, to a lesser extent, consumption taxes to raise revenues to finance the bulk of their expenditures. Most locally raised revenue (about 86 percent) is obtained from

the property tax. In addition, many local governments receive significant amounts of financial aid from federal and state governments.

As the discussions in previous chapters of this text indicate, both consumption and property taxes tend to have regressive distributive effects. Taxing jurisdictions often have no option but to rely on these regressive taxes, in view of the practical problems involved in implementing progressive taxes at the local level. A local community that introduces a progressive income tax is likely to initiate a migration of both business firms and households that do not think they are receiving commensurate local benefits and already are paying high federal and state income tax bills. The local income base can be considerably elastic with respect to local progressive rates of taxation. Local regressive taxes are, in fact, efficient if they serve to internalize local externalities that upper-income groups are forced to consume.

The constraints on taxation at the local level caused by the elasticity of the tax bases led the Advisory Commission on Intergovernmental Relations to conclude that there is a "fiscal mismatch" of local public expenditure requirements and the ability of local taxing jurisdictions to raise the necessary revenues to finance the expenditures. That is to say, the levels of government that currently are experiencing the sharpest increase in demands for public services and increases in unit costs in supplying those services are least capable of acquiring the resources necessary to finance such services. Under current institutions, local governments are, by and large, responsible for financing the bulk of education expenditures and significant amounts of welfare costs. These demands strain local budgets. Competitive effects of taxation make it difficult for local taxing jurisdictions to obtain revenues from sources other than the property tax. Increased social conflicts and problems in central cities created the need for large amounts of public expenditures on education, crime prevention, welfare, and other public services. This, in turn, necessitated sharp increases in local tax rates in the central cities, coupled with a deterioration in the quality of many municipally supplied services. High tax rates, in part, encouraged the flight of many middle-income households to surrounding metropolitan suburbs that boast lower tax rates and greater expenditures on educational facilities. However, low-income households effectively are barred from the suburbs by overt discrimination in housing, zoning restrictions, and lack of resources. This movement eroded the tax bases in the central cities by reducing property values in many areas and put further demands on city budgets through the concentration of low-income households in the central cities. This increased local expenditures and tax rates, further encouraging migration of middle-income households.

The existence of problems that create a mismatch of needs and resources for many local governments suggests a need for reform. Among the suggestions most often discussed are the creation of metropolitan governments with powers to internalize external costs and benefits within metropolitan areas, and the reallocation of responsibility for financing some services, such as education and welfare, to higher levels of government (state and federal). The relative merits of these proposals will be discussed later in this chapter.

Fiscal Capacity and "Revenue Effort"

While all local communities are concerned about the elasticity of their tax bases, some communities have distinctly low tax-base values relative to other communities. In a sense, the fiscal capacities of local governing units are likely to vary with the values of local tax bases. Taxing jurisdictions with relatively low tax bases in dollar terms find it more difficult to raise tax revenues than do wealthier high-income jurisdictions. Insofar as the demands for local public services do not increase with fiscal capacities, low tax-base communities are likely to encounter difficulties in supplying acceptable minimum levels and qualities of public services.

For example, consider the fiscal consequences of different per-capita income levels among states. If each state supplies the same per-capita amounts of public services to its citizens and finances all these expenditures by income taxes falling solely on residents in the state, then it follows that the proportionate per-capita tax burdens are higher in those states with lower-income residents. Alternatively, if tax rates are the same in all states, and all public expenditures are financed by state taxes, then those states with lower per-capita income households supply less and lower-quality public services. Such differences in the "fiscal capacities" of states and local taxing jurisdictions suggest that some federal intervention is necessary to assure that all communities supply "minimum" acceptable amounts of public services. In effect, federal aid to "disadvantaged" communities redistributes resources from wealthier states and local communities to communities with relatively low-value tax bases in the belief that there are external benefits for all citizens to consume at least a "minimum" amount of certain local public services. A program of "fiscal equalization" assures that no United States citizen is forced to consume markedly inferior local public services merely because he happens to live in a poverty-stricken taxing jurisdiction. Federal aid usually takes the form of specific grants-in-aid with expenditures restricted to one purpose (for example, education). In recent years, there have been suggestions to replace many of the specific grants with a form of federal revenue sharing among the states that would remove many of the "strings" that usually are attached to federal funds. In addition, many state governments provide aid to local taxing jurisdictions designed to equalize fiscal capacities.

It is difficult to obtain a measure of relative fiscal capacities and performances for the various states and localities in the federal system. One measure that often is used is the concept of "revenue effort."[5] Revenue effort measures the extent to which a taxing jurisdiction is tapping its tax base relative to

---

[5] For some data on revenue effort among the states, see James A. Maxwell, *Financing State and Local Governments*, rev. ed., Brookings Institution, Washington, D.C., 1969.

some national average. Although it is usually computed on the state level, it also can be used to compare the taxing effort of a local government. Revenue effort gives the ratio of tax collections from all sources in a taxing jurisdiction per $1000 of personal income in that jurisdiction to the national average among taxing jurisdictions of revenues raised per $1000 of personal income.

$$\text{Revenue effort} = \frac{\text{revenue per \$1000 of personal income}}{\substack{\text{national average of revenue raised} \\ \text{per \$1000 of personal income}}} \qquad (12.2)$$

This measure has a number of serious shortcomings. Basically, it is designed to measure the extent to which a taxing jurisdiction is tapping its local tax base. However, it does not consider the fact that jurisdictions with low levels of personal incomes require high relative revenue efforts to maintain the same level of per-capita public expenditures financed in jurisdictions having high levels of personal incomes. Furthermore, differences in revenue efforts can be explained by different expenditure needs and demands among the taxing jurisdictions. In general, areas with higher population densities and greater percentages of their populations living in cities require greater levels of local public expenditures. Differences in revenue efforts also reflect differences in collective choices among communities for the allocation of resources between public and private uses. Communities that desire high-quality school systems are likely to surrender significant amounts of their property rights to private resources in the form of taxes to finance expenditures on schools and, thus, have high revenue efforts.

Thus, a value for revenue effort that is greater than the average value for the type of taxing jurisdiction implies that the jurisdiction is raising a greater amount of revenue than the national average per $1000 of personal income. This, in turn, can mean a number of things. First, it is possible that citizens in this taxing jurisdiction have strong preferences for local public expenditures compared to other communities. Second, it can mean that the community has a low level of per-capita income relative to other communities and, therefore, requires greater revenue effort to maintain the national average of per-capita public expenditures. Finally, it can mean that this community, because of either geographic or demographic characteristics, requires more expenditures per capita than the national average to meet the basic needs for public services by its populace.

The chief shortcoming of the revenue-effort measure is the fact that it ignores the expenditure side of the budget. Any concept of "taxable capacity" tends to be without meaning, because the extent to which a community wishes to tax itself depends on the collective choices it makes concerning the allocation of resources between public and private uses. To compensate somewhat for these faults, some economists prefer to calculate "benefit-effort ratios" to compare the fiscal performances of taxing jurisdictions.

A benefit-effort ratio is computed as follows:

$$\text{Benefit-effort ratio} = \frac{\text{expenditures per capita}}{\text{revenue effort}} \tag{12.3}$$

Of course, expenditures per capita are adjusted for price differentials in inputs among regions. In addition, some economists prefer to include only that amount of personal income above the poverty line of about $800 per capita when computing revenue effort to partially adjust for differences in income levels among states.[6] Using this adjustment, very poor states and other taxing jurisdictions have negative benefit-effort ratios. The adjusted benefit-effort ratio gives a more balanced indication of fiscal performance than does ordinary revenue effort. Since it considers both sides of the budget, it provides better information concerning the need for fiscal equalization. Areas with low or negative benefit-effort ratios are good candidates for transfers designed to pull their quantities and qualities of local public services up to those of the average national level.

LOCAL GOVERNMENTS AND EXTERNALITIES

As previous discussion suggests, collective choices made by local governing units concerning the allocation of resources between public and private uses can have effects that "spill over" to residents in other communities who do not participate in the collective decisions. The spill-over effects are non-compensated costs and/or benefits. In other words, they are externalities caused by an improper size of the collective decision-making unit. Not all collective choices made by communities within the federal system generate external effects. Effects are most likely to occur for public activities such as air pollution control, sewage disposal, transportation, public health, urban planning and renewal, water supply, and educational facilities. On the other hand, the probability of intercommunity spill-over effects are much lower for local public services such as recreational facilities, libraries, museums, and police protection. When externalities exist among communities, economic analysis suggests that some form of coordinated public decision-making is desirable to internalize the external effects. Coordination can take the form of governmental consolidation, regional planning, or intergovernmental transfers designed to force communities to consider the spill-over effects of their collective actions.

Taxes can "spill out" as well. Local governments may succeed in "exporting" some of the costs of financing projects that yield only local benefits. When

---

[6] The benefit-effort ratio is computed in this manner for states and some localities by Lester C. Thurow in "Aid to State and Local Governments," *National Tax Journal*, March 1970.

this is the case, one expects, other things being equal, an overexpansion of local governmental activities for the community that succeeds in exporting its taxes. Local citizens are not bearing the full marginal costs of governmental activities, and they can be expected to vote for expansion in local public expenditures beyond the point where marginal benefits are just equal to marginal costs, if the political process itself is costless. Of course, if some taxes "spill in" from other communities while others "spill out," the effect on the level of governmental activities becomes more difficult to predict.

Governmental Consolidation

In principle, the motive for consolidation of neighboring units into larger collective decision-making units is to internalize external effects and reap benefits of economies of scale in the supplies of certain public services. In addition, consolidation allows an expansion of the tax base and reduced opportunities for economic units to avoid local taxation by changing locations. On the other hand, consolidation can serve to limit the opportunities for political participation and to reduce the capacity of the federal system to accommodate a wide array of preference patterns for public services. In other words, the diversity of quality and quantity of local public services is reduced by consolidation. This leads to inefficiencies unless consolidation internalizes interjurisdictional externalities.

Consolidation can take the form of a metropolitan government that comprises many governing units in an economically integrated area. It can also take the form of a merger between two bordering communities on terms mutually agreed upon by residents of both communities. Among the factors to be considered in consolidation, or merger, are the benefits of internalizing externalities, economies of scale, and the costs of possible reduced political participation and reduced diversity in the supply of public services. Furthermore, although consolidation reaps economies of scale for the supplies of some public services, it also can result in diseconomies of scale in the supplies of other public services. Most empirical studies show that significant economies of scale in local public services beyond a supply level of 100,000 residents occur only in water, electric, gas, and sewage-disposal services. Thus, consolidation of communities larger than 100,000 residents is likely to result in net diseconomies of scale. The consolidation approach to internalizing externalities is, therefore, clumsy in the sense that it coordinates decision-making on a bundle of public services not all of which truly generate spill-over effects and/or economies of scale. This suggests that regional planning commissions and other forms of intergovernmental cooperation and bargaining in specific areas are more effective methods of internalizing intergovernmental externalities. Such cooperation should be limited to areas of collective action in which intercommunity spillovers are prevalent, while retaining the identity and independence of local governing units to deal with collective problems not generating significant spill-over effects. This can be accomplished by "special districts" created to purchase particular public services from higher levels of government and private business firms. This enables citizens to satisfy their preferences for public services by remaining members of relatively small communities with diverse public budgets, while bargaining with other communities for internalizing the external costs and benefits associated with the supply and financing of particular public services.

Intergovernmental Transfers and Regional Planning

Intergovernmental transfers can be used to compensate for regional income differentials accounting for varying capacities among state and local governments to provide essential services. However, such grants are most useful as a device to help correct distortions in collective decision-making induced by interjurisdictional spill-over effects. The categorical grant-in-aid can be considered as a method that attempts to internalize the external effects of local collective decisions on specific expenditure projects by substituting some federal control for complete local autonomy.

A *categorical grant-in-aid* is a transfer of funds from a higher level of government to a lower level with specified conditions attached to the expenditure of the funds. Some federal grants contain the requirement that recipient jurisdictions match each dollar of federal aid with a certain amount of locally raised revenue. General unconditional grants differ from categorical grants by sharing revenues among governments with no "strings" attached to the use of the funds.

Federal aid to encourage expenditures on particular projects is used as an inducement to state and local governments to pursue activities in general accord with "national goals." Perhaps the most famous example of an early categorical grant-in-aid program is the nineteenth-century Morrill Act, which established the so-called land-grant colleges in the states. Essentially, this program granted both land and funds to states that agreed to establish colleges of various kinds. In effect, this served to internalize some of the external interjurisdictional benefits associated with higher education by subsidizing state expenditures for public colleges.

The bulk of federal intergovernmental transfers in the United States today are in the form of the categorical grant-in-aid. In 1968, total federal aid to state and local governments totaled over $18 billion, or 16 percent of the federal revenues. Most of this aid was to state governments, while lesser amounts were given directly to local governments. The three most important categories of federal aid to states are for highway construction, public assistance (welfare), and educational expenditures. These three categories include about 85 percent of total federal aid to state governments. As previous discussion indicates, these three areas of governmental activities tend to have various inter-regional and interjurisdictional spill-over effects. The major functions for which federal transfers are made directly to local governments include education, housing and community redevelopment, waste-treatment facilities, and airport construction. Again, these are areas of expenditure with likely spill-over effects.

If categorical grants are to be efficient tools for internalizing externalities, then they must be allocated according to a system that accurately evaluates spillovers and their ranges. In point of fact, precise measurement is often impossible. Instead, formulas for allocating federal grants among functions and governmental units often are based on rough approximations of spill-over costs and benefits and distributive considerations in relationship to collective notions of national goals and priorities as manifest through the Congress and executive branch of government. Often, specific grant-in-aid programs outlive their usefulness but are retained because of political patronage and/or bureaucratic entrenchment. Perhaps some grant-in-aid programs for agricultural purposes currently fall into this category. In addition, if there are opportunities for communities to engage in bargaining to internalize externalities, then categorical grants are unnecessary and their use may result in inefficiencies.

There also are significant amounts of aid designed to internalize externalities granted directly by the states to their own local governmental subdivisions. As in the case of federal aid, the bulk of such funds appear to be designed to internalize externalities caused by inappropriate sizes of the collective decision-making units. The major local functions subsidized by state-aid programs are education, public welfare, and highways.

When spillovers exist, there is a tendency for either overspending or underspending depending on whether costs or benefits are spilling over and the extent of spillovers among communities. When it is determined that the spillovers lead to an undersupply of public services, categorical grants-in-aid are reasonable tools to use in order to subsidize governmental activities that generate external benefits. The existence of a categorical grant program for a particular function has the effect of inducing an increase in local expenditure. However, in the case of most functions that generate external benefits, all the benefits are not appropriable by the communities that are responsible for supply decisions. For example, in the case of educational expenditures, there tends to be spillout, because some of the recipients of education relocate to other areas after they finish their schooling. On the other hand, many recipients of educational services do remain in the community in which they are educated. Thus, efficiency considerations imply that some matching of funds is desirable. Ideally, the federal share of costs for a program is equal to the percent of net benefits spilling out from a particular local area. The local share is based on an estimate of the benefits retained by the community. While this, in principal, is desirable, accurate computations of spillouts virtually is impossible because of problems in quantifying and evaluating collectively consumed goods. However, some reasoned estimates of appropriate matching formulas are useful and are likely to improve resource allocations.

Finally, grant-in-aid programs can be used to promote regional planning and program coordination on functions that yield collectively consumed benefits over an area that encompasses many governmental jurisdictions. Examples of this form of extensive coordination include the efforts of the Appalachian Regional Commission, which attempts to coordinate planning and public investments in a geographical region that shares common problems but extends over the areas of many states. In addition, programs of community planning for urban redevelopment are sponsored by the U.S. Department of Housing and Urban Development and other federal agencies.

Thus, intergovernmental transfers and coordination, while not providing a panacea for problems unique to a federal system, do appear to be more delicate techniques for internalizing interjurisdictional externalities than does governmental consolidation when bargaining among communities is relatively costly. Intergovernmental aid permits diversities of supplies for those services that do not generate significant spillovers, while permitting extensive aid in functions where spillovers are significant. To improve the effectiveness of grants-in-aid it is desirable to further the understanding of spillovers and to improve methods for quantifying and evaluating their effects.

REVENUE SHARING

An alternative form of intergovernmental cooperation is direct revenue sharing. Revenue sharing, in its broadest form, attaches no strings on the expenditure of funds transferred among levels of governments. It simply transfers responsibility for raising revenues to the level of government that does so most efficiently—namely, the federal level—and allocates the funds among state and local governments on the basis of predetermined formulas that do not specify any conditions for expenditures. Unconditional revenue sharing would not be as effective in internalizing interjurisdictional externalities as categorical grants-in-aid, but it would increase the powers of state and local governments to supply their own public services without competitive effects of local taxation. It could, therefore, serve to broaden the opportunities for state and local political diversity.

Any revenue sharing plan specifies four basic policy variables:[7]

1. A formula for determining the total amount of federal revenues to be distributed among the states per year.
2. A formula specifying the allocation of total revenues to be shared among the alternative states.

[7] See Murray L. Weidenbaum and Robert L. Joss, "Alternative Approaches to Revenue Sharing," *National Tax Journal*, March 1970, for a more complete discussion and specifications of the variables.

3. A formula specifying the percentage of funds that should go to local governments in each state and the levels of local government that should be included in the sharing arrangement.
4. A specification of any restrictions to be placed on the expenditures of the federally shared funds.

Revenue sharing has been politically advertised as both a method for solving the fiscal crisis currently faced by many local and state governments and a technique for injecting a new vitality into the federal system of government. President Nixon titled his initial request for revenue sharing as "The New Federalism." Early versions of revenue-sharing plans stipulated that about 10 percent of federal tax collections should be set aside for the states.[8] A trust fund would be established to make periodic distributions to the state governments as the needs for expenditure accrued. The method of allocating funds among states was based on population in the early proposals. Each state was to receive the same per-capita share of funds although some states would contribute relatively more to the fund on a per-capita basis. The plan would, therefore, have the effect of redistributing income away from the relatively richer states to the relatively poorer states. Finally, early versions of the plan proposed that all funds be given directly to the state governments with no restrictions at all on the use of these funds and no specified formulas to direct the states to allocate a portion of shared federal revenues among their political subdivisions. However, some versions of the plan specified a "minimum pass-through" of, say, 50 percent, of funds allocated to each state to be earmarked for expenditures by cities on urban problems.

The benefits of revenue sharing to the citizens of any particular state or locality depend, in part, on the method chosen to finance the plan. If the plan is financed by an increase in federal taxes, and appropriations are made on the basis of population, then citizens in states whose appropriations are equal to the increase in taxes will not experience any opportunities for increased local public expenditures or reductions in local taxation. However, there may be some mild redistributive effects because of the change in the methods of collecting taxes if the federal income tax is substituted for, say, local property taxes. On the other hand, citizens in those states and localities where appropriations exceed the increased federal tax will experience net benefits, while in those states and localities where the increased federal tax exceeds appropriations, there will be a net loss in resources available for public and private expenditures. A likely consequence of such a revenue-sharing plan is, therefore, some redistribution of purchasing powers for both public and private goods among the citizens of the various states and political subdivisions.

If, however, the plan is financed through a reduction in federal expenditures, its impact is more difficult to trace. Insofar as the benefits of federal

---

[8] For example, see W. W. Heller, R. Ruggles, et al., *Revenue Sharing and the City*, Johns Hopkins Press, Baltimore, 1968.

expenditures are not the same for all citizens irrespective of the state or locality in which they reside, a plan with appropriations based on population is again likely to result in some redistribution of net benefits among citizens of alternative states and political subdivisions. Since it is difficult to impute benefits of many public services to individual citizens, this redistribution cannot be assessed easily.

The method of financing and appropriating revenue-sharing funds presumably will be determined through the political process on the *federal* level. If there are no "strings" attached to the expenditures of revenue-sharing funds by federal legislators and administrators, then the uses to which these funds are put will be determined by collective decisions on the *state and local* levels. The political processes on the state and local levels will determine whether the funds will be used to increase public expenditures or to reduce state and local taxes, thereby permitting an increase in private expenditures by citizens of particular states and localities. If citizens of states and localities collectively choose to use the funds to lower state and local taxes so as to offset the burdens of any increased federal taxes, then the revenue-sharing plan will have virtually no affect on the allocation of resources among public and private uses and will only result in some mild redistributive effects caused by shifts in tax burdens.

The Nixon Plan

The initial proposals for revenue sharing submitted to the Congress in 1970 by the Nixon administration contained specific plans for implementing a revenue-sharing program on a national basis. The President argued that this proposal would decentralize decision-making and, by giving more power to state and local governments, would enhance the responsiveness of governments to the collective needs of the populace.

The Nixon proposal specified an annual appropriation for any fiscal year of a fixed percentage of total taxable income to be set aside for revenue sharing. Under the initial proposal, this percentage was fixed at about 1 percent to be phased in over a period of years. This specifies the first policy variable for revenue sharing: the total amount of funds. Second, the Nixon plan specified a formula for state-by-state distribution of revenues. Essentially, the formula would distribute funds among states according to population with an adjustment for "revenue effort." That is, each state would receive a percentage of the total revenues equal to its proportion of total national population adjusted by the extent to which the state is tapping its tax base relative to the national average. States that are collecting more revenues per thousand dollars of personal income would obtain premiums from the federal government that are equal to the products of their shares computed on a population basis and the percent by which their revenue efforts exceed the national average. The effect of the revenue-effort adjustment is to provide an incentive for state governments to tap their own revenue sources. A proposed alternative by Senator Jacob Javits to the Nixon method of allocating revenue among states stipulates that only 85 percent of the revenue-sharing funds be distributed in this fashion. The remaining 15 percent would be allocated only to those states whose residents have an annual per-capita income below the national average, with the largest share of these funds going to the poorest state. The effect of this amendment would be to redistribute more income from the relatively rich states to the poorer states.

The initial Nixon plan further suggested that the states pass on a percentage of their revenue shares directly to local government that equals the ratio of locally raised general revenues in the state to the sum total of all state and locally raised revenues in the state. Each local government in any state would then receive a share that is equal to the ratio of their local general revenues to the total general revenues of all local governments in that state. This, of course, implies that local taxing jurisdictions currently raising the greatest amounts of taxes would receive the greatest shares of revenues. It is questionable that this formula would result in an efficient allocation of funds among local governments. A high relative tax-collection rate in a local community can mean many things. It can mean that the community has a decided preference for public goods or that it is experiencing unique problems necessitating high tax rates. A more recent version of the Nixon plan leaves the distribution of funds among local governments to the states, with a premium given to states that work out an "acceptable" local-government sharing arrangement.

Finally, most revenue-sharing plans specify only minimal restrictions on the usage of shared revenues. The revenue-sharing proposal submitted to the Ninety-Second Congress in 1971 by the President specifies a total appropriation of $16 billion for revenue sharing. Of this sum, $5 billion would represent new funds that would be shared with state and local governments on an unconditional basis. State and local governments could use these funds for general purposes at their own discretion with only minimal constraints imposed by the federal government. The remaining $11 billion would come largely from older federal programs. The expenditures of these remaining funds would be limited to six broad categories: urban development, rural development, education, transportation, job training, and law enforcement. The state and local governments would, however, be free to allocate their shares among projects in these categories in any manner they wished. It should be noted that the above six categories represent areas where interjurisdictional externalities are likely to prevail.

An Evaluation of Revenue Sharing

The fiscal implications of general unconditional revenue-sharing plans raise some interesting theoretical questions. The Nixon plan represents only one of many possible revenue-sharing arrangements. Each possible plan differs according to the specifications of the four basic policy variables listed. Consider the implications of revenue-sharing plans that specify absolutely no restrictions on the utilization of shared revenues.

The theory of public expenditure suggests that there is an interdependence between the revenue and expenditure sides of public budgets. That is, the level and mix of public expenditures demanded by the citizen is contingent, in part, on the cost-sharing arrangements. Efficient allocation of resources between private and public uses and among alternative public uses requires that those citizens directly affected by the public-expenditure decisions participate in the collective decisions. Insofar as general revenue sharing applies to expenditures that do not have national spill-over effects, one expects inefficiencies to result. The separation of expenditure and revenue decisions implicit in general revenue sharing is, therefore, likely to result in collective decisions that do not satisfy the Pareto criterion. The revenue decision will be made on the federal level, presumably in the Congress, while the expenditure decisions will be made on the state and local level. This could result in taxation without adequate representation. On the other hand, forcing Congress to consider and determine annual appropriations earmarked for state and local expenditures can serve to highlight social trade-offs among public uses that may not be obvious otherwise. For example, it might make clearer to the executive branch of government and to many congressmen the opportunity costs of increased allocations of resources to defense uses in terms of foregone public expenditures for state and local needs.

There are further problems involved in choosing and implementing formulas for allocating shared funds among state and local governments in order to channel resources to areas of use where the social returns are highest. In particular, it is questionable whether rigid formulas can be helpful in channeling resources toward solving the problems of large central cities in this country. While the distribution of funds among states is fairly straightforward, distribution of funds to local governments on any national basis may prove difficult because of inadequate data on local incomes and inadequate indicators of local fiscal requirements. Although it is often argued that state governments are likely to be more responsive to the needs of their residents, this is debatable. The relative efficiencies of the political processes on the federal and state levels is an empirical question that has not as yet been resolved. Some argue that substitution of state responsibility for some programs administered currently on the federal level will result in transfers of benefits of public services from certain minority groups to other groups. In addition, state and local governments are unlikely to formulate adequate social policies on issues that generate interjurisdictional spill-over effects.

Perhaps the most serious criticism against general revenue sharing is its limited scope for internalizing inter-regional externalities. Insofar as revenue sharing replaces current programs designed to internalize externalities, it may serve to impair efficient resource allocations. Federal aid to state and local governments on issues of truly national concern, in the sense that public expenditures have national spill-over effects, may be more desirable on efficiency grounds. For example, federal assumption of all public welfare costs may provide the same fiscal relief to state and local governments, while permitting national collective decision-making on a problem having national spill-over effects.

SUMMARY

In a federal system of government, there are alternative levels of government through which public services can be supplied. The optimal division of responsibility for supplying particular public services among levels of government depends on the relative efficiency of alternative governments. In general, collective activities that affect all citizens irrespective of their places of residence are most efficiently supplied on the federal level. Activities that are collectively consumed on the state or local levels are usually supplied most efficiently by state or local governments. When spill-over effects cross political jurisdictions, the result is inefficient collective choices even when the local political process is perfectly efficient. Interjurisdictional externalities can take the form of spill-out costs or spill-over benefits.

A federal system of government can improve efficiency by accommodating a wider array of preferences for public services than would be possible if there were only one level of government. Insofar as citizens are mobile, they can "vote on their feet" by choosing to locate in the community that best satisfies their tastes for public expenditures. According to this approach, local taxes are viewed as "prices" for a bundle of local public services. Citizens "shop" for a community in much the same way as they shop for a car. The mobility of taxable activities within the federal system acts as a constraint that may prevent local governments from pursuing inefficient public policies.

Interjurisdictional externalities can be internalized by informal bargaining among communities, governmental consolidation, regional planning, or intergovernmental grants. Governmental consolidation is somewhat more clumsy that the other alternatives as an internalization method because it merges a whole bundle of public services, while the other techniques allow subsidization and bargaining among communities on the output levels of particular public services. Direct revenue sharing is a form of intergovernmental transfer that specifies only minimal restrictions on the use of funds. Revenue sharing on the national level is likely to result in some redistribution of purchasing power for citizens in different states and localities but will not be effective as a means to internalize interjurisdictional externalities.

13

Urban Problems

In recent years, urban problems have reached "crisis" proportions in the United States. The problems faced by central cities include congestion, concentrated poverty, inadequate housing and education, increased pollution, and soaring crime rates. Many cities appear to be on the verge of bankruptcy because of the erosion of their tax bases and increased expenditure needs. This has led to the demand for increased state and federal aid by mayors and city managers.

Much of the analysis formulated in previous chapters can be applied to urban problems. The theory of public expenditure is useful in analyzing allocative effects of alternative sources of supply of local public goods and the demand for local public expenditures. The theory of taxation provides a basis for evaluating alternative urban financing arrangements in terms of their allocative and distributive effects. Furthermore, many of the problems of the cities and high-density living can be conceptualized as externalities. The problems may be solved by choosing the minimum-cost method of internalizing the externality once the interdependence has been defined and, if possible, measured.

THE CITY

Cities are exciting places. Although it is rather difficult to define a city in specific terms, certain characteristics appear common to all such geographic entities. It appears that cities are something other than simply "large towns."

Perhaps the most distinguishing feature is diversity. Cities supply diverse services both to their residents and to visitors. The population of a city is large and heterogeneous in terms of individual preferences. The diversity of tastes among inhabitants enables the city to support many kinds of economic activities for which markets do not exist in smaller municipalities. These include such cultural services as opera, dance, concerts, and theatre as well as other services including exotic restaurants, rare-book stores, and medical specialists. Furthermore, business activities are diversified and characterized by high-export rates to other communities and foreign countries. This implies that much of the income accruing to residents and business firms located in the city is derived from goods and services not consumed in the city itself.

How do cities develop? Some develop in response to certain natural advantages, such as proximity to a waterway (for example, a natural harbor or a river), while others develop in response to man-made industry. Examples of the first kind include New York City, London, and St. Louis. Examples of the second include Gary, Indiana, and Detroit, Michigan, which became centers for steel and auto production respectively. Other cities develop as centers for the distribution of agricultural produce. Kansas City, Missouri, is a good example of this.

Cities that rely too much on the production of a narrow range of goods and services can be subject to severe disruptions in economic activities in response to shifts in demand for their narrow range of outputs. In particular, successful and prosperous cities appear to develop a process of import substitution and adaptation that enables them to change their product mix quickly in response to shifts in relative demand.

Thus, in economic terms, a city represents a complex of inter-related markets for goods and services. Some goods and services produced can be viewed as primary outputs, while others can be considered supportive, or secondary, outputs contingent on the major services. Furthermore, the city comprises one very large labor market which the many business activities tap for their diverse man-power needs. And finally, one particular input appears to be used intensively in cities. This, of course, is land. Cities are characterized by intensive land use. The density of both people and physical capital relative to land is very high. For example, the average number of inhabitants per square mile of land in the United States was 50.5 for the year 1960, while in the City of New York, average density was 25,966 persons per square mile in the same year. Cities are not noted for "wide-open spaces." Land use is economized by building very tall buildings and locating them very close to one another. Cities, therefore, can be described as having very high labor-land and capital-land ratios relative to other kinds of geographic communities.

An economic description of a city cannot be expected to capture all complex features of one particular place. Many cities have unique characteristics of their own that stem from physical designs, geographical characteristics, and their inhabitants. There is a great deal of social interaction within and among "neighborhoods" in the city that cannot be explained in economic terms. The existence of various subcultures as well as ethnic and racial concentrations within the city gives rise to sociological problems that cannot be analyzed by the economist but that are, nonetheless, inherent in the nature of cities and their problems.

THE CENTRAL BUSINESS DISTRICT

Most cities appear to have "hearts" from which much of the economic activities are generated. This is a city's "central business district" (CBD). It is characterized by a complex of industries. Some of these industries serve world markets, while others serve local markets. For example, in New York City, the central business district includes industries that provide financial services and produce garments consumed on a national and global level as well as many retail-trade establishments, such as restaurants and department stores, that serve the local and tourist markets. The land in the CBD, therefore, is used mainly for commerce. There are few residences located in this area of the city. Apparently, there are some economies obtained through such intensive land use for commerce in the central business district. Insofar as the economic activity of the firms located in the CBD are interdependent and transportation and communication are costly, close proximity to each other serves to reduce production costs. This has, in the past, led many business firms to locate their economic activities within the central business district. Many cities have zoning laws that restrict land use in the central business district to commerce.

The CBD usually is surrounded by a residential area within the city limits. Residential areas usually have land devoted to apartments, private homes, and retail food and service outlets as opposed to commerce producing "exports" designed to serve larger national and local markets. The city residential areas are characterized by somewhat less intensive land use relative to the central business district. That is to say, the capital-land ratio usually is lower in the residential areas than in the CBD. Much of the labor power used within the central city during the day is housed in the city residential areas.

Finally, the city itself is surrounded by a ring of suburbs employing land for residential use. These suburbs typically are characterized by still less intensive land use than that which prevails within the central city and residential areas within the city limits. The suburbs tend to employ both lower capital-land and labor-land ratios than anywhere within the city. Furthermore, in the United States, these suburbs are separate political entities from the city itself. They have their own governments, raise their own revenue, and supply a bundle of public services to their residents. Since the end of World War II, there has been a migration of middle- and upper-income residents from the central cities to the surrounding suburban areas and political jurisdictions. The result is termed "urban sprawl." Much of the labor utilized in the central business district during the work week now resides in suburban areas and no longer pays property taxes to the city. The apparent preference for suburban living by middle-income citizens has contributed to the physical and financial problems of many cities. The suburbs offer more "open spaces," less congestion and pollution, sometimes less crime, and often lower taxes for a bundle of public services more in line with the tastes of middle-income citizens. Some business firms are also relocating their activities in the suburbs because the relative cost advantages of doing business in the CBD of the cities apparently have declined in recent years. Since many workers already live in the suburbs, the relocation of manufacturing and other businesses from the CBD to the suburbs raises the possibility for real cost savings in terms of reduced transportation time and expenses for employees and possibly a reduction in labor costs. These trends have contributed to decay and lagging growth in many urban centers in recent years. Furthermore, many cities are experiencing increased unemployment rates among their remaining residents as a partial result of the migration of human and physical resources to suburbia. This implies that cities are inefficient production locations under current economic circumstances. An additional problem created by the migration of middle-income residents to the suburbs is the resulting concentrations of poor people who remain as residents in the central cities. Furthermore, many of these poor residents are non-white. This gives a distinctly racial characteristic to urban poverty. Many of our largest cities are projected to have populations composed of over 50 percent non-whites by the year 1985. Aside from soaring income maintenance costs, this poverty results in many other costly societal effects that contribute to the decay of the city. These include increased welfare rates and educational costs.

URBAN LAND USE

A key factor in urban development concerns the decisions by private economic units to locate physical capital in urban space. In acquiring land as an input to combine with physical capital, an investor may be considered as purchasing two goods: land and location.[1] The price of the land reflects its opportunity cost in alternative uses at that point in urban space. In general, one expects land in more "desirable" locations to command relatively higher prices (other things being equal). Of course, the "desirability" of a location depends on the use to which that land can be employed as an input. This, in turn, depends on the profitability of the output produced on that land by combining it with other inputs at that location. The price of the land is a function of its most profitable use. If the profitability of land use varies inversely with distance from

---

[1] This is discussed in more detail by William Alonso, "A Theory of the Urban Land Market," *Papers and Proceedings of the Regional Science Association*, vol. 6, 1960, pp. 149–157.

the central business district, then one expects the price of land to vary inversely with its distance from the CBD.

A relevant question to pose is, "What factors determine the relative profitability of land use in the CBD?" One factor is transportation cost. Another is the external effects of economic activity that tend to be internalized in the central business district. These internalized costs are known as "agglomerative economies." They are caused by the close proximity of complementary economic activities.

In explaining the formation of central business districts of cities in the nineteenth century, Leon Moses and Harold Williamson argue that a key factor in the development of such urban "cores" was the high relative costs of moving physical resources within cities as compared to the costs of moving human resources within cities and physical resources between cities.[2] The economies of scale in rail transport are such that one central freight station handles incoming shipments most efficiently. On the other hand, prior to the early twentieth century, the dominant mode of moving goods within the city itself was the horse and wagon—a relatively costly mode of transport. This led firms to locate relatively close to the central rail station and, thus, relatively close to one another to minimize the freight-transport costs of doing business. Furthermore, there were economies in moving people within the core-dominated city because the compactness allowed the construction of trolley and city rail systems. Thus, Moses and Williamson suggest:

> The cost of moving goods was, therefore, high relative to the cost of moving people. This relative cost relationship played a crucial role in the emergence of the core-dominated city. The lower transport costs associated with location in the core exceeded the reduction in cost possible from lower wages and rents at sites in the satellite area. A prerequisite for decentralization was the breaking of the transport tie to the core.[3]

Such a prerequisite emerged in the early twentieth century in the form of the motor truck, which greatly lowered the relative costs of moving goods within the central city. Furthermore, improvements in highways later in the twentieth century reduced reliance on railroads for shipment of freight between cities and, hence, further reduced the relative advantages of locating economic activities near the central rail stations. The final *coup de grâce* for the central business district occurred in the post-war era, with the proliferation of the private automobile and an improved road system that greatly broadened the urban labor market. All these factors contributed to the decentralization of economic activities in metropolitan areas, the consequent "urban sprawl," and the economic decline of the central business districts. The relative cost advantages of locating economic activity in the CBD diminished to zero very

[2] Leon Moses and Harold F. Williamson, "The Location of Economic Activity in Cities," *American Economic Review*, May 1967, pp. 211–222.

[3] Moses and Williamson, p. 213.

quickly and may, perhaps, even be negative for some forms of activity. The transportation and communication innovations of the twentieth century have simply eliminated many of the "agglomerative economies" that led to the formation of large core-dominated cities. This, in turn, implies that, under existing technology, cities are inefficient locations for many types of business activities.

URBAN GOVERNMENTAL ACTIVITY
AND PUBLIC SERVICES

In a federal system of government, the city is a political unit with its own political institutions designed to articulate demands for public services and supply the collectively chosen amounts to citizens. If the city government pursues inefficient policies, one expects (other things being equal) those citizens who are mobile and feel that the marginal costs of city public services exceed their marginal benefits to leave the area if substitute political communities are available. In political terms, a city is only one of many alternative types of subcentral governing units. If its political process imposes excessive external costs on residents, then one expects that the city will not survive as a political unit. Citizens will turn to higher levels of government or move to alternative localities to satisfy their demands for services which they believe are being inefficiently supplied by the city government.

When the marginal cost of correcting a city problem exceeds the marginal gain, it is inefficient to attempt a solution. It is possible that some large cities already have reached a state where it is inefficient under existing technology to attempt solutions for many problems. When this is the case, the efficient public policy simply may be to let the city deteriorate as alternative land-use patterns and political arrangements are sought by existing residents of the city. The city land eventually will be redeveloped for more socially productive uses.

Every city must supply certain basic public services to support the activities of its residents. Included in such basic services are water and sewer facilities, police, fire, and sanitation services, as well as inspection, health, judicial, and educational services. The city government should supply only those services that are inefficiently provided by private enterprise and other levels of government. In recent years, city governments encountered sharp increases in the costs of supplying many basic services. These cost increases are attributed to a variety of causes. Included in such explanations are inept city administrations, difficulties in increasing the productivity of local civil servants, and the lack of competitive forces in the public sector.

The unit cost of supplying any good or service depends on the technology available to produce the output and the costs of the optimal input combination. City governments purchase inputs in the form of labor services, capital, and land from the private sector and transform them, according to the available technology, into the collectively agreed upon levels of public outputs, such as police or sanitation services. Since much of the output of the urban public sector tends to be collectively consumed, one encounters difficulties in defining the output in physical (that is, measurable) terms for the purpose of economic analysis.

In order to determine whether economies of scale do exist in the supply of any of these local public services, a consistent definition of output must be chosen. Often, it is necessary to choose that which, in actuality, is an intermediate output in order to obtain quantitative measures of public outputs. These intermediate outputs are only proxies for the true collectively consumed public services, and in many cases, they must be adjusted to reflect quality differences. For example, in the case of police protection, the true final output is likely to be something called "public safety." An intermediate output necessary to produce public safety is police patrolling. This intermediate output can be measured by some estimate of the degree of surveillance, such as the number of times a city block is passed by police patrolmen per day. The level of actual public safety provided by these patrols depends not only on their quantity but also on the quality of surveillance. Presumably, a policeman in an electronically equipped patrol car provides more effective surveillance than a foot patrolman with inadequate communication equipment. Raw data on patrols, therefore, have to be adjusted by quality indexes to obtain a consistent measure of outputs.

Another complication in measuring public outputs stems from the fact that differences in environmental factors require varying amounts of intermediate outputs to produce the same level of final public outputs. For example, in a crime-prone neighborhood, more patrols per city block per day may be necessary to supply the area with the same level of public safety as a more tranquil area of the city. The fact that one neighborhood in the city has more police patrols than another in no way implies that the first neighborhood is consuming a higher level of public safety. It may merely mean that the ratio of required police patrols to a unit of actual public safety is higher in the crime-ridden area. This implies that intermediate public output, even when adjusted for quality differences, may be a poor measure of final public output. Environmental variables have to be considered, and intermediate public output should be adjusted to reflect the environmental differences.[4] Of course, these adjustments are not necessary for publicly supplied outputs that are not collectively consumed to any great degree. Included in this latter category are water, sewer, and transportation services supplied by city governments.

The terms at which intermediate public output can be transformed into final public output depends on the technology available. For example, in the case of public educational services, the intermediate outputs are lessons in

---

[4] For a more rigorous discussion of this point, see D. F. Bradford, R. A. Malt, and W. E. Oates, "The Rising Cost of Local Public Services: Some Evidence and Reflections," *National Tax Journal*, June 1969.

particular areas of learning. The final outputs are some kind of learned skill. If there is some sort of innovation in teaching methods (for example, programmed learning combined with computer use), one expects a decrease in the number of lessons required for students to reach particular levels of skill (as measured by uniform objective tests).

With the complications in mind, consider some of the explanations of sharply increasing costs (about 5 to 7 percent per year) in supplying local public services in recent years. First, consider the manner in which unit cost varies with output when the cost of inputs remains constant and technology is fixed. Under these conditions, if there are economies of scale, one expects average costs of production to fall as output is increased. Insofar as output varies directly with the population of an urban area, population can be taken as a proxy measure of level of output in some cases. Most studies of public utilities (electricity, gas, sewage, and so forth) supplied by local governments indicate that average costs of production fall with increased outputs. There are thus advantages of producing these services with a large population base. On the other hand, empirical studies of police protection, refuse collection, and public education have indicated that there are neither economies nor diseconomies of scale in the supply of these services. For these services, average costs of production under conditions of fixed input prices and technology tend to be invariant with population.[5] Other services, such as fire protection and hospitals, show economies of scale over low output levels but diseconomies of scale over higher output ranges. The cost curves for these activities tend, therefore, to be U-shaped over population. One study by Robert Will, for example, indicates that the unit costs of fire protection fell with increased population to a point of 300,000 residents.[6] Thereafter, unit costs tend to rise with population. Depending on whether economies of scale outweigh diseconomies of scale, one expects average costs of urban public services to rise or fall with population under conditions of fixed input prices and technology.

In reality, input prices and technology are not likely to be fixed. Thus, the observed variance in average costs of public services over time and across communities depends on economies of scale, changes in input prices, and changes in technology. William Baumol argues that the sharply rising costs of supplying urban public services in recent years can be explained by rising input costs and lagging technological innovation.[7] Baumol argues that the technology of supplying most urban public services is such that increases in productivity are hard to achieve. Most urban services, such as police, education, sanitation, and

[5] For a summary of studies on economies of scale in local public services, see Werner Z. Hirsch, *The Economics of State and Local Government*, McGraw-Hill, New York, 1970, pp. 178–184.

[6] Robert E. Will, "Scalar Economies and Urban Service Requirements," *Yale Economic Essays*, vol. 5, Spring 1965, pp. 1–62.

[7] William J. Baumol, "Macroeconomics of Unbalanced Growth: The Anatomy of Urban Crisis," *American Economic Review*, June 1967.

inspection activities are highly labor intensive. The opportunities for substituting capital for labor are limited by the nature of the services performed. Baumol argues that urban public services are subject only to "sporadic" increases in productivity. This implies that there is a basic difference between the manufacturing sector of the economy (which Baumol refers to as "technologically progressive") and the public sector. Wage increases in the progressive sector can be offset by innovations that increase labor productivity, while in the "non-progressive" sector, such innovations are not readily obtainable.

Costs increase because wage levels in the "non-progressive" urban public sector are tied to wage levels in the "progressive" manufacturing sector. While the increases in wage levels in manufacturing are being offset by increases in productivity, this is not the case in the urban public sector. As a result, unit costs of production are rising for public services relative to manufacturing outputs.

The major explanation of the link between civil servants' and industrial workers' wages is the existence and growth of labor unions in the urban public sector. These unions have increased labor costs, which comprise the major input in urban public services, in the last 20 years. But there have been only periodic increases in productivity to offset the wage increases. The problem is further complicated by the fact that the demands for urban public services tend to be income elastic. Thus, the size of the urban public sector tends to increase in greater proportion than gross national product increases despite increases in unit costs. The result is ever-increasing expenditure burdens for city budgets, with no apparent end in sight. The strength and power of municipal employees' unions appears to be increasing steadily over the years. This implies that city governments have to attempt to achieve productivity increases by more rational budgeting techniques to offset the rising labor costs.

Empirical support for Baumol's hypotheses is provided by Bradford, Malt and Oates.[8] In a study of education, health and hospital, police and fire protection, and welfare administration services they conclude that rising unit costs of production in these activities have been a major determinant of the sharp increases in local public expenditures since World War II. Furthermore, their analysis indicates that the major source of these cost increases have been increases in the wages and salaries of municipal employees, while there have been no major cost-saving innovations.

A final explanation of the "cost-squeeze" faced by cities is that city government administration is inefficient. It is argued that since public servants and bureaucrats do not face market tests of profit or loss, there is inadequate incentive to seek and employ input combinations embodying minimum costs and to seek innovations in technology. If this is, in fact, the case then it appears that innovations in budgeting policies (such as instituting program budgeting techniques on the local level) may be needed to stop the trend to

[8] Bradford, Malt and Oates, pp. 189–202.

rising costs of supplying urban public services. Such budgeting techniques, if they are effective, force bureaucrats to define their missions (outputs), delineate alternative ways of accomplishing those missions, and choose the minimum cost alternatives. Other alternatives include transferring the responsibility for supply of certain urban public services to other levels of government or to private enterprise, if they can be supplied more efficiently by other means. If, for example, the administration of income maintenance services are more efficiently supplied by the federal government in the presence of interjurisdictional spillovers, then these services should be transferred from local and city governments to the federal government. If sanitation services can be supplied more efficiently by having citizens contract for the services of private sanitation firms, then this can be a better alternative than having the city attempt to run its own sanitation service. Competition among private sanitation firms might promote productivity increases and keep the costs of sanitation service down.

URBAN PROBLEMS AND PUBLIC POLICY

Among the problems confronting urban areas and governments today are the supply of adequate housing and transportation facilities, the supply of education, and increased crime. Governmental activities at all levels as well as private initiative are alternative means to implement solutions to these problems. The following sections discuss some of the problems confronting cities today and evaluate some alternative solutions.

Housing and Urban Renewal

A major portion of any city's physical capital takes the form of housing units. The housing within the city is quite diversified and consists of both single-family homes and multiple-family dwellings. The residences within the city are of varying ages and in varying states of repair. In recent years, there has been increasing concern about the quality of housing in many of the major cities in the United States. The stock of housing in many cities has deteriorated into a state of decay. Poor-quality housing is usually the only kind within economic reach of low-income residents of the city. It, therefore, is profitable for landlords to devote some land to substandard housing rather than convert it to alternative uses. In many cases, demolition of substandard housing actually can worsen the plight of the urban poor by raising the cost of housing.

Most housing in the United States is privately supplied. Although the federal government does subsidize homeownership through liberal income tax deductions and subsidies to the mortgage markets and through public housing projects, the incentive to develop land for housing uses is, by and large, controlled by the profit motive. In the case of blighted urban areas, that motive apparently is inadequate to encourage redevelopment and reinvestment in housing units. The lack of private incentive to redevelop housing in slum areas can be comprehended in terms of the theory of externalities. For the purposes of this discussion, a *slum* is defined as a constrained geographic area within which all structures are substandard or in a general state of disrepair. Furthermore, it is assumed that the housing in the slum area currently is owned by a multitude of landlords. Each landlord is confronted with the choice of reinvesting his scarce capital resources in his existing housing stock or employing his capital in some alternative use (for example, investing in stocks or bonds). Naturally, the landlord seeks to use his capital in such a manner as to obtain the highest expected return adjusted for risk. If any one property owner in the slum decides to invest in the improvement of his property, the net return he earns is likely to be lower than the return he earns from alternative investments. This is because the value of his property does not depend solely on his investment in it but also on the neighborhood in which it is located. That is to say, the return from his investment in his own property is dependent not only on his actions but also on the actions of other property owners in the community. As long as only one property owner invests, the character of the neighborhood does not change substantially, and the increase in the investor's property values are likely to be minimal. On the other hand, any one investor, by renewing his property, is likely to increase the return on neighboring properties at no cost to those property owners. This is because it marginally improves the quality of the neighborhood, thereby increasing the demand for all housing surrounding the renewed property and increasing rents (assuming no rent control). In view of such interdependence and the lack of compensating arrangements for external benefits bestowed, any one property owner tends to have more to gain from not investing in his property.[9] Although it might be profitable to invest in property when *all* owners do so simultaneously, individual action is wanting because of the lack of a means for extracting compensation for the external benefits bestowed upon neighboring property owners. In the absence of institutional arrangements to coordinate investment decisions, renewal of the neighborhood is not likely to occur through individual action.

In view of these problems, Davis and Whinston have offered a precise definition of *urban blight*: "Blight is said to exist whenever (1) strictly individual action does not result in redevelopment, (2) the coordination of decision-making via some means would result in redevelopment, and (3) the sum of benefits from renewal could exceed the sum of costs."[10] Governmental action to eliminate blight is justified only when such action is deemed the most efficient method of coordinating the investment decisions of the individual

---

[9] For more detailed analysis of this, see Otto A. Davis and Andrew B. Whinston, "Economic Problems in Urban Renewal," in Edmund S. Phelps (ed.), *Private Wants and Public Needs*, rev. ed., W. W. Norton, New York, 1965, pp. 140–153.

[10] Davis and Whinston, p. 147.

property owners in the area. This definition implies that, in some cases, slum housing may in fact be the most efficient use of land where coordination of investment decisions does not result in profitable investments. In such cases, the residents of the area can be better compensated by direct income transfers rather than indirect transfers through improved housing.

When, then, is governmental subsidy of urban renewal justified? One can argue that governmental subsidization of renewal is desirable when the benefits of renewal spill over among neighborhoods. That is to say, even if coordination of investment decisions within the community does not provide the incentive to invest, there may still be some external benefits collectively consumed by the whole region (or even nation) generated by renewal. If this is, in fact, the case, collective subsidy of renewal can be desirable. This reasoning apparently underlies housing policy in the United States.

Both the National Housing Act of 1949 and the subsequent Housing Act of 1954 established federal subsidies for urban-renewal projects. Under the provisions of the 1949 act, the federal government subsidized the costs involved in clearing urban land and selling it to private interests for redevelopment. The 1954 act provided additional funds to subsidize public improvements (such as recreational and educational facilities) in urban renewal areas and Federal Housing Administration insurance for mortgages secured by new properties in the renewal areas.[11] The Housing Acts had the effect of channeling federal revenues into the rehabilitation of central business districts in urban areas. Essentially, an urban-renewal project clears land of residential "slums" and subsidizes coordinated reinvestments in the land in the form of new residential and business structures.

As is pointed out by Alan Campbell and Jesse Burkhead, any urban renewal program has three essential elements:[12]

1. The utilization of the state's power of eminent domain for the purpose of site assembly in the renewal area. This includes the process of eviction and relocation of displaced households and firms.
2. The use of federal subsidies to "write down" land values to a point where private development of the area is economically profitable.
3. The development of a workable plan for renewal by the local authorities designing the project.[13]

It remains to evaluate the efficacy of urban-renewal programs in rehabilitating the aggregate stock of housing in urban areas.

[11] For details of the 1954 Housing Act, see Jerome Rothenberg, *Economic Evaluation of Urban Renewal*, Brookings Institution, Washington, D.C., 1967, p. 7.

[12] Alan K. Campbell and Jesse Burkhead, "Public Policy for Urban America," in Harvey S. Perloff and Lowdon Wingo, Jr. (eds.), *Issues in Urban Economics*, Resources for the Future, Johns Hopkins Press, Baltimore, Md., 1968, p. 591.

[13] For a discussion of the "workable plan," see Rothenberg, p. 6.

The Costs and Benefits of Renewal

Urban-renewal projects have been widely criticized for undervaluing costs and overvaluing the benefits associated with redevelopment. In addition, it has been charged that, by and large, such projects reduce the real income of the poor. As a final indictment of the program, some question whether urban renewal is a proper activity for the federal government.

Among the benefits of urban renewal is an upgrading in the physical capital of the city. Insofar as the project improves housing quality, there is a net benefit to society. In addition, it is argued that there is often an "aesthetic" benefit to the city as a result of the elimination of the "eyesore" of substandard, dilapidated housing in the city's core. Although this may, in fact, be a true benefit, it is likely to be collectively consumed and very difficult to measure. Aesthetics, after all, is a very subjective phenomenon. Some may very well argue that the new architectural styles that replace the old slum structures are, in fact, "uglier" than the displaced structures. It is also argued that the elimination of slums tends to reduce crime rates by ridding the city of a crime-infested neighborhood. Finally, it is argued that the renewal aids the economic redevelopment of the CBD, thereby expanding the local tax base.

It must, however, be emphasized that the listed benefits are true benefits to society if and only if they are not offset by other costs in the form of reductions in incomes and welfare in other parts of the city and region. Insofar as the benefits of the renewal project are capitalized into higher property values, the preceding proposition may be restated in the following manner: Urban renewal produces a net gain to society if and only if there is a net increase in property values within the city or region. That is to say, property value increases in the renewal area must not be offset by property value decreases elsewhere.[14]

A key to answering the questions is to trace the movements of the households and business firms displaced by the project. These individuals are likely to have low incomes and will, therefore, seek relatively inexpensive housing. Unfortunately, it appears that the net effect of urban renewal to date has been to reduce the city's stock of low-cost housing. If this is, in fact, the case, families are forced to "double-up" in the remaining units available in order to live within their budget constraints. This suggests that low-income residents, in seeking to relocate subject to their budget constraints, are likely to form another slum in some other area of the city. If this reduces property values in this area of the city, the net gain to the community is the increase in value of the renewal property less the decrease in property values in the newly created "slum" areas. One empirical study yields results that suggest

---

[14] See Hugh O. Nourse, "The Economics of Urban Renewal," *Land Economics*, vol. 42, February 1966.

that the increments in property values as a result of renewal are just offset by property value decrements in other areas of the city.[15] That is to say, the net benefit of the renewal project is zero! This leads Nourse to conclude: "The notion that renewal of the complete clearance type merely shifts slums around implies that slums are due to the poverty of people and that this class of person will always be with us."[16] Insofar as the housing problem is really a poverty problem, this analysis suggests that rent supplements that enable low-income families to afford the higher quality housing in the renewal area, after the project is complete, can improve the efficacy of renewal projects in truly redeveloping the city.

On the costs side, it is often argued that actual resource costs of acquiring and clearing land in the renewal area understate the true social costs of the project. This is because these costs do not include the disruptive effects of relocating displaced families and business firms. It can be argued that these represent true social costs to society because the time and effort in relocating involves a real loss of output and welfare. Unfortunately the disruptive costs of the demolition of a neighborhood are extremely difficult to measure. All too often no effort is made to estimate these costs of the project. They are simply ignored.[17]

On the other hand, the subsidization of land in the area often results in windfall gains to the private interests that develop the renewal area. All this suggests that, to date, many of the "net benefits" of urban renewal really are transfers. Furthermore, the transfers reduce the quality of life for the poorest residents of the city, while aiding those that are least in need of aid. The program can be improved, it would appear, by concentrating on supplying quality housing to low-income groups, with a minimum amount of disruption to their lives. Rent subsidies can increase the demand for quality housing sufficiently to encourage private investment in housing without direct federal intervention in the housing market.

Finally, it is questionable whether federal subsidies of urban renewal are justified. Subsidies lower the costs of renewal to local governments and, thereby, result in more renewals than would be forthcoming in the absence of subsidies. This is desirable on efficiency grounds only to the extent that benefits of renewals are, in fact, collectively consumed on the national level. Since cities are, in fact, "national assets" that can be visited by any resident of the country, their states of repair are in the national interest. But, if the extent of these national spillovers are overestimated in determining the federal subsidies, one expects an overallocation of resources to renewals and a consequent reduction in efficiency for the economy at large. Since these national spillovers from urban renewals are collectively consumed, they are difficult to measure precisely. The current federal subsidies are equal to two thirds of all

[15] Nourse, p. 68.
[16] Nourse, p. 69.
[17] For a discussion of these costs, see Campbell and Burkhead, p. 593.

planning and site preparation costs for localities of over 50,000 in population and three fourths of these costs for communities with less than 50,000 residents.

Urban Transportation

A vital capital input into the functioning of a city is its transportation network. Included in this capital input are roads, bus and subway systems as well as rail stations, air and sea ports. The latter provide transport links to other communities, while the former mainly provide transport services within the city. Currently, it appears that virtually all levels of government as well as private enterprise play roles in shaping urban-transportation policy. Some transportation facilities are publicly supplied in urban areas, while others are privately supplied. Among the key factors necessary to formulate a rational urban-transportation policy are knowledge of factors that influence the choice of mode of transport by citizen consumers, knowledge of present and future land-use patterns in urban areas, and knowledge of the technology of urban transport.

Many of the problems in urban transportation stem from the public's apparent preference for the private automobile as a mode of transport and the urban residential "sprawl" that increased availability of the automobile, in part, made possible in the post-World War II era. Most urban central business districts were designed prior to the automotive revolution of the twentieth century. In the CBD, there is inadequate separation of truck, bus, automobile, and pedestrian traffic. As a result, the CBD typically suffers from acute traffic congestion during business hours. This contributes to loss of commuter time, traffic accidents, air pollution, and other social costs. Many of these costs are external to users of private automobiles. Campbell and Burkhead have referred to the private automobile as "the greatest generator of externalities that civilization has ever known."[18] This suggests that some of the problems of urban transport can be alleviated by raising the relative price of automobile utilization in urban areas in such a manner as to "internalize" the external effects associated with its use. However, in many cases, this can be accompanied by increased supply of alternative modes of transport in the CBD if automobile usage is to be elastic with respect to the new user charges.

Furthermore, planning cannot be done rationally without considering those factors that influence the locational choices of business firms and households. The location patterns, as well as the prices of alternative transport modes, influence the demand for transportation facilities in the metropolitan areas. If the trend toward decentralization of economic activities continues, this has to be taken into account in planning future transportation networks.

There has been a marked increase in the construction of roads since the end of World War II. Interstate highway networks are planned and built by

[18] Campbell and Burkhead, p. 601.

the federal government. The interstate highway system is financed directly from earmarked revenues from the gasoline tax. There is no direct governmental subsidy of the transport system. Adequate revenues are raised by the gasoline tax to support the federal highway system. On the other hand, urban roads are the responsibility of local governments. There is some reason to believe that local and state governments that supply roads in and to cities do indirectly subsidize motorists who use these roads during peak hours.[19] This is because peak users are not charged their full marginal costs (including congestion costs) of using urban arteries. This leads to an overuse of urban roads.

Among the methods suggested to eliminate overuse are user charges. These include higher tolls on roads and bridges leading into the cities as well as higher registration and parking charges for cars using city streets. Tolls and charges could be regulated according to the time of the day. Such "peak-load pricing" could have the effect of internalizing the external costs associated with urban usage of private automobiles. Higher charges could be applied during rush hours to discourage auto use in the cities during those hours. Other similar methods involve using lanes of certain roads for buses only during peak-load hours, thereby increasing congestion costs for individual motorists in the remaining lanes. Of course, the effectiveness of such user charges depends on the price elasticity of demand for automobile use as a mode of transport. This, in turn, depends on the alternative transport modes available to commuters to and within the cities.

Alternative transport available within the metropolitan areas includes rail, bus, and, possibly, boat service. In many cities, the rail and bus services are publicly supplied and heavily subsidized. There apparently are economies of scale involved in constructing such systems for high-density population areas, but cost considerations make it difficult to construct rapid-transit links to many low-density suburban areas surrounding the cities. One possible solution to this problem is to develop a few strategic rail or bus terminals in suburban areas along with large parking lots to encourage commuters to leave their cars in suburbia while riding mass transit to the city. In addition, jitney service—small buses responding to telephone calls and not following a fixed route—might discourage the use of the automobile for short trips and provide an economical mode of transport between mass-transit stations.

There is, no doubt, some interdependence between transportation facilities available, their prices, and residential choices. One expects that a sufficient increase in the relative price of private automobile usage in and to cities would ultimately alter the metropolitan residential pattern. If low-cost mass transit is available at various terminals in suburban areas, one expects a clustering of residences near the terminals. Of course, if it is difficult to reduce congestion in the CBD and provide inexpensive mass transit into the cities,

[19] See J. R. Meyer, J. F. Kain, and M. Wohl, *The Urban Transportation Problem*, Harvard University Press, Cambridge, Mass., 1965, pp. 62–69.

the effect may eventually be elimination of remaining economic advantages of locating activities in the CBD and a move to further decentralization of economic activities. Unless there are innovations in the technology of urban mass transport, this may be the ultimate effect.

Many urban residents are already "reverse commuters" in the sense that they travel out of the cities to work during the incoming rush hours, and vice versa. Many of these are low-income urban residents who are unable to reside near their suburban work places because of the relatively high cost of housing in these areas. Current commuter pricing methods result in the same fares for both the low-income people and the high-income suburban residents, who cause high congestion costs during peak-use hours. A change in pricing policies for mass transit that discriminates by length, direction, and time of travel may serve to internalize externalities and benefit low-income "reverse" commuters.

Solutions to the urban transportation problem may, therefore, require a redesigning of the CBD, investment in new mass-transit systems, and a significant change in the pricing of existing alternative modes of transport. The solutions may require considerable amounts of resources. Depending on the method of finance chosen, it may also entail increases in tax rates if public subsidy is deemed desirable. Some regional planning among local and state governments may also be necessary to internalize some of the interjurisdictional spillovers of fragmented public transportation policies.

Education

It has been estimated that 42.2 percent of the metropolitan poor were under eighteen years of age in 1968.[20] If the vicious cycle of poverty is to be broken, investments must be made in education for the children of the urban poor. However, there are some unique problems in supplying educational services to children in poverty-impacted neighborhoods. It is often argued that there are environmental factors, such as low motivation, poor study atmosphere at home, or poor diet, that make it difficult to transform traditional educational inputs (for example, teachers and books) into the required final output (for example, reading proficiency). This suggests that expenditures per pupil on educational services in ghetto areas may have to be significantly higher than those in areas where the students are not "disadvantaged" in order to produce the same educational results.

Until recently, per-pupil expenditures were, in fact, higher in the central cities' school systems relative to those in the surrounding suburban communities. However, the migration of middle-income residents to the suburbs in the past twenty years has reversed this trend by removing to the suburbs the

---

[20] Anthony Downs, *Who Are the Urban Poor?* rev. ed., Supplementary Paper number 26, Committee for Economic Development, New York, 1970.

tax base that traditionally supported city school systems. Since 1957 in the United States, per-pupil expenditures have been higher, on the average, in suburban communities than in the central cities.[21] The central city school has deteriorated in terms of the quality of both its inputs and outputs in recent years.

Cities apparently lack the resources to finance the type of educational system necessary to meet the needs of residents, particularly those residents of low-income households. Although there is significant state and federal aid to local governments to support education, this aid often is inadequate in increasing expenditures per pupil in the central cities' school systems. State aid often is distributed on a population basis and ignores some of the unique problems in supplying effective education in low-income areas. Since the spill-over benefits of education are likely to be consumed on a national level (for example, increase in literacy makes citizens more productive and decreases income maintenance costs), aid to education is considered an appropriate federal activity. It is sometimes argued that the role of the federal government in this area should be to assure that every citizen of the country receives a certain minimal amount of effective education irrespective of his place of residence. The Advisory Commission on Intergovernmental Relations argues that improved educational opportunity can be achieved by transferring the source of supply of both elementary and secondary education from local governments to the states. The commission argues that state assumption of public education costs would "release the local property tax for use in meeting growing non-educational costs, would halt much of the existing inter-local competition for industry and would mitigate exclusionary zoning practices directed against large, low-income families."[22]

Effective policies designed to improve urban education require measures of educational outputs and estimates of the "production functions" in urban education. Carefully designed objective tests may serve as a useful tool in evaluating the effectiveness of schools in transforming teacher services and capital inputs into such final outputs as reading and quantitative skills. Most studies of educational success among students show that the best prediction of educational achievement is family income, which apparently is a proxy for various environmental factors that affect student motivation.[23] This suggests that greater expenditures per pupil may be required for low-income students to achieve the same results as those achieved with lesser expenditures for middle-income students. Drastic innovations in the curriculums, teaching methods, and expenditures in central city schools may be necessary to offset the effects of growing concentrations of low-income families in the central cities. On the other hand, the celebrated Coleman Report argues that inte-

[21] Campbell and Burkhead, p. 612.

[22] Advisory Commission on Intergovernmental Relations, *Urban America and the Federal System*, GPO, Washington, D.C., 1969, p. 3.

[23] Campbell and Burkhead, p. 612.

gration of students from low-income families with students from middle-income families in schools may be the most efficient method of improving the educational achievement of disadvantaged children.[24]

Others argue that the basic problem with large central city school systems is the fact that they monopolize the supply of education and reduce competition in curriculums within the city.[25] Advocates of this argument believe that community control of schools and consequent decentralization of the school system is an effective method for assuring innovations designed to increase educational outputs in poverty areas. In order to be implemented, such a policy requires freedom of choices by families to decide where to send the children to schools within the city. Innovations presumably would be dispersed throughout the system under the pressures of public demand.

Crime

In recent years, there has been increasing concern about rising crime rates in urban areas. Crime is wasteful in economic terms because it destroys or impairs both physical and human capital. While some crimes are pure transfers (for example, burglary, embezzlement, and so forth), they involve wastes for society because criminals can presumably devote time and capital used in perpetrating crimes to legal uses that involve positive marginal social products for society. In addition, the potential for crime induces "honest" economic units to expend resources for precautions against criminal activities. These resources also reflect the costs of crime. In order to develop an effective public policy against crime in urban areas, it is necessary to study the factors that influence the potential criminals' choices between legal and illegal economic activities.

Clearly, if everyone is "honest," there is no crime. Under these circumstances, the valuation of incomes received through illegal economic activities is uniformly zero. Unfortunately, in the real world, everyone is not "honest." One expects individuals to engage in illegal activities if their return when adjusted for risk is significantly higher than that which they can receive through legal activities. This suggests that low-income individuals who lack skills that can be sold in markets for legal labor services are likely candidates to choose careers of crime. If they have skills but cannot put them to their best use because of, say, racial discrimination, the probability that individuals will choose criminal activities over legal activities also is high. In other words, the lower one's income in legal activities, the lower the opportunity costs of crime from that individual's point of view.

With the potential criminal's decision process in mind, one divides public policies designed to alleviate crime into two categories. One type of public

[24] James S. Coleman, *Equality of Educational Opportunity*, U.S. Department of Health, Education, Welfare, GPO, Washington, D.C., 1966.

[25] See Anthony Downs, *Urban Problems and Prospects*, Markham, Chicago, 1970, pp. 264–292.

expenditure decreases the expected return to crime for the criminal by increasing the probability of apprehension or the severity of punishment.[26] A second type of policy increases the opportunity cost of crime to the criminal by providing him with skills to enhance his income-earning potential in legal activity.[27] Ideally, a community chooses the minimum-cost combination of these two types of policies to achieve any given reduction in the amount of criminal offenses.

An interesting question to pose concerns the level of government to be responsible for police enforcement activities designed to decrease the returns from crime. If a city government pursues an effective crime-control program through increasing the probability of apprehension for any offense and criminals are mobile, then the effect of such a program merely can be to redistribute criminal activities within the region or nation. This suggests that police enforcement activities can have significant interjurisdictional spill-over effects. This in turn implies that optimal police activities can be those that are regionally or nationally coordinated. Crime control appears to be an appropriate public activity for federal aid.

Furthermore, the fact that training programs designed to increase the opportunity costs of crime for low-income individuals can be an effective method for reducing the costs of criminal activities in cities suggests that public budgeting for crime control might include such programs in the same category as police and correctional costs. This enables the public to make trade-offs between these two methods of reducing costs of criminal activities. Some activities, such as drug addiction, may best be considered health rather than crime problems. There is a need for research into both the costs of and motivation for crime to help determine rational public policies in urban areas to minimize the costs of crime.

SUMMARY

The brief survey of urban problems comprised in this chapter suggests that these problems are complex and inter-related. Adequate solutions are likely to require significant amounts of resources diverted from other uses. There is some doubt as to whether the citizens of the United States will agree collectively to the sacrifices of alternative public and private expenditures to help solve the problems of the cities. The trend toward decentralization of economic activities can bring an end to urban life and all its cultural amenities (and costs). More data are needed to determine whether or not it is efficient to devote resources to solve urban problems.

[26] For an analysis of these variables, see Gary S. Becker, "Crime and Punishment: An Economic Approach," *Journal of Political Economy*, vol. 76, no. 2, March–April, 1968.

[27] For a study of the effect of socio-economic variables on crime, see Belton Fleisher, *The Economics of Delinquency*, Quadrangle, Chicago, 1966.

There are, however, some conclusions that can be made concerning urban-policy actions. There appears to be a lack of coordination among the various federal, state, and local programs designed to seek solutions to urban problems. Fragmented decision-making in this area often results in inconsistent policies that do not result in feasible solutions. There is a need for more coordination of urban policies among different levels of government. Long-range metropolitan or regional planning may be necessary to assure that policies on housing, transportation, and other aspects of urban life are consistent with each other. The development of "new towns" or cities, such as Reston, Virginia, and Columbia, Maryland, planned to avoid the mistakes of earlier city development may represent a future alternative to urban living as it exists now.

Finally, it is clear that the cities themselves lack the resources to finance their own rehabilitation. Federal financing is necessary to assure the commitment of resources necessary to solve urban-redevelopment problems. This, in turn, means that the nation as a whole has to become aware of the trade-offs between, say, defense projects and urban-renewal projects to make the necessary collective choices. Federal financing need not imply federal control of the destinies of the cities. Properly handled, federal aid should be designed to internalize the interjurisdictional externalities that currently make difficult a coordinated attack on urban problems. The Demonstration Cities Program is a federal program designed to encourage local participation in metropolitan planning with the aid of federal funds. Federal aid to education and mass transit as well as other areas of urban concern where coordinated planning is necessary may be a necessary ingredient to any solution of the "urban crisis" in the United States.

14

Conclusions

This text shows that much of governmental activities can be explained in economic terms. Many services generating externalities either in production or consumption are more efficiently supplied through political institutions rather than through market institutions. But the fact that private action is inefficient in undertaking any particular activity need not necessarily imply that governmental control of that activity improves efficiency. Collective action through political institutions has costs as well and there is no a priori reason to believe that the external and decision-making costs of the political process are always less than those generated by unrestrained private action.

There remains a vast empirical problem to determine the relative costs and benefits associated with alternative courses of action designed to solve social problems. Much of the political issues of the day can be interpreted as arguments concerning the existence, specification, and measurement of externalities. Since much of the external effects are subjectively evaluated, measurement remains a difficult problem. Many economists are currently engaged in research to generate information on the consequences of alternative public policies with respect to resource allocation and income distribution. Such research is important insofar as it allows citizens to make more informed collective choices. Publication of information on the costs and benefits of alternative public policies enables individual citizens to more accurately determine the relative merits of alternative policies in light of their own preferences. Information on the costs associated with political institutions could lead to more efficient laws of collective decision-making.

Although economic theory can be very useful in delineating the role of government in coping with social problems, economic theory cannot be used in isolation. There is a need to consult other social sciences as well as natural sciences to predict the consequences of alternative policies and to understand social trade-offs. Political theory is useful in understanding the viability of alternative political institutions. Knowledge of biology, chemistry, and physics is necessary to compute costs and benefits associated with technological advances in the public and private sectors. In addition, sociology can help understand the basis for preferences and attitudes held by groups of citizens and the manner in which such attitudes change.

Much of the discussion undertaken here has been concerned with principles to help determine "optimal budgets" at all levels of government. Governmental activity is desirable on economic grounds only when it promotes efficiency. This is most likely to be the case for the supply of services whose costs or benefits are collectively consumed by a relatively large percentage of the community, and when it is difficult to assign property rights to these external costs and/or benefits. In such cases, governmental supply of the service accompanied by compulsory financing of costs through taxation is likely to improve efficiency. Collective choices on the supply of public services are most likely to achieve efficient outcomes when tax shares of individual citizens reflect the marginal benefits they receive from governmental activities. Information on the distributive effects of alternative taxes can enable citizens to compute their tax shares and compare these with the benefits they receive from public services so as to permit more efficient collective choices.

At this point, some predictions may be hazarded concerning the future scope of governmental activities in the United States. It appears that there is a consensus of increasing concern about problems of poverty, pollution, and other domestic problems in this country. Furthermore, given the unfortunate involvement of our nation in an Asian land war during the past decade, there appears to be growing distrust among large groups of citizens concerning the activities of the military establishment. Economic growth is no longer the "sacred cow" it once was, and citizens are collectively concerned about external costs associated with unbridaled growth. There is increased demand for an improved "quality" of life that often is not complementary with increases in GNP or the "quantity" of goods and services. Although some new environmental and antipoverty programs can be financed by displaced military and space-exploration programs, it is likely that a net increase in tax rates may be necessary over the next decade or so to finance these social programs. More likely than not, the role of government, as measured by the percent of GNP it absorbs, will increase rather than decrease over coming years. This prediction is inclusive of all levels of government in our mixed economy. Insofar as government represents an efficient mechanism for internalizing externalities within the framework of our social institutions, there will be increased demands made upon government by coalitions that represent all sorts of special interests (including poverty and ecology) to interfere with private decision-making.

Name Index

Subject Index

A

Ability-to-pay approach, 150, 151
Accrual accounting, 128
Advisory Commission on Intergovernmental Relations, 274, 288, 318
Agglomerative economies, 305, 306
Air pollutants, 59
Air pollution, 59–68
  as an example of an externality, 45
  as representative of an inefficient utilization of fuel resources, 54
  control costs, 61–62
  control policies, 63–66
  effects, 51–60
  identifying victims and perpetrators, 62–63
  measurement of costs, 60
Appalachian Regional Commission, 295
Assessment, 256–257
  fractional, 257–258

B

Benefit approach to taxation, 150
  and Lindahl solution, 150
Benefit-effort ratio, 291
Budget, administrative, 127n

cash, 127n
constraint, 34
definition, 125
of the United States Government, 126
capital, 161
cycle, 130
interdependence of revenue and expenditure sides, 84, 85
NIA, 127n
optimal, 80
  voluntary exchange approach, 84
Presidential Commission on, 127
unified, 126–130
Budgetary process, 126
Built-in stabilizers, 128
Bureaucrats, 122

C

Capital gains, and the concept of income, 200
definition, 203
taxation of, 202–203
Central business district (*see* Cities)
Cities, central business district, 303–304
  core-dominated, 305–306
  development of, 302